The Celluloid Atlantic

THE SUNY SERIES

HORIZONS OF CINEMA

MURRAY POMERANCE | EDITOR

RECENT TITLES

John Caps, *Overhearing Film Music*

Benedict Morrison, *Eccentric Laughter*

Hannah Holtzman, *Through a Nuclear Lens*

Matthew Cipa, *Is Harpo Free?*

Seth Barry Watter, *The Human Figure on Film*

Daniel Varndell, *Torturous Etiquettes*

Jonah Corne and Monika Vrečar, *Yiddish Cinema*

Jason Jacobs, *Reluctant Sleuths, True Detectives*

Lucy J. Miller, *Distancing Representations in Transgender Film*

Tomoyuki Sasaki, *Cinema of Discontent*

Mary Ann McDonald Carolan, *Orienting Italy*

Matthew Rukgaber, *Nietzsche in Hollywood*

David Venditto, *Whiteness at the End of the World*

Fareed Ben-Youssef, *No Jurisdiction*

Tony Tracy, *White Cottage, White House*

Tom Conley, *Action, Action, Action*

Lindsay Coleman and Roberto Schaefer, editors, *The Cinematographer's Voice*

Nolwenn Mingant, *Hollywood Films in North Africa and the Middle East*

Charles Warren, edited by William Rothman and Joshua Schulze, *Writ on Water*

Jason Sperb, *The Hard Sell of Paradise*

A complete listing of books in this series can be found online at www.sunypress.edu.

The Celluloid Atlantic

Hollywood, Cinecittà, and the
Making of the Cinema of the West,
1943–1973

Saverio Giovacchini

SUNY PRESS

Cover: Jamie Foxx and Franco Nero in *Django Unchained* (2012; dir. Quentin Tarantino). The Weinstein Company/Photofest.

Published by State University of New York Press, Albany

© 2025 State University of New York

All rights reserved

Printed in the United States of America

No part of this book may be used or reproduced in any manner whatsoever without written permission. No part of this book may be stored in a retrieval system or transmitted in any form or by any means including electronic, electrostatic, magnetic tape, mechanical, photocopying, recording, or otherwise without the prior permission in writing of the publisher.

Links to third-party websites are provided as a convenience and for informational purposes only. They do not constitute an endorsement or an approval of any of the products, services, or opinions of the organization, companies, or individuals. SUNY Press bears no responsibility for the accuracy, legality, or content of a URL, the external website, or for that of subsequent websites.

For information, contact State University of New York Press, Albany, NY
www.sunypress.edu

Library of Congress Cataloging-in-Publication Data

Name: Giovacchini, Saverio, [date] – author.
Title: The celluloid Atlantic : Hollywood, Cinecittà, and the making of
    the cinema of the West, 1943–1973 / Saverio Giovacchini.
Description: Albany : State University of New York Press, [2025]. | Series:
    SUNY series, horizons of cinema | Includes bibliographical references
    and index.
Identifiers: LCCN 2024018918 | ISBN 9798855800562 (hardcover : alk.
    paper) | ISBN 9798855800586 (ebook) | ISBN 9798855800579 (pbk. : alk.
    paper)
Subjects: LCSH: Motion pictures—United States—History—20th century. |
    Motion pictures—Italy—History—20th century. | Motion pictures—Social
    aspects—United States. | Motion pictures—Political aspects—Italy.
Classification: LCC PN1993.5.U6 G4965 2025 | DDC
    791.430973/09043—dc23/eng/20240724
LC record available at https://lccn.loc.gov/2024018918

Per Sahar, dal babbo.
Con tutto l'affetto del mondo.

Contents

List of Illustrations	ix
Acknowledgments	xi
Introduction: Frozen Contrasts	1
1 Atlantic Showmen	19
2 The Celluloid Atlantic between Fascism and the Cold War	57
3 Atlantic Soldiers	105
4 Race and Atlantic Exceptionalisms: The Atlantic Journey of John Kitzmiller	143
5 The Spaghetti Western as Atlantic Genre	189
6 A Cinema of Camouflage: Spaghetti Sensibility and the Postcolonial World	219
7 The Last Dance of the Celluloid Atlantic	255
Conclusion	287
Notes	295
Bibliography	355
Index	371

Illustrations

1.1 In the 1950s, next to those who moved back and forth from New York to Los Angeles, *Variety* routinely listed people in the film industry who moved across the North Atlantic, from Europe to the USA and vice versa.   45

2.1 *Ossessione*. The credits.   75

2.2 Spagnolo (Elio Marcuzzo) in *Ossessione*.   79

2.3 Gino (Massimo Girotti) in *Ossessione*.   81

2.4 Vittorio Gassman and Doris Dowling in *Bitter Rice* (1949).   96

3.1 Peter Falk impersonating the myth of the good Italian soldier in Giuseppe De Santis's *Italiani Brava Gente* (1964).   140

4.1 Giuseppe Viviani, *Le Segnorine* (1945).   151

4.2 Pietro Tacca, *Monument of the Four Moors* (1620–1624) in Livorno, Italy.   152

4.3 Giorgio Casini, *Prostitutes at Tombolo*, circa 1948.   159

4.4 Japanese poster for *Dolina Miru* (1957).   171

4.5 Italian poster for *Vite Perdute* (1958).   173

4.6 Totò (Antonio de Curtis) in blackface in *Tototruffa '62* (1962).   179

4.7 The Ambassador of Katonga (John Kitzmiller) glares at Totò (Antonio de Curtis) in blackface in *Tototruffa '62* (1962).   179

4.8	John Kitzmiller dancing with Constance Dowling.	183
4.9	John Kitzmiller joking with Carla del Poggio.	184
5.1	"Budd" Boetticher's *Buchanan Rides Alone* (1958). The US and Mexico mirroring each other.	201
6.1	A homage and a critique of the spaghetti Western: Glauber Rocha's *Antonio das Mortes* (1969).	238
6.2	Masks and haberdasheries. The Mexican bandit "El Chuncho" sartorially confronts the Yankee bandit "El Niño" (Lou Castel) in the finale of *Quien Sabe?* (1967).	242
6.3	Gian Maria Volonté in *Faccia a facia* (1967).	244
6.4	Tomas Milian in *Faccia a facia* (1967).	245
6.5	Axum obelisk in Rome in 2001.	247
6.6	Boy Scouts Order of the Arrow Shenshawpotoo Lodge #276 meeting, summer 2018.	253
7.1	Bertolucci and Brando on the set of *Last Tango in Paris* (1972).	271
7.2	The places of *Last Tango in Paris* (1971). Île aux Cignes, Pont de bir-Hakeim, Avenue du Président Kennedy.	276
7.3	The Statue of Liberty of Paris (on the Île aux Cignes).	277
7.4	The memory of European colonialism in *Last Tango in Paris* (1972).	281

Acknowledgments

My father, or *babbo* as we say in Tuscany, was born in Florence in 1925. He lost his father in 1944, a few months before the Allies and the Italian partisans liberated the city. After the war ended, he went to the movies almost every day. He lived in the working-class section of the city center, and there was not much to do in the semidestroyed city. Watching movies in the few functioning city theaters was a way to have some relief, some fun, and some time away from the relatively small apartment he shared with his sister—my aunt Ella—and their mom, Linda. My father never really liked radio, so people, movies, and novels were his entertainment. When I asked him which kind of movies he sought and saw, he answered vaguely, "mostly Hollywood films but also some Italian ones." When he went to the movies, my *babbo* never looked up the day program; he just bought the ticket and watched whatever was playing. I soon learned, however, that his tastes were somewhat defined, even though he generally made no distinction between Hollywood and Italian cinema. "At the end of the day," he once told me, "they are the same film." He did have some preferences within this Euro-American congeries of celluloid. A poet and a student of Italian art and literature, *babbo* liked Rossellini's *Open City* and the neorealists, but he also adored Hollywood Westerns. The politics of the Cold War never influenced his choices. I think he voted for the Italian Socialist Party his entire life, but socialism never got in the way of his enthusiasm for John Wayne and especially for the specific way the actor walked. My father loved and remembered actors more than directors—though he was never in general good with names—and told me stories about the deep impression Anna Magnani and Aldo Fabrizi made on him when he saw them in *Open*

City. He also talked about falling in love—though he did not use these words—with Ava Gardner. An intermittent presence when I was growing up, my father became more intriguing and comprehensible to me after he died in 2002. This book is really a meditation about the origins of my father's Euro-American film menu and the coming together of Italian and American celluloid into a continuum of moving images that shaped the filmic tastes of my *babbo*, as well as those of many other people on both sides of the North Atlantic.

Writing this book has been a long journey, and I am delighted to have the opportunity to thank the many people who contributed to its making in so many ways. At State University of New York Press, Murray Pomerance, James Peltz, and Ryan Morris gave me advice and invaluable support when I needed them. Copyeditor John Raymond prevented misspellings, neologisms, and other crimes against American English. I want to thank the College of Arts and Humanities at the University of Maryland for providing financial support. Valentina Knox gracefully shared with me her memories of her father, writer and actor Mickey Knox, and of his pivotal role in Rome's "Hollywood on the Tiber." At the very last moment, Antonio Cariello generously provided me access to his extraordinary collection of drawings by the painter and art critic Giorgio Casini and secured a reproduction of a painting by artist Giuseppe Viviani. I owe him more than an aperitif in Borgo Stretto!

My thanks also go to all the archivists and librarians that made this book possible. I owe a debt of gratitude to the archivists of the Centro Sperimentale di Cinematografia; to Louise Hilton, Adam Foster, and Taylor Morales at the Margaret Herrick Library of Motion Picture Art and Sciences; to Joy L. Bivins at the Schomburg Center for Research in Black Culture; to all the wonderful staff of the Billy Rose Collection at the New York Public Library; to the archivists of the Fondazione Gramsci and the Fondo Luchino Visconti; to Ted Jackson at Georgetown Archives; to the archivists of UCLA Special Collections; to the late Ned Comstock and Sandra Garcia-Myers at USC Warner Brothers Archives; to Megan Moulder at the Special Collections Department of the Z. Smith Reynolds Library at Wake Forest University; and to all the amazing colleagues at the Interlibrary Loan Office and Rare Book Room of the University of Maryland Library System.

Acklnowledgments

Many colleagues have read and commented on segments of the manuscript over the years. The peer review readers at State University of New York Press gave the book manuscript insightful and truly helpful readings. Ira Berlin, Vincent Brown, Audra Buck-Coleman, Anne-Sophie Cerisola, Mario del Pero, Caroline Eades, Jason Farman, Ruth Feldstein, Andreas Killen, Marco Mariano, Robyn Muncy, Nancy Mykoff, Mauro Resmini, Peter I. Rose, Ingalisa Schrobsdorff, Judith Smith, Thomas Zeller, and Howard Wach all made important suggestions on individual chapters and on the project in general. Elsa Barkley-Brown offered advice and archival suggestions, especially for the chapter on John Kitzmiller.

I have a particular debt of gratitude toward Richard Abate, Jonathan Auerbach, John Baick, Thomas Bender, James Gilbert, Paul Landau, Mary Nolan, and Karin Rosemblatt for the time they spent reading, editing, and discussing my work and their belief in its value. Richard and Karin advised me at key moments in the journey. Tom, Jonathan, Molly, and Paul read the entire manuscript and gave me very insightful suggestions. James and John read the whole thing, discussed it with me, and challenged me about the choice of a word or the turn of a phrase—something that nonnative English speakers usually need at some point when they write in English, unless they are named Billy Wilder. You all went above and beyond the boundaries of friendship and collegiality and offered enormously useful suggestions and aid. If I have lived up to one-tenth of your expectations and suggestions, this book is really in good shape!

I presented parts of my work at several venues, and the spirited comments and debates that followed my presentations have helped me immensely. I want to thank the "Brainstorms in Good Weather" colloquium at CUNY's Bronx Community College for letting me present some early thoughts about *Confessions of a Nazi Spy* and the Warren Center for Studies in American History at Harvard University for letting me present my early work on Giuseppe De Santis—and for a generous yearlong fellowship that got the whole project started. In more recent years, I presented my work at the CUNY Graduate Center, the Program in Cinema and Media Studies and the History Department at University of Maryland—College Park, the Dipartimento di antichità filosofia e storia of the Università di Genova, the Université du Québec à Montréal, SUNY Purchase, Sciences Po in

Paris, and the Università del Piemonte Orientale in Bergamo, Italy. The directors of these workshops and seminars—Simon Davis and the late Jim Ryan at Bronx Community College, Laurel Thatcher-Ulrich at the Warren Center, Nando Fasce and Massimo Rubboli at the Dipartimento di antichità filosofia e storia, Greg Robinson at the Université du Québec à Montréal, Paula Halperin at SUNY Purchase, Mario del Pero at Sciences Po, and Marco Mariano at Università del Piemonte Orientale—were incredibly generous hosts and helpful interlocutors. Parts of chapter 4 were published in revised form as Saverio Giovacchini, "John Kitzmiller, Euro-American Difference, and the Cinema of the West," *Black Camera, An International Film Journal* 6, no. 2 (Spring 2015): 17–41.

The making of a book is also a technical challenge, and here too I received help. At the University of Maryland, great technical support was offered by Jon Boone, Dana Getka, and David Herrera Orosio. Dana, herself a very promising historian, lent her sharp and precise mind to the compilation of the bibliography and the index.

Stefanie Bloom shared with me mad laughter and her gifts of wisdom, generosity, and joy. I am so lucky to have met you! My daughter, Sahar, inspired me with her courage, resilience, and humor, which I will never be able to match. She is no longer a "piccina," though I hope she will still let me call her that, at least sometimes. This book is dedicated to her.

Introduction

Frozen Contrasts

I wanted to achieve nothing more but stimulate your thoughts and contribute to a certain liquefaction of congealed contrasts.

—Theodor W. Adorno

ↄ

ON JULY 7, 2018 THE cover of the British weekly the *Economist* featured a dramatic visual rendition of the continental divide. The North Atlantic Ocean between Western Europe and the United States is cracking and the West and East sides of "the Pond" are drifting apart.[1] The split pivoted on politics and military spending. With the meeting in Brussels, Belgium, of the North Atlantic Treaty Organization (NATO) on the horizon, President Donald Trump was threatening to pull the United States, one of the founding members of NATO, out of the treaty. Trump had accused the leading European powers, mostly the same Western European countries that had negotiated the treaty with the United States back in 1949, of being delinquent by not contributing a fair share of the military budget of the NATO alliance.

The *Economist* editorial board was both surprised and alarmed at Trump's behavior. The Western alliance had faced challenges including the Suez Canal crisis of 1956, the launching of the French "force de frappe" in 1966–1967, the French and then the American interventions in Vietnam, and the second Iraq invasion in 2003. Europeans were "from Venus" and Americans "from Mars," Robert Kagan had written that year. The bloodbath of World War II had made Europe wary of war, and sixty subsequent years of peace had made its governments soft. Europeans believed in a Kantian perpetual peace, whereas Americans, who had not suffered as much during World War II, had come to see the world as Hobbesian anarchy in need of stern, and strongly armed, leadership, Kagan noted.[2]

Even amid the 2003 diplomatic crisis, however, the breaking up of NATO had never been on the table, and fifteen years later the *Economist* marveled at the American president's unorthodoxy. NATO "won the Cold War" with the Soviet Union; given the twenty-first-century's new authoritarianism, the alliance was still "worth saving." "NATO is an inheritance that is all the more precious for being irreplaceable," the magazine's editors concluded.[3] Politically, the West had been one and needed to remain so.

If the divorce Trump threatened in 2018 had been about culture rather than policies, however, his divergence would have been considered a description of the status quo. Culturally, most observers had long seen the two sides of the Atlantic as separate, in a permanent state of collision. The rise of American cinema had made things worse. Many influential Europeans had disparaged American culture since the founding of the Republic, but in the twentieth century the main difference between Europe and the United States became the presence of Hollywood as the core of the American mind. Political scientist Edward W. Chester noted in 1962 that Europeans saw mass culture as the center of American culture and Hollywood as the "epitome" of American mass culture.[4] For Harold Laski, the British political theorist and Labour politician, European countries had national cinemas, but Hollywood was a different animal. American cinema changed the nature of American power. Hollywood films were everywhere and the films by the other European industries did not compare: "Everyone knows that Hollywood is the capital city of the [world's] film industry and that, though ardent efforts have been made to challenge its preeminence in its economic aspect, no rival has even come near to the hope of success." The world was no better for it, since "Hollywood is a mass of unfathomable contradictions, where men who know nothing of anything act upon the assumption of their omniscience."[5]

Introduction

This discourse of cultural divergence has thus run orthogonal to military alliances and foreign policy goals that have emphasized coordination and unity. Politically, America and Europe have largely behaved like Siamese twins, joined at the hip by the North Atlantic and by Cold War necessities and accepting of their intertwined political, economic, and military destinies. Culturally, however, they have projected the image of untethered "frenemies" and denied their cultural kinship. How could such an alleged foundational diversity coexist with such long-standing cooperation and coordination?

My goal in this book is to solve this apparent contradiction by unpacking the discourse of cultural difference at the level of the cinema. In the following pages I offer a new cultural geography and analyze the making and the unmaking of what I call the Celluloid Atlantic from the middle of the Second World War to the beginning of the 1970s. I argue that the Celluloid Atlantic existed as an integrated cultural zone where the financial, cultural, and human capital coming from both sides of the Atlantic flowed together and created a largely homogenous "cinema of the West."

That such an important phenomenon has escaped the attention of many critics requires an explanation. Although diffuse and powerful, the processes that made possible the Celluloid Atlantic were largely obscured. The Celluloid Atlantic came to life behind a discursive veil that exalted difference and concealed the ties that subterraneously bound it. By bringing this history to light, my book contributes to the history of American, Italian, and Western European cinemas and analyzes the interrelation of these film cultures and film industries in the second postwar period. By grounding my analysis in a precise historical moment and geographical zone, I also want to offer a transnational history that is both concrete and theoretically informed by critiques of the nation-state and national cultural histories.

Congealed Contrasts

In a lecture about Euro-American cultural differences he delivered in Germany in 1958, but did not publish during his lifetime, German philosopher and sociologist Theodor W. Adorno, who had spent eleven years in the United States and had become an American citizen in 1943 before returning to Germany in 1951, noted that Europeans and

Americans saw themselves through "congealed contrasts" (*geronnener Gegensätze*) that needed "liquefaction" (*Verflüssingung*).[6]

These "congealed contrasts" had a long history. Faced with the new American nation in 1783, Europeans averred their cultural superiority, while Americans struggled to unbecome British.[7] In the nineteenth century, even a sharp-eyed observer like Alexis de Tocqueville saw American cultural production as shoddy. Commodities were plentiful in the United States, but their mediocre quality reflected a spreading equality of tastes and means and the lack of an aristocracy to demand perfection.[8] Tocqueville remained ambivalent as far as the American "power of the middle" was concerned, and was convinced that America was the future. Most of his fellow Europeans, however, saw American culture in condescending terms, an inferior copy of the original. After the end of World War II, when American political and military hegemony became undeniable, most Western Europeans turned their sense of superiority into self-pity and concurred with British philosopher Bertrand Russell that their supremacy was gone and their "inheritance is now divided between Russia and America."[9] Europe was left with a choice. It could let itself be conquered, its culture wiped out by the inferior American intellectual imagination, or, like Athens had allegedly done with Rome two thousand years before, Europe could conquer its captor at the cultural level. This binary assumed no possible fusion of the North Atlantic culture.

Among intellectuals, Europe and North America deemed difference acceptable and worth preserving. As many scholars have documented, European intellectuals from Antonio Gramsci to André Siegfried and Jean-Paul Sartre saw American and European culture as opposite. Gramsci was writing about the United States in 1934, while in a Fascist prison, after the election of Franklin Delano Roosevelt and before the onset of the Cold War. Given his circumstances, he was on the fence about whether or not European culture needed saving and American culture needed condemnation. Gramsci's posthumous prison notebook *Americanism and Fordism* (published in1949, after the philosopher's death in 1937 in a Fascist prison) elicited "surprise" among Communist cold warriors in Europe. "Apology of the US? Certainly not, but there is no doubt that we can trace in it a certain fascination [with America], and that its argument is complex and not devoid of ambiguities," writes one of Gramsci's most recent biographers.[10] The "$5 a day per 8 hours of work," the comparatively

Introduction

high wages Henry Ford granted factory workers were not to last, but American Fordism created a "civilization of quantity" that, at least temporarily, benefited the working class. The Italian Communist stood out for his dislike of a European cultural "civilization of quality" and its parasitical aristocratic supporters. Quality is irrelevant to those who cannot afford it.

Most of Gramsci's successors agreed with his assessment of Euro-American difference, but they have endorsed more clearly one form or another of *exception culturelle* and argued that European cultural civilization is both fragile and in need of preservation from the American onslaught.[11] At least in cultural terms, European elitarian "quality" was better than American massified "quantity."

In the second postwar period, in fact, much of the cultural difference between Europe and the United States pivoted on the latter's deployment of mass culture. In his 1958 lecture, Adorno rejected European self-righteousness vis-à-vis America while still stressing difference. The United States had created a culture directed at the exterior world, a technological imagination aimed at the "taming of nature, and the control of resources," Adorno suggested. Europe's was an inward "Kultur," which had failed to shape reality and had, thus, directed its energy inward, toward "spiritualization" (*Vergeistigung*). Neither was to be uncritically embraced. The former was insufficiently utopian and had not proved capable of imagining a reality beyond what was already "real." The latter had, instead, "split off" from reality.[12] In this lecture, Adorno distanced himself from previous writings and stood out among European left-wing intellectuals in his even-handed treatment of American culture. Europe, he held firm, was neither intellectually superior nor necessarily freer than the United States. Sealed off in the realm of the spirit (*Geist*), the great European culture had not prevented the Holocaust, and the SS officers who managed the ovens at Auschwitz notoriously appreciated a symphony by Anton Bruckner after a day spent burning their victims' corpses. One central tenet of Adorno's thought, however, stood firm. In the twentieth century American culture overlapped with "the powerful system of the American culture industry." Mass culture was, in Adorno's conception, "the cellophane with which [America] wraps everything."[13]

Two historical trends flowed into the philosopher's emphasis on American mass culture as the signifier of Euro-American difference. In the first place, the Fordist revolution of the interwar period had established, to use Gramsci's words, a "civilization of quantity" confronting Europe as a "civilization of quality."[14] American culture was made for the masses, whose tastes the American culture industry also contributed to create. Second, World War II had placed a great emphasis on the new media. Coming in the wake of the radio decade of the 1930s,[15] World War II had been, among other things, a propaganda conflict, waged on the screen and on the radio waves as much as on the battlefields.[16] The United States had won the war, some Europeans thought, because of its unrivaled supremacy in the production and distribution of mass culture. Emerging from the conflict as one of the two world hegemons, America's mass cultural supremacy was only to continue.

There was one problem with this interpretation. Any celebration of Euro-American difference flew in the face of economic data that pointed to the similarities of the Euro-American consumption of film and of popular culture in general. Twentieth-century Americans and Europeans had increasingly been reading the same books, watching the same movies, and appreciating the same art.[17] That Hollywood movies exercised what Stephen Gundle called a *fascino polimorfo* (polymorphic charm) on the European working classes was the bane of Communist organizers who, correctly, understood American films and American culture as weapons some in the United States intended to deploy during the Cold War.[18] A French member of the Communist Party Central Committee observed in 1950 that "in the [working class] suburbs, in spite of the well-known [Communist-leaning] political opinion of the majority of the population the share of American film increases year after year."[19]

In *Bellissima* (1951), a film about the people living and working around the Cinecittà film ateliers in Rome, and made at the tail end of the neorealism movement, Communist film director Luchino Visconti acknowledged the varied film diet of Italian spectators, even those who voted for the Communist Party. In the film, a stage dominates the courtyard where Maddalena (Anna Magnani) and Spartaco (Gastone Renzelli), her Communist husband, live with their little daughter Maria (Tina Apicella), for whom Magnani hopes to build a future in Cinecittà. The courtyard is a contested terrain where Atlantic cultures and politics meet and clash. Visconti shows it in daylight, when it is occupied by rehearsals for a traditional vaudeville act, but also at night, when the screen behind the stage shows Hollywood movies such as

Howard Hawks's *Red River* (1948). A close-up of Montgomery Clift dominates the canvas: "Isn't he a nice man?!," Magnani comments of Clift. "'A' Maddale,' do not waste your time on cinema," Spartaco retorts. "They are all fairy tales," he continues, but his wife disagrees: "They are not tales. Look how beautiful it is!," she retorts, looking at the landscape of the American Western.

This Euro-American consonance in consumption has been explained via an argument derived from the musings of Adorno and his friend and colleague, Max Horkheimer. Adorno and Horkheimer wrote their seminal *Dialectic of Enlightenment* in 1944 and circulated it among the refugee community in Los Angeles. They finally set it in press with the small Dutch publisher Querido Verlag in 1947. The two German-born sociologists, who had migrated to America in the 1930s, theorized cultural hegemony as the reason for the rise of fascism and the resilience of capitalist domination. "Knowledge, which is power, has no limits either in its enslavement of creation or in its deference to worldly masters," they wrote.[20] Preeminently effective in the enslavement of the masses was the American cultural industry, which both Adorno and Horkheimer knew firsthand from living near Hollywood, in Pacific Palisades, the "German California" of Los Angeles.[21] According to Adorno and Horkheimer the culture industry "can do as it chooses with the needs of the consumers—producing, controlling, disciplining them." The culture industry, and Hollywood in particular, was the strong arm of capitalism and had weaponized culture in its defense. Rather than violence, modern capitalism has made the entertainment industry into the main instrument of class domination and "to be entertained means to be in agreement."[22]

Diluted and banalized, Adorno and Horkheimer's cry against the power of mass culture could be appropriated by all those who saw American culture as a threat. Their critique and its updating of Marxian thought turned into the cultural imperialism thesis, which according to British historian John Tomlinson reached ubiquity in the early 1960s and saw Europe and much of the rest of the world as a cultural colony of the United States.[23]

The cultural imperialism approach was well founded, given the ongoing confrontation of the West with the Soviet Union, the power of the United States, and its intention to use this power to also win the hearts and minds of the Europeans.[24] Conveniently enough, however, cultural imperialism explained the consonance of Euro-American tastes and consumption while maintaining difference and discounting European agency, and, with it, responsibility in the political, economic, and cultural project of the West.

Had we only been free, the cultural imperialism argument went for many European intellectuals, we would not have watched Hollywood films. Americans seemed to make film central to their effort to win the hearts and minds of the Western Europeans; this was a case of inauthentic, manufactured "consciousness" producing consumption choices that could then be misinterpreted as consent. But the consent was artificial. America could impose its cinema on Italy via its troops and economic power, but authentic Italian cinema was to remain different. Cesare Zavattini, the screenwriter of *Bicycle Thieves*, declared in 1952 that American cinema, even the most intellectually advanced, "was just the antithesis of our own."[25]

This book is a study of a contradiction. In politics, economics, and military choices, Americans and Europeans considered themselves part of the same economic geopolitical zone, distinct from the Second and Third Worlds. They acted accordingly. Yet what about "cultural production"? During the twentieth century any Atlantic convergence had been elusive and had remained so since the founding of the American republic. America and Europe defined themselves with a slogan that forms the title of Richard Pells's study of the Euro-American cultural attitudes: *Not like us*.

Yet the fragmentation of the West was also a discursive performance. If we open the conversation to non-Western observers, rigid divisions within the West disappear or lessen. For example, the Afro-Caribbean poet and politician Aimé Césaire refused to distinguish between the imperialism of the Dutch oil company Shell or American Standard Oil because for those oppressed by fossil fuel conglomerates the difference was minimal or nil. In 1973 the Nigerian historian Chinweizu Ibekwe set out to explore the relations between "the West" and "the rest of us."[26] As for cinema, postcolonial filmmakers did not trust Hollywood but had few positive things to say about European cinema either. The founder and theorizer of Brazilian Cinema Novo, Glauber Rocha, distinguished his "tropicalist" cinema from both Hollywood and Europe. European and Hollywood masters influenced the early phase of Cinema Novo, but the movement had outgrown them and was now free to delve into "the real plastic visage of Brazil."[27]

Introduction 9

From Rocha's perspective the routes that crisscrossed the Celluloid Atlantic revealed complicity and had made differences between national cinemas almost illusory: "The films of all the great Italian filmmakers—Visconti, Antonioni, Fellini—are produced by American companies. A film which Carlo Ponti produces is financed by American money. Italy does not really have a national film industry."[28] Senegalese filmmaker Ousmane Sembène rejected the assimilation of his cinema (from the camera movements, to his work with actors, to the stories he liked to tell) to neorealism.[29] Even *Borom Sarret* (1963), Sembène's splendid debut short film about Dakar's working class, revealed in the words of Sembène's critic and biographer Nwachukwu Frank Ukadike, a "uniqueness that is non western, non European, and non conventional [*sic*], signaling a different mode of representation and introducing indigenous aesthetics."[30] Ukadike notes that "African filmmakers and neorealists share the view that film is a political tool." But the former had to revise the latter's "cultural codes and political ideology" to make these relevant to Africa.[31]

For some of these filmmakers, European avant-gardes and Hollywood were so linked as to make the co-optation of vanguard film practices problematic. The "third cinema" theorized by Argentinians Fernando Solanas and Octavio Getino situates the cinema of the developing world between Hollywood's first cinema and a second cinema of the European avant-gardes that was still contained within the dominant system.[32] Glauber Rocha once commented that "Italian neorealism and the French New Wave" offered little to his movement. European avant-gardes were as unpalatable as Hollywood because they were "bought off" by Hollywood, with the exception "of [Jean-Luc] Godard and a few others."[33] By 1970 the German-Italian-English-French-Spanish title of his film manifesto *Der Leone Have Sept Cabeças* (The Lion Has Seven Heads, 1970) proposed at the level of language the hydra-like, multinational imperialism of the Cold War and beyond.

My book builds on the intuition of these non-Western critics and considers the cinema of the West as a coherent unit, though one that is of course not devoid of regionalisms and internal contradictions. I am not suggesting that Cinecittà and Hollywood ateliers were producing the same film, the equivalent of the Hegelian night where all cows are black. Rather, I am arguing that they were both parts of a politically, economically, and culturally integrated zone that produced the cinema of the West or, as I call it, "the Celluloid Atlantic." The cinema of the West admitted regional differences and the input of individual authors without losing its cohesive nature. Genres that began in one region of the West could be "creolized" in another, and then recirculated back into the whole. Hollywood Westerns were given an Italian accent by, for example, Sergio Corbucci, whose spaghetti Westerns were then offered back to American film audiences among whom sat, smitten, a young Quentin Tarantino. In Europe, the American loner of Westerns like *Shane* (1953) by George Stevens became the more lethal *Django* (1966) by Corbucci, and Django was then blackened and "unchained" in the United States by Tarantino in his *Django Unchained* (2012).

All these products were coherent with one another and compatible with the tastes of the Euro-American spectator—be she mass or niche. *The Celluloid Atlantic* explores the inner workings of this integrated film industry and culture and challenges the prevailing canons of European and American difference. It intends to "thaw" the "congealed contrasts" that Adorno noted, and replace an argument and a spatial logic pivoting on difference and separation with one centering on hybridization, cohesion, continuity, and complicity.

Explaining the Coherence of the Celluloid Atlantic

The West grew politically and economically homogenous in the three decades following the end of World War II, but its film history has remained divided at almost all levels of discourse. In the history of film, a subfield of cultural and intellectual history of the twentieth century, the strictures of national cultural history have been tightened by the role culture in general and mass culture in particular have had in defining Euro-American difference. Both sides have much to gain by denying similarities and integration. Separation has been the unchallenged assumption. When the hybridization of themes, genres, cultures, styles, and personnel was undeniable, as in the case of what we call the spaghetti *Western*, this was seen as the exception, rather than the rule.

The result is often an exercise in downplaying contradictions in one's argument. A recent anthology of writings about European cinema titles itself, flamboyantly, *The Europeanness of European Cinema*.[34] As Michel Foucault would have had it, discourses are shriller when their position is more contested. In the introduction to this collection, which contains important essays by leading film historians, the editors focus on *The Artist* (Michel Hazanavicius, 2011) as a model for the *Europeanness* of European cinema. Yet how "European" is Michel Hazanavicius's Academy Award–winning film? As the editors dutifully mention in their introduction, the plot of *The Artist* is set in the Hollywood silent period rather than Europe and is inspired by the affair between two Hollywood stars, the American-born John Gilbert and the Swedish-born Greta Garbo. *The Artist* also assumes the viewer's fluency not so much in European cinema, but in Euro-American cinema, as the film is "peppered with cinephilic [*sic*] winks and in-jokes aimed at cine-literate viewers and critics," many of them coming from Hollywood movies like Orson Welles's *Citizen Kane* (1941).[35] The film itself would not have been noticeable had it not garnered a respectable $45 million at the box office in Europe and the United States (the only territories where the film was released) and won a record five Academy Awards in 2012 at the Los Angeles gala of the American film industry.

If we add to the above the fact that *The Artist* was a Euro-American (Franco-Belgian-American) coproduction it becomes clear that the Europeanness of European cinema is blurred. When we seek to sharpen its contours, we wind up bringing to the fore the concept of Euro-American integration rather than European autochthony. *The Artist* is a nationally hybrid product and calls into question the application of any national, or even "American" or "European," label. Referencing Italian and American productions in the immediate second postwar period, Giuliana Muscio correctly wrote that to understand this cinema "it is necessary to follow labyrinthine transnational itineraries within a patchwork of rich, creative, and industrial relations."[36]

To stay with films contemporaneous to this writing, *The Artist* resembles Quentin Tarantino's *Once Upon a Time . . . in Hollywood* (2019). In that film, everything is a Euro-American mix including the title, which references Sergio Leone's *Once Upon a Time* trilogy (*Once Upon a Time in the West*, 1968, *Once Upon a Time in the Revolution*, aka *Duck You Sucker*, 1971, and *Once Upon a Time in America*, 1984), the advertising campaign ("the ninth film from Quentin Tarantino"), which references Federico Fellini's *8 1/2* (1963), the story, which is a homage to François Truffaut's *Day for Night* (1973), and the new kind of Western films and television product (the TV episode shot in Hollywood that is part of Tarantino's film's diegesis and the other Westerns that are mentioned in its story and that Rick Dalton, Leonardo Di Caprio's character, ends up interpreting during his European trip) that all belong to the same genre revolution and sensibility that I analyze in chapters 5 and 6.

This separatist way of thinking about cinema has obfuscated the history of film in Europe and the United States. Until recently we have uncritically accepted the autochthony of Italian neorealism, which Robert Sklar and I, on the contrary, have termed a "transnational style." More recently, Karl Schoonover has noted how neorealism was "comfortable" with transnationalism and "transnational geopolitics" and Giuliana Muscio has written about "transnational neorealism."[37] Continuing this work, I stress that transnationality was at the very origins of neorealism. I shall argue that neorealism can be traced back to an international debate about realism in the 1930s, which became Italianized into neorealism as a result of the cultural Cold War and continued to draw on American cinema. I shall stress, for example, the intense collaboration between the aforementioned Zavattini, Hollywood, and more generally American culture in the postwar period and how this collaboration was also based on the screenwriter's prewar interest in Hollywood.

To give another example, at least until the pioneering work by James Naremore, film noir has remained "a conceptual black hole."[38] In fact, two French critics invented the term *film noir*, and then declared that the films they classified this way were part of a Hollywood genre (ignoring for instance that the first two filmic renditions of *The Postman Always Rings Twice* were made in Europe in 1939 and 1943 and that many of the Hollywood practitioners of the genre, like Edgar G. Ulmer, Otto Preminger, Fritz Lang, and Billy Wilder, were European refugees).[39] Andrew Spicer has correctly suggested that film noir is a "transnational cultural phenomenon, one that operates (commercially and conceptually) both as part of various national cinemas and as a wider cultural phenomenon." Or "a discursive construction that was from its beginnings transcultural, an idea that the French projected onto American cinema that the Americans later adopted and then re-exported. And . . . this reciprocal discursive appropriation and re-appropriation unsettles the traditional conception of national cin-

Introduction 13

emas as fixed and self-contained entities, showing, instead, complex and interwoven histories of influences and interferences."[40] Building on these examples and giving a synthetic coherence to the story of the cinema of the West in these decades, the pages of *The Celluloid Atlantic* are ruled by attention to cultural mélanges and suspicion of cultural separatism. I argue that the North Atlantic constructed an economic, political, and culturally integrated world. This world created the Celluloid Atlantic, a cinema so interconnected as to be almost a single cultural entity.

The Scope and the Method of The Celluloid Atlantic

Let me forewarn my readers about the scope and the methodology of my book. I have not written an encyclopedic history of the cinema of the West. *The Celluloid Atlantic* is an interpretive effort that hopes to open a debate rather than close it. To cite Adorno one last time, what I have written functions more like an essay than a monograph. Rather than exhaustive it "is more open in so far as, through its inner nature, it negates anything systematic and satisfies itself all the better the more strictly it excludes the systematic."[41]

My book focuses on neorealism, World War II cinema, and the spaghetti Western revolution and uses the transnational career of African American star John Kitzmiller to examine the Atlantic dimension of the color line. I could think of other genres, such as the cop movie (*poliziesco*), or the peplum genres that could, and should, be revisited, through an Atlantic lens. In my book I want to examine in detail a few specific themes and genres because of their centrality in the hope that more studies will tackle others. The debate about realism in the immediate aftermath of World War II had neorealism as its pivot. In addition, the cinematic organization of the memory of the Second World War was central to Euro-American cinema and the spaghetti Westerns' genre revolution that occurred in the midsixties had enormous underestimated dimensions. In 1967 almost 30 percent of Italian films and 10 percent of all European movies were spaghettis, and the contemporary cinema of Quentin Tarantino, among others, shows in depth the continuing relevance of this revolution. The neglected career of John Kitzmiller helps me gauge W. E. B. DuBois's idea that the problem of what he called the "color line" informed cultural productions outside of the United States as well.

To avoid the encyclopedic approach, I am using the Celluloid Atlantic as a historically contingent concept, situated in a precise geography and chronology. Arguably the cultural reorganization at the center of my book engaged the entirety of Western Europe and its cultural relation to the United States. It did so, however, in different ways, and the scope of this book is the United States and Italy in the three decades following World War II. In the decades I take into account, I contend that *all* Western European film industries had a "special relation" with Hollywood.[42] With the exception of some references and the occasional excursus I am, however, confining my argument to the Italian case.

There are many reasons for this choice. Partly this is because, *si mihi licet parva componere magnis*, like Theodor Adorno, "I have lived in America for too long to not have at least become Americanized insofar as that for me Europe in certain respects, having come together, has formed a unity."[43] But the choice of Italy makes historical sense. Vanessa Schwartz has argued, in a book on the intersection of French and American cinema, that the "Hexagon" may have had the upper hand in terms of film festivals (Cannes) and the relevance of its critical discourse, in particular Bazinian realistic criticism and *Cahier du Cinéma* auteurism.[44] Yet in the decades I consider, Italian cinema was second only to the United States in terms of films produced and tickets sold. While New Wave cinema was a hybrid that deserves to be taken into account and be fully explained in another book, the influence of the New Wave may be compared to the cultural phenomenon of neorealism and, I argue, its numbers and genre influence pale compared with the spaghetti revolution.

My idea of a cultural geography that privileges connections and transnational integration over separation and nationhood does not mean to discount the works of many scholars who have analyzed the relation between Hollywood and Cinecittà from a nation-based perspective. Focusing on a very thorough and deeply researched notion of all aspects of the cinematic apparatus including production, distribution, and spectatorship, Gian Piero Brunetta has given us a study of Hollywood influence on Italian spectators of unparalleled depth and detail in his multivolume study.[45] In this book, however, I have not dealt with spectatorial interactions with the screen but rather

Introduction 15

I have focused on intellectual, political, and economic conversations between film people, be they filmmakers, critics, or financiers. I have also intentionally created a new, more transnational geography and stayed away from any "contributionist" approach to the history of the relationship between Hollywood and Cinecittà. I do not deny that states and nations exist and scholars like Mary Ann McDonald Carolan have described with great acumen and elegance the "profound impact Italian cinema has had on filmmaking in the United States." I suggest, however, that in the period I take into account these contributions and these relations were too strong and too many to be fruitfully counted in their individual terms. Instead, I argue, these connections formed a shared space where people, films, capital, and ideas traveled with such frequency and ease to suggest a communality of space.[46]

As a historian, I also like to hold fast to the idea that things happen for specific reasons at specific times. Scholars like Giorgio Bertellini and Giuliana Muscio have written powerfully on the interaction between American and Italian cinema in the first interwar period.[47] My argument, however, is that this interaction intensified during the second postwar decades because of the political necessities of the Cold War and the decolonization process. Joined at the hip by NATO and a capitalist economy, Europe and the United States together confronted a newly rambunctious world, while the US invested $1.4 billion, or "$1,000 per minute," in Italy, and a total of $13 billion (or $110 billion in 2016 dollars) in Western Europe in the successful reconstruction of the subcontinent as a Fordist society.[48]

While collaboration and integration were present before the Second World War and would be there again in the aftermath of 1973, the period this book covers has a particular intensity and flavor. My story begins in earnest at the close of World War II and ends when the reverberations of the fiscal policies of the first Nixon administration and in particular the Tax Revenue Act of 1971 make themselves felt in Western Europe. In the three decades following the Second World War, the classical Hollywood system dissolved, was displaced, and finally re-created itself, and great, non-Western film industries, like the Chinese, Mexican, Korean, Indian, and Iranian—to name only a few of those now intensely interacting with European and American cinemas and critical discourse—were already on the map, but still not as globally relevant as they became in the last decades of the twentieth century and the first twenty years of the ensuing one, when "world cinema" developed into both a viable category and one of the possible qualifiers for the modern moment.[49] The cinema of the West between 1945 and 1973 was both a viable, politically coherent entity, tempered by the heat of the Cold War, and *the* dominant economic construct. It was, as well, an increasingly integrated cultural zone.

History and film do matter to each other and methodologically I also make the case for the possibility of a history of cinema or, perhaps, more precisely, about the necessity to build bridges between film studies and cultural and intellectual history. The two fields have had a difficult relation. Famously, in 2013, Jacques Aumont gave a provocative title to a very thoughtful essay, "The History of Cinema Does Not Exist." What Aumont suggested was that insofar as cinema is a series of images perceived by an infinite multitude of spectators, the writing of its history is per se problematic: "Cinema is made up of an infinite variety of images which appear to the human subject as a presence, and it is not truly possible to write the history of either this variety or these subjective phenomena."[50] The conclusion of the essay is more optimistic than its title, however. The history of moving images may be elusive and yet, Aumont states, the history of their "social existence" (*leur être socializé*) is much needed. We need studies about "the history of devices, the invention of cinema, or specific periods within the film industry," he concludes.[51] My attempt is, rather trenchantly, to construct the "Celluloid Atlantic" as a double step between a historically specific context and the representations it produced. In each chapter, specific films converse and dance with their historical context. My close analysis of specific scenes is shaped by my conviction that these scenes were the product of intellectual debates to which these films also, in turn, contributed. History explains cinema just as much as cinema is an essential component of cultural history. Ultimately my book follows the conclusion of another French scholar, Pascal Ory, who argued, more than forty years ago, that cultural history amounts to the "social history of representations."[52]

Chapter Outline

My book's structure is grosso modo both chronological and thematic. An introductory chapter sets up the context and describes the initial making of the integrated Celluloid Atlantic thanks to the work by

Introduction 17

several politicians interested in using cinema to promote Atlantic politics, and by a cohort of visionary European and American producers that included Joseph E. Levine, Carlo Ponti, and Dino De Laurentiis. The scene having been set, the following three thematic chapters make clear how the Atlantic film industry collaborated tightly and produced a surprisingly homogenous cinema. Chapter 2 is about realism and reveals the hidden Atlantic legs of postwar neorealism. My aim here is to extend Karl Schoonover's argument in his *Brutal Vision* (2012) and my own and Bob Sklar's in our *Global Neorealism* (2012) to demonstrate that Italian neorealism has Atlantic legs.

The third chapter is about the representation of the Italian World War II soldier. Using the National Archives in College Park and the Department of Defense archives at Georgetown University, I will show that the mythology of the hapless Italian World War II soldier was not solely created by Italian postwar filmmakers as a way to dodge responsibility for World War II and escape an Italian Nuremberg or Tokyo, but it was, again, an Atlantic construction where Italians built on preexisting Anglo-American cultural, military, and political strategies fashioned during the conflict.

The fourth chapter is about race and follows the Euro-American career of African American actor John Kitzmiller. At the core of Euro-American difference is a mutual notion of exceptionalism. The idea of American exceptionalism usually pivots on the alleged absence of a national aristocracy or rigid class system.[53] Much less studied is what I identify as European exceptionalism, which, in the second postwar period, posited Europe as untouched by a global color line that Europeans displaced onto their American cousins. Kitzmiller's peripatetic career exposes the differences and similarities of racial cinematic discourses within the Celluloid Atlantic. One of the key stars of postwar European cinema, Kitzmiller was the first performer of color to win a prize at a major international film festival (Cannes in 1956). With some recent exceptions, he has been ignored by film historians.[54] The analysis of Kitzmiller's career serves less as a confirmation of Euro-American difference than a Rorschach test that reveals color as an organizational principle in the cultural practices of the North Atlantic film industry.

The last three chapters of my book describe the end of the Celluloid Atlantic, though it starts at the moment of its clearest affirmation, the 1960s. In chapters 5 and 6, I reinterpret the great genre revolution of the spaghetti Western outside the confines of national cinemas but as an Atlantic phenomenon. I argue that the traditional historical geography of the spaghetti production is limiting. I analyze the culture and politics that lay behind the new spaghetti Western aesthetics and connect it to the new historical sensibility developing out of the decolonization process and the rise of the so-called West and Third World.

Chapter 7 details how the tax policies of Richard Nixon undermined the foundations of the Celluloid Atlantic and renationalized cinemas. I use historical and textual analysis in tandem throughout the book, and this chapter is no exception. The collapse of the economic structure of the cinema of the West is echoed by my reading of Bernardo Bertolucci's *The Last Tango in Paris* (1972) as a critique of American *and* European colonialism couched in a misogynistic text. Bertolucci's most controversial film shows that the concept of the cultural West had also become untenable after the aftershock of Vietnam and Algeria. A Euro-American coproduction, *Last Tango* becomes a commentary on the collapse of the structure that produced it.

1

Atlantic Showmen

Cinecittà is just like Hollywood. Just an expression.

—Oriana Fallaci, "Dietro le luci di Cinecittà"

⟿

THE THREE DECADES COVERED by this book were a period of profound transformation for film culture and filmmaking in the Western world. Atlantic filmmakers between the late 1930s and the late 1950s were both participants and spectators of a show that went on at festivals, in hotel suites, and in the smoky offices of film producers and, as importantly, film distributors. "It starts here, in a hotel lobby: Hollywood, New York, Paris, Cannes, Rome, wherever the deals are made and movie stars gather." Thus begins the voiceover of *Showman* (1960), the penetrating documentary by Albert and David Maysles about one of the front-runners of this new, roving film world, the producer and distributor Joseph E. Levine.

Radical change was afoot and the Maysleses' film is telling us about it via the story of Joe Levine. "Is the movie business dying?," the Maysles brothers rhetorically ask the producer. After being smashed to pieces by the 1948 Supreme Court decision in the anti-trust case against Paramount, Hollywood studios had been hounded by McCarthyites till the mid-1950s and faced a shrinking audience lured away by television. The entire film world was on the verge of transformation, but in the middle of the mayhem the Maysles brothers thought: "There is one man who does not believe this talk or he is too busy to listen. He is film distributor Joseph E. Levine. He hunts down films all over the world. He builds up a title or a star until you buy one or the other. Either way he gets a piece of your dollar. The stakes are high, the market is the world." The documentary was far from hagiographic and the Maysleses' voiceover was not bombast.[1] This chapter will show how Levine and other filmmakers like him navigated the troubled waves of the post-1945 Celluloid Atlantic and sailed their firms, films, and film industries to safer harbors. The key to their navigation skills was their understanding of the global nature of their art and business and of the special importance of the North Atlantic region within this new film world. Together they ushered in the Celluloid Atlantic.

As the documentary argued, Joe Levine's playing field was now larger than the US domestic market because Hollywood was truly becoming global. This was not new: the film routes of the Atlantic had seen traffic since the Franco-American birth of cinema at the end of the nineteenth century.[2] As well, the notion of purely national film industries and cultures had already been challenged by many, be they the Hollywood studios' hunt for European talent in the 1920s, the attempts at constructing a European integrated film industry and market in the same decade, or the politically motivated migration of European filmmakers in the 1930s.[3] But after 1945 the change accelerated to become both quantitative and qualitative.

Some data may help us gauge the dimensions of the new phenomenon. During the 1930s around 35 percent of Hollywood revenue was gathered outside of the United States.[4] In 1949 the percentage had risen to 39 percent, to reach 53 percent in the early sixties.[5] In 1985 UCLA media sociologist Susan Christopherson stated to a California Assembly Committee that in the 1950s the motion picture industry had begun to move away from the old studio system that concentrated production in California and was based on the vertical integration of production, distribution, and exhibition. The 1950s saw cinema becoming, in her words, a "fragmented, contractual, organization," where movie production was separated from the other two sectors and no longer concentrated in the ateliers of the famous Hollywood majors. Fragmentation led to separation, and production slowly abandoned the Los Angeles area and embraced the world, or at least, at first, Western Europe. Christopherson noted that in 1960 50 percent of movie production financed, partly or wholly, by American capital still took place in Los Angeles. Ten years later, in 1970, the Los Angeles quota had dropped to 22.5 percent. Before the tax cuts of 1970 that called back to the United States American capital that had been invested abroad, Christopherson argued that most non–Los Angeles production occurred in Europe.[6]

And it was not only the west coast of the Pond that "blindly plunged like fate into the lone Atlantic" during these decades. European cinema was also internationalizing. In March 1945 the Italian film magazine *Star* interviewed Renato Gualino, the top producer of Lux, the most forward-looking of Italian studios. Gualino was eager to report that the possibility of high-quality "Italian" movies was predicated upon the film industry's ability to cross national borders. "The sole Italian box office," reported Gualino, "cannot by any means cover the current production costs of a high-quality film so it is indispensable that [Italian producers] succeed in selling their movies abroad." Gualino proposed the integration of the Italian film industry into a global film market. Italy had exported movies to France, Switzerland, Spain, Belgium, and Central and South America, Gualino noted. Now the producer thought that the "Anglo-Saxon" market was crucial, and that, with the Allies invested in Europe, it was at hand.

The producer made clear that state protectionism was counterproductive. The Italian film industry needed integrated film markets and its prosperity was predicated on abolishing any tax on film imports, the so-called *tassa sul doppiaggio* or dubbing tax, and all government controls on the import and export of films.[7] In his study of the postwar West German film industry Tim Bergfelder argues that "from the mid 1950s to the late 1960s, most European film industries witnessed a decline in purely national productions and a rise in bilateral, or multinational co-productions."[8] A few years after Gualino's remarks, his former employee Carlo Ponti, now the head of his own production company, repeated his former boss's ideas and specified the necessity of integrating Italy into America. "The American film industry produces fewer films and it needs the cooperation of internationally minded producers more than ever before in order to fill the gap in its domestic and international market. . . . We (in Italy) can no longer shoot films [solely] for the Italian market. The costs are too high and there is no possibility to recoup them in our own market [alone]. We need American capital, we need the American market, and we need American companies that can distribute our films globally."[9] Reflecting this new international landscape, the documentary *Showman* begins with Levine in Cannes orchestrating the world release of Vittorio De Sica's *Two Women* (La ciociara, 1960) with Italian star Sophia Loren, a film that Levine had produced together with Loren's husband, Carlo Ponti. At the end of the documentary, Levine is back in his native Boston from Rome, where he has gone to give Loren the Oscar statuette she had received in absentia. Back in Boston, Levine is shooting the breeze, relaxing with his pals from the old neighborhood, and checking his calendar for the coming weeks. "Where do I go next?," the mogul wonders aloud tongue-in-cheek before the adoring circle of friends: "In the month of July, I have to go to London, Hong Kong, Berlin, I am trying to consolidate, Rome, of course, and . . . there, there won't be, can't be, just one trip." The man of the movies was himself on the move.

This chapter focuses on Levine and his cohort of innovative producers from Europe and the United States. My concerns here are about the economic and political processes that brought together the Celluloid Atlantic in the decade following World War Two. I am aware that many films and their makers were still tethered to national and subnational contexts. The "big" films of the era, however, were mostly Atlantic films involving personnel, moneys, and networks crisscrossing the ocean. And it was not only the commercial fare—the spaghetti Westerns, the James Bond actioners, or the *maggiorate fisiche* ("shapely women") vehicles, for example—that made the Celluloid Atlantic. Tino Balio has also shown that art films produced in Europe relied on a booming art venue distribution network that dipped well into the United States.[10] The producers who emerged from this milieu, Levine, Euan Lloyd, Carlo Ponti, Samuel Bronston, and Dino De Laurentiis, among others, reinvented how cinema was made in the West and each deserve a separate book. In this chapter, I shall deal with them as a group to tell the story of the structural changes in film culture, production, and consumption that they represented.

The End of the Studio System and the Fall of the American Studio Producers

To understand the rise of the Celluloid Atlantic, the first element to keep in mind is that these were turbulent times for the makers of mass-marketed cinema in the West. During this period the nature of their job changed and adaptive skills were required to excel. At the end of the war Hollywood seemed flush with prosperity. In 1946, close to ninety million Americans—or 57 percent of the entire US population—bought movie tickets every single week, the largest agglomerated box office ever. Yet for the movie citadel the days of stability and confidence were numbered.[11] And so were those of the typical, California-based movie producer.

Studios were soon besieged from all sides. After the war US attorney general Tom Clark resurrected an antitrust lawsuit that had been dormant since 1938. While not directed at the studios, a midwar Supreme Court decision in the 1944 *US v. Crescent Amusement* case had already questioned the legality of large, unaffiliated theater circuits using their quasi-monopolistic powers to harass small, independent exhibitors.[12] In May 1948 the Supreme Court almost single-handedly sank the old studio system by ordering the divorce of the production branch from exhibition in the famous *United States v. Paramount* decision. The government also castigated the unaffiliated large theater circuits that had long strangled independent movie venues by working in conjunction with the studios and compelling independent theater owners to accept the blind block-booking of packages of films.

The Court could not have rendered its opinion in the *Paramount* case at a less propitious moment in the studios' history. After the World War II bonanza and record revenues and profits in 1946, the studio balance sheets were offering a more and more somber spectacle. Attendance was down and by 1949 the increase in ticket prices could do little to mask the revenue downturn.[13]

Motion pictures had more and more competitors for Americans' entertainment dollars. Television conquered America before laying siege to the entire world. Between 1947 and 1948, American ownership of TV sets increased by more than ten times to 175,000 sets.[14] Film attendance in American households with TV sets decreased by 10 percent.[15] The same American families that purchased a TV set also moved out of the city and into the new, mostly theater-less, Levittowns. When they could, Americans bought new homes outside of cities and TV sets for their new living rooms. Both the suburban homes and the TV sets kept them away from the rapidly deteriorating downtown movie palaces.

Drive-ins took their place, at least temporarily, and visionary producer Joseph Levine opened one in Springfield, Massachusetts, in the early 1950s.[16] Yet the construction of "ozoners" and the increase in the nominal value of ticket sales could only partially make up for the loss of the mostly white, urban, middle-class customers who moved away from the cities and their entertainment districts.

Film producers' social status changed along with the crisis of the studio system that had dominated Hollywood, grosso modo, from the inception of sound onward. Under the studio system a limited number of firms—five majors and three minors—controlled production of the majority of big budget and big revenue films in America, secure in their domination of the three branches of the movie business: production, distribution, and exhibition. A clear geography assigned to Southern California the system's control over talent and the production process, and to New York the oversight of financial management and long-term investment and strategies. Power relations were clear. Creative talent—not just directors or auteurs, but actors, screenwriters, directors of photography, and composers—was influential, and distinct authorial traces are often visible in the studios' filmic output. What French critic André Bazin called "the genius of the system," however, was the producer, and "the chief architects of a studio style" writes Thomas Schatz, "were its executives, which any number of studio chroniclers observed at the time."[17]

The producers established their control over their star employees via binding seven-year studio contracts. They may not have had their photos in the papers as regularly as the stars, but everyone knew who were the top dogs in the pound. Hundreds of associate producers shepherded a few hundred features a year under the guidance of studio executives, who oversaw all from their plush offices on studio backlots. The main executives, most famously Louis B. Mayer, Harry Cohn, and Jack Warner, were the visible masters of Hollywood. In 1941 Leo C. Rosten dedicated two chapters and about fifty pages of his portrait of the California movie colony to the professional category of producers—twice the amount of space he allotted to directors, actors, and screenwriters.[18] Producers, Rosten acknowledged, were the targets of some of the harshest criticism leveled at the Hollywood colony. Studio executives were alleged to be ignorant and unschooled.[19] Ordinary Americans imagined them as parasites. In an age that celebrated Fordist productivism, Rosten noted that Americans perceived film producers as fundamentally unproductive, un-American, hangers-on.

Perhaps as a consequence, most of the public believed that many Hollywood producers were foreign born.[20]

It was a narrative that manifested a threat—that the owners of the dream factory might be non-, if not un-, American. The allegations, however, were not true. After the screenwriters, producers were the Hollywood group with the highest percentage of college graduates, 85.6 percent. And more importantly, most of them were born in the US. Only 14 percent of them were born abroad.[21]

Criticism notwithstanding, in the early 1940s producers were the bosses of Hollywood, commanding the highest salaries—"glittering figures" in the neighborhood of $250,000 with Louis B. Mayer scratching the million dollar ceiling and topping everybody else in Hollywood.[22] But in the years immediately following 1946, the year when Hollywood earnings reached an all-time high, much of the confidence Hollywood producers enjoyed went the way of the silent film. The great Hollywood self-portraits of these years, Billy Wilder's *Sunset Boulevard* (1950), Vincent Minnelli's *The Bad and the Beautiful* (1952), George Cukor's remake of *A Star Is Born* (1954), Edward Dmytryk's *The Carpetbaggers* (1964), and Gordon Douglas's *Harlow* (1965), are hardly celebrations of the film industry's classical studio years or hagiographies of the studio executives. Rather, they are fraught with images of death and moral and physical decay.

Billy Wilder's tale about an ill-fated romance between an aging star, Norma Desmond (Gloria Swanson), and a younger screenwriter, Joe Gillis (William Holden narrating his own story via a perversely unrealistic flashback), famously ends and begins in death.[23] *Harlow*—the film drawn from Jean Harlow's life and one of two released in 1965 that dealt with the star's life—also associates the classical studio system with decay and death. The film depicts the young Jean Harlow (Carroll Baker) ecstatically taking stock of her new personal dressing room bungalow on the studio lot after she has made it out of the starlets' ranks.[24] Compared to what she is used to, the bungalow is a grand improvement. But, as the more seasoned Hollywoodian, director Jack Harrison (Mike Connors), warns her, the flower ornaments mean that her bungalow "looks like a funeral. And it is! Yours."

Some producers were incensed by these portrayals of the system's impending demise. The story goes that Louis B. Mayer picked up on this at the premiere of *Sunset Boulevard* and called Wilder out.[25] By

1953 Dore Schary, then the main executive at MGM after leaving RKO in 1947, was pouring his time and his considerable writing skills into fending off attacks on Hollywood by the "happy undertakers who stand ready to bury the motion picture industry."[26] Others were resigned. The producer of Minnelli's movie, John Houseman, wrote in his autobiography that the time was right for a picture "about the Great Days" given Hollywood's visible decline.[27]

That the studio system was waning was, ironically, in evidence during postwar Hollywood's political blacklist, which the producers themselves allowed and enforced. In the eyes of many, the outcome of the hearings of the House Committee on Un-American Activities (HUAC) was a blow to producers' status. For progressives, the spectacle of Jack Warner—a "clown," according to blacklistees Maurice Rapf and John Wexley[28]—and Louis B. Mayer defending themselves and then committing their firms to a politics of blacklisting and political repression was at best disgraceful, and at worst a crime against American principles. For the reactionaries and much of the nation, the producers had proved that Hollywood was truly awash in all kinds of sins. They had kowtowed to the FDR administration and produced pro-Soviet films, employed Communists, and—as in the case of one of the Hollywood Ten, Adrian Scott—been Communists themselves.[29]

This was a crisis that invested the entire class of the studio producers regardless of their age and status. On the surface, the old guard and the young guns had behaved differently. The old producers had squirmed but bowed to the committee with the partial exception of the Twentieth Century Fox head, Darryl F. Zanuck.[30] As for Dore Schary, the RKO's liberal-minded "Wunderkind" had initially voiced doubts about the committee's claims. Communists had little influence in Hollywood, Schary had told the *Los Angeles Times* at the end of October, and studios had no power to hire or fire people because of their political opinions.[31] However, by the end of November, Schary had participated in the formulation of the Waldorf Statement and supported the blacklist it de facto unleashed.[32]

Independent producers fared little better. These were producers renting studio facilities for their own films and, while less tied to a single studio, they still belonged to the California-based industry. After voicing some objections in New York, powerful independents like Walter Wanger and Samuel Goldwyn did not oppose the resolution and neither did the president of the Society of Independent Motion

Pictures Producers, Donald M. Nelson.[33] Of particular note, Wanger, one of the Hollywood producers most committed to liberalism, did not publicly respond to any of the charges leveled against him or his direct collaborators and later promoted his Eagle-Lion films as "tools in the anti-Communist fight."[34] When his friend and associate, writer Carl Foreman, came under the committee's fire in 1951, even Stanley Kramer—a young and liberal independent producer—repudiated the screenwriter and later bought out his partnership in their production firm, Screen Plays, Inc.[35]

Italian New Beginnings

It is easy to be too harsh with the Hollywood studio producers. Their about-face before HUAC needs to be cast within the collapse of the Hollywood studio system itself. The emergence of the Celluloid Atlantic happened when many factors were challenging the very foundations of Hollywood. The winds of change were also felt on the other side of the North Atlantic Pond. In Italy, however, the local film industry was electrified by the changes brought about by the reconstruction of the Atlantic film world after World War II as this industry was coming out of the stultifying Fascist *ventennio* (twenty-year dictatorship).

In fact, the Fascist dictatorship had been a turbulent period for Italian cinema. The regime had invested in the construction of modern facilities like the Cinecittà studios that opened in 1937. It had also exhibited less than clear-cut cultural xenophobia. It encouraged the international exchange of ideas about cinema both at the Venice Film Festival (launched in 1932) and at the newly created national film school, the Centro Sperimentale di Cinematografia, which opened in Rome in 1935. The regime allowed the import of foreign films, including those of the Hollywood majors, until the Alfieri Law of 1938, which was followed by the creation of a government monopoly over film imports and the American majors' decision to boycott the regime. Hollywood had previously exported up to 220 films a year to Italy including 190 the year before the Alfieri Law was passed; the regime's move was quite unexpected.[36]

Following 1938, Italian cinema survived and actually increased its output. In 1942 Cinecittà surpassed the famous *quota cento* (100 films produced in one calendar year). However, few of the films

Cinecittà manufactured were exciting. The cinema of the *telefoni bianchi*, or "white telephones" (often in the shot's foreground), was mostly entertainment fare. Some of the war propaganda stood out, like Roberto Rossellini's Fascist trilogy (*La nave bianca*, 1941, *Un pilota ritorna*, 1942, and *L'uomo della croce*, 1943), but Fascist cinema was generally dull and unwilling to speak to the country's reality. With the armistice of September 1943 things took a turn for the worse as the Italian industry split between the Nazi-Fascist North and the Allied-occupied South. The lack of raw stock, the dispersal of talent and personnel, and the scarcity of film development facilities produced what Steven Ricci termed a "downward spiral" in both segments of the boot. In the liberated talon, the Allies operated according to two strategic principles: dismantle what Fascism had tainted, and prepare the way for the return of Hollywood. By the end of April 1945, when Italy was finally liberated, the studios of Cinecittà were in disarray and mostly used as a refugee camp.[37] According to several historians, US admiral Ellery Stone suggested that the entire Italian film industry should be dismantled and not reconstructed ever again. Since it had been a tool of Fascism and since Italy was "an agricultural country, so what would she need a film industry for?" the military man allegedly proposed.[38] Hollywood would suffice.

Stone's remarks may not have been reported verbatim but they do reflect a well-documented American desire to regain entry to the Italian market. These words are paradoxically compatible with the Italians' yearning for a tabula rasa, a complete break from the Fascist past. Even among Italians who thought that a free kind of Italian film could, and should, exist in the aftermath of the war, many were happy to forget a past intertwined with guilt and complicity. It was time Italy gave birth to a more democratic culture. An anti-Fascist cultural nationalism arose, with films a key component of it. In its portrayal of Italians as victims and its claims of originality and autochthony, neorealism became the dominant intellectual "brand" of Italian cinema. It slaked this thirst for the new, while largely denying war guilt. It also attenuated the memory of 1930s debates that had occurred during the Fascist tenure of the Venice Film Festival, something that *Open City* screenwriter Sergio Amidei may have suggested when he stated that Rossellini's film was the "continuation of preceding films" rather than the expression of something novel.[39]

The new, innocent, autochthonous culture imagined in these films was part of an attempt to build some kind of democratic and empathetic national pride. Critics, filmmakers, and cultural commentators may have overemphasized innocence, but some pride was justified when it came to cinema. As neorealism made Italian cinema famous all over the Atlantic, the Italian film industry was also a success story, well before the general resurrection known as the "economic miracle" in the early sixties. The Italian government attempted to protect the local renascent film industry while also heeding the liberators' forceful advice not to close Italy's borders to their films. Like other European nations, Italian governments refused to impose a quota on imported American films, but established a *programmazione obligatoria* (compulsory scheduling) that obliged exhibitors to show Italian films on at first eighty (Cappa Law, no. 379, 1947, and the Andreotti Law, no. 958, 1949) and later 100 (in 1956, law no. 897) days during any calendar year. It also compelled importers to loan the Italian Banca Nazionale del Lavoro 2.5 million liras per dubbed film, a sum that could be used to finance Italian films, which also received fiscal encouragement (a reimbursement or *ristorno* of up to 18 percent of the taxes). Italian producers would also get a "dubbing bonus" for each film they produced in Italy, which would allow them to import one foreign film—that is, one that needed dubbing—without having to lend money to the Banca Nazionale del Lavoro.

The results of this joining together of an esthetic rebirth nourished by newly recovered freedom and of a cautious protectionism that was ever mindful of the desires and demands of a powerful ally and former occupier were impressive. Many Italian intellectuals feared the American film invasion, but in 1948 Cinecittà reopened with the production of the Italian colossal film by Alessandro Blasetti, *Fabiola*, and between 1949 and 1953, economic historian Barbara Corsi writes, "the Italian film industry went from the fourth to the second place in the world: the produced films and the investments increased by 100%, the box office of national films increased by 120%, the volume and export profits grew by 300%."[40]

Traveling Pictures

Always the booster, producer Dore Schary argued that TV was no threat to Hollywood. There were unspecified "constant factors that remain in the human mind" that brought people to prefer theaters to TV. The "end of the theaters" was an "absurd predictio[n]. . . . If we ma[ke] our pictures good enough and big enough, TV will start worrying about us," Schary assured recalcitrant exhibitors in 1952.[41] Many were skeptical about Schary's boosterism, however, and also unsure what a good picture was.

The Italians may have provided inspiration and the Celluloid Atlantic may have thus been built on a middle ground where hope lost met hope regained. As Hollywood emerged hopeful after World War II and lost steam in the following decade, the Italian film industry emerged out of World War II in pieces, but soon regained its footing. Neorealism won over many an Atlantic film critic and intellectual, but it was the industry itself that regained strength after the war. The best of Italian producers were good sailors, *capitani coraggiosi* (brave sea captains) to repeat the title of a pathbreaking collection about them, and they aptly divined the directions of the Celluloid Atlantic winds.[42]

The smartest of the Italian set, as Renato Gualino had already said in March 1945, thought that "good" pictures were traveling pictures. On the other side of the Pond, American producers agreed. In his landmark study of Hollywood box office, John Izod writes that "the foreign earnings of the American industry had amounted to some 40% of theatrical revenue in the 1950s, and increased to about 53% in the early 1960s. Europe returned about 80% of those overseas rentals."[43]

Europeans had long seen and enjoyed pictures that were made far from their homes and were showing interest in American pictures and coproductions with Hollywood or other Western European partners. "In 1953, of the 104 films produced by West German companies, only 15 had foreign involvement," Tim Bergfelder writes. "These figures would fluctuate throughout the decade but went dramatically up in the early 1960s. Between 1963 and 1964 alone the number of co-productions more than doubled, and for the rest of the decade they consistently outnumbered purely indigenous films. Similar developments occurred in Italy and France."[44] Coproduction ruled the Celluloid Atlantic: between 1950 and 1965, Italy coproduced more than 1,100 films with the United States and with European partners.[45]

European producers could take heart in the fact that some of their films were finding an audience overseas, as American audiences, too, were adjusting to a cosmopolitan film diet. A 1956 survey of exhibitors showed that 76 percent of all theaters—and a remarkable 64 percent of small-town theaters—had exhibited at least one foreign picture during the 1955–1956 season.[46] In 1955 Anna Magnani received an Academy Award for her role in *The Rose Tattoo*. Sophia Loren, another Italian-born actor, got hers for *Two Women* in 1962. American audiences had embraced foreign glamour since the age of Greta Garbo in the 1920s, and were now growing accustomed also to foreign films.[47]

Because of the relative shrinkage of the domestic market, foreign markets became paramount for American studios' survival. In 1957 *Variety* calculated that "far more than most American industries, films are dependent upon export—up to 50% of total revenues. Overseas box-office helps U. S. films hold their own at home against television."[48] Producers thus tried to give 1950s blockbusters what John Izod calls "universal appeal."[49] Since the 1920s the "worldwide hegemony of classical Hollywood cinema" had been achieved because, to cite Miriam Hansen's justly famous line, they had provided the world with "a sensory-reflexive horizon for the experience of modernization and modernity."[50] As the foreign market became a greater source of profits, any serendipity in this was surpassed by conscious studio strategy. In 1955 former Office of War Information analyst Dorothy Jones analyzed how economic concerns had shaped Laszlo Benedeck's *Bengal Brigade* (1954). Eager to please non-American audiences, and especially the massive Asian Indian one, Universal's producers radically modified the film's narrative line to give space to Indian characters and stress the necessity of human brotherhood.[51] Hollywood producers were both more concerned with, and more outspoken about, foreign markets and their importance. Confronted with a "stable US domestic market" *Variety* noted that most companies had realized "the still growing potential of the overseas box-office."[52] "For many, many, years we all know that certain pictures were almost specifically made to get back their real gravy in the foreign markets," Arthur Loew told *Variety* in 1956.[53]

Cold War Atlantic: Politics and Pictures in the Early Celluloid Atlantic

Politics also welded the Celluloid Atlantic together, with contested power dynamics. Neither of the above-cited Italian producers, Gualino and Ponti, were eager to mention political necessities among their motives for branching out into the West. In their biography of Atlantic producer Dino De Laurentiis, Alessandra Levantesi and Tullio Kezich summarize why De Laurentiis came to work across the Atlantic:

> Partly it was the war that made Rome closer to California, partly the impact of neorealism and of that new and winning way of casting characters in real environments. And in addition, one needs to take into account American studios' necessity to reinvest the revenues gathered in Europe and their keen interest in lower production costs and fiscal advantages for those American actors working in Europe. There are various elements that create the premises for that specific phenomenon of commixture that is called Hollywood on the Tiber.[54]

Like Ponti and Gualino, tellingly, Kezich and Levantesi do not mention politics among the reasons for De Laurentis's Atlantic collaboration. They may not have wanted to discuss collaborating with the United States political machine. On the North American side of the Pond, however, Atlantic politics more obviously helped American producers answer the question about which movie to make, where to make it, and for whom. The soft stance the American film executives took before HUAC in late 1947 was motivated by their increasing dependency on the government's brawn to help sell their movies abroad; there was simply too much to lose in antagonizing Washington. And, for Washington, there was much to gain in trying to get Hollywood to produce politically useful movies. M. Todd Bennett has analyzed what he terms the "corporatist partnership" that Washington and Hollywood developed during the Second World War. While at war with the Axis and their allies, the US government had come to rely more and more on Hollywood to disseminate its "strategy of truth"[55] inside the United States, among its allies, and in the liberated areas. In turn, having lost much of its overseas market after September 1939, Hollywood depended on Washington and its armies to navigate the troubled waters of a world at war.[56] If Hollywood produced politically useful films, the government would make sure that they would reach an audience inside and outside of the United States.[57] As Bennett recognizes, this partnership had been rocky at times but it had worked well enough, especially in the case of the British market, the largest venue for Hollywood products.

As Laura Belmonte and others have documented, this corporatist bargain only intensified with the end of the conflict and the beginning of the Cold War. "We must formulate and put forward for other nations a much more positive and constructive picture of the sort of world we would like to see than we have put forward in the past," George Kennan concluded in his famous 1946 "Long Telegram." Films were meant to play a major role in this expanded propaganda war. Already in 1944 one of the leaders of the Psychological Warfare Division of the US Army in France, L. W. Kasner, had written Robert Riskin, the famed Capra screenwriter who had joined the ranks of the producers at Metro in 1942,[58] that "the French are planning all kinds of restrictions against . . . American films and I am very much afraid that unless someone from the [Motion Picture Producers and Distributors of America] and a film attaché from the American embassy is sent over rapidly they will try to push through their nefarious plans and beat us to it."[59]

In 1945 Hollywood executives decided to create a branch of the Motion Picture Producers and Distributors of America that was devoted to building and securing foreign markets.[60] In partnership with the government, this branch, called the Motion Picture Export Association, was directly charged with the export and distribution of American films in the territories of the former Axis powers.[61] The corporatist pas de deux was expected to be even more coordinated in the aftermath of the conflict. In 1946 Assistant Secretary of State Adolf Berle circulated a document from the State Department that argued that "the [State] Department desires to cooperate fully in the protection of the American motion picture industry abroad." The State Department "expects in return that the industry will cooperate wholeheartedly with this government with the view to insuring that the pictures distributed abroad will reflect credit on the good name and reputation of this country and its institutions."[62] The federal government became a Janus-faced presence for the studios, its judicial branch condoning the very monopolistic practices overseas that it actively dismantled at home.[63]

American producers had much to gain from collaborating with the State Department. The European Recovery Plan (ERP), better known as Marshall Plan, pumped $13.5 billion into Europe, thereby alleviated the shortage of dollars;[64] the studios also believed that the Motion Picture Producers and Distributors of America could lobby effectively to get at least five million dollars directly out of the ERP pot of money, to aid film companies that "have money frozen abroad by currency restrictions."[65] The Marshall Plan could also enlarge the studios' take in Europe simply by making Europeans richer, as ticket sales proved that richer people went to see more movies more often. While in the US the number of sold tickets kept shrinking from 1946 onward, the European market surged. In Italy the number of movie tickets sold jumped from 411 million in 1946 to 819 million in 1955 and 745 million in 1960 just as the Italian Gross National Product, aided in no small part by the ERP, followed the same upward direction.[66]

In January 1948 Congress also passed the Smith-Mundt Act by a large bipartisan majority. The act was endorsed by a Democratic president and bore the name of two Republican congressmen, Karl Mundt from Minnesota and H. Alexander Smith from New Jersey. The Smith-Mundt Act is mostly known because it ensured the expansion of Voice of America, but it also authorized the secretary of state, "when he finds it appropriate, to provide for the preparation, and dissemination abroad, of information, about the United States, its people, and its policies, through press, publications, radio, motion pictures, and other information media, and through information centers and instructors abroad."[67] By the middle of 1948, *Variety* estimated that the studios were going to earn an extra $3 million from the Smith-Mundt Act, which had made $28 million available to private firms supplying material deemed educational by the US Information Agency.[68]

Mimicking the collaboration between Hollywood and the Office of War Information during World War II, Smith-Mundt promised something to everybody. In the words of Senator Smith, Hollywood was to make an effort to "maintain the highest possible quality of production (meaning for export)." In return, Smith promised to throw the full support of the federal government behind the studios, even to the extent of "relieving the producers of the embarrassment of foreign currencies which they received for their services."[69] Smith proposed that the US government establish a flow of dollars into European countries to aid the spread of favorable information about the United States. In turn, these dollars would allow the studios to earn more from Western Europe.[70] Both the ERP and the Smith-Mundt Act helped project Hollywood into Western Europe and showed the governmental underpinning of the Celluloid Atlantic. As for Western Europe, government, audiences, but also local filmmakers, were actually—*pace* the cultural imperialism thesis—interested in the opportunities it offered.

Rethinking Cultural Imperialism:
The Corporatist Push

Regardless of its benefits, the political underpinning of the Celluloid Atlantic was mostly taboo on the east side of the ocean. The cultural imperialism thesis—popularized in these decades and pivoting on the idea that Europe was the victimized cultural colony of the American empire—silenced that part of the story.[71] The problem is that cultural imperialism may not fit the reality of the postwar West. Seeing Europe as the passive victim of American advances does not do justice to the international ambition of many Italian producers or the simple fact of the Italian—and European—film industry's good fortune during the years taken into account in this book. The Celluloid Atlantic was about an interrelated prosperity.[72]

Political scientist Stefano Cambi has recently suggested that the thesis should be softened, if not abandoned altogether, when it comes to Washington's use of Hollywood in Europe. The Hollywood-Washington relation "was not the expression of a coherent political plan . . . in sum, defining American politics in the field of cinema as bent on [cultural] hegemony seems excessive if not entirely wrong-headed." Hollywood was not "the mediatic prosthetic arm" of Washington.[73] This provocative revision may be excessive: the corporate pas de deux between industry and government did pan out, however haphazardly, and not all the calls of foul play and accusations of propaganda were unfounded. There was more than a kernel of truth in the Italian intellectuals' fear of the role Washington wanted to have in Hollywood, a fact that the language of the Smith-Mundt Act made abundantly clear. In addition, European countries and their governments were keen on reconstructing their own film industries, especially after World War II demonstrated the power of domestic propaganda. Exhibitors' gain from the importation of popular Hollywood movies was more immediately visible than the expansion of the Italian film industry itself, which reached its peak in the 1960s, more than a decade after the passing of Smith-Mundt and ERP. On February 20, 1949, 20,000 people marched in Rome demanding government protection for the Italian cinema against the flood of foreign products. "[Italian film] has been able to break free of the isolation that has engulfed the national creative intellect during [fascism], has created a new expressive language, and has offered the world a new message of human brotherhood [*fratellanza*] and peace," as one observer put it. It was a rare success story and deserved to be safeguarded from the American cultural invasion.[74]

Endorsed by the US Congress as a weapon in the struggle for the hearts and minds of the Europeans, American films were increasingly rejected by Italian intellectual authorities for that same reason. No longer did American culture amount to the "spices and the gold that those vessels carr[ied] across the Atlantic," as Italian radical antifascist intellectual Giaime Pintor had poetically defined it in early 1943 when Fascist Italy was still entangled in a struggle to the death with America.[75] Cold War American culture was becoming a plague. Americans, commented Italian Communist and prominent literature scholar Carlo Salinari in the mid-1950s, "are completing the work of destruction by reducing great sectors of our culture to the rank of a colonial culture."[76]

The economic crisis of postwar Western Europe did not help either. It was, at times, more a perception than a reality—the "gloom" Tony Judt has written about in his magisterial *Postwar*.[77] But expectations do make an economy tick and the crisis was real. Among the buyers of the Hollywood product, Western Europe accounted for a larger market share than any other corner of the globe, and within Europe the UK, France, and Italy counted more than any other countries, selling respectively 1,182 million, 417 million, and 411 million tickets in 1946.[78] By 1948 Great Britain, France, and Italy had all enforced anti-Hollywood measures. In 1947, Great Britain, America's closest wartime ally, was remitting $70 million in rentals to Hollywood, more than 50 percent of the studios' foreign market revenue. The British and American film industries were also deeply intertwined: in 1946, J. Arthur Rank had orchestrated the merger between Universal and his International Pictures; in 1947, Eagle-Lion had bought a controlling interest in Producers Releasing Corporation. Great Britain, however, was on its way to become the new "sick man of Europe." Importing Hollywood meant thwarting British domestic production and depleting the country's reserves of hard currencies. In 1947, the Board of Trades imposed a whopping 75 percent tax on all earnings a Hollywood film could be expected to make in the British market, provoking a Hollywood boycott of the British market. The American State Department intervened, and the tax was lifted the following year. The new regulation allowed $17 million in revenues to be reexported by the studios back to the States, a figure to be augmented by the amount British pictures garnered in the United States—an obvious encouragement to American distributors to give a fair chance to British films.[79]

France and Italy also tried to eschew Hollywood films. In the Italian case the antidote to Hollywood was an admixture of "compulsive exhibition" (*programmazione obligatoria*) of Italian films[80] and government fiscal and financial aid to domestic products.[81] Italy partly followed the example set by the French. In 1946, France renegotiated the 1936 so-called Accord Marchandeau that legislated a maximum yearly contingent of 150 American films into the French market (out of 188 import licenses for foreign films).[82] The Accord had become untenable given that many theaters in postwar France were either in trouble or in rubble. Facing a potential boycott of their product, the studios appealed to the State Department. The situation was favorable to the Americans, as the French badly needed US economic aid, and the resulting agreement was a mere two-page addendum to a larger commercial agreement between the two nations. Negotiated by the French special envoy, former Popular Front prime minister Léon Blum, and James F. Byrne, the American secretary of state, it aimed principally at securing coal and wheat for the war-ravaged nation to enable it to survive the coming winter months. The brawn of Washington won Hollywood favorable terms. The so-called Blum-Byrne agreement replaced the contingent system with a quota that initially allotted four weeks (five in 1948) per quarter to French films, de facto leaving the rest to Hollywood production. Given the studios' opposition to quotas, the increased economic and political might of the United States, and the enormous backlog of the studios, Léon Blum and his negotiator on film issues, Pierre Baraduc, probably got the best deal they could. Still, many French filmmakers accused them of selling out. Some French independent distributors also loathed losing the box office brought in by American films and sabotaged the agreed-upon screen quota reserved for French films. Thus, Blum was unjustly accused by many French politicians of "depriv[ing] our artists, musicians, workers, and technicians of their daily bread."[83]

Yet Italian cinema hardly lost in its collaboration with America. The benefits of the Celluloid Atlantic were not easy to discern at first amid interlocking pretenses and intellectual and political Cold War posturing. Just as both sides of the Atlantic benefited from the

Marshall Plan and the rapid rebirth of European economic prosperity and consumption power, many Western European film industries benefited from American investments that also profited US shareholders. After the initial postwar crisis, in 1964 *Fortune* magazine reported that "this year . . . [Hollywood's next box office] should come close to the all-time pre-television high of 1.6 billion in 1946."[84] Italy was doing even better. By the beginning of the 1950s it had established itself as the second most capitalized and profitable film industry on the planet. The Italian film industry had slumps but grew until the 1970s. By 1960 *Variety* was remarking on Cinecittà's "current resurgence" with film exports totaling $18 million for 1959 and the artistic dominance that had won Italian films prestigious awards at Cannes (Federico Fellini's *La dolce vita* and Michelangelo Antonioni's *L'avventura*), at Mar de la Plata (Valerio Zurlini's *Estate violenta*), and Venice (Mario Monicelli's *La grande guerra*, Vittorio de Sica's *Il generale della Rovere*). The American trade paper noted that the domestic success of Italian films had contained the inroad of American films into Italy. *La dolce vita* had scored the largest box office in Italy in 1960, beating Billy Wilder's *Some Like It Hot*, and the success of Italian films or coproductions on the Italian market had limited the take of exclusively Hollywood-made films to "an unprecedented low of 29%" of the Italian box office.

The intertwining showed. The focus of *La dolce vita* was itself the Celluloid Atlantic, the famous "Hollywood on the Tiber" where the Italian *paparazzo* Marcello (Marcello Mastroianni) and the Swedish American Hollywood star Sylvia (Anita Eckberg) interact. *La dolce vita* beat Hollywood by showing American cinema's new face and novel relations. The film demonstrated what Robert Gordon has called "the porous interface between Hollywood and Italy in the 1950s, in production terms and also, by way of this, in patterns of fantasy."[85] As we shall see, however, enfolded by the divisive politics of the Soviet-American confrontation and in the neo-nationalist discourses that followed the war, both sides often feigned ignorance of this porousness and declined to declare how much their prosperity depended on their integration.

Slimming Down

American propaganda and European protests and regulations notwithstanding, both sides of the Atlantic profited. Extracting revenue from abroad while protected by Washington was for the American studios a way to unshackle themselves from their Southern California soundstages, which had been the productive, but capital intensive, backbone of the Golden Age of Hollywood. As the 1950s turned into the 1960s, Hollywood studios welcomed independent producers and TV crews, and their soundstages lay fallow with their own crews at work on their own productions. This did not necessarily bode ill for American cinema. American producers did better than in the previous decade and found viability in a landscape mutated by the *Paramount* decision and Americans' flight into TV parlors and Levittown's ranchers (ranch houses) and colonials.

This revolution decentered the classical Hollywood production system, eliminated fixed capital investment, and embraced the Atlantic. Hollywood, so to speak, maintained its profitability by becoming less of Hollywood, more invested in the world. In the aftermath of Blum-Byrne, the *Los Angeles Times* quoted Motion Picture Producers and Distributors of America chief Eric Johnston: "Revenue from foreign distribution is the lifeblood of the American motion picture industry." Johnson also praised Washington's performance in the negotiation of the Blum-Byrne agreement, for it had ensured that at least France was not going to stop the lifeline of overseas revenues. Johnson also announced the opening of the Motion Picture Export Association offices in New York City headed by Twentieth Century Fox executive Irving Mass.[86]

There were losers. Hollywood labor, especially below-the-line technical workers, protested the hemorrhage of jobs from Southern California. During the post–World War II studio strikes, Roy Brewer, the moderate leader of IATSE, the International Alliance of Theatrical and Stage Employees, had used "Communist" smears to condemn the more radical Conference of Studio Unions. Brewer was now vocal in identifying the movies Hollywood produced abroad as the reason for the "precarious employment position" of film workers in the Los Angeles area.[87] Producers used Brewer's own anticommunist slogans to argue that Hollywood was not fattening its above-the-line talent but actually spreading the American way of life as a bulwark against the Soviets, and furthermore suggested that the decrease in jobs was due to other causes, like the decrease in production after the 1948 *Paramount* case, or the rise of television. Responding to the unions in 1950, producer Arthur Hornblow Jr. told *Variety* that "Hollywood would fall upon its worst days if income from overseas sources were restricted." Fresh from teaming up with John Huston on *The Asphalt Jungle* (1950), the producer was about to go back to Europe to shoot two films. His central argument was that "the money earned by the industry overseas helps to carry it. . . . The industry puts that money back in the employment of people in Hollywood."

This notion may not have convinced the unions confronted with a radical decline in the Hollywood payroll from 24,000 in 1946 to 13,000 in 1950.[88] Yet Hornblow described the hard logic of what existed: Hollywood had "only just started our spread overseas." When, in 1953, Brewer resigned from being head of Hollywood's IATSE, writes Camille Johnson-Yale, he took "with him much of labor's zeal in fighting producers on the issues of overseas production" and from the union perspective this issue died down till the early 1970s.[89]

Slimming down was part of a reorganization of film labor, a segment of what Toby Miller and others have called the New International Division of Cultural Labor.[90] Studios and excessive capitalization were becoming anathema to the Celluloid Atlantic, where the old physical studios seemed to melt into the proverbial capitalist air. "The era of the majors as we knew it in the so-called golden age of Hollywood is over. . . . the fact that you are loaded down with real estate and backbreaking overhead only makes you a major candidate for a major financial headache," Paramount Pictures chief executive officer Martin Davis told *Variety* in 1969.[91] The most alert among the old regime's stalwarts jumped ship. One of the great producers of the studio heyday, Hal Wallis, abandoned Warner, where he had helmed the production of classics the likes of *Casablanca* (1943, Michael Curtiz), and moved into a semi-independent role at Paramount, and later at Universal.[92]

More Alike Than We Think

Writing about the 1970s, Italian economic historian Lorenzo Quaglietti noted "the transformation of the American studios from production and distribution conglomerate to essentially distribution firms . . . We can say that the American production structure [*struttura produttiva*] has become very similar to the Italian one, with the difference that it has an unlimited source of capital."[93] Remarkably, Hollywood may have been following Italy, where the film industry had long been characterized by low investment in fixed capital and the predominance of semi-independent producers. Until 1997, when it was largely privatized, it was the Italian government, what Marina Nicoli has termed the "visible hand" of Italian film history, that owned Cinecittà's soundstages and postproduction facilities. This created the notorious dependency of the Italian film industry on the Italian state but it also allowed Italian producers to remain functional even with lower levels of capitalization.[94] Among the Italian studios, only Titanus, owned by Gustavo and later Goffredo Lombardo (Gustavo's son), was a vertical trust controlling production, distribution, and exhibition branches.

Italian Lux's founder, Turin-born entrepreneur Riccardo Gualino, had long opposed fixed capital investments like soundstages. Like Joe Levine's Embassy, "Lux does not own, does not want to own, ateliers and soundstages," writes Luigi Farassino in one of his essays on the studio. "It is one of the most peculiar and most crucial characteristics of the studio throughout its existence." Curiously enough, Gualino modeled the structure of his firm on an American model and was a card-carrying member of the "Italian Fordists."[95] But in the entrepreneur's own words his was not a Hollywood studio but a Fordist production process: "The example of Ford is interesting . . . nothing is more dangerous than trying to manage a product [in all its production phases] from origins to marketplace. . . . Ford continuously demands the production by others of the pieces he needs for his cars," the Turinese wrote.[96] To make movies for Gualino "was mostly thinking them, willing them into existence, organizing them."[97] After 1945–1946 Gualino's Lux ceased to produce movies directly. Instead, Gualino devised a system of independent producers similar to the model Hollywood studios adopted in the same period, especially at United Artists. According to this model, producers "have a steady relation, but not an exclusive or subordinate one, with the studio." They headed their own firms, though these were all domiciled in Via Po 36 (the address of Lux's rather imposing building in downtown Rome) and all had the same telephone number. They made their movies for a fixed cost (*prezzo bloccato*), which meant that Lux allocated each of them an amount that was to cover all the costs for a movie to be completed by a certain date. Individual producers were then responsible for all costs exceeding the *prezzo bloccato* and could pocket any unused money as part their own compensation, which also consisted of a fee and a quota of the film's box office.[98]

Like Wallis at Paramount, semi-independent producers navigated the Lux universe with ease and this allowed the completion of a variety of projects with varying budgets and attending to different audiences and tastes. Take the case of Atlantic producers Agostino "Dino" De Laurentiis and Carlo Ponti. Unlike Titanus's boss, Goffredo Lombardo, "Dino" came neither from money nor from a family long invested in the film industry. His father was a pasta maker in Torre Annunziata, close to Naples. Pasta sold wide and far, making the young Dino aware of the importance of the Atlantic market, and particularly of the American one, for the success of an Italian business. Yet selling pasta was not to be his calling. After moving to Rome, Dino passed the selective entry exam for the acting class of the newly founded Centro Sperimentale di Cinematografia directed by leading Italian film intellectual Luigi Chiarini. Dino had an intelligent face, strong features, and a powerful, thundering voice—as many would later attest—but he was no thespian. After a brief acting career in film he moved on to production, first for the Turin studio FERT, then founding his own firm, Realcine, and then in 1939 joining Riccardo Gualino's Lux as a semi-independent producer. Here he met Carlo Ponti, the lawyer turned filmmaker with whom in 1950 he founded the Carlo Ponti–Dino De Laurentiis firm, and left Lux though remaining close to Gualino and cofinancing many films with the firm of his former boss.

Ponti and Dino came from opposite parts of the peninsula (Ponti was from the northern city of Magenta, close to Milan), but they shared almost everything else. Like the older Gualino, they were both the offspring of Italian productive commercial middle classes whose growth depended upon transnational commercial networks (Ponti's father was the owner of an international music printing shop in Milan and Carlo had studied law before devoting himself to cinema). Both were new to the film business; both married prominent Italian actresses (Dino married Silvana Mangano, Carlo wedded Sophia Loren); and both profited from, as much as they aided, their spouses' celebrated Atlantic careers.

Carlo and Dino were keen observers of America, not just its cinema but also its Fordist notion of a consumer-centered economic modernity. Every morning both producers drove American cars to Lux's Roman offices (Dino a Packard, Carlo a Buick), famously prompting Gualino, who himself drove a more modest *milleccento* Fiat, to ask, "Are we paying them too much?"[99] Dino de Laurentiis produced *Riso Amaro* (Giuseppe De Santis, 1949), whose American and

Atlantic success, which we will examine in the next chapter, made an Atlantic star of Mangano and himself. Carlo Ponti was responsible for *La ciociara* (Two Women, 1960), which won Loren an Oscar and launched her Hollywood career.

Both used the Atlantic market to overcome the limited capitalization of the Italian and European film economies. After founding Ponti–De Laurentiis in 1950, the duo kept producing cheap films for the domestic market but also produced big budget films that needed a transnational market to recoup their production costs. The first of these was *Ulysses* (Mario Camerini, 1954), written by an Atlantic team of star writers comprising directors Camerini and Franco Brusati, Italian screenwriters Ivo Perilli and Ennio de Concini, and Hollywood literary powers Ben Hecht and Irwin Shaw. Shaw wrote about this experience in his partly autobiographical novel, *Two Weeks in Another Town* (1960), and the making of the film was also the inspiration for another famous Atlantic production, Jean Luc Godard's *Le mépris* (1964), where a German filmmaker (before hiring Fritz Lang, Dino's choice had originally been Georg Wilhelm Pabst) comes to Cinecittà to film Homer's epic poem and clashes with an American producer à la Levine interpreted by Jack Palance. The cast of *Ulysses* was Atlantic too. In the title role was Hollywood's Kirk Douglas, then at the top of his box office power, while De Laurentiis's wife, Mangano, did double duty as the magician Circe and Ulysses's wife, Penelope. The film was a coproduction between Ponti–De Laurentiis, Lux, and Paramount.[100]

Sometimes the Atlantic collaboration occurred almost by chance. Ponti–De Laurentiis produced *Mambo* (Robert Rossen, 1954), discussed in chapter 4, because Rossen was in Europe trying to escape McCarthyism's turmoil (he had first refused to name names and later collaborated with HUAC). Mangano's participation and Rossen's name enabled them to secure Paramount US distribution and financing. Carlo and Dino continued to work with Paramount when the budget exceeded national investors' capacities. The adaptation of Leon Tolstoy's *War and Peace* (George Cukor, 1955), which they also produced before going their separate ways in 1957, had an American at the directing helm and a collection of Atlantic stars in key roles including Belgian-born Audrey Hepburn, her husband Mel Ferrer, *Bitter Rice* star Vittorio Gassman, and Swede Anita Eckberg. In their biography of De Laurentiis, Tullio Kezich and Alessandra Levantesi describe the quintessentially Atlantic financing of the film. In preproduction, Ponti and De Laurentiis went to Gualino's Lux and got 20 percent of the budget in exchange for the Italian distribution rights. "I then decided that it was worth my while going to America and see how [the studios] responded to my proposal. On the strength of *Ulysses* and *Mambo* we had established good relations with Paramount."[101] After securing King Vidor as the director, the budget was in place, and after he delivered the finished film Paramount invested one million dollars in its promotion.[102]

The availability of state-owned soundstages and postproduction facilities in Cinecittà was a strong incentive. Ponti and de Laurentiis balanced external financing and capitalization with differing results. As he partnered with Ponti, De Laurentiis bought his own first studio at the Vasca Navale on the outskirts of Rome. "A studio is essential for [our] work," he noted. "Without facilities one cannot plan a certain kind of production, and it is useful to minimize the costs."[103] The studios of Vasca Navale became part of Ponti–De Laurentiis in 1950. Balancing fixed capital and external financing was not easy. When the two producers went solo in 1957, they both embarked in expensive investments in studio structures that did not pay off. De Laurentiis attempted creating an integrated studio at Dinocittà on the Via Pontina in 1964.[104] Ponti purchased the former Fascist studios of Pisorno, between Pisa and Livorno, in the hope of creating an alternative to Rome and Cinecittà, but both enterprises were unsuccessful.[105] Titanus, the only heavily capitalized Italian studio, went belly up in the 1960s and abandoned production for almost three decades. The same fate befell the other big Italian studio, Lux.[106]

Untethered to national structures, people moved back and forth across the Atlantic. In the early 1950s, next to the column detailing comings and goings between Los Angeles and New York, *Variety* debuted a record of industry people going "NY to Europe" and "Europe to NY."

The Marshall Plan encouraged American entrepreneurs to invest in Europe, an economic process that followed from a political project. Films and people followed both. In 1956, a study funded by the American Federation of Labor looked at Hollywood's employment record in California and found that fewer and fewer movies were shot there. The author of the study, labor economist Irving Bernstein, found that in 1957, Hollywood studios had shot fifty-five films abroad. Because of language, proximity, and the so-called Eady Pool, which since 1950 had secured American firms coproducing in England substantial financial aid from the British government, the

Figure 1.1. In the 1950s, next to those who moved back and forth from New York to Los Angeles, *Variety* routinely listed people in the film industry who moved across the North Atlantic, from Europe to the USA and vice versa. *Source*: *Variety*, February 2, 1956, 4.

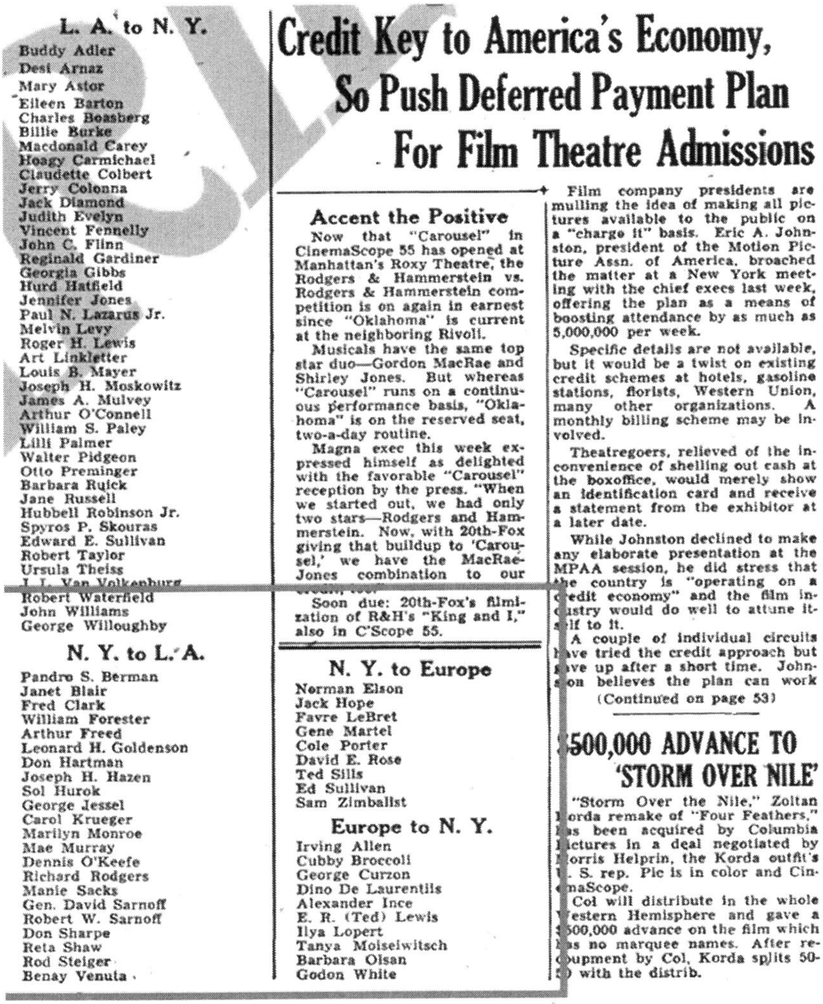

L. A. to N. Y.

Buddy Adler
Desi Arnaz
Mary Astor
Eileen Barton
Charles Beasberg
Billie Burke
Macdonald Carey
Hoagy Carmichael
Claudette Colbert
Jerry Colonna
Jack Diamond
Judith Evelyn
Vincent Fennelly
John C. Flinn
Reginald Gardiner
Georgia Gibbs
Hurd Hatfield
Jennifer Jones
Paul N. Lazarus Jr.
Melvin Levy
Roger H. Lewis
Art Linkletter
Louis B. Mayer
Joseph H. Moskowitz
James A. Mulvey
Arthur O'Connell
William S. Paley
Lilli Palmer
Walter Pidgeon
Otto Preminger
Barbara Ruick
Jane Russell
Hubbell Robinson Jr.
Spyros P. Skouras
Edward E. Sullivan
Robert Taylor
Ursula Theiss
J. J. Van Volkenburg
Robert Waterfield
John Williams
George Willoughby

N. Y. to L. A.

Pandro S. Berman
Janet Blair
Fred Clark
William Forester
Arthur Freed
Leonard H. Goldenson
Don Hartman
Joseph H. Hazen
Sol Hurok
George Jessel
Carol Krueger
Marilyn Monroe
Mae Murray
Dennis O'Keefe
Richard Rodgers
Manie Sacks
Gen. David Sarnoff
Robert W. Sarnoff
Don Sharpe
Reta Shaw
Rod Steiger
Benay Venuta

N. Y. to Europe

Norman Elson
Jack Hope
Favre LeBret
Gene Martel
Cole Porter
David E. Rose
Ted Sills
Ed Sullivan
Sam Zimbalist

Europe to N. Y.

Irving Allen
Cubby Broccoli
George Curzon
Dino De Laurentiis
Alexander Ince
E. R. (Ted) Lewis
Ilya Lopert
Tanya Moiseiwitsch
Barbara Olsan
Godon White

Credit Key to America's Economy, So Push Deferred Payment Plan For Film Theatre Admissions

Accent the Positive

Now that "Carousel" in CinemaScope 55 has opened at Manhattan's Roxy Theatre, the Rodgers & Hammerstein vs. Rodgers & Hammerstein competition is on again in earnest since "Oklahoma" is current at the neighboring Rivoli.

Musicals have the same top star duo—Gordon MacRae and Shirley Jones. But whereas "Carousel" runs on a continuous performance basis, "Oklahoma" is on the reserved seat, two-a-day routine.

Magna exec this week expressed himself as delighted with the favorable "Carousel" reception by the press. "When we started out, we had only two stars—Rodgers and Hammerstein. Now, with 20th-Fox giving that buildup to 'Carousel,' we have the MacRae-Jones combination to our credit too.

Soon due: 20th-Fox's filmization of R&H's "King and I," also in C'Scope 55.

Film company presidents are mulling the idea of making all pictures available to the public on a "charge it" basis. Eric A. Johnston, president of the Motion Picture Assn. of America, broached the matter at a New York meeting with the chief execs last week, offering the plan as a means of boosting attendance by as much as 5,000,000 per week.

Specific details are not available, but it would be a twist on existing credit schemes at hotels, gasoline stations, florists, Western Union, many other organizations. A monthly billing scheme may be involved.

Theatregoers, relieved of the inconvenience of shelling out cash at the boxoffice, would merely show an identification card and receive a statement from the exhibitor at a later date.

While Johnston declined to make any elaborate presentation at the MPAA session, he did stress that the country is "operating on a credit economy" and the film industry would do well to attune itself to it.

A couple of individual circuits have tried the credit approach but gave up after a short time. Johnson believes the plan can work

(Continued on page 53)

$500,000 ADVANCE TO 'STORM OVER NILE'

"Storm Over the Nile," Zoltan Korda remake of "Four Feathers," has been acquired by Columbia Pictures in a deal negotiated by Morris Helprin, the Korda outfit's U. S. rep. Pic is in color and CinaScope.

Col will distribute in the whole Western Hemisphere and gave a $500,000 advance on the film which has no marquee names. After requipment by Col, Korda splits 50-50 with the distrib.

UK had the lion's share of these with twenty-one, Italy was already second with nine, while France was the third European country with six.[107] Tax incentives actually encouraged American performers to work abroad. The Revenue Act of 1951 allowed Americans who had resided abroad for seventeen out of eighteen months to avoid paying federal income tax altogether. According to Rebecca Prime, this was intended as an "encouragement to America's titans of industry to expand internationally,"[108] but the measure was also an encouragement to American filmmakers to transfer jobs from California to Europe. Representatives from states where film producers yielded less power protested it, and had the law amended to twelve months in 1953. In August 1953, Representative Daniel Reed (R-NY) remarked angrily that Congress had passed the proviso to facilitate managerial experts exporting American know-how but that "it has been subject to a great deal of abuse. Some individuals with large earnings have seized upon the provision as an inducement to go abroad to perform services that were customarily performed at home."[109]

The American New Breed of Producer

The twists and turns of Italian Ponti's and de Laurentiis's careers echo those of their American counterparts. Like them, not only did Hal Wallis go independent, he also went Atlantic and pursued talent outside the Hollywood reservoir. He launched the American career of an Italian star, Anna Magnani, who received the 1956 Academy Award for Best Female Actor for *The Rose Tattoo* (1955) by Daniel Mann. This screen adaptation of the play by Tennessee Williams targeted audiences both in the United States and in Italy, by then the second largest market for American films in the world.[110] As an independent producer using Paramount facilities, Wallis optioned Williams's play and recruited Magnani for the role of Serafina delle Rose. Magnani was Williams's choice for the role he had written. But the actor was a risky choice for Wallis, who knew her reputation for being demanding. Audrey Wood, Williams's agent, wrote Wallis that she knew that the producer considered Magnani's terms to be "exorbitant." The actor wanted director approval—she ultimately accepted Daniel Mann—and she was not going to participate "at a cheap figure." Besides, her command of English was poor and she was self-conscious about this; she had refused to play Serafina on Broadway for that very reason. Wallis accepted the steep terms, which included a dialogue and speech coach, and actually went to great lengths to persuade Magnani to do the film. Studio records show that at $91,000 she was the second highest paid member of the cast after the male star, Burt Lancaster, who earned $100,000.[111] Wallis also paid an American expat in Rome, Mickey Knox, as dialogue coach (at a cumulative $2,417) and a technical advisor, Natalie Murray, who got $100 per week for four weeks.[112] At 75 percent the size of the film title, Magnani's credit was the same size as Lancaster's.[113]

Wallis was willing to invest in the actor because he was investing in the Celluloid Atlantic. In 1954, the producer went to Rome to meet Magnani.[114] She had box office draw overseas, and her American reputation had been cemented by the success of Roberto Rossellini's *Open City* immediately after the war. In 1949 the *New York Times* dedicated a long article to the "tigress of Italy's screen," followed the next year by a thirteen-page spread in *Life*.[115] Her first Atlantic film, William Dieterle's *Vulcano* (1950), a melodrama about a prostitute exiled to the Aeolian islands by the Fascist regime, banked on her international success in *Open City*. It was also a public rebuke of *Open City*'s director Roberto Rossellini's love affair with Hollywood star Ingrid Bergman. Rossellini, Magnani's former lover, was filming *Stromboli* (1950) with Bergman on another Aeolian island with RKO financing.[116]

Vulcano did not do well, but that did not dent Magnani's international fame. In 1953 critic Howard Thompson argued that Magnani was "the most awesomely familiar surname since the abdication of Garbo."[117] Paramount distributed *The Rose Tattoo* and touted Magnani as an "international star" all the way to the Academy Awards.[118] On the other side of the Pond, Italian critics saw Mann's filmic melodrama as a descendant of neorealism, unwittingly highlighting the cultural exchange of the Celluloid Atlantic. Commenting on the location shooting and the naturalism of the sets, Giorgio N. Fenin wrote in left-leaning *Cinema Nuovo* that "it is interesting to see the influence of neorealism in Mann's film."[119]

In the process, Wallis and Magnani became close. The actor considered *The Rose Tattoo* one of her favorite films along with *Open City*, *Bellissima*, and the episode "Il Miracolo" in Rossellini's anthology feature *L'Amore* (1948).[120] And both Magnani and her supporters played on her Atlantic success as evidence of her bankability. *Variety* noted that the Academy Award to Magnani had made headlines in Rome and cited the implication of Rome's main daily, *Il Messaggero*, that Magnani's rediscovery in America would help her in Italy. "The [*Messaggero*] piece points out that again, as in the case of the post-war Italian neorealist successes, they have been discovered abroad."[121]

After *The Rose Tattoo*, Wallis recruited Magnani for one more film, *Wild Is the Wind* (1957), a prestige production helmed by star director George Cukor. The film, a melodrama that cast Magnani as the mail-order bride of a rich, crustaceous Nevada shepherd, Anthony Quinn (Gino), did not do particularly well, but Magnani's Atlantic career soared on Sidney Lumet's *The Fugitive Kind* (1960) from Tennessee Williams's *Orpheus Descending*, which prompted Bosley Crowther to salute Magnani's and Marlon Brando's performances as "brilliant."[122]

Pervasive ageism and sexism caught up and hindered the star's career, which, however, kept spanning across the ocean and involved Atlantic producers. Her last Atlantic film, *The Secret of Santa Vittoria* (1969), was produced and directed by Stanley Kramer, who was also a member of the new breed of Atlantic producers. By then, Magnani had not made a film for Hollywood in seven years and her last starring film role, in Pier Paolo Pasolini's *Mamma Roma*, was released in 1962, but she was still a bankable star in America, as critic Mark Shivas noted in the *New York Times*.[123] Like Wallis, Kramer pursued the star for the film, which, like many of Kramer's movies, was a gamble. The story of *Santa Vittoria* read—it still does—as a farce. It is a choral story of a village in northern Italy that begins resisting the German occupiers as they retreat north up the peninsula. The villagers confront the taint of Fascism and collaboration embodied by the character of the wine shop owner and town mayor, Bombolini (Anthony Quinn), who erases the pro-Mussolini slogan that he himself had painted on the city tower. Magnani plays Rosa, his wife, a powerful woman skeptical of her husband's intellectual and political judgment. It was not a starring role for her—the film was more a collective effort than anybody's star vehicle. Kramer told this to Magnani, and wrote to Abe Fogel that "it is my opinion, for what it is worth, that she cannot miss making a gigantic imprint for the part."[124] She did, although the film was not a hit. The marketing files of *Santa Vittoria* in the UCLA Special Collections also reveal the lengths the producers went to market the film internationally, banking on their Atlantic cast.[125]

The choice of *Santa Vittoria*, which was entirely shot in Italy in the village of Anticoli Corrado close to Rome, was not an odd one for Kramer. When his career at Columbia ended bitterly in 1955, Kramer happily moved to United Artists (UA) where he became a producer-director in the "studio without a backlot." His first film for UA was *Not as a Stranger* (1955), which he shot in the old Chaplin

Studio in La Brea and the smaller California Studios on Melrose that was then mostly used for television. Kramer also went Atlantic and traveled to Spain to produce *The Pride and the Passion* (1956), the second film in his two-picture deal with UA, which starred an Atlantic star triptych formed by Frank Sinatra, Sophia Loren, and Cary Grant. Both films were released by UA.[126]

In Spain Kramer came across Samuel Bronston, an Armenian-born Hollywood producer who produced a series of Atlantic hits like *El Cid* (Anthony Mann, 1961) and *The Fall of the Roman Empire* (Anthony Mann, 1964) in Spain, the latter in his own giant studio in Las Matas, close to Madrid. After Bronston's falling out with his financing muse, Pierre du Pont, Philip Yordan picked up the torch of Hollywood production in Spain.[127]

The new producers were a novel breed. Describing the old studio system, Kramer quipped that "the old American dream was you go to work at MGM when you're twenty-one years old, and if you keep your nose clean for twenty years you become whatever you want to become. A director, a producer, or writer, whatever."[128] He exaggerated, as the "old American dream" was never exactly that. Yet ambitious and successful Hollywood producers did disengage their careers from the Southern California environment that had nourished their Golden Age predecessors. In 1964 Katharine Hamill, the groundbreaking societal and financial analyst at *Fortune* magazine, was writing that "producers . . . have become in effect entertainment companies rather than simply makers of movies."[129]

Hamill was specifically referencing Joseph Levine, the subject of *Showman*, the Maysles brothers' documentary. A former clothing salesman from a tough Boston neighborhood, Levine had cut his teeth in the exhibition sector and then graduated to distribution and production. Having founded Embassy as an independent film business company in 1938, Levine reorganized it as Embassy Picture Corporation in 1956 and soon became the most important producer of the Celluloid Atlantic. Levine was adept at providing complete packages for a movie, including financing, distribution deals, and stars' commitments, but he eschewed the daily work on sets as executive and associate producers had traditionally done. Geography militated against this, as Levine had no soundstages of his own and his productions were all over the Atlantic.

Packaging sometimes meant *re*-packaging and Levine often repackaged foreign films for the Western market, as with the Japanese hit *Godzilla* (1954) by Ishirō Honda, a tale of the rampage of Japan by a forty-story-high monster created by radiation. Levine treated the Japanese version as raw material, reedited it with an experienced director/editor, Terry O. Morse, and retitled the film *Godzilla, King of the Monsters*.[130] Levine then hired veteran publicist Terry Turner to launch a "monster campaign" to ballyhoo *Godzilla*. In 1956, the film opened in 400 theaters, 150 in New England alone, a campaign that *Variety*, years ahead of the similar opening of Steven Spielberg's *Jaws* in 1975, termed "saturation."[131] In June the film was still playing in 250 theaters, an abysmally bad review by Bosley Crowther in the *New York Times* ("incredibly awful film") notwithstanding.[132]

Film wares were easier to sell in the Celluloid Atlantic if they conformed to its racial codes (see chapter 3). To make *Godzilla* palatable to Western audiences, Levine and Morse invented a Caucasian character, the American reporter Steve Martin, played by Raymond Burr. Atlantic films needed less intervention. Levine repackaged several Italian films like *Attila the Hun* (1953) and *Hercules* (1958), both by Pietro Francisci, and added no new characters. Embassy bought the Canadian and US distribution rights of *Hercules* for $120,000. In *Hercules*'s case, Levine repackaged the film by reediting and redubbing all in English. Once again, he distributed the film using a saturation strategy, and released it in 600 theaters. He also spent $1.5 million in publicity, $250,000 in tie-ins with television, $350,000 on newspaper ads, and $40,000 in a plush "explodation" banquet for 1,200 exhibitors and journalists at the New York Waldorf Astoria.[133] *Hercules* took in an amazing $20 million at the box office.[134]

As with the old studios, Levine's Embassy was involved in all branches of the business, from the exhibition to the distribution and even, though more rarely, in actual production. But talking to the *New Yorker*'s Calvin Tomkins in 1967, Levine happily distinguished himself as a producer without a studio: "Embassy owns no production equipment. [It is a studio] owning nothing. Not so much as a movie camera. And Levine plans to keep it that way."[135] On a transnational scale Levine's role was similar to the one Tino Balio describes for United Artists, the studio that "ushered the industry into a new era," after being taken over by Arthur Krim and Robert Benjamin in 1951.[136] In return for distribution rights, Levine provided local producers and talent with a large share of production financing, complete control over production, and a share of the profits.[137]

Levine understood the job of the producer as that of a transnational provider of films whose largest constituency, but by no means its sole one, was American moviegoers. In this context, some of the protectionist practices enacted by European countries represented a possibility rather than a constraint. Tied to a simplistic notion of "national product," these provisions could be fairly easily manipulated. For example, since 1946 the Italian state had tried to protect its industry by freezing some of the revenues accrued in Italy by foreign imports and by financial aid to the "national" product. To qualify as "national" the film needed to be shot in an Italian studio or, if shot on location, postproduced in Italy; its cast and crew needed to have a majority of Italian actors, but the stars could be foreign born. If these conditions were met, the film received fiscal aid from the Italian state and could qualify for a prize if it met vague quality requirements. Finally, its producer was allowed to import one foreign film without paying the tax on dubbing. Meeting these requirements was fairly easy for Levine and other American producers who associated themselves with modern Italian producers, namely Carlo Ponti and Dino De Laurentis. The idea was to make films in Italy that could be reexported into the American market, either in the commercial circuit or in the blossoming art circuit that by 1966 counted close to 700 houses in the United States.[138]

Business boomed for Levine and for an Italian film industry that in 1967 was nominally producing more films than Hollywood.[139] Busy stages and hundreds of coproductions also protected Levine from nationalist criticism.[140] Within the Celluloid Atlantic, not all players had equal power, but profit-sharing helped assuage fears of American domination. At the time of Magnani's Oscar, the Communist press had momentarily embraced America: "The commie press . . . for once credits Hollywood, the Yank industry, etc.—hence the p.r. value is immeasurable," as *Variety* noted.[141] As Greg Elmer and Mike Gasher note, "As countries around the world increase their stake in the Hollywood film industry, . . . they are less likely to oppose politically American films' box office dominance."[142]

In 1963, when Levine and Carlo Ponti struck a coproduction deal, even the Communist daily, *L'Unità*, reported the news without reference to cultural imperialism. Levine named four films under the deal, per *L'Unità*: *Casanova 70* (1965, Mario Monicelli), *Ieri oggi e domani* (Yesterday, Today, and Tomorrow, 1963) by Oscar winner Vittorio De

Sica, *La noia* by Damiano Damiani from the novel by Alberto Moravia, and Jean-Luc Godard's *Le mépris*. The piece concluded by citing the producer's praise for Italian cinema. "I am not sure I understand how anybody may venture [the notion] that Italian cinema is in a crisis when it features directors like Vittorio de Sica and Federico Fellini. *La Ciociara* (Two Women, 1960) and *Boccaccio '70* (1962) are currently being exhibited on American screens and their box office is great. In its six month run at the Paris [theater] in New York *Divorzio all'Italiana* (Divorce Italian Style, Pietro Germi, 1961) has garnered $ 335,000."[143] By 1967 Levine had "produced" 150 films[144] and had been profiled in *Esquire* and the *New Yorker*.[145] He was the showman of the Celluloid Atlantic. When Gulf & Western Industries replaced Martin Davis, their top producer at Paramount Pictures, in 1969, *Variety* reported that the mother company was thinking of "an independent indie producer who is as attuned to independent filmmaking as his successor" and the idea was to reduce overhead and embrace "the United Artists pattern." The following sentence mentioned Joe Levine's Avco Embassy as a model on how to be a new "mini-major" with no overhead.[146]

Conclusion

The new Atlantic producers shared characteristics. They were not as wedded to capitalization and studio structures as their predecessors had been and they all believed in "ballyhoo." Cinema was once "a daily habit" (*un'abitudine*), declared Federico Fellini, rather than an act of volition for a particular movie.[147] Before World War II and television, many people just "went to the movies." But this had changed. Tino Balio has noted that in postwar America and certainly by 1960, American audiences "had become selective . . . Motion pictures became special events, which had the effect of widening the gap between commercial winners and losers."[148]

The producer himself was part of what drew Atlantic spectators to the movies. Irving Thalberg, the greatest producer of classical Hollywood, had famously effaced himself and kept a low profile separated from his pictures.[149] In the Celluloid Atlantic, the producer was part of the package that made the picture a sound financial investment. "We, American [*sic*] producers, regard ourselves as showmen," De

Laurentiis told Moritz de Hadeln.[150] The Levines and the Dinos were selling movies and selling themselves.

In a 1964 profile of Joe Levine, *Fortune* framed the producer as the most representative of his generation: "When Hollywood gets around to doing a movie about the triumphs and heartbreaks of this transition period (as it inevitably will), the picture may well be entitled *The Joe Levine Story*."[151] A. T. McKenna, the author of the only scholarly work on Levine, notes that the producer put his name everywhere he could. When he allowed the Maysles brothers' generous access for *Showman*, their 1966 documentary about him, he wrongly thought that by augmenting his own fame he would be adding value to all "Levine Productions."

But the new producer was not necessarily a hero, as the Maysleses showed in a portrait that was anything but hagiographic. The film begins with a shot of the beautiful Sophia Loren saluting the crowds in Cannes from the back of her open car. The Maysleses then cut to showing Levine, overweight, sweating, and not particularly handsome, haggling with other film moguls including Loren's husband, Carlo Ponti, about money and sales for her film. It is an unpleasant, ironic montage bound to remind the viewer of a slave market, one where women are sold and stereotypically Jewish men are buying. According to McKenna, Levine hated the Maysles brothers' documentary and effectively halted its distribution.[152]

Though accused of being anti-Semitic at its release, the film was less *Jud Süß* (1940) than something in the vein of Jean-Luc Godard's *Le mépris* (Contempt, 1963), another portrait of a greedy—and, needless to say, white and male—producer in the age of the new Hollywood. The brothers were Jewish themselves and their film was a cogent portrait of a Hollywood producer in the age of the Celluloid Atlantic. As opposed to *Le mépris*, the Maysles brothers documented the Atlantic world where Levine operated. Much of the film shows Levine outside of the United States; he neither represents the Hollywood studio system nor is he a metonymic stand-in for capitalist America. Rather, *Showman* built on the cliché of the Hollywood-based "mogul" while showing that he was increasingly unmoored from Southern California and more and more tethered to Western cinema's Atlantic reality.

Ponti and De Laurentiis were also showmen. In her serial portrait of Cinecittà in the late 1950s published in *L'Europeo*, journalist Oriana Fallaci anointed the producers, not the stars, as the great modernizers, among them Dino De Laurentiis and Carlo Ponti in particular. They were remaking Cinecittà by "sleeping at night with a hand on the phone," awaiting a call from Los Angeles or Mexico City.[153] Dino and Carlo promoted the Atlantic stardom of their wives because they knew that they were also promoting themselves and their films in general. When Dino was distributing Alberto Lattuada's *Il bandito* (1946), about an outlaw in Italy's immediate postwar, he even plotted to have himself kidnapped by real bandits to make his own life part of the marketing of the movie.[154]

The two Italians were comfortable navigating the Celluloid Atlantic. Members of a booming ocean-crossing and jet-setting crowd, their lingua franca was English even as they made their colorful accents part of their cosmopolitan charm. Dino may have been barely comprehensible in English, but he was a well-known presence all over New York City and Los Angeles where he moved in the early 1970s. Arrigo Colombo, who produced Giuliano Montaldo's Atlantic film *Grand Slam* (1967) with Janet Leigh and Klaus Kinsky, had left Italy in 1939 because of its racial laws and moved to the United States. He came back to Europe with an Americanized nickname (Harry), a deep knowledge of America, and flawless English.[155] The producer of Fellini *La dolce vita*, Peppino Amato, had been a silent film actor in America.[156] One of the rare women in this group, Marina Cicogna, who produced Sidney Lumet's *Pawnbroker* (1964) with Rod Steiger and Luis Buñuel's *Belle du jour* (1967) with Catherine Deneuve, suggested that being a cosmopolite had been crucial to her career: "We had been raised like Gypsies," she told Stefano della Casa. "Because my parents were anti-Fascists we had lived in England when we were young. My first language was English, Italian was almost an afterthought." This helped her casting choices, as "there were no frontiers in my head, so I used people I felt right and it's always a good thing for a producer to have actors of quality."[157]

These changes were bound to remain. In the mid-1950s William Murray, the son of Magnani's English interpreter and confidante, Natalie Murray, described "Hollywood on the Tiber" in his novel *The Fugitive Romans*.[158] In 1968, in the middle of the spaghetti Western revolution, Almeria, Spain proclaimed itself the "movie capital of the world" with eight coproductions shooting there simultaneously (one more movie than in Southern California).[159]

The Celluloid Atlantic was making its partners' geographies "uncertain," as Oriana Fallaci noted for Hollywood and Cinecittà.[160] Hollywood may not have ended when the old "moguls" and the system they helped create died out,[161] but studios were literally "thinning out." The sale of some of the studio lots in the sixties, which were turned into Los Angeles's Culver City and Century City real estate developments, made the process apparent.[162] The other side of the Pond was also morphing. Cinecittà, like Hollywood, was becoming less a concrete place than a brand and, as we shall see, Cinecittà Westerns were being shot in Almeria, Spain with international casts. "Cinecittà is like Hollywood, a linguistic construct," rather than a real place, concluded Fallaci in 1958.[163]

If Italian producers, like their American counterparts, were not easily pinned to one place, the Celluloid Atlantic had its own new centers, such as the bohemian Trastevere in Rome or the world-famous promenade of Via Veneto. It launched new salons like the one run by Mikey Knox, a former Hollywood actor and a friend of Norman Mailer, who served as Magnani's English language coach and would leave his imprint in the spaghetti Western revolution examined in chapters 5 and 6. In June 1967, a member of the Kramer Production Company marveled to the producer's uncle, Earl, that "Rome is a beehive of activity at this time for motion pictures. The following studios are represented for the future. MGM, Fox, Columbia (shooting), Paramount (shooting one) and preparing three including ours." "Things are not cheap," but "it is impossible to get a bad meal here."[164]

It will always be possible to get a good meal in Rome, but the frantic engagement of the city's movie ateliers with the Atlantic film economy and culture was specific to this era. Something special was occurring, and the denizens of the Celluloid Atlantic would remember it. "Rome was different then. Everybody was there and everybody came from, and went back, continuously, across the ocean," Mickey Knox's daughter, Valentina, told me in her comfortable Los Angeles home, "and when they were there, Italian and American alike, they all passed by my father's apartment."[165]

2

The Celluloid Atlantic between Fascism and the Cold War

Ferrara is not Annapolis.

—Antonio Marchi, review of *Ossessione* (June 14, 1943)

⤳

M ASS CULTURE IS OFTEN USED to characterize the gap between the United States and Western Europe. A number of European intellectuals, from Umberto Eco to Jean Baudrillard, have used cinema as a starting point to typify the "otherness of American culture compared to European culture."[1]

That American and European filmic cultures would be so at odds is more than a little surprising. If there is a segment of twentieth-century American culture through which foreigners, and especially Europeans, have moved fairly undisturbed, it is cinema. In the 1930s a massive antifascist migration brought many European filmmakers to Hollywood.[2] But even before the refugee crisis of the 1930s the influx of European filmmakers had transformed Los Angeles. In 1928, the Italian journalist Arnaldo Fraccaroli remarked that the charm of Hollywood was its being "a formidable, chaotic assemblage of humanity, a mix of races and of languages."[3] In the 1930s German filmmakers were so prominent that foreign visitors like French writer

Blaise Cendrars remarked that MGM was dominated by a "powerful German-American trust" and characterized by what he termed a "German order" and "the solid accent of the majority of the studio's employees."[4]

Of course, Europeans did stand out in Hollywood. But already in the postwar years after 1918, this separation was the result of marketing done by the studios and by the foreigners themselves. The "foreign"—especially if associated with the high end of European culture—defined actors or directors as exotic "geniuses" and their films as highbrow masterpieces. British journalist Cedric Belfrage noted that "it is undoubtedly true that many foreigners are getting contracts at the studios on reputations abroad which are entirely mythical. . . . Hollywood casting directors still make remarkably little effort to check the claims of actors from foreign countries."[5] Greta Garbo—herself a beneficiary of the cultural capital of European origins—quipped that "in Hollywood a Rumanian is not a nationality, it is a profession."[6]

Belfrage's and Garbo's notations are crucial, though they need context lest we assume that foreignness signified complete alterity. Already then the Euro-American difference was a discursive performance. As much as it was a biographical reality, some of the Hollywoodians' Europeanness was a strategy to make a stereotype work for their careers. To paraphrase historian David Roediger's famous terminology, like whiteness, Europeanness produced its own "wages."[7]

This Euro-American dichotomy has characterized twentieth-century Atlantic intellectual history, unattenuated by the intensity of the contacts and the exchanges. When Jean-Marie Messier, the former French CEO of Vivendi, bought an American studio, Universal, and declared that "the French cultural exception is dead," a committee of French citizens petitioned to have his citizenship taken away.[8] Messier had flamboyantly created an Atlantic bridge where there were to be none. Or consider the words that Gian Piero Brunetta, one of the most acute and relevant of European film historians, chose to define the coming of the Hollywood films in Italy in the aftermath of World War II: "the barbaric invasion of the Hollywood horde."[9]

Yet this horde may not have committed much pillage. As we have seen, European cinema was actually flourishing in the central years of the Celluloid Atlantic, when Western Europe was supposedly overrun by the American barbarians. Italy and the US occupied the first and second place in Western film production, and the third spot was taken by France, which produced 120 films in 1967.[10] But these numbers are unpersuasive to the Atlantic Jeremiahs who lamented that Hollywood was turning Europe into a cultural colony of the United States. Also crucial to my argument is that the economic and linguistic apparatus related to what I call the Celluloid Atlantic bloomed during the Cold War, when many intellectuals produced a discourse of Euro-American difference that involved rethinking Western colonialism and European victimization.[11]

To describe the roots of this process and its articulation, I shall examine the relation between American cinema and Italian cinema during the Fascist *ventennio*. I shall then examine the making of *Ossessione* (1943), Luchino Visconti's forceful call for a new cinema that could break the Fascist filmic and cultural schemata. I shall pay particular attention to the role of American culture in this film, which was released during the last months of the Fascist regime. In the last part of the chapter, I shall look at the first postwar years of the Celluloid Atlantic and deal with the emergence of the contradictory notion of radical cultural difference that I link to the onset of the Cold War. Here, the focus will be on Giuseppe De Santis's *Riso Amaro* (Bitter Rice, 1949), which exemplifies the changes occurring in the years when the economic structure of the Atlantic film industry was first shaped. As we shall see, this was a moment of bicoastal integration and emulation that *Riso amaro* confirmed yet rhetorically denied.

The 1930s

While Atlantic integration accelerated in the decades after World War II, its foundation was laid before the conflict. In his provocative essay on the German, Italian, and American 1930s, Wolfgang Schivelbush argued that "the great postwar synthesis that created the trans-Atlantic 'West' spanning the United States and Europe would have been impossible without the cross fertilization of the 1930s."[12] At the turn of the twentieth century Europeans noticed American mass culture in their midst,[13] but it was only after 1918 that they realized the pervasive power of its technological inventions and mass-marketed media fabulations.

"Everywhere there emerged the centrality of America—whether loved or loathed—as the crucial term of comparison when the topic was building the future in any form," historian David Ellwood writes.[14]

He is correct, yet love dominated the intellectual circles that this book is concerned with, at least till the late 1940s. By then cultural imperialism had gained the upper hand among European intellectuals on the left. For the notion of an endangered and radical Euro-American difference to emerge, it took the onset of the Cold War and the US government's enrolling of culture in the anticommunist struggle for European hearts and minds.

European contempt for Hollywood is a relatively new idea. In a pioneering essay, Michela Nacci illustrated the scorn that Italian Fascist propaganda heaped on America and Hollywood cinema for what it termed the American "savage notion of comfort" (*barbarie del comfort*).[15] Nacci's work only began to reveal the vibrant and complex story of the regime's involvement with the United States and its culture. Emilio Gentile has suggested that "anti-Americanism based on a total aversion to modernity was only one aspect of the Fascist perception of the United States. Many other Fascist [intellectuals] neither considered modernity as evil in itself nor saw Americanism as a nightmare which threatened the future of Italian civilization."[16] Even when a series of Black Thursdays and even darker Tuesdays seemed to erase the mythical strength of American capitalism in the late twenties and early thirties, the Fascist regime was reticent about trumpeting America's troubles. Fascism was superior, but Americans were not enemies, and their nation hosted many expatriates that were financing the Italian economy from afar. On New Year's Day 1931 Mussolini sent his regards to the American people and "the President of your great republic."[17]

As far as cinema is concerned, in 1932 Luigi Freddi, whom Mussolini was to handpick as head of the General Directorate of Cinematography in 1934, went to Hollywood to study the American system. Upon his return, he proposed to create in Italy "a state owned MGM" (*MGM statalizzata*).[18] The son of the Duce, Vittorio Mussolini, headed *Cinema*, an important intellectual magazine that viewed Hollywood cinema with curiosity if not admiration. Mussolini junior was a film producer manqué; he liked American cinema and tried to set up a new production studio with American producer Hal Roach, RAM (Roach and Mussolini), to make Hollywood-style films of Italian operas.[19] This admiration partly echoed the Fascist enchantment with Fordist productivism that Vittorio wanted to copy for Cinecittà, which opened in 1937.[20]

The Celluloid Atlantic between Fascism and the Cold War   61

This attitude did not extend to the whole of American cinema, and it varied according to the politics of the commentator. Fascist censors hated the more mature examples of Hollywood democratic modernism of the thirties such as *The Grapes of Wrath* (John Ford, 1940) or *Confessions of a Nazi Spy* (Anatole Litvak, 1939). Here Fascism and anti-Fascism parted ways and the regime banned both films. Fascist censors considered Ernst Lubitsch's *The Merry Widow* (1934) unfit for Italian distribution because of the frivolity with which the institution of monarchy was treated.[21] On the other side of the political spectrum, Hollywood realist cinema inspired anti-Fascist intellectuals through their energetic representation of America's social reality. In his extraordinary autobiography *Questo novecento*, a socialist leader of the anti-Fascist resistance, Vittorio Foa, remembered how "even in the bleakest times of the Fascist propaganda in the 1930s, a large part of the Italians had sensed the energy charge coming from the other side of the ocean: one has just to think of the success of the American novel. . . . and of Hollywood cinema."[22]

Unlike the Fascist censors, the anti-Fascist group gathered around the publishing house Einaudi in Turin had only praise for American cinema. One of the key figures in Italian postwar intellectual circles and one of the innovators behind Einaudi's success, Cesare Pavese, was already interested in cinema and the United States in the 1920s. He had studied American literature at the University of Turin, writing his doctoral thesis on Walt Whitman. Throughout much of his short professional life (he took his life in 1950, in his early forties) Pavese worked as an editor and translator at Einaudi. If his translation of Herman Melville's *Moby Dick* is a major contribution to that field, his 1950 novel *La luna e i falò* (The Moon and the Bonfires), about Anguilla ("eel"), an Italian who spends the Fascist *ventennio* in America only to go back to Italy after the war, is, according to Mark Rudman, "the most American novel ever written in a foreign language."[23]

Next to literature, Pavese had long admired American cinema and its democratic appeal. "After a brief infancy and underdevelopment, American cinema has reached and overtaken the Italian one," Pavese wrote in 1927. "Part of the reason [for this rapid development] has been the American genius for organizing and rationalizing production." America cinema, however, was more than a reflection of Fordism. Hollywood understood "the revolutionary impulse harbored in that small black machine," Pavese wrote, referring to cinema's technological apparatus. This achievement, according to the young writer, had much to do with American film's ability to speak to its public. "The American films, even the least dignified, are all awash with, and full of . . . a frank and young conception of life, an enthusiasm that shapes all lives [centering] on a joyful seriousness about one's existence and work."[24]

Three years later, Pavese was arguing even more clearly that American cinema was the vanguard of a new civilization. A letter he wrote in English to a new American friend, the musician and educator Anthony Chiuminatto, whom he had met the year before in Turin, is worth citing in a slightly modified version that clarifies young Pavese's expressive, though Italianized, syntax and grammar (the original is in the footnote).

> In this century you Americans are going to dominate the civilized world, just like Greece, Italy, and France have done. What American movies have achieved in Old Europe in their relatively narrow sphere of action, the whole of your art and thought will achieve as well. (And I have always fiercely disagreed with those who maintained that it was Hollywood's financial organization and advertising power that made its movies successful. I'd say, in fact, that their success is due not simply to their artistic value, but to the surpassing strength of their vital energy—it does not matter whether of a pessimistic, or joyful, nature.) Each of your worthy writers discovers a new field of existence—a new world—, and writes about it with such down-to-earth-ness and immediate-ness of spirit that it's useless for us to even try and match it.[25]

In an essay contemporary with this letter, Pavese repeated that America cinema was "an art of, and for, the crowd and the reason for its vitality is . . . just that it constitutes an art not exceptional but entirely popular, that is, one that is able to speak to all audiences."[26] In this essay, "Di un novo tipo d'esteta," the twenty-two-year-old Pavese professed the customary European admiration for Charlie Chaplin as well as a dislike for American Westerns. He went further, theorizing cinema as the preeminent form of modernist, vernacular, and democratic art. He railed against elitist literature and reminded his readers that American cinema was "un arte di folla" (an art for the masses).[27] The third-run neighborhood theaters (*cinemini da due lire*), Pavese argued, were the places where spectators could come across "the most earnest of masterpieces" (*capolavori dei più schietti*). These little theaters were "the altars where art banquets are held, [which would be] impossible [*inaudite*] in less popular venues."

On the same wavelength Alberto Lattuada, one of the young Turks of Italian film criticism and realist photography—and later an early exponent of neorealism—imagined a more democratic role for Italian intellectuals and the same interclass audience as Pavese did. Lattuada argued in his 1939 "Meditazione" that cinema can be entertainment "or a contact point between the intellectual and the masses."[28] "Until today," Lattuada wrote in another essay, "intellectuals have had no loudspeaker; cinema has given them that, and has made things bloody complex. . . . Cinema . . . offers really the means to meld and fuse the masses and the intellectuals [*le masse e il pensiero*]."[29]

Central to these intellectuals' musing was the role of realist cinema in engaging the masses, which would offer them an image of "themselves with their problems and the issues that deeply engage them." And American cinema—"when not hampered by the dictatorship of [William] Hays"[30]—has led the way in films "of social character" like those by Fritz Lang, Mervyn LeRoy, and William Wyler.[31] A gifted photographer, Lattuada manifested his profound interest in American culture in his first published book of photos, *L'occhio quadrato* (1941), which contained little celebration of Italian economic and social life and much resonance with the work of the Farm Security Administration photographers, whose work he had seen in Paris. The book attracted the attention of the regime. "You see only rags and poor people, and thus it derogatively operates against us," a police inspector for the Milanese district told Lattuada rather convolutedly, when the volume saw print.[32]

National boundaries stand in the way of writing a coherent history of Western intellectuals' attitudes toward cinema. This story is not just about the intellectual tastes of a cadre of Italian intellectuals but the consolidation of a novel intellectual and cultural geography. What is remarkable is not solely that during the Fascist regime Hollywood cinema, as Umberto Eco noted, constituted for Italian intellectuals a "sort of alternative education, a real flow of "counterpropaganda" to that of the regime,[33] but also the fact that these Italian intellectuals (who later became the protagonists of the neorealist generation) were part of the same transnational modernist movement as their American counterparts. Consider, for example, how Pavese's or Lattuada's words resonate with those written in the 1920s by American playwright, and later screenwriter, John Howard Lawson. In 1927 Lawson, who embraced Communism in the 1930s and was blacklisted in Hollywood after World War II, wrote that "dullness" was the capital sin of American theater.[34] Theater should excite a vast audience and reject any intellectual exclusivity. "I have endeavored," Lawson wrote in the preface to his 1925 play, *Processional*, "to create a method which shall express the American scene in native idiom, a method as far removed from the older realism as from the facile mood of expressionism."[35] Far from any "anxiety of contamination" between the high and the low of cultural production, the young playwright wanted his play to be a veritable hybrid between what he called "vaudeville," avant-garde expressionism, and the "legitimate theater," which he deemed "in a feeble trance, totally removed from the rush and roar of things as they are, a sanctuary with doors barred against the world."[36] Writing the foreword to Lawson's coming of age tale, *Roger Bloomer*, John Dos Passos argued that theater needed a large national audience: "Like everything else about American theater," Dos Passos wrote, "a criterion of judgment exists if at all, only in vague conditional prophecy. Before we can have standards, we've got to have plays, an audience, a tradition."[37]

Thus, ideas echoed across the Celluloid Atlantic and national perspectives are not sufficient to characterize the modernism of the interwar period—or even thereafter. Not only were some of the Italian young intellectuals in Rome in awe of American cinema, they also appreciated it for some of the same reasons that gave hope to a new generation of progressive Hollywoodians like John Howard Lawson: cinema was a way to connect intellectuals to the masses. For some of the more or less openly anti-Fascist Italian intellectuals, this task was made more urgent by the international threat of fascism, which high modernism had failed to oppose. "I think that this is just the moment," wrote Alberto Lattuada in 1941, "to break the shell that protects a certain kind of modernism and to renovate the flux of love that moves men toward unity."[38]

That Italians saw many American movies facilitated the Atlantic dialogue. The Hollywood majors stopped exporting Hollywood movies into Italy only at the beginning of 1939, when they retaliated against

Mussolini's decision (the Alfieri law of September 1938) to institute state control of the distribution of foreign films by withdrawing their movies from the Italian market.[39] Critics and cinéphiles could watch American films at the Esposizione Internazionale d'Arte Cinematografica, the Venice Film Festival, which opened in 1932 and where Pare Lorentz's *The River* was recognized as best documentary in 1938.

America also appeared in Italian literature and Italian films, albeit framed into a heavily biased depiction. Emilio Cecchi, the former executive producer at the most modern of Italian film studios, Stefano Pittaluga's Cines, visited the United States in 1930 and again in 1937–1938 and became the main interpreter of things American for middle-class Italians. His *America Amara* (1939) was the most popular travelogue by an Italian visitor to America before the war. Not surprisingly, given his professional interests, Cecchi noted the importance of cinema in American life and culture, its reliance on formulas, and its ability to generate new ideas and recruit talent from all over the world.[40] He observed that the typical gangster film plot changed after the implementation of the Hays Code in 1934, turning gangster film stars like James Cagney into FBI agents in *G Men*. Cecchi noted, however, that "the element that makes it interesting [to the audiences] remains the same" (*l'elemento di fondamentale interesse rimane immutato*).[41]

Cecchi's interpretation of American society left little to the unexpected. Next to the obligatory descriptions of American women as masculine (*alte, membrute, violente*, "tall, strong, violent"),[42] American literature as dominated by formulaic bestsellers (*fabbricata su ricetta*, "made according to a formula"),[43] and American cities populated by gangsters, whom Cecchi saw as the natural heir to the pioneer,[44] Cecchi's racism showed in his interpreting the Italian conquest of Ethiopia as "necessity of expansion" and as evidence of "military glory [and the superiority of] Latin civilization."[45] He depicted African Americans in contemptuous terms, comparing, for example, African American women in their Sunday dresses to "working nags pulling the vegetable peddler's horse-carts."[46] He did not hesitate, however, to call out American hypocrisy in racial relations. Americans were ready to criticize Italy and Germany for their anti-Semitism, but hypocritically feared the Jewish control of Wall Street;[47] they passionately loved the "negri d'Etiopia," but refused to pass laws to stop lynching in their own backyard.[48]

Summed up in his best-selling travelogue, Cecchi's views of America returned in *Harlem* (1943), which Cecchi wrote for director Carmine Gallone together with Sergio Amidei (later a protagonist of the neorealist season and the writer of many of Roberto Rossellini's and Vittorio De Sica's films). Like *America Amara*, *Harlem* was not original in its themes. The African American neighborhood of Harlem gave the title to this film and suggested how much race was a crucial component of the Fascist imagination about the United States. But Harlem was also tangential to three-quarters of this film, which dealt with the entire New York City as synecdoche of America. The plot depicted the American trip of an Italian boxer, Tommaso (Massimo Girotti), who arrives in New York City to visit his older brother Amedeo (Amedeo Nazzari), a successful architect. Amedeo has been framed by local gangster Chris Sherman (Osvaldo Valenti), and sentenced to jail. To post bail, Tommaso agrees to fight the brutish African American boxing champion, Charlie Lamb (played by the real Charlie Lamb), and he defeats him, thus affirming the physical superiority of the Latin "race." The film was rereleased in postwar Italy with a happy ending that sees Amedeo's vindication in the American court and his release from prison. The original ending was much more explicitly anti-American. The gangster has Amedeo gunned down upon his release from jail, and he dies imploring his brother on his deathbed to return to Italy for good.[49]

As a potboiler of popular American themes, *Harlem* synthesized the conundrum of Italian Fascist cinema: how to make anti-American movies that looked like Hollywood movies. In *Cinema*, Giuseppe De Santis noted the film's dependence on American genres and style, its fast cars and tall buildings part of a "'lexicon' typical of American films, with situations that were fully copied [from Hollywood films]" (*'terminologia' da film americano, con situazioni ricalcate di sana pianta*).[50] The film was poor propaganda because, in failing in its attempt to mimic the fresh styles of Rouben Mamoulian's gangster movie *City Streets* (1929), the effect was not realism but its opposite. The film referenced real America the same contrived way most American movies depicted Italy. De Santis pointed his finger at Dorothy Arzner's *The Bride Wore Red* (1937), which featured a papier maché northern Italy as a setting for an unbelievable romance. Likewise, *Harlem* was all about a fake America, and De Santis used his review to praise, tongue-in-cheek, the literature of the country Italy was then at war with:

The Celluloid Atlantic between Fascism and the Cold War   67

William Faulkner's *Sanctuary* and *Pylon* brilliantly depicted American "mental slumber" (*sonnolenza mentale*), he noted. Similarly, Antonio Pietrangeli reviewed the film in *Bianco e Nero* and suggested its writer should have known better: "The authors have aimed at impressing on the film the surrogate of an American movie. It is surprising that among these authors is [Emilio] Cecchi who passes for an expert of things American."[51]

Wearing America on One's Sleeves: Ossessione (1943)

In 1943, when he directed his first film, *Ossessione*, Luchino Visconti was a thirty-six-year-old scion of large means but no definite profession. His father, Giuseppe Visconti, was the descendant of Gian Galeazzo Visconti, the first duke of Milan. His mother, Carla Erba, was the daughter of Carlo Erba, the founder of the most important pharmaceutical firm in Italy. Gifted but restless, Luchino had bred race horses with some success and traveled extensively, including to the Sahara Desert where he had gone in 1929 following the death of a friend in a car crash that he, himself, had caused. On frequent trips to Paris he had assisted French director Jean Renoir in *Toni* (1935), *Les Bas-Fonds* (The Lower Depths, 1936), *Partie de Campagne* (A Day in the Country, 1936) and, perhaps, *La grande illusion* (The Great Illusion, 1937).

The work with Renoir and his crew and the France of Léon Blum and the Popular Front probably contributed to shift the young aristocrat's views from apolitical to antifascist. When Renoir went to Italy to direct *Tosca* (The Story of Tosca, 1941) in 1939, Visconti followed the French maestro on a trip back to Italy. By then, Visconti had chosen his profession and was calling himself a filmmaker. When the French director left Italy following the Italian attack on France in June 1940, Visconti collaborated with Carl Koch to complete *Tosca*.[52]

Visconti's intellectual curiosity pointed him, like many of his generation, toward the United States. Unlike most of his peers, who had to content themselves with American literature and Hollywood films, Luchino possessed the means to investigate America firsthand. From the end of 1937 to the first months of 1938, Visconti traveled in the United States and visited California and Hollywood,[53] igniting an intensified interest in American culture. Critic Gianni Rondolino reports that prior to *Ossessione*, Luchino encouraged many of his collaborators to work on American subjects, including adaptations of Herman Melville's *Benito Cereno*, Erskine Caldwell's *Tobacco Road*, and John Steinbeck's *Of Mice and Men*.[54] After *Ossessione*, *Cine Magazzino* reported that he was hard at work on film adaptations of William Faulkner's *Sanctuary* and John Steinbeck's *The Grapes of Wrath*.[55]

It was Renoir who suggested that Visconti consider James M. Cain's American short novel for his screen debut. The French auteur probably knew the 1934 novella from its first screen adaptation, *Le Dernier Tournant* by French filmmaker Pierre Chenal, that dated to 1939. Chenal's film had gone mostly unnoticed by critics, but Renoir may have been drawn to it by the working-class setting of Cain's novel and by its violent and tragic ending, themes he had just engaged in his *The Human Beast* (La bête humaine, 1938).

Ossessione was thus the second film adaptation of James Cain's *The Postman Always Rings Twice*, and the European success of this novella exemplifies European attention to 1930s American realist literature. *Postman* centered on adultery, insurance money, and murder among working-class white Californians in the middle of the Great Depression. While one of the characters, Nick Papadakis, the cuckolded husband, and the owner of the Twin Oaks Tavern, is an immigrant from Europe, little of the story evoked the eastern border of the Pond. On the contrary, Cain uses quintessential American types only to denude them of any romantic mythology. Frank Chambers, the drifter who has an affair with Nick's young wife, Cora, and eventually murders him, is the classic hobo traveling the great American road. Cora herself is a type. The winner of a local beauty contest given the archetypal American surname of "Smith," Cora Smith has come to Los Angeles from Iowa to try her luck in Hollywood, but stardom is not in her cards. Having failed a screen test, she ends up in a "hash house," where Nick finds and marries her out of pity and lust, making her the mistress of his miserable roadside inn.

In addition to Cain's typified American characters, the plot of *Postman* involves complicated transactions with insurance companies and the American justice system: "I've got all the insurance I need," the exasperated judge tells District Attorney Sackett during the murder trial of Frank and Cora after the lawyer has paraded several insurance representatives before the bench.[56] The trial's denouement involves laborious transactions between Frank and Cora's defense

The Celluloid Atlantic between Fascism and the Cold War   69

attorney, Mr. Katz, and insurance companies, corporate entities that, as Jonathan Auerbach has shown, very much concerned early American film noirs.[57] Famously, Cain had Katz save Frank and Cora from death row by pitting one insurance company against another (if Cora is found guilty of the murder, one insurance company will save the $10,000 of Nick's life insurance premium but the other company will have to disburse $20,000 to Frank because he had been badly hurt, as a passenger, in the car crash that killed Nick). The life insurance representative then testifies that he does not believe Cora is guilty, thus foiling the DA's strategy as no jury would be willing to convict her when the insurance company itself deems her innocent. In the end, fate determines Cora's and Nick's death. Ironically, Cora dies in an accidental car crash and Frank will hang on the assumption that he caused the accident to get at Cora's property.

Postman was a cynical look at a specific kind of American modernity, one modeled after a Southern Californian anomie of car culture that would prove almost incomprehensible to European viewers. The profound Americanness of the novel notwithstanding, Pierre Chenal, the director of the first European adaptation of the story, and his screenwriters, Charles Spaak and Henry Torrès, closely followed its plot. They maintained the names of Cora (Corinne Luchaire) and Frank (Fernand Gravey) for the two adulterous lovers and the cuckolded immigrant husband and innkeeper Nick (a terrific Michel Simon), though they changed Nick's nationality from Greek (Papadakis) to Italian (Marino). They preserved the name of the tavern in its French translation, Taverne des Chênes Jumeaux (Twin Oaks Tavern). Like the American inn, the French inn has a badly illuminated sign, a diegetic element that sets in motion the first murder attempt, causes the electrocution of an innocent black cat, Nick's hospital stay, and Cora and Frank's initial weeklong romance.

Chenal and his screenwriters are kinder to Cora than Cain is. After the second, and successful, murder attempt, the novelist has Frank Chambers sign a deposition accusing Cora Papadakis of masterminding the plot. Upon learning this, Cora signs a counterdeposition detailing how they organized the murder together. In the French film, Cora Marino is more subdued and loyal. "I do not want to sign anything against him and I have nothing to say," she tells the lawyer, although, like her novella's alter ego, she soon becomes angry and distrustful of Frank. Beyond this, the film is remarkably faithful to Cain's novel. *Le dernier tournant* includes the novella's seaside setting and a simplified insurance ploy to let Cora and Frank off the hook. It also repeats Cora's visit to her ailing mother, Frank's affair with a woman whose surprising (even more so in a French setting) profession is taming wild mountain lions, and the foiled blackmail attempt that prompts the reconciliation between Frank and Cora. The French film and novel also end the same way. Cora dies in a fateful road accident, which triggers the justice system to reopen the case and sends Frank to the gallows. The final thoughts of Frank (Maurice) are also modeled after those of Frank (Chambers). His only hope for the afterlife is another chance to see Cora so that he can tell her that her death was accidental.

The film was not a hit, but it did fit French audiences' and critics' interest in realism. Chenal and his dialogue writer, Charles Spaak, were both Belgian (Chenal was born Philippe Cohen in Brussel and trained as a chemist) and were both interested in realism and socially engaged cinema (Spaak also collaborated to Renoir's *Les Bas Fonds* in 1936 and *La grande illusion* in 1937). Reviewing Chenal's *La rue sans nom* (1933) in *Cinémonde* in 1933, French critic Michel Gorel applied the term "poetic realism" to the film, a definition that followed the French realist school of the 1930s comprising Marcel Carné, Marcel Pagnol, and Renoir among others. *Le dernier tournant* emphasized the popular origins of its main characters through a careful choice of clothes, accents, and dialogue. In addition, the film uses real locations, which prompted film historian Allan Williams to see the film as an "adumbration (along with Renoir's *Toni* and most of Pagnol's work) of postwar neorealism."[58]

In contrast to Chenal's, Visconti's choice to film *The Postman* has been seen as separate from the novel's singular qualities. Scholars often repeat that the script of *Ossessione* was written without close knowledge of the book, but while the film and the novel often part ways, Visconti and his screenwriters knew their source well. Renoir had most likely seen Chenal's film, a close rendition of the novella, when he first suggested that Visconti adapt it. We also know that writer Giorgio Bassani, who was then translating Cain's novel, gave one of Visconti's close collaborators, the future director Giuseppe De Santis, a copy of the draft of his own translation of *Postman*, and was often on set while the film was shot at the outskirts of Bassani's native Ferrara. The script was, by then, probably complete, but De Santis does not

The Celluloid Atlantic between Fascism and the Cold War   71

discount Bassani's contribution and Visconti's attentive reading of the book. According to De Santis and to Bassani's own daughter, Paola, the Italian writer made welcome on-set suggestions about locations and even the "comportamenti psicologici" (psychological behaviors) of the characters.[59]

It is also unlikely that Visconti chose the inspiration for his first feature film lightly. On the contrary, it is evidence of the intense intellectual Atlantic traffic of the 1930s. What attracted European filmmakers and intellectuals to Cain and other American artists of the 1930s was their realistic address of the American social milieu—what Pavese had called their "downrightness [sic] and immediateness of spirit."

In this context the choice of Cain makes sense. In his *New York Times* review of *The Postman* Harold Strauss wrote that the "intense realism" of Cain's sparse and direct style made "[Ernest] Hemingway look like a lexicographer and [Erskine] Caldwell like a sob sister" and forced us "to revalue our notion of the realist manner, for no less than reality itself."[60] Seen from the perspective of the Celluloid Atlantic and of anti-Fascism, the choice of Cain's novella becomes a gesture within the long tradition of Italian intellectuals' engagement with American culture as an antidote to the conservative fairy tale optimism typical of Fascist cinema. Besides, though comprehensible to most Italian intellectual young Turks, or those disenchanted with and opposed to the regime, the covert anti-Fascism in Visconti's choice of subject was unlikely to be detected by Fascist censors who had not read the novel.

Yet admiration for American realist style did not necessarily translate into recasting American stories into an Italian context. Many of the Italian filmmakers involved in the realization of *Ossessione* thought Italian cinema's engagement of Italian reality was woefully minimal; as De Santis's pointed critique of *Harlem* shows, they wanted Italian, not American, stories. American realist cinema and literature could serve as models when it came to form, but not content. Visconti had in fact considered several 100 percent "Italian" possibilities for his directorial debut and in 1941 he had bought the rights for Giovanni Verga's *I malavoglia* (The House by the Medlar Tree, 1881), a classic of Italian, late nineteenth-century literary realism.[61] Two of the screenwriters of the film, Giuseppe De Santis and Mario Alicata, had also suggested Verga as an inspiration for the new Italian cinema.[62]

What complicates the issue may then be the "excessive" Americanness of Cain's novel, its characters, and its landscape. Its translator, Giorgio Bassani, shared the progressive Italian intellectuals' admiration for American stories and American cinema, and his anti-Fascist education and politics echoed those of *Ossessione*'s crew.[63] In "Chiacchiere," a piece he wrote for "La Pagina del Cinematografo" of the *Corriere Padano* in 1936, Bassani displayed his loyalty to the same principles as De Santis, Lattuada, and Pavese. He expressed doubts about "liberal arts" that have become too "difficult and specialized" (difficili e professionali). He manifested a keen interest for the "popolarissima Musa" of cinema that is "on everybody's mouth" (sulle bocche di tutti). He also showed that he was paying attention to Hollywood, whose recent experiment with color (he cited *Becky Sharp*, 1935, by Rouben Mamoulian, and Henry Hathaway's 1936 version of John Fox Jr.'s 1908 novel *The Trail of the Lonesome Pine*) Bassani celebrated as pathbreaking against the Italian *misoneisti* (haters of the new).[64]

When he gave his friend his own copy of Cain's novella while De Santis was on the set of *Ossessione*, Bassani added a note warning the filmmaker that "to translate the [American] landscape, to try and see it in Italian" (tradurre il paesaggio [Americano], cercare di vederlo in Italiano) was a difficult task though a tempting intellectual challenge ("stimolo infinito").[65] De Santis soon realized that the young writer was correct. Born in the countryside around Rome in 1917, before moving to Rome and enrolling in the Centro Sperimentale di Cinematografia, De Santis had grown up in the midst of the bogs and the malaria-infested ponds of Ciociaria and lower Maremma, a part of Italy that, until the land reclamation by the Fascist government, was among the most primitive of the peninsula. Nothing could seem more distant from Cain's America than that land, he wrote, with its "archaic quiet, proud immobilism, patriarchal dogma."[66] In 1942, just a few months before beginning the shoot of *Ossessione*, then still called "Palude," Alicata and De Santis wrote in *Cinema* about the necessity to cast Italian films into an Italian landscape ("paesaggio italiano") to enhance their realism ("veri").[67]

That Visconti and his circle could advocate filming Italian stories in an Italian landscape while making a film drawn from a very American novel may thus seem intellectually contradictory in addition to being personally dangerous. By 1942, when the shooting of *Ossessione* began, Italy had been at war with the United States for almost a year.

The Celluloid Atlantic between Fascism and the Cold War   73

It is important to keep in mind, however, that *Ossessione* remained a deeply creolized (to use Rob Kroes's useful expression) cultural import that only indirectly gave credit to its American origin.[68] Admiration for the novel and American realist style was only one of the elements of a shaping cultural force field that also comprised anxiety about censorship and intellectual and political concerns that called for the Italianization, rather than Americanization, of Italian cinema.

All three earliest versions of Cain's *Postman* (Chenal's, Visconti's, and Tay Garnett's 1946 *The Postman Always Rings Twice*) start where the novel begins, with the arrival of—respectively—Gino (Massimo Girotti in *Ossessione*) and Frank (Fernand Gravey and John Garfield, respectively, in *Tournant* and in Hollywood's first *Postman*) at the small roadside business owned by Nick (Michel Simon and Cecil Kellaway, respectively) and Giuseppe Bragana (Juan de Landa). All also end where the novel ends, with the drifter arrested for the murder of the innkeeper, and the adulterous wife Giovanna Braganza (Clara Calamai) or Cora (Corinne Luchaire and Lana Turner, respectively) dead in an accidental road crash.[69]

Ossessione also radically differs from these films, however. Take, for example, the very beginning. Like the novel, the action begins with Frank's arrival at Nick's store, the Twin Oaks Tavern, which is called "Ex dogana" (former custom house) in *Ossessione*.[70] But here the similarities stop. The "threshold" of Chenal's film is both classical and unremarkable. Garnett's Hollywood film is obsessed with copyright issues, and Visconti's with America and the uncertainties of modernity.

Chenal depicts Nick's arrival at night. The camera films a mountain road and the director interrupts this shot by showing the visage of his actors—in particular Corinne Luchaire—as the credits roll down. The incipit shows the film for what it is, a movie with well-known French stars. Garnett's film shows no action and no face in its initial credit sequence, the threshold of the film, instead centering the image of the cover of Cain's novella. Garnett's film, the third adaptation of the novel but the first American one, was also the first based on a legally obtained copyright because MGM had acquired the right to Cain's story from its author.[71]

Visconti introduced the viewer to the story of Gino and Giovanna differently. In a manifesto he published in *Cinema* in October 1943, the young director argued for the centrality of human beings in any aesthetic of film. The human body was the only phenomenon that could fill ("colmare") a photogram. Visconti sought a humanist cinema ("cinema antropomorfico") aiming at the depiction of "real persons" (uomini vivi).[72]

Remarkably, then, his first film begins with an empty landscape. *Ossessione* began by showing a progression of things rather than human beings. Visconti and Aldo Tonti, his director of photography, placed the camera in the cab of the truck carrying Gino to his fateful meeting with Giovanna and Giuseppe Bragana. Hewing to the novella's timing ("noon"), the camera is filming in daylight, as opposed to the night shot in Chenal's version. Inside the moving vehicle, Visconti and Tonti pointed the camera outwards, toward the windshield, recording the dull, repetitive landscape of the banks of the Po as the credits scroll. The 88-second sequence communicates a sense of inexorable momentum, and connects this thrust forward to modernity. *Le dernier tournant* title sequence showed a nocturnal, primitive, mountainous French countryside. Over *Ossessione*'s credits, the screen records the opposite of a traditional agricultural land. The highway is paved and the banks of the powerful river are contained by cement levees. The slight wobbliness of the images show the camera's presence inside a rapidly moving truck, another reference to a modern, slightly un-Italian world, as automobiles and trucks were a relatively new addition to Italian agriculture, their spread often connected to the American model of Henry Ford. Coming from the more traditional *meridione*, Giuseppe De Santis noted how the countryside around Ferrara was exceptionally modern compared to the rest of Italy and dominated by a "management of the soil . . . already on the brink of technology . . . no longer managed traditionally and with no imagination . . . but already at the heart of a rich [technological] experimentation."[73]

Despite taking greater liberties with the American novel's text, Visconti is far more interested than Chenal in the United States. The credits of the film begin his conversation with America on a disturbing note. The opposite of the "cinema antropomorfico" Visconti had proposed, the sequence depicts an agricultural world that is both mechanized and strangely vacated by human beings. It is a mechanical world manifesting the critique of American modernity as fundamentally dehumanizing.

But Visconti's is far from a simplistic rejection of America and its Fordist modernity of highways and cars. *Ossessione* also offers another possible America, one that becomes Visconti's cypher for freedom

Figure 2.1. *Ossessione*. The credits. *Source*: Author's collection.

itself. Gino's existence, like Frank's, centers on movement: his story and fate is about his progressive loss of mobility, his being inexorably penned in. The beginning of the film depicts him literally driving, or being driven, into his destiny. He will not cease moving, or dreaming about moving, throughout the rest of the film. *Ossessione* emphasizes the geographical consequences of this continuous motion by filming on location outside the stages of Cinecittà (Ancona, Ferrara, or the plains around Ferrara, for example). As Gino moves, or wants to move, Cora's alter ego Giovanna demands that they stay put. She is the one who wants to stay in the "Ex dogana" and keep Gino there. "Now you will never leave me, right?" (Adesso non mi lascerai più vero?), she tells the drifter after sleeping with him for the first time, "not even to go back on the road!" (nemmeno per tornartene sulla strada!).

When the lovers try to escape Giuseppe Bragana, the young woman becomes physically unable to walk forward. In the novella, exhausted, Cora stops and goes back home and Frank proceeds further to San Bernardino, where he wins money in a poolroom. He thinks of going to Mexicali, but loses all his prize money. He meets Nick, and sheepishly goes back to the tavern, Cora, and his destiny. In Visconti's film, Gino and Cora try to escape from "Ex dogana" almost immediately after they meet (the film has no first murder attempt) and, just like in the novel, they part ways when she cannot go on. As Frank does in the novella, Gino continues alone, but unlike Frank he goes far. His destination is the harbor of Ancona, two hundred miles south of Ferrara, in whose rural outskirts the film begins. In comparative and absolute terms, Gino goes further than Nick in the novella and in both of the other earliest film versions. Cain and Garnett imagined Nick going from Glendale to San Bernardino (a mere fifty mile trip on a comfortable California highway) and Chenal does not posit any long journey either.

In theory, Gino would want to go even further. As imagined by Visconti and his crew, Gino's movements may connect him to the world. Gino makes it to Ancona where he considers boarding a freighter, and we see the powerful, modern ships leaving the port. In an early draft of the film's treatment, the scope of Gino's travel plans were global. In that treatment, he goes to Ancona and "once arrived, winds up in a café, spending days playing pool and waiting for a chance to land a job on a ship directed to the [overseas] colonies."[74] The reference to the colonies is not in the final film or script, most likely because Italy had by then lost control of all its overseas possessions to the British army, but Gino's *Wanderlust* remains as central as his dedication to modern means of transportation. In *Ossessione*, Gino rarely walks, but often travels via mechanical means, in contrast to the rest of the characters in the film. In the beginning, as we said, he is hiding on a truck. He is often shot at the wheel of Braganza's car. When he leaves for Ancona, he boards a train, a scene added to the story by Visconti and his screenwriters. Conversely, Cora walks and works about the house and the inn, and Bragana rarely drives. He prefers riding his bicycle, alongside the priest, who represents another marker of Italian antimodernism.

Movement and a passion for the wide and modern world is not the only difference between Gino and all the Franks in Cain's novel and Chenal's and Garnett's renditions of the story. In *Postman* Cain insists on the moral equivalence between Cora and Frank. "We are just two punks, Frank," Cora tells her lover, acknowledging their similarity. "We were trying to fly to the sky by putting an airplane engine in

The Celluloid Atlantic between Fascism and the Cold War   77

an old Ford car but one cannot do that," she tells him. "That's what we are, Frank, a couple of Fords. God is up there laughing at us."[75]

In 1939 Chenal was forgiving toward his "Cora." Of the pair, she is the more romantic. Visconti unbalances the equilibrium with a subtly misogynist twist. Unlike the novella, *Ossessione* notes her desire to pen Gino in. She is the force confining Gino's dreams: "Once the world looked so large to me, now only this store exists," he reproachfully tells her. Though already in the text, this claustrophobia is sharpened in the Italian film. Cora and Bragana run the "Ex dogana," its name, "the former custom house," underscoring exactly the borders imposed on Gino's travels and freedom.

In the novella, and in both Chenal's and Garrett's films, Frank is shown at his worst: he betrays Cora as soon as the investigation for the murder of Nick starts closing in on him (and, in retaliation, she turns against him). Cain also has him confess that he considered killing her before she revealed her pregnancy because she threatened to turn him in and have him "dance on air" upon discovering his infidelity.[76] She is, of course, no gentle soul, and the gloomy novella is about two people who deserve their fate and each other. Visconti's script, however, eschews the subtle discourse of moral complicity and its implication of gender equality, in part by omitting the entire trial scene that is at the center of the other *Postman* (the novel and Garnett's 1946 version and also of *Dernier Tournant*). After the accident, the lovers are dismissed by the inspector with a warning that he may need to see them again—in contrast to the protracted trial section that in the novel allowed Cain the opportunity to showcase his knowledge of insurance practices and corporate America and emphasize the weak moral fiber of both his characters. During the trial, Frank suspects that Cora has used him and agrees to file a complaint against her. This fragility is in line with the character Cain has shown us to be impulsive and unprincipled. Frank is no good: he cheats at pool and is unfaithful to Cora as soon as she leaves to be with her dying mother.

"Gino" is subtly, but unquestionably, made of a different cloth than all these literary and filmic "Franks." The omission of the trial allows Visconti to eliminate Gino's betrayal of Cora. Gino is, in the end, sexually unfaithful to her, but Visconti makes excuses for his character's behavior: Gino cheats only after he finds out that she will collect a large life insurance payout. Rather than a gambler, a murderer, and a cheat, Visconti's young man emerges as principled, a free spirit, a vagabond dressed exactly like the American progressive tramps familiar to Italian spectator in the films of Frank Capra, George Cukor, or Charlie Chaplin.[77]

Visconti makes the direction of Gino's quest even clearer with the addition of a character, Spagnolo (the Spaniard), that is neither in the novel, nor in Chenal's film, nor even in the first versions of *Ossessione*'s treatment when the film was still called "Palude" (bog). Interpreted by the antifascist and gay actor Elio Marcuzzo, who was later lynched by a mob of anti-Fascist partisans in one of the most tragic episodes of the Italian civil war, Spagnolo is a cypher gesturing toward homosexuality and an antifascist invocation of America.[78] A brilliant invention by Marcuzzo, Visconti, and his crew, Spagnolo is what Gino aspires to be: he stands for freedom and for what Gino could be if only he were to live up to his ideals. When the latter meets Spagnolo on the train to Ancona, Spagnolo pays for Gino's ticket so that he is not thrown off the train. Marcuzzo is dressed almost identically to Charlie Chaplin's famous tramp, but unlike Chaplin's vagabond, Spagnolo is a talker. In obvious reference to the Spanish Civil War, he tells Gino that he has been in Spain, hence his nickname. We simply *know* that he did not fight for Mussolini or Generalissimo Franco. He is an artist, travels with a parrot he has named Robespierre, is generous, and explains his generosity with money via a vernacular Keynesianism that sounds like New Deal economic policy ("Money has legs and must walk. If it stays in the pocket, it grows moldy. Rather [than keeping it], you take a bite of it and then pass it on to someone who then lives on it. Thus, the liras we earn in Rome make possible a decent living for someone in Turin or Palermo").[79] For Spagnolo, traveling represents freedom, which, as he implies, means more than (hetero)sexual freedom. He encourages Gino to travel further, "as far as you can." The Superego to Giovanna's Id, Spagnolo is what Gino should be, and wants to be, and yet no longer can, possibly because of his attraction to Giovanna.

In her provocative essay on the film, Cristina della Colletta remarks upon the final scene where we see Spagnolo. It takes place at the police station and della Colletta suggests that the character is actually turning in Gino to the police for the murder, after Gino has refused to follow his friend on the road.[80] The scene is more ambiguous than this. It takes place during a weekend when the "Ex dogana" is doing a brisk business. Bragana has been murdered and Gino and

Figure 2.2. Spagnolo (Elio Marcuzzo) in *Ossessione*. *Source*: Author's collection.

Giovanna have hired musicians from Polesella, a town fifteen miles north of Ferrara. People are dancing and drinking. Spagnolo appears out of nowhere, Gino spots him from his window, rushes out, and warmly welcomes the friend. Spagnolo has come to the inn because he wants to see Gino, and, as everybody is talking about him and Giovanna, finding him has been easy. Spagnolo is again "on the road" and, in one of the film's most poetic lines, he invites his friend to join him and go to Genoa: "One can walk for hours along Genoa's docks. It is like a road and you come across so many friends! Because everybody goes to Genoa."[81] Gino refuses. He tells his friend that he wants to stay at "La dogana" with Giovanna and give up "being a hobo" (fare il vagabondo). The two men argue and come to blows. Overpowered, Spagnolo puts on his ragged jacket and misshapen hat, and leaves. Gino shouts for him to come back, but he keeps walking. Visconti frames Spagnolo from the back and his clothes and limping gait remind the viewer of Charlot (Charlie Chaplin).

After a brief scene at the inn, Visconti cuts to the inspector's office in Ferrara and to a figure shot from the back, framed by the door and wearing neither coat nor hat. The glass door soon closes, leaving us on the outside. Before cutting back to Gino and Giovanna, Visconti lets us hear words through the glass: a cop identifying the man as "Lavorato, Giuseppe, aka 'lo spagnolo.' "

It is an ambiguous scene. Maybe Spagnolo, if he is the person we see from the back, is acting out of jealousy. The spat with Gino follows Visconti's depiction of the intense bond between the two men. In Ancona, before Gino meets again with Giovanna and Giuseppe, the two friends share a bed and talk all night about their common dreams of freedom. Visconti, however, shows that whatever the person was doing at the police station, he was not informing on Gino. The final denouement of the story, when the police apprehend Gino, is set in motion later in the film. Two truck drivers are shown reporting to the police inspector that they observed Gino and Giovanna on the road as Braganza's car was going off the cliff. It is only then that the inspector tells his men that he wants to know Gino Costa's thereabouts, and he still seems uncertain of Gino's guilt: "Let me ask you something . . . what about that guy, Costa?" (ma sentite un po' . . . quel Costa?), he asks his underlings.

If Spagnolo was not informing on Gino and Giovanna, what was he doing at the police station? Perhaps, as a known anti-Fascist, Spagnolo was required to register with the local police wherever he was. While Visconti and his collaborators may have wanted to mark their realistic approach by avoiding hagiographic character construction, Spagnolo is mostly defined as an ideal character, the stand-in for a life of personal, political, and perhaps sexual freedom that Fascism, and Giovanna, prevent Gino from enjoying.

Remarkably, the Fondo Visconti at the Gramsci Institute in Rome possesses two early versions of the "Palude" script. Both are undated and unsigned, but have quite a few handwritten notes. Neither of them features the character of "Spagnolo." In one of these two treatments, marked C10–003043, there is a report of the Ministero della Cultura Popolare dated January 26, 1942. After 1939, the Fascist Ministero di Cultura e Propaganda (Department of Culture and Propaganda) inspected all treatments before they were placed into production. In the report the department "expresses favorable opinion for the further development of the treatment with the goal of its being filmed." It stands to reason that the crew of anti-Fascist filmmakers around Visconti added the character of Spagnolo on set to avoid censorial suspicions.[82]

The American imagery of Visconti's hobo is clear in the costumes Maria De Matteis designed for Girotti and Marcuzzo. While Marcuzzo dresses like Chaplin's tramp, Gino wears a tank top that gestures toward the notorious one worn by Clark Gable in *It Happened One Night* (Frank Capra, 1934).[83]

Contemporary critic Walter Ronchi noted the reference, and remarked that, when he played the harmonica, Girotti reminded him of "a character from [Frank] Capra."[84] Adriano Baracco marked the film's obsession with Girotti's body and Visconti's propensity to show the actor in sleeveless undershirts.[85] The script Visconti discussed with De Matteis is full of handwritten specifications that his characters look like "gente vera" (real people),[86] but Gino and Spagnolo looked as if fashioned from a steady stream of American celluloid.

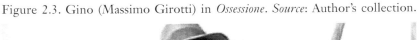
Figure 2.3. Gino (Massimo Girotti) in *Ossessione*. *Source*: Author's collection.

Commentators noted the incongruity of the film. Dramatic and crudely realistic in its theme and exterior locations, *Ossessione* shrilly stood out among the Fascist output of "white telephone" films and melodramas about past and present national heroism. The film was shot on location with characters that spoke heavily accented Italian. Mira Liehm has written that the film is "Visconti's most realistic film. It subverts reality as little as possible."[87] It could actually do that, while doing the opposite. The "realistic" portrayal of the film's Italian landscape flew in the face of the *Ossessione*'s borrowings from other nations' filmic traditions. At the premiere of the film Vittorio Mussolini is supposed to have shouted "questa non è l'Italia!" (this is not Italy!) and, at some level, he was correct. The notion of a vagabond traveling around Fascist Italy dressed in rags and sporting a harmonica seemed, then and now, to be preposterous. A more sympathetic critic, film director Carlo Lizzani, still noted that among the characters in *Ossessione* Gino and Spagnolo were the most outlandishly "unrealistic . . . The hobo, for example, is a literary figure drawn from [American] literature. No vagabond [in Italy] would go around the way [they do]. . . . A hobo would have been arrested immediately. During fascism and in the middle of the war he would have ended up like that."[88]

The doubtful Italian-ness of the film was front and center in the *querelle* that immediately followed its premiere, and it was a curious outcome, given the filmmakers' published manifestos advocating the necessity of featuring Italian stories, literature, faces, and landscapes. In *La Fiamma*, the organ of the Parma section of the National Fascist Party, future film theorist and filmmaker Antonio Marchi correctly identified the intellectual pedigree of the film.

> *Ossessione* is born out of Giuseppe De Santis's film criticism which he published on *Cinema*, a criticism that well synthesizes in a way that is both direct and precise the opinions of those who really love cinema in Italy, and especially the young generations: "grab [Italian] reality! Create *our* cinema! Show *this* Italy!," these have been for the last two years the slogans we have heard the most often; "realism, realism, realism!" these have been the most commonly used words.

The problem with *Ossessione*, he continued, was its internal contradiction: a reality at odds with Italy. According to the critic, the film was "on a level of profound realism, but it is not *real* [*vero*]." Visconti's crew has grabbed the "piñata of the purest of realism, the American one . . . and they have transplanted it inside our real, identifiable cities, Ancona and Ferrara." But it did not work. The film was "far from any tradition and any truths. Look at the main character, Gino Costa. . . . Ferrara is not Annapolis, just like Rome is neither London nor Berlin. . . . Italy is not the kind of land for a man like [Gino] fit for the limitless skies of Russia and the monotonous streets of America."[89]

Nonetheless, there were positive reviews. Giovanni Meneguz saw the transplant as a successful adaptation to the Italian tradition.[90] Guido Aristarco, the founder in 1952 of the Marxist-inspired *Cinema Nuovo*, championed it as the "most significant film" of its time and "destined to remain in the history of cinema." He applauded the "duro realism" (hard realism) of its dialogues and the "naked and unrelenting description of its humble and forlorn characters, of the minimal chronicle of their everyday gestures and actions." But Aristarco also noted that *Ossessione* wore its America and its France on its sleeve, and noted that *Ossessione* drew on the models of John Steinbeck and the French "neo realism" of Chenal, Renoir, Carné, and Julien Duvivier.[91]

Even the reviewers who applauded the political élan of the film resented its cosmopolitanism. The French and, obviously, Chenal's influence were frequent targets. Cinema should be a creation of culture derived from the national mind, whose moral health defined culture's health, they contended. Thus the French "sick and crippled psyche" had generated French cinematic realism that could not be adapted to Italian cinema or Italian culture as both of these sprouted out of "our healthy and fecund nature."[92] Some, like the Bologna daily *L'avvenire d'Italia*, urged the authorities to ban the film.[93] Some went further and advocated violence: "Some criticism is to be done with catcalls and bats rather than with pens and [written] words," wrote *Italia Giovane*, the Fascist Party's daily from Novara.[94] On June 18, Bologna's *Resto del Carlino* announced that the film had been banned by the city authorities.[95] The film was also banned in Ferrara, with Ancona one of the two cities *Ossessione* somehow celebrated.[96] The support of a young Guido Aristarco, who advocated projections followed by open discussions, could do little to save the film.[97]

History settled the critical debate. On July 25 Mussolini was deposed by the Gran Consiglio of the National Fascist Party and replaced by Marshal Pietro Badoglio, the conqueror of Ethiopia. The Duce was exiled to the Hotel Campo Imperatore, a ski resort on the Gran Sasso in the Apennine mountains. Those who had saluted *Ossessione's* message of freedom rejoiced.

A week after the Duce was deposed, an exhilarated Aristarco wrote to De Santis about his hopes for his generation of filmmakers: "The Fascist regime is finally dissolved. Do you remember how much we looked forward to this moment? . . . My dear Beppe, we are free. Now Italian cinema is expecting much of you."[98] *Ossessione* itself, however, did not much benefit from the Liberation. After a German commando set Mussolini free on September 12 and placed him in northern Italy to head the Fascist government of the Salò Republic, Italy was temporarily divided, and its cinema reduced to shambles. *Ossessione* was banned in the north and proved too controversial and gloomy for the south, which was then being rid of Nazis and Fascists by partisans and the Allies. Rome was liberated on June 4, 1944, but *Ossessione* was released there only in April 1945, a few weeks shy of the fall of the Salò Republic and the German final retreat.

Ossessione was a difficult movie to watch in either Fascist or liberated Italy. Its call for freedom was undercut by a somber meditation on human nature and desire that couldn't be channeled into simple, anti-Fascist rhetoric, and the film wore its non-Italian symbols and style—its Americanness—proudly, on the ragged sleeves of the ragged clothes of its characters.

In her perceptive essay about the two first Italian translations of Cain's novel, Rita Filanti argues that the first unpublished Italian translation of *Postman*, by Ada Prospero, dating to circa 1940, abided by the Fascist instructions and translated all American expressions of the book into Italian words. Visconti's team, who most likely did not know Prospero's text, chose a different strategy in their creolization of this American story and instead created a film that gestures in the direction of Giuseppe Bassani's strategy in translating the novel.

Born in 1916 to a prosperous Jewish family from Ferrara, in 1942 Bassani was a schoolteacher and an aspiring writer. Though his father had joined the party in the 1920s, Bassani was openly anti-Fascist, so much so that in April 1941 the security division of Bologna's railroad police (Commissariato di Publica Sicurezza presso la Direzione Compartamentale delle Ferrovie dello Stato di Bologna) requested information about the young man from the local police (Questura)

The Celluloid Atlantic between Fascism and the Cold War   85

in Ferrara, worried that Bassani would "use the railroad service to enact more easily his antinational propaganda work."[99] But Bassani managed to stay out of prison, and by 1942 was hard at work on his translation of *The Postman* that Milan publisher Bompiani released in 1945, in the immediate aftermath of Italian Liberation. [100]

Bassani's translation, Filanti argues, was radically different from Prospero's. The two versions "incarnate two ostensibly opposite translating strategies and two different ways of dealing with the *foreign-ness* of the source text. . . . While Prospero circumvented the Fascist constraints through the practice of self-censorship thus signaling the culmination of Fascist repression, Bassani rejoiced about the regime's final defeat by anticipating its catastrophe" [emphasis added]. In contrast to Prospero's all-Italian translation, Bassani left many words in the original English: some, like "whisky," because he assumed Italian readers' familiarity; others, like "ice cream soda," because he thought their meanings were clear from context. Bassani went further and preserved other words, like the derogatory "wop" for Italian immigrant, just adding an explanatory footnote.[101] The choice, according to Filanti, represents Bassani's refusal of "the Fascist program of linguistic appropriation." He instead emphasizes his "acknowledge[ment] of the complete alterity of his source text, and surrender to the untranslatability of the other."[102]

In its handling of America, *Ossessione* echoes Bassani. The film stakes its American origin in glaring contrast with its Italian surroundings. The Chaplinesque hobos embodied by Spagnolo and "Gino" or their diegetic desire to take to the "open" road of 1943 Italy are, as it were, "foreign words" set against an Italian context made all the more visually striking by Visconti's decision to film all on location. Spagnolo was a figment of a cinematic imagination that had long communed with American stories, and the incongruity was not accidental but programmatic. Visconti and his crew's invention of this character and the morphing of Frank into Gino make clear that these intellectuals wanted to maintain what Filanti called "the untranslatability of the other," amid the stifling jargon of Fascist Italian cinema and culture. In *Ossessione*, screenwriter Giuseppe De Santis later admitted in an interview on the film, "there is no Italy. . . . there is the insertion of a cinema culture that is ready to see reality in a different way."[103]

The untranslatability of America was the point. *Ossessione* wore its America confidently in Chaplinesque rags, as its creators used its "untranslatable" symbols to mark their own desire for freedom. But this was going to change soon. Paradoxically enough, America was proclaimed most openly when it was prohibited.

"Then" and "Nowadays":
Atlantic Dialogue in the Cold War Context

It was the disruptive nature of the American signifier that interested Visconti in *Ossessione* and this attitude did not change immediately after the war. The Atlantic exchange was given only more import by the bloody experience of the war, which urged the rebirth of a democratic cinema in Italy.

It helped that in 1945 American cinema and American culture became increasingly accessible. Born in 1929, director Sergio Leone was sixteen on that fateful April 25, 1945 when the war was finally over in most of the peninsula. Leone remembers the effect the sudden inrush of American cinema and culture had on people like him.

> In sum, American cinema turned out to be a beautiful, cultural slap across the face. We still bear on our cheeks the red imprint of that slap. We, young people in particular, were drunk with America from morning to evening. Nowadays America is manufacturing its own image, but in those days, we were taking sides spontaneously, nobody and nothing was telling us to do it, but our age and our lust for a different life, a different world. We developed a sort of addiction, a cultural drug addiction. . . . Its being right was a particularly charming kind of being wrong. We wanted the "Martians" to invade us.[104]

Leone's words and their implicit timeline are telling. There is a *then*, at the end of the war, when America was a positive model, but there is also a *nowadays* (the interview dates from the late seventies or early eighties) when this is no longer the case. This transformation in attitudes is central to the politicized discourse engulfing the Celluloid Atlantic. In his "Cinema e narrative," an essay he published immediately after the Liberation in June 1945, Giuseppe De Santis repeated the terms of 1930s democratic modernism. American cinema, and Westerns in

The Celluloid Atlantic between Fascism and the Cold War   87

particular, had created a new type of Gramscian "national popular." This was a cinema that "by drawing on the popular narrative mode and on indigenous tales could . . . speak the language of the masses and stir their sentiments."[105] In July 1945, Alberto Lattuada argued in *Il Mondo* that Italian cinema still lacked the ability "to speak to all men," once again citing as exemplars the cinema of Charles Chaplin, King Vidor, and D. W. Griffith and praising the "collaborative spirit" of the Hollywood film industry.[106]

In the months following the war filmmakers bounced ideas back and forth across the Atlantic, producing increasingly hybridized products. Take the famous case of film noir, a subgenre of crime film inspired by American hard-boiled writers like James Cain. Film noir became popular in the first years after the war, when Tay Garnett directed the American version of *Postman*, and *Ossessione* has often been associated with it. It is doubtful that Garnett saw Visconti's film, but the multiple Atlantic versions of Cain's novel suggest a contemporaneity of sensibility spanning the Pond. Film historian James Naremore has rightly suggested that "*film noir* has no essential characteristics and that it is not a specifically American form."[107] Naremore concludes that *noir* actually occupies "a liminal space somewhere between Europe and America, between high modernism and 'Blood melodrama,' and between low-budget crime movies and art cinema."[108]

Ossessione can be interpreted as early Italian noir but its makers favored linear emplotment, eschewing flashback narrative framings, overwrought plots, and femme fatales to tell the story of present-day Italy as it emerged from the Fascist *ventennio* and Nazi occupation. Like noir, however, the style they were concocting, later popularized as "neorealism," eschewed rigid norms, evoking a cultural and political attitude toward life and esthetics rather than a well-defined style or genre. *Ossessione*'s crew and their filmmaking successors wanted to tell about the present of Italy. To do so they applied devices from earlier cinema, often haphazardly.[109] These devices, most critics concur, include a reliance on nonprofessional actors, working-class protagonists, simple dialogue, natural lighting, and location shooting. Some of these choices were due to necessity, as Italian ateliers were in shambles. Cinecittà was used as a refugee camp until 1947. Yet all these stylistic features ended up being subsumed into a mythological coherence of Italian neorealism and as evidence of the *italianità* (Italian-ness) of the style.[110]

We are on less mythical and more coherent terrain when we associate neorealism with themes. Like *Ossessione* had done in 1942–1943, neorealist films were interested in the downtrodden and the socially marginal. It prompted Giulio Andreotti, the conservative Catholic politician who was the government's supervisor of Italian postwar cinema during the early 1950s, to vent that Italian "dirty laundry" should be washed at home and not in public for the world to see.[111] It could not be helped, though, as neorealism was an answer to novelist and critic Elio Vittorini's call for Italian art that would not simply comfort humanity but that would "prevent its suffering" by promoting social change.[112] Screenwriter Cesare Zavattini told an interviewer that his work was about the "discovery" of the reality before his eyes, one that he had avoided throughout the Fascist era. It was the "moral" choice to engage this neglected world because "to have evaded reality had been to betray it."[113]

It would be a grave mistake to take literally the discourse that soon surrounded neorealism and often stressed its Italian autochthony. As we have seen in *Ossessione*, the United States was stylistically and physically present in the first experiences of neorealism. Furthermore, on the other side of the Atlantic, neorealism was seen as a continuation of the movement toward realism that had begun in the last years of the thirties. Maybe for this reason, some neorealist films were more successful in America than in Italy. *Ossessione* was not distributed in the US till the early seventies because of copyright issues, but the film was not a popular and critical success when it came out in Italy. Visconti's second great neorealist film, *La terra trema* (1948; The Earth Quakes) did not even find a distributor for the Italian market though it was nominated for a prestigious prize at the Venice Film Festival. On the other hand, Hollywood progressives welcomed Roberto Rossellini's neorealist manifesto, *Roma città aperta* (Open City, 1945), which in 1946 beat all New York box office records for a foreign film and remained in the program for one year and a half; in Milan it had stayed on the *cartellone* (marquee) a mere fifteen days.[114] The film was distributed in New York by Arthur L. Mayer, the progressive owner of the Rialto theater. *Hollywood Quarterly*, the organ of the progressive film intelligentsia in Los Angeles, glowingly praised the film.[115] James Agee, the author of a 1930s clarion call for socially engaged literature, *Let Us Now Praise Famous Men*, had by then become a film critic for *Time Magazine* and the *Nation*. He was

The Celluloid Atlantic between Fascism and the Cold War 89

on its way to a career as a Hollywood screenwriter interrupted by his untimely death at forty-six in 1955. He was so taken by *Open City* that he told his readers that he could not write about it for at least a few weeks. When he did, he called it "magnificent" and connected it to American work, like that by "Hollywood cameraman" Karl Brown in *Stark Love*.[116] In naming *Open City* the best film of 1945, Agee was not disturbed by James T. Farrell's accusation that the film was "communist propaganda" because—as an American intellectual who had more than dabbled in 1930s progressive modernism—he saw "much of the spirit and grandeur of this film" as coming out of its being "socially or politically hot under the collar."[117] So did Bosley Crowther, the progressive modernist critic of the *New York Times*, who called *Open City* "a screen drama of tremendous power in which the techniques of realism—and the attitudes—are [illegible] employed."[118] Another protagonist of Hollywood modernism, refugee magazine *Aufbau*, linked *Open City* with Billy Wilder's use of real exteriors in his *The Lost Weekend*: like Wilder's film, *Open City* abandons "Cock-tailatmosphäre" and "with a single blow has placed Italian cinema in the first rank" (Mit einem Schlag hat sich die italienische Filmkunst in die erste Reihe gespielt).[119]

The second chapter of Rossellini's war trilogy was also infused with transatlantic conversations. *Paisà* (Paisan, 1945) was written by Alfred Hayes, a young American writer with strong roots in 1930s progressivism. It was inspired by the refugee writer Klaus Mann, the son of Thomas Mann, and funded by Rod Geiger, a young American would-be producer and entrepreneur.[120] Hayes had been a Communist in the 1930s and had written two famous labor anthems, "Into the Streets, May First," set to music by Aaron Copland, and "I Dreamed I Saw Joe Hill Last Night" (aka "Joe Hill"), which Paul Robeson also recorded, and Joan Baez famously sang at Woodstock in 1969. Divided into six episodes that marked a journey from southern to northern Italy, each section of *Paisà* depicted the encounter between Italians and Americans. The film made obvious its authors' concern for the Euro-American liaison in its confusion of languages and accents (mostly recorded in postproduction),[121] and in its multinational cast. English words and American actors seemed to outnumber Italian ones. In all episodes American and Italian anti-Fascists collaborated and tried, at times painfully, to understand one another. The film and the Euro-American relationship culminated in the last episode on the river Po where American OSS (Office of Strategic Services) operatives and Italian partisans die together fighting the Nazi Fascists.

Paisà was actually better received in the United States, where it won the New York Critics' Award and the National Board of Review's award, than in Italy, where the film received a lukewarm welcome at the Venice Film Festival. "This is a film to be seen—and seen again," Crowther breathlessly concluded in *The New York Times*.[122] James Agee found the film even *too* pro-American: *Paisà* is "painfully sycophantic towards the United States," he wrote. "So much of it is recorded in English that one wonders whether it was made for home [Italian] consumption at all."[123]

Embraced by progressive filmmakers within and outside Italy, neorealist films rejected stories of elites and formulaic genre narratives. They were far, however, from explicitly proposing socialism, or endorsing the Soviet Union's side against the United States and the West in what was shaping up to be a global confrontation. As we have seen in the previous chapter, the West was an integrated political construct that also constructed its own integrated culture. Neorealism was no exception. Karl Schoonover has captured this element well. The scholar has argued that neorealist films, if "not tailored for a transatlantic geopolitics that recognized the category of the human while allowing the flow of consumer capitalism to determine the shape of postwar recovery and emerging modes of international connectivity, certainly appear to be comfortable with it."[124]

What is striking is that this "comfort" was increasingly obscured by a denial of Atlantic dialogue. Agee need not have worried about Italian film intellectuals' excessive Americanism. Things were to change radically and quickly. Film historian Gian Piero Brunetta saw the turning point of the American myth in Europe in the years after World War II. Among Italian intellectuals the myth was at its strongest at the beginning of the Second World War; for Brunetta it was "first the Cold War, then the Korean one" that disassembled it.[125] Leone's *nowadays* that I cited at the beginning of this section were shaping up.

Bearing witness to the rise of Euro-American difference is a wonderful letter in the De Santis archives by a then-young filmmaker, Carlo Lizzani. Born in Rome in 1922, Lizzani had grown up during the Fascist *ventennio* like De Santis, who was five years older. He had joined the Roman Gruppi Universitari Fascisti and written for Vittorio Mussolini's *Cinema*. In an essay published immediately

The Celluloid Atlantic between Fascism and the Cold War   91

before the end of the regime, in May 1943, the budding filmmaker showed an ill-concealed admiration for American cinema. Hollywood appreciated its many "craftsmen" (mestieranti) like George Cukor as opposed to Italian cinema, which showed contempt for craft and was in the hands of a "crowd of Italian pseudo-intellectuals" that hated film and thought of art as a "miraculous rain that falls from the sky and can just be gathered and offered up" to an audience.[126]

Lizzani's letter to De Santis was dated August 17, 1947, when Lizzani was in Berlin assisting Roberto Rossellini's work on the third and last chapter of his War Trilogy, *Germania Anno Zero* (Germany Year Zero, 1947). This film was a dark portrait of postwar Berlin seen through the eyes of a traumatized German boy, Edmund. On the instructions of his unrepentantly Nazi teacher, the youth murders his ailing father and then, unable to find solace, kills himself. By then Lizzani had joined the Communist Party and begun his career in cinema as an actor in *Il sole sorge ancora* (Antonio Vergano, 1945) and in the Resistance "Western" by De Santis, *Caccia tragica* (1946). The letter showed that changes were coming fast. The story Lizzani told his friend in Italy differed greatly from the rhetoric of their World War II *Cinema* essays and Visconti's Americanism of *Ossessione*.[127] He compared Rossellini's work with Billy Wilder's as Wilder was also in Berlin to film *A Foreign Affair* (1948). There could have been remarkable ground for mutual dialogue: both *Germania Anno Zero* and *A Foreign Affair* were somber meditations on the aftermath of the war and the German psyche. Wilder's film dealt with a congressional investigation into moral, sexual, and financial corruption in the midst of the American occupation army (of which Wilder had temporarily been a member). A biting satire, it was denounced in the halls of the US Congress. The Defense Department issued a press note refuting the film's portrayal of American troops in Berlin and the Military Government Screening Committee forbade its distribution in the German area under its control.[128] Herbert G. Luft, the drama editor and book reviewer for the Los Angeles B'nai B'rith *Messenger*, accused the refugee director of "decadence," "luxurious cynicism," and "unhealthy boulevard witticism" at the expense of American military and Allied occupying forces stationed in Germany. Wilder's portrayal of American troops as complicit in Berlin's postwar black-market economy was bound to "increase animosity against Americans" in Germany.[129]

Neither film was a celebration of American heroism and both were pessimist assessments of postwar Germany and denazification. Yet the story of the directors' meeting manqué in Berlin is also the story of two cinemas and their increasing, real or imagined, separateness. The two film crews, Lizzani told De Santis, dined together but Wilder was "rather nasty" (*piuttosto antipatico*) and he and Rossellini did their best to show not what they shared, but what set them and their cinema apart. The Italian director tried to scandalize ("épater," in French in the original) Wilder, telling him that he had no script for his movie, only a vague idea of the story that he was shooting day by day. According to Lizzani, Wilder was "flabbergasted" (costernato) by the declaration. The chasm between Italian and American cinema production looked even more gaping on set the next day, where Wilder's team appeared with "six cars, two trucks, three jeeps and a lot of people," while Rossellini's featured a taxi cab, a small private car (una "centoventi"), and no director. Wilder was again stupefied, but joked that Rossellini was not there because he was at home writing the script for his movie. Lizzani called the meeting "a rather significant encounter between American and European cinemas" (un incontro abbastanza significativo tra il cinema Americano e quello europeo).

The anecdote is telling. After all, Rossellini had previously been influenced by American traditions to the point of being called a pro-American sycophant. And Wilder was no brainless America booster, with his realism cited by *Aufbau* as an inspiration of *Open City*.[130] But neorealism's Atlantic connection was being obscured in the increasingly frosty climate of the Cold War. Ten years after *Ossessione*'s release, screenwriter Gianni Puccini mentioning only once in describing its production "una copia dattiloscritta del *Postino* di Cain" (a typed draft of Cain's *Postman*).[131] The same year, De Sica's screenwriter Cesare Zavattini, who as we shall see had been no stranger to collaboration with American realist artists and Hollywood cinema, told *La rivista del cinema italiano* that the "American position [on realist cinema] is the antithesis of our own.[132] Far from visually stressing the American "untranslatable," most film intellectuals increasingly and mistakenly agreed that the style was autochthonous and that the US had learned realism from Italy. Reviewing Willian Wyler's *Best Years of Our Lives* (1946), *Bianco e Nero* reported that American audiences were "flabbergasted and stupefied" (sconvolto e stupefatto) "by a realism to which only the latest Italian successes had tried to accustom it."[133] In the same paper, the most important film studies periodical in postwar Italy, Vinicio Marinucci noted that "Hollywood has certainly not ignored realism" but it has done so "with the delay typical not just [of Hollywood] but of all the United States when compared with the European vanguards."[134] Dmytryk's *Crossfire* was, according to Marinucci, "almost a film *a la* Rossellini," and Tay Garnett's *The Postman Always Rings Twice* was of course inferior to Visconti's *Ossessione*, "the progenitor of our realism."[135] In a 1953 interview in *Cinema Nuovo*, American director and McCarthy blacklistee Jules Dassin defended Hollywood directors against plagiarism of *neorelism* by describing "an unconscious relation of sympathy, in the literal sense of the term, a phenomenon I would call parallelism."[136]

Mentioning the neorealist links to Hollywood was rapidly becoming bad manners in Italian film circles. In December 1947 Enrico Emanuelli wrote to De Santis that as he was composing an essay for *Occident: Revue Intercontinentale* he had met an American editor, Bill Richardson. The two had talked cinema, but once again roads that were intertwined had become hopelessly separate. "Imagine that young Bill had so vague an idea of Italian cinema that he could believe that our so-called realism was born out of contact with American literature: those damned Faulkners, Hemingways, Caldwells! I gave myself permission to explain to him that, should we have needed [realist literature], we had our Giovanni Verga."[137] It was a historical paradox. After the Liberation, the American culture made glaringly visible by the makers of *Ossessione* in Fascist Italy at their own personal risk had become an embarrassment.

The Embarrassment of America: Riso amaro

The transformed rhetoric of the Celluloid Atlantic is clear in a comparison between Visconti's film and Giuseppe De Santis's *Riso amaro* (Bitter Rice, 1949). De Santis's film shared much with Visconti's. There was continuity of personnel: De Santis and Gianni Puccini, two of the scriptwriters of the earlier film, wrote the script of *Riso amaro*, which De Santis also directed. The politics of the two crews were similar and both De Santis and Visconti were active members of the Italian Communist Party. The films also shared a neorealist concern with the Italian working classes. *Ossessione* and *Riso amaro* even shared the dense humidity of similar locales. Visconti shot *Ossessione* (first called "Swamp," "Palude") in the bogs of Comacchio between Ravenna and Ferrara, and De Santis filmed *Riso amaro* in the soggy *risaie* (rice paddies) of northern Piedmont that belonged to the Agnelli family, the owners of Italy's automotive giant Fiat.

While Visconti implausibly posited the "untranslated" America of highways and hobos at the center of his film, De Santis concealed his glamorous American star, Doris Dowling, whom the production needed to guarantee the film's export, under the heavy clothes and the bandanas of an Italian peasant. As opposed to *Ossessione*, *Riso amaro* wanted desperately to be "Italian" and reflected De Santis's attempt to draw his films from the chronicle of Italian everyday life. His first film, *Caccia tragica* (Tragic Pursuit, 1947), had dealt with a real-life robbery of a farmers' cooperative. His later *Roma ore 11* (Rome 11 O'Clock, 1952) focused on the notorious collapse of a building in Rome.[138] Sandwiched between these two films, *Riso amaro*, though not taken from the headlines, places realistic people in a plausible situation. Francesca (Dowling) and Walter (Vittorio Gassman) are two small-time jewel thieves who try to abscond with a hot score. Chased by the police at the railroad station, Francesca joins the *mondine* (rice pickers) traveling to the *risaie*. She befriends Silvana (Silvana Mangano), a young picker obsessed with American music, and Marco (Raf Vallone), a sergeant in the Italian army and the moral conscience of the film. Walter follows Francesca to the *risaia* and woos the naive Silvana when he realizes that Francesca has become more and more reluctant to follow his criminal lead. When the jewels turn out to be fake, Walter decides to steal the rice crop to sell it on the black market. In the gun-blazing finale, the two couples square off and Walter and Silvana die while Francesca and Marco are given a new opportunity to live and love.

Critics and historians group together *Riso amaro* and *Ossessione* as examples of neorealism.[139] Both films use real locales populated by working-class characters interpreted by both professional actors and novices. Both films also nod toward American culture, though in opposing ways. Drawn from an American source, *Ossessione* centers on a hobo, Gino, who aims at escaping the fog of Comacchio and the "Ex dogana." In *Riso Amaro*, instead, the United States *is* the fog preventing Silvana from seeing her fate.

The narrative threshold of the latter film shows that the subject matter is not modernity per se, but its disruptive encounter with tradi-

The Celluloid Atlantic between Fascism and the Cold War   95

tional labor relations. Over the credits, De Santis has his DP (director of photography), Otello Martelli, who had worked on Rossellini's *Paisà*, pan over real *mondine* at work in the Vercelli rice fields. The shot reproposes what Brunetta called De Santis's "constant dialectic between long shots and close-ups."[140] The camera quickly moves from the water to a higher point of view where the women become a mass of faceless bodies ankle-deep in the water. As the credits end, the shot fades into an extreme close-up of a man speaking directly into the camera, recounting the global history of rice culture. His retelling excludes the United States, then the largest exporter of rice to Italy, instead stressing how rice has been cultivated in Italy for "centuries the same way as it has been in India and China." The narrator also emphasizes this as a story of female labor. Women have impressed their mark on the earth itself in an agricultural tradition dictated by the "eternal" laws of nature, he concludes. Only women can do the work of rice farming because they have small and nimble hands that can as aptly attend a newborn baby as the delicate stem of a rice plant. Suddenly the camera sways backward and the man's face (actor Attilo Dottesio) is revealed as that of a well-dressed radio broadcaster reporting about the *mondine* for the fictional "Radio Torino." The movement aptly juxtaposes "nature" and traditional lifeways against the rise of a postwar modernity dominated by mass media and new gender roles.

De Santis then shifts from the well-dressed man to another. Close to the radio man and chased by the police, Walter (Vittorio Gassman) hides among a crowd of laborers waiting for a train. He reaches his lover, Francesca (Doris Dowling), and the couple hide on a train that has stopped at the station. As Walter is talking, he suddenly stops and directs his gaze elsewhere. Without cutting De Santis and Martelli have the camera slowly sway leftward to reveal, first another train, then Silvana (Silvana Mangano) provocatively dancing the boogie by herself on the platform, the sound provided by her own portable record player.

Silvana is a study in contradictions. "A Rita Hayworth from the suburbs of the Italian working class" according to De Santis, she is both primitive and modern, the most "Americanized" of the film's central characters and, perhaps because of this, the most credibly Italian.[141] Dressed in simple clothes, similar, though less ragged, to those of the *mondine*, she dances to modern American music. Walter is ensnared. He tells Francesca to hold the jewels and board the train

Figure 2.4. Vittorio Gassman and Doris Dowling in *Bitter Rice* (1949). *Source*: PhotofestNYC.

along with the rice pickers. He then approaches Silvana after grabbing a wide-brimmed straw hat to conceal his face. When he begins to dance with her, their sensuous twirling shows a shared familiarity with American modernity and foreshadows that their pairing will work better than their previous ones. Walter and Silvana are a better fit and it is their attitude toward America that shows it. Like Silvana, Walter knows how to boogie, executing a "lindy hop" according to the *New York Post*'s Archer Winstein.[142] Like Walter, Silvana is chewing gum, another symbol of American cultural and financial penetration.

Silvana's ownership of the vinyl record and player increases her seductive power. After their first encounter, she lures Walter once more via music. This time is nighttime in the *mondine* encampment. Walter is there to try and make contact with Francesca and Silvana and her peers have decided to have fun. The women climb the fence around the camp barracks and join the men waiting for them in the fields surrounding the dormitories. Silvana has adorned herself with Francesca's jewels and she carries her record player. She uses the latter to bait Walter to dance again.

As opposed to the train station, this time the natural setting of trees and wild vegetation contrasts with the record player's mechanical output. Silvana again begins to dance by herself, the center of the circle of the peasants around her. And again, Walter matches her dancing skills. He rejects Francesca, contemptuously telling her that she stole a fake necklace and, conspicuously chewing his gum, approaches Silvana. This time Marco is there and he challenges Silvana for wearing what he still thinks are real stolen jewels. Walter punches him and the two men fight. The brawl is nominally about Silvana's wearing the jewels but it is really over Marco's romantic claims on Silvana. The pairing of the four young people, however, has already shifted. Francesca has met Marco and is falling for him and Silvana has lost interest in the soldier. In the afternoon, she and Marco quarrel when he told her that he wanted to start over in South America after serving in uniform for ten years. Silvana wants to go to the US instead, where "all is electrical." "Yes, even the electric chair," Marco drily comments.

The second dance signals Silvana's switching sides. She abandons Marco and her own social class to team up with Walter and his unscrupulous social climbing. The scene also suggests the political moral of the film that, in its simplest terms, is a rejection of Americanization. Silvana is guilty of surrendering to the boogie, to Walter and to his chewing gum, and she will pay the price. In the final confrontation Francesca kills Walter, and Silvana commits suicide by throwing herself from a tower as Francesca climbs to save her. In the final scene, the *mondine* toss handfuls of their hard-earned rice rations on Silvana's dead body. The gesture goes beyond the rituals of job solidarity and the reidentification Silvana as a *mondina*. It also grounds her body in the native soil of Italy, and in a culture she was trying to escape via her record player.[143]

The Contradictions of Silvana

Via Silvana, De Santis made his film about Americanization. It was not a particularly original theme. After the onset of the European Recovery Program in 1947, Americanization was everywhere in

Western Europe. Even the studio that produced *Riso amaro* reflected this new climate. *Riso amaro* was produced by Riccardo Gualino's Lux, which was, as we have seen, the most modern of the Italian postwar film companies. Lux historian Alberto Farassino writes that it was the "only Italian studio that was able, if not to compete, to be at least comparable with the great Hollywood studios."[144] Ugo Pirro, an Italian screenwriter, describes the Lux top personnel of the immediate postwar as very "Hollywood": they were "young, elegant, always busy, quick on their feet."

Lux was also one of the Italian pillars of the Celluloid Atlantic. Riccardo's son, Renato, was the president of the Italian Film Export, and IFE's Releasing Corp. Interested in producing big budget films, the Gualinos needed to tap into markets outside of Italy and in particular the rich American box office. Lux had created a sister company, Lux Releasing Corporation, in 1948 with the idea of releasing Italian pictures in the US. By 1950 it had already released in the US the critically acclaimed *Senza Pietà* (Without Pity, 1948) by Lattuada, starring African American actor John Kitzmiller. In February 1950 Bernard Jacon, Lux vice president in charge of the American market, promised to release fourteen Italian language pictures in the US.[145] In July, ahead of the September release of *Riso amaro*, Lux circulated a fifty-eight-page "profusely illustrated" brochure advertising the film.[146]

From the beginning Gualino wanted to produce a film with international appeal. Though openly a Communist, because of his experience in *Ossessione* and the success of his first film *Caccia tragica*, young director De Santis seemed a sensible choice. The studio's other casting choices followed the international aims of the studios and the transatlantic popularity of neorealism. At the studio level, the creation of a "national" film did not preclude international ambitions. The latter dictated hybridization rather than autochthony and the film needed an American star. Lux chose Doris Dowling, who had gathered good notices for her work in Billy Wilder's *The Lost Weekend* (1945) and was in Italy at the time.[147] Dowling was the highest paid performer on the set of *Riso Amaro*, earning three million liras, just like director De Santis. Vittorio Gassman, the male lead, made only two million, although in the Italian market his name came before Dowling's in the credits.[148]

The American presence in the film, however, is a study in contradictions. Gassman and Dowling are acknowledged as the stars of the film and their contracts were the first to be drafted and signed (May 4, 1948) after De Santis's. In contrast, the novice Silvana Mangano was added last to the cast and Giuseppe De Santis remembers that he considered the reigning Miss Italy, Lucia Bosè, and French actress Martine Carol for the role, before finally deciding on Mangano.[149] Historian Sergio Toffetti suspects that she was hired through the producer of the film, her future husband Dino De Laurentiis.[150] Yet reviewers and the audience agreed that Mangano stole the film. For Katie Cameron, she was "an unwashed beauty of the Ingrid Bergman type," and for the *New York Times*'s Crowther she was "a sensation on the international film scene . . . Anna Magnani minus 15 years, Ingrid Bergman with a Latin disposition and Rita Hayworth plus twenty five pounds." Crowther also made a comparison with Dowling, "pallid and physically unimpressive" though her role gave the film its "moral substance."[151]

Propelled by Mangano's body, *Riso amaro* was an international hit that stands out in De Santis's filmography for its popularity. His *Caccia Tragica* had done well at the box office but *Riso amaro* quickly eclipsed it. Audiences lionized Mangano and the film more than the critics, who were divided. *Bitter Rice* premiered at the Cannes Film Festival where it received good notices although the Catholic world was appalled. *Riso amaro*, concluded the Centro Cattolico di Cinematografia, "it is nothing but the summary of a perversion ("bad fact"). As for its realization, all looks scattered, the performances, the direction, the photography."[152]

Given the political pedigree of its director and its screenwriters, the division of the Communist press is even more remarkable than the Catholic and conservative reservations. In *L'Unità*, Ugo Casiraghi called the film "spectacular and compelling" (spettacolare e avvincente), though he noted that De Santis's penchant for the spectacular was sometimes at odds with the necessity for political education.[153] This criticism snowballed among leftist critics. De Santis remembers a polemical exchange with union leaders on *L'Unità*, who argued that "no *mondina* danced the boogie woogie on [Italian] fields where, according to them, people only danced traditional tunes." According to the director, however, Communist Party secretary Palmiro Togliatti agreed with him and congratulated him.[154] Still, in *Vie Nuove*, Antonello Trombadori, one of the main cadres of the Italian Communist Party cultural *nomenklatura*, called the film ambiguous and confused.[155]

For Trombadori the problem was the character of Mangano. She ably represented a new social category: the Americanized Italian youth, for whom "a better life cannot but be the one described in the American movies (sentimentalism and sexual prowess) or in the comic books she reads." The problem was that De Santis had made Silvana attractive. Though ultimately punished, she was a more powerful screen presence than the "redeemed" Francesca. Thus the film was a "passive documentation of our age, or better, of the cultural and moral confusion of some social groups who live in our age." *Riso amaro* was as confused as those it purported to rebuke.[156] An American actress was the quintessential Italian woman, the moral center of the film, and the Italian actress, Mangano, represented the corrupting temptation of America.

Trombadori's criticism was harsh and De Santis resented it throughout his life, sometimes blaming Trombadori for the limits of his later career. Yet Trombadori's opinion should not be confused with an official party verdict. Togliatti, the general secretary of the Italian Communist Party, defended the film, as did art critic Carlo Muscetta and film critic Umberto Barbaro in the party press.[157] Neither Muscetta nor Babaro contested Trombadori's point about American culture, which they agreed was deplorable. They only accepted De Santis and his film as condemning US culture rather than celebrating it.

America had become a plague, an attitude summed up in 1948 by Communist leader Pietro Secchia who indicted "the American trusts" and American "gangsters" for "flooding our country with their books, their films, and their lowbrow ideological rubbish meant to weaken, disorient, and corrupt our people."[158] De Santis would have mostly agreed with Secchia. *Riso amaro* was a condemnation of the corrupting American culture ushered in by the American occupation and the 1947 Marshall Plan. Silvana's fall and Francesca's surge that the script placed at the end of the film were clear testimonies to those intentions.

Yet Trombadori's shot was, essentially, on target. Silvana's appeal was undeniable, as De Santis had shown in the two dancing scenes. Both scenes use traveling and long shots and depth of focus to show the reactions of those who are also listening to the music and watching Silvana. The traveling shot of the first scene reveals an interclass audience of men and women. Some women are obviously objecting to the excessive interest in Silvana by their male partners, one of them even slapping a flower from the hands of her male companion.

The Celluloid Atlantic between Fascism and the Cold War 101

But the camera lingers on Silvana as she dances alone and the deep focus shows women in the background dancing and clasping their hands to the rhythm. The same participation is revealed in the second dance scene when De Santis shows women of different ages swaying and clapping to the "Lindy Hop" rhythm, alone or coupled to other women or to male companions.

Bitter Rice thus contains two separate and contradictory utopias. It features the utopia of class solidarity that Marco embodies, animated aurally with the traditional songs referenced throughout the film and especially in the scene when the *mondine* sing together in the rice paddies about labor issues. This utopia links people in a collective demand for social change. But in the film there is also the utopia of Fordist consumption, which is embodied by Silvana's record player, her *Grand Hotel* magazines, and her chewing gum. *Bitter Rice* links the latter with Americanization, but does not dispel, or hides, its appeal. The former utopia is about liberation *of* work while the latter is about liberation *from* work. The ultimate fate of Silvana makes clear which one De Santis thinks is the better, or more realistic, option. Yet the contradiction that Trombadori pointed out was real. The righteousness of the former is insufficient to silence the obvious and sensual appeal of the latter.

Silvana's relation to American culture resembles that of Gino and Spagnolo in *Ossessione*. In both films, American culture, openly cited in *Riso amaro* and referenced tongue-in-cheek in *Ossessione*, is taken as utopian. Like the freedom to travel that Spagnolo professed in 1943, Silvana's dances gestured toward the promises of a new world, one associated with the United States. In the earlier case, Gino's "American" desire to bum around opposed the regime's constraints on the movement of Italians. In the later film, Silvana proposed a new way of being, freed from the scarcity and gendered oppressions of traditional rural life. And this is what Italian audiences related to. This was the substance of her victory over Francesca that the film's finale denies.

The context of the Atlantic is helpful here. The opposition to Silvana's liberationism was part of a transnational front. Just like the Italian conservative and leftist critics, American cultural conservatives worried about Silvana's utopia. The files of Hollywood's Production Code Administration (PCA) attest to the opposition of American censors to the film. Lux tried to release the film in the US in 1950 when the PCA was trying to control the release of foreign films into the

United States by collaborating with the MPAA's newly created Advisory Unit for Foreign Film headed by B. Bernard Kreisler. Without having seen the film, Kreisler had proposed to support the release of *Bitter Rice* in the United States and asked for the PCA *placet*. PCA chief Joseph Breen scoffed that "from what I heard it would appear that the picture is a new low" and the PCA had been founded "to prevent the distribution of pictures of this type."[159] The PCA strongly advised the Advisory Unit for Foreign Film not to aid the distribution of a film that Gordon White deemed the most "morbid and depressing film" he had ever seen.[160]

The PCA, however, was aging. After the 1948 Supreme Court's *Paramount* decision, the American studios had lost control over exhibitors, and in 1951 Breen lamented that *Bitter Rice* "is being shown in a number of FOX [*sic*] west coast theaters" without the PCA seal of approval.[161] And Gordon White wrote Sidney Schreibner that "the attitude of the big circuit theatres toward the production code seal following the divorcement of these theaters may well, in my humble opinion, present the most important problem we have to face in the near future."[162]

He was correct. The PCA denied *Bitter Rice* approval though it agreed to forgo a formal letter of rejection.[163] The censorship offices of individual states also requested cuts.[164] Yet not only did *Riso amaro* break box office records in Italy, it also performed impressively throughout the Celluloid Atlantic. By December, the film was "a hit all over Germany," according to *Variety*, and scored "record-breaking" box office in many American cities including the US capital.[165] In 1951, *Riso amaro* was nominated for an Academy Award for best original story.

In a few years, the invocation of the American utopia had changed direction. Communist scenarist Franco Solinas, one of the protagonists of the spaghetti Western revolution that we will examine in chapters 5 and 6, summarized the development. "There was a time when we were looking across the ocean and we were dreaming of the immense Statue of Liberty opening the harbor of New York," he wrote in the leftist daily *Paese Sera* in 1950. His reminiscence is typical of his generation: it is the story of an international debate about realism that the war and the postwar period increasingly nationalized. The origins of neorealism lay there as well, because our young filmmakers "nested" (covavano) their neorealism while looking at the films by

"Vidor, Stroheim, Chaplin, Ford, and other renowned people who were then making and, were allowed to make cinema, and really do this." But in this account America had betrayed the whole ideal and created a postwar cinema where "the oranges must always be lucid and ripe, the trees full of beautiful pomes, and everything must be clean, pleasant, colorful." Solinas now cast Italian films and Hollywood cinema as antithetical, denying the existence of any conversation, and extolling difference. "The 'gray' of *Ladri di Biciclette* breaks out from the schemes and the conventions and shows another way of living. . . . So [to Americans] de Sica becomes 'Communist,' the film is boycotted and, to try and prohibit, [Americans] reference a morality that cannot tolerate the image of a child peeing."[166] As we shall see in the next chapters, this assumption of Atlantic difference obscured much more than it revealed. Of the remarkable transformations that occurred in Italian and American cinema, few can be understood referencing a purely national context. The filmmaking Solinas participated in—be it *Burn!* (Queimada, 1967) by Gillo Pontecorvo with Hollywood star Marlon Brando, or the spaghetti Westerns he scripted—was deeply imbricated with Hollywood and its genres. Nonetheless, it is striking how effectively the discourse of difference and autochthony pushed under the surface any reference to hybridization and Atlantic cross-pollination. And so it happened that a discourse rife with cultural nationalism and anti-Americanism was produced within a context that was truly international and transnational.[167]

3

Atlantic Soldiers

> The massacres were not committed only by the Germans. We have equally killed, raped, wounded sensibilities, violated souls. Thus, it may be high time we did some accounting of our own debts, and acknowledge our own debt toward the recent history of Europe.
>
> —Valerio Zurlini

In the aftermath of World War II, Hollywood became an increasingly material presence in Italy and Western Europe. Interrupted by the conflict, Atlantic relations resumed in its aftermath. In 1955, *Ladri di Biciclette*'s (Bicycle Thieves, 1946) writer Cesare Zavattini, by now a world-famous scenarist, collaborated with the great realist American photographer and filmmaker Paul Strand. In the 1930s, Strand had been the cinematographer of two much admired masterpieces of realist cinema: Pare Lorentz's *The Plow That Broke the Plains* (1936) and Fred Zinnemann's *Redes* (The Wave, 1936). The war then froze the Atlantic routes, but in the 1950s Zavattini and Strand brought the American and Italian streams flowing back together when they collaborated on the photo-story of the small Italian village of Luzzara in the photo-book *Un paese*.[1] The two had met at the 1949 International Filmmakers Congress in Perugia where film people discussed the postwar resurrection of realism as a transnational film style. Like James Agee and Walker Evans's *Let Us Now Praise Famous Men*, Strand and Zavattini's *Un Paese* combined the stories of ordinary people with the American 1930s' tradition of realist photography, and also with village-centered collective narratives à la Edgar Lee Masters (*Spoon River Anthology*, 1915) and Sherwood Anderson (*Winesburg, Ohio*, 1919).

The collaboration between a prominent neorealist screenwriter and a protagonist of the American 1930s realist film and photo movement attests to the renewed intertwining of Atlantic intellectual routes and to the shared attention on neorealism. Zavattini was, by then, engaged in direct collaboration with Hollywood studios. In the early 1950s David O. Selznick produced an American neorealist blockbuster in Rome, *Indiscretions of an American Wife* (Stazione Termini, 1954). He anchored its international marketing prospects in two American stars, his wife, Jennifer Jones, and Montgomery Clift, and also secured its Atlantic intellectual pedigree: *Ladri di biciclette*'s director, Vittorio De Sica, was to helm and produce, and Zavattini collaborated on the script with fellow Italians Luigi Chiarini and Giorgio Prosperi as well as Americans Truman Capote and Ben Hecht.

Even genres like the musical were being shaped by the crosscurrents of the Celluloid Atlantic. The film version of *West Side Story* (1961), a gritty story of gangs and murder written for the stage in 1957 by blacklisted playwright and screenwriter Arthur Laurents, was set in a real New York City slum and conversed as directly with the cinema of De Sica, De Santis, and Visconti as with the theater of William Shakespeare. Transposed on the screen by Jerome Robbins, the politically progressive director and choreographer of the stage production, and by *Citizen Kane*'s editor Robert Wise, the filmic version of *West Side Story* used real settings and exterior shooting in a stunning beginning that had the spectators' gaze descend from an aerial shot of New York City into the unvarnished Upper West Side of Manhattan. The powerful incipit of the film paraded rarely seen images of a city of slums within the city that never slept and positioned itself in a dialectic and almost polemical relation to soundstages.[2] "Except for one brief bit against a red wall," the *New York Times* reported about the film's exteriors, "the film's first fifteen minutes were photographed here."[3]

Atlantic political, economic, and military alliances also flourished. Italy was a founding member of the North Atlantic Treaty

Organization (1949) as well as a recipient of more than one billion dollars from the European Recovery Plan (aka Marshall Plan) funds. The previous chapter has also shown the role America played in the formulation and marketing of Italian neorealism. Albeit often denied by European filmmakers, America played a role in neorealism, and, as Karl Schonoover has argued, neorealist cinema played a role in America as well, constructing what he calls an American "ethical spectatorship," a "kind of surrogate seeing," and eye-witnessing of the tragedy of postwar Europe that only a minority of Americans had witnessed.[4]

Italian intellectuals, however, often underplayed and contested this Atlantic cross-pollination. As we have seen in the previous chapter, in the aftermath of the conflict many downplayed the inspiration of American realism in Italian cinema and others lamented what they saw as the Americanization of Italian culture. Novelist and film critic Alberto Moravia, who had been initially tapped to write the script for *Stazione*, lamented the contaminating effect of American money and talent on the *Italian* style par excellence, neorealism. *Stazione Termini* was a "hybrid film," Moravia wrote, and it "cannot aspire but to a fair commercial success. An Italian director who works with foreign actors is like an Italian writer who writes some of his books in French or English."[5]

And yet this discourse of difference was ever more an intellectual performance than a reflection of reality. Along with its economic, political, and military foundation, in the West, culture too was becoming integrated. An important sign of this amalgamation was the way Atlantic culture and cinema coherently memorialized World War II and rapidly produced a coherent Atlantic representation of the conflict. Embracing a case study methodology, in this chapter my focus will be on the cinematic figuration of the Italian soldier during World War II, and my argument is that themes and types central to the Italian and American depictions of the most transformative event in the twentieth century were also becoming more and more integrated.

Hollywood and the Good Italian Soldier

My story begins in Hollywood where the three pillars of the Celluloid Atlantic's representation of the European front were already taking shape during the conflict. Of these three pillars two are well known: "the idealized figure of the [American] combat soldier"[6] and the cruel and efficient Nazi military operative. Shaped during the war, the types of the good American and the bad German flowed seamlessly into postwar Western cinema.

Recently, new historiography has identified a third pillar of this cultural representation: the *italiano brava gente* (Italians, nice folks). In the aftermath of World War II, this scholarship argues, Italian elites constructed a self-serving myth of Italian soldiers as victims of World War II rather than the perpetrators of its bloody opening act. Victimhood granted amnesty for previous war crimes, a process based on amnesia and resulting in the absence for Italy of any counterpart to the Nuremberg or Tokyo trials. In turn, this lenience stabilized Italy's loyalty to the nascent Atlantic political alliance.[7]

Italy, however, was not the initiator of this process.[8] I shall argue in this chapter that the celluloid myth of the good Italian soldier was grounded as deeply in American wartime propaganda as it was consistent with Italian postwar strategies. It was at its core an important aspect of the Celluloid Atlantic.

On December 7, 1941, Franklyn D. Roosevelt issued Proclamations 2525, 2526, and 2527 that established a category of "alien enemy," or "enemy alien," for those German, Italian, and Japanese nationals in the United States who had not become American citizens. Enemy aliens could not own weapons, radios, cameras, or even documents that may contain "invisible writings."[9]

Draconian though they were, these measures were not applied evenly, and the enemy alien policy of the FDR administration was fraught with ambiguities and racist overtones. "By order of the president," Japanese Isei and Nisei were deported from the West Coast to concentration camps in the middle of the country.[10] Germans too were subjected to constraints, including a "dusk-to-dawn" curfew on the West Coast[11] that irked refugees who felt wronged by a provision that confused victims and oppressors. To use the words of the German refugee film director Henry Koster, "I was more American than many Americans I met."[12]

Koster's reaction was comprehensible, but the Germans and the Italians were still treated better than the Japanese, and the Italians had it better than the Germans. Attorney General Francis Biddle famously reminisced that Roosevelt once told him that he was not concerned with the Italians: "They are a lot of opera singers, but the Germans are different; they may be dangerous."[13] It may have motivated the president that Italian migration, peaking in the 1890s and the first decade of the twentieth century, was more recent and substantial than the dwindling German influx. Italians voted as a bloc and controlled key electoral college votes; Germans did not, and had integrated after the anti-German hysteria of World War I. Much could be lost by antagonizing the Italian American community and there was little fear of an Italian fifth column. Even after entry into the war, the FBI reported that the community's subversive elements were either under control or marginal.[14]

As the war progressed, it became clear that Italy might break away from the Axis if properly handled. Since the beginning of the conflict American propaganda, which after June 1942 was coordinated by the newly created Office of War Information (OWI), distinguished between the regimes and the regimented, Fascist leaders and citizens of Fascist states, but this distinction was soon articulated more clearly for Italy than it ever was for Germany and Japan. The opera-singing Italians were less dangerous because they were less committed to the Nazi-Fascist cause. Their unsteady allegiance to the Fascist regime could be exploited. American propaganda thus aimed to construe Italians in a different way than it did the Germans and the Japanese. Out of the ashes of World War II, the foolish, innocent Italian soldier, the Italian soldier as *Italiano brava gente*, was to join the righteous GI and the evil German as the military pillars of the Celluloid Atlantic.

Possibly, the first articulation of the *Italiano brava gente* was ironically a World War II film made by a prominent member of the German speaking anti-Nazi refugee community in Hollywood, Billy Wilder. Wilder's *Five Graves to Cairo* (1943) begins on a bleak note. It is June 1942, the aftermath of the battle of Gazala, a locality west of Tobruk in the Italian colony of Libya. German and Italian forces led by Generaloberst Erwin Rommel have just fought and defeated Allied forces (mostly British, South African, Indian, and Free French) led by General Claude Auchinleck and pushed them back deep into Egypt. A British tank erratically climbs and descends impressive desert dunes. Wilder reveals the grim reason for the machine's irregular behavior. The tank is full of the corpses of Allied troops, all dead but for the barely alive Corporal John Bramble (Franchot Tone). Having slipped out of the ghostly vehicle, Bramble reaches the Empress of Britain hotel in Sidi Halfaya where a French maid, Mouche (Anne Baxter), and an Egyptian hotel manager, Farid (Akim Tamiroff), reluctantly help him hide from the incoming Afrika Korps of Field Marshal Erwin Rommel (Erich von Stroheim) by letting him assume the identity of a waiter, Davos, who perished in the German bombings.

A sort of remake of *Hotel Imperial* (Robert Florey, 1939), which was, in turn, a remake of the 1927 film by the same name by Mauritz Stiller, and, like both of these previous movies, was based on Lajos Bíro's story *Színmű négy felvonásban*, *Five Graves*'s plot is fraught with masquerades and misunderstanding. The waiter, Davos, was actually a German spy working behind British lines, a fact Bramble learns and exploits to get close to Rommel, who has never met the real Davos. Eventually Bramble learns the location of the five supply deposits (the five graves of the title) the German general has hidden in Egypt.

Wilder does not play the plot for laughter, down to the grim last scene. Bramble returns to Sidi Halfaya with the victorious British Eighth Army and discovers that Mouche, unable to conceal her joy about the Nazis' coming defeat in North Africa, has been executed by the Germans. But the screenwriter-turned-director does allow comedy in juxtaposing the Germans to the Italians. Rommel was played by Erich von Stroheim, an actor who embodied sadistic German rigor both onscreen and off (even though he was born in Vienna from a Jewish family). Facing Stroheim/Rommel was the Italian general Sebastiano played by Spanish tenor Fortunio Bonanova. Wilder introduces both leaders when the Axis powers jointly take over the hotel. Rommel, as played by the physically fit Stroheim, is commanding and frightening. In contrast, the paunchy Sebastiano is friendly and fun loving, an easy target for German contempt. German lieutenant Schwegler (Peter van Eyck) assigns him a room that has no working bathroom because the room with running water is to go to Rommel. When he finds out, Sebastiano is accommodating though annoyed. When Rommel sends Bramble/Davos to ask the Italian general to cease his incessant opera singing, Sebastiano complies, but wonders aloud to Bramble about the future of the Axis: "Can a nation of belchers understand a nation that sings?" War is obviously not his métier; singing is. At the dinner table, where Rommel boasts of his conquests and cunning before captured Allied officers, the Italian again plays the part of the fool. Sebastiano unwittingly asks Rommel to reveal his plans before enemy

Atlantic Soldiers

officers. Rommel rebukes him, and notices that his army has fewer soldiers than the Allied forces because "nobody counts the Italians."

Sebastiano's treatment is humiliating but, remarkably, it also lets off the hook a country that initiated European fascism, was one of the three original members of the Axis, invaded and cruelly defeated Ethiopia, and joined the war in June 1940. When Bramble returns to the hotel as an officer of the victorious British Army, Sebastiano is filing out before the building, a POW prodded along by a baby-faced British soldier. Bramble treats him as a friend. He is happy to see him alive, and tells him so. Sebastiano hardly recognizes him in British military attire, but seems unconcerned with his fate, or that of his country. He is singing Puccini and all will be well.

The OWI was only moderately impressed by the film. It seemed too bleak in its depiction of Rommel's skills, and the Italian general was drawn too broadly. "Some of the comedy business with the Italian general could be eliminated," wrote OWI reviewer Peg Fenwick.[15] Luigi Luraschi, the London-born Paramount liaison with OWI and later a CIA asset in Hollywood, agreed. "I am glad that you are recommending that the buffoonery of the Italian general be toned down," Ulric Bell wrote Luraschi.[16]

The German v. Italian binary continued to be a staple of World War II American war movies. The itinerary through OWI's bureaucracy of the script for *Sahara* (Zoltan Korda, 1943) is revealing, especially because the film was often proposed as the model of the "useful" Hollywood war movie by government agencies and American progressive film circles. *Sahara* shared its North African setting with *Five Graves*, and followed a ragtag gang of soldiers from several armies disbanded by the early victories of Rommel's Afrika Korps. The soldiers are aboard a stranded American tank commanded by Sergeant John Gunn (Humphrey Bogart), which picks up more men along its way, including a Free France soldier, a British medical corpsman, Sudanese officer Tambul (Rex Ingram) and his Italian prisoner Giuseppe (J. Carrol Naish), and even Captain von Schletow (Kurt Kreuger), the pilot of a German Stuka the group has shot down. This motley crew ends up contributing to Rommel's defeat at El Alamein by defeating a German battalion trying to take possession of a vital water well. With the exception of von Schletow, who is killed by Tambul as he attempts to inform his comrades that the well has actually gone dry, and of Gunn and the Irish soldier Ozzie Bates (Patrick O'Moore), who survive the ordeal, everybody else dies a hero's death while contributing to the important Allied victory.

Sahara was directed by Zoltan Korda, the brother of producer and British secret agent Alexander Korda, and scripted by Korda and John Howard Lawson, the leader of the Communist Party cell in Hollywood, with the uncredited contribution of fellow traveler Sidney Buchman. The film's cosmopolite cast comprised, among others, Humphrey Bogart, Bruce Bennett, J. Carrol Naish, Lloyd Bridges, Rex Ingram, German Kurt Kreuger, Frenchman Louis Mercier, Englishman Guy Kingsford, and Irishman Richard Aherne. *Sahara* had a worldly and progressive pedigree with Korda at the helm, several Hollywood Europeans in the cast, and the story's foundations in the Soviet film *The Thirteen* (1937) by Mikhail Romm (about Red Army soldiers fighting Afghan bandits), which had been a hit in American urban and intellectual circles in the late thirties.[17]

The film aimed to celebrate the ecumenical nature of the anti-Nazi front, but by foregrounding national and ethnic differences, *Sahara* was also a classic model of Hollywood commerce in racial and ethnic stereotypes. OWI manuals argued the necessity of depicting the ethnic, and sometimes racial, variety of both the American nation and the nation-states composing the anti-Axis front. Hollywood, sometimes and somewhat, complied. The multiethnic platoon, as Richard Slotkin has noted, was the hallmark of *Bataan* (Tay Garnett, 1943) and other World War II American films.[18] These films depicted an America that was more inclusive and less insular than it really was, and also ironically reinforced stereotypes. Accents and physiques made Jewish soldiers easily recognizable to non-Jews. They had names like Jake Feingold (*Bataan*) and spoke with heavy Brooklyn accents. Irishmen like Sam Malloy (Tom Dugan) in *Bataan* had paunches, tempers, or reddish skin complexions, especially around the nose, that made them out as regular denizens of the neighborhood bar. Even before he appeared on the screen doing the platoon's laundry, African American private Wesley Eeps (Kenneth Spencer) was introduced in *Bataan* via the soundtrack that had the black soldier gleefully, and tellingly, sing a gospel song.

Likewise, *Sahara* depicted a world where everybody's behavior—be this ethnic or racial—was predetermined. More than uniforms, racial and ethnic stereotypes made it easy for the American film spectator

Atlantic Soldiers 113

to recognize who came from where. Each character was marked in name or nickname by his geographic origins even when it was at odds with the actor's biography. Irish actor Richard Aherne was supercilious and hyper-English as Captain Jason Halliday of the Royal Army Medical Corps since everybody in America knew that the "limeys" were haughty and hierarchical, the "Jerries" authoritarian and cruel, and the "Frenchies" obsessed about Camembert cheese. Rex Ingram, a graduate of Northwestern University Medical School where he had been the first African American to receive the Phi Beta Kappa key, was "Tambul," a Sudanese sergeant major who spoke in pidgin English and is fooled by Gunn into thinking naively that he has captured an enemy tank by himself. Even the American soldier was a stereotype of sorts. His name is "Waco" after the Texan town from whence he comes. Only sergeant John Gunn (Bogart) and the tank itself, Lulubelle, bore names that did not immediately reveal their origins, gesturing only toward their professions (with explicit irony in the case of the machine). This marked their own superiority over the rest of the cast. Gunn replies to the question about his personal geography: "I come from nowhere, I come from the army."

Sahara's Italian stereotype is performed surefootedly by a non-Italian, New York City–born actor J. Carrol Naish. Giuseppe is short, hairy, and adorned with a prominent Catholic cross. He places his faith in Jesus and loyalty in his family, whose pictures he carries in his wallet. The French soldier is the only one who distrusts him given recent history. "I have been fighting them since 1936 . . . in Spain," he says. At first, Gunn agrees with the Frenchman. There is no space on Lulubelle for "this load of spaghetti." But to no avail: conventional Italian familism binds Giuseppe to America. His wife has a relative (a "cousin," or maybe an "uncle") who works in a steel factory in Pittsburgh. Gunn has to change his mind and let him in with the others.

Giuseppe's Italian-ness is defined in conjunction to Tambul's Africanness and in opposition to Captain von Schletow's German-ness. The Italian and the African are introduced together, from a distance, framed by the oval lenses of Gunn's binoculars. Korda picks the immediate characterization of the Italian soldier out of the slapstick tradition also referenced by the silent cinema visual convention of the "iris" impressed on the frame by Gunn's lenses and immediately recognizable as such by most adult spectators in 1943. Giuseppe is comically loaded with his and Tambul's gear, and the latter prods him on with the butt of his rifle. When Waco shoots a couple of warning shots ahead of the duo, Giuseppe amusingly falls down the dune. He remains comic relief till his tragic and heroic death.

Captain von Schletow is Giuseppe's opposite. He strafes the tank and its crew from his Stuka and, once downed, demand the group's surrender. Dressed in white garb, he recoils when Tambul searches him for weapons. He does not want to be touched by a man from an inferior race. After Schletow murders Giuseppe, he almost succeeds in betraying the group to the German Afrika Korps, but Tambul suffocates him by stuffing his head in the sand.

The violence of von Schletow's death at the hands of the Sudanese soldier is a remarkable visual spectacle, Tambul violently pushing the man's head into the sand till the German officer's body stops twitching. It is more than an ordinary combat death and everybody knows it, including the performers and the spectators. It plays with well-established stereotypes as it radically modifies them. It signifies that Africanness and blackness seemed on the verge of being deeply altered by the war as Tambul is allowed to fight and kill a white man. But it is an uncertain victory, and the racial order is recomposed when the African is soon afterward downed by enemy bullets.

Unlike the "Jerry," Giuseppe is clearly the victim, rather than the initiator, of the war. He hates the Duce and dies trying to stop his German fellow prisoner from communicating with the German troops. Like Tambul, Giuseppe is a good man by instinct and lives and dies as a victim rather than as an oppressor. The real ally of the German is the Libyan guide, who is guiding the Afrika Korps battalion to the water wells and prominently wears an Italian military uniform.

Compared with General Sebastiano, Giuseppe was less comedy, more melodrama, and the OWI approved. The OWI review of the script had reservations about the character of the "Negro" Tambul ("sort of Gunga Din") but was effusive about the portrait of the German enemy and the distinction between Italians and Germans. Reviewers Margaret Ruthven and Dorothy Jones called the film a "real contribution to the war information program," enthusing that "the nature of the enemy is convincingly shown in the portrayal of von Schletow, the arrogant, young, Nazi in his contempt for his Italian fellow-prisoner." The script also did a good job at expressing "the inarticulate longing of the Italian prisoner in his dreams of 'peace and labor.' "[19] Of the finished film OWI noted that Giuseppe was "so well presented . . . that the picture could be possibly shown in Italy itself with constructive results."[20] The office recommended the film for foreign distribution with no reservation: *Sahara* was "one of the best jobs this office has seen."[21]

By the end of the conflict, Hollywood was, if anything, going too far in the representation of Italian innocence and German evil. The former were too innocent, the latter so evil as to appear frighteningly too effective. OWI was appalled by Alfred Hitchcock drama *Lifeboat* (1944), another story of an unlikely ethnically and racially varied group of survivors gathered on a lifeboat as a result of a merchant marine ship and a German U-boat sinking each other in the Atlantic. The wiliness of von Schletow in *Sahara* had morphed into the superhuman capacity of Captain Willi (Walter Slezak) to harm his enemies. His evil power had preoccupied OWI since the beginning of production and in the final feature film, the German U-boat captain still outwitted the other survivors for a good while by hoarding water and energy pills. He is finally revealed as an "ersatz super man," his superiority due to cowardly plunder rather than power, but his ability to outmaneuver the other passengers did "combine to give the impression that the Nazis are superior to the people of the democracies."[22]

On the other hand, in some Hollywood films Italians seemed too innocent. *A Bell for Adano* (1945) dealt with the successful attempt by US Army major Victor Joppolo to bring the values of democracy back to the coastal southern Italian city of Adano. Based on a John Hersey novel, which was to become a bestseller and win the 1945 Pulitzer Prize, the Twentieth Century Fox film followed the novel closely and was applauded by one of the early American champions of Italian neorealism, the *New York Times*'s Bosley Crowther. He declared *Adano* one of the notable films of 1945, praising "the reportorial accuracy of director and scene designers" and, using a word energized by postwar debate about realism and neorealism, noting that director Henry King "has made the story of Major Joppolo a moving and thrilling *document*."[23]

OWI was not so impressed. While finally greenlighting *A Bell for Adano* (Henry King, 1945) as suitable for overseas distribution, the Office did not recommend it, and the OWI's staff criticized both the script and the finished film for its elevation of all Italians, military and civilian, from supporters of the Duce to unqualified victims of fascism. Already in January 1944, Dorothy Jones and Sandy Roth had reviewed a seventeen-page synopsis and two-page summary of the yet unpublished novel prepared by Hersey himself, and found it lacking. Fox, they contended, needed to show that there were at least "one or two Italian Fascists" in Adano or, for that matter, in Italy. Otherwise "the impression could be created that we are under the illusion that fascism in Italy began and ended with Mussolini." The finished film seemed hardly any better, and the office still found that *Adano*, while "well produced . . . sidestepped any conflict of pro- and anti-Fascists."[24]

Yet the OWI had been complicit in creating the image of the good Italian, even beyond movie screens. When in the early spring of 1943 the OWI planned an exhibit at the Rockefeller Center in Manhattan on "The Nature of the Enemy," Italy received only scant attention. Mussolini was referenced by radio personality Raymond Gram Swing in the radio program accompanying the opening of the show on NBC's Blue network in May 1943,[25] and the attacks on Ethiopia and Albania in 1935 and 1939 were mentioned in the tableau for "The Enemy Strikes." While the exhibit timeline listed the national socialist takeover of the German government after the January 1933 election ("1933: Nazis seize power in Germany"), it did not mention the 1922 March on Rome, nor the Italian conquest of Libya (completed by Mussolini's army in the late twenties), nor the Italian invasions of Yugoslavia and Greece. No other mention of the earliest European Fascist state and member of the Axis was made throughout the exhibit.

Organized around "six centrals aspects of the enemy's philosophy" (regimentation of labor, abolition of justice, concentration camps, the desecration of religion, the suppression of free thought, and the militarization of children), the exhibit cited enemy manuals, propaganda, and the regimes' intellectual interventions—all of which came from German and Japanese sources. The six speakers invited to comment, who included Italian American jurist Ferdinand Pecora, made no mention of Italian Fascism, while reminding all listeners that, among other things, "the governments of Germany and Japan are against God."[26]

It is remarkable that this attitude prevailed *before* the removal of Mussolini from power in July 1943. It was clear that the Allies wanted to make sure that Italians did not side en masse with the Germans. Almost immediately after the battle for Anzio the Italian

Atlantic Soldiers

soldier in liberated Italy was transformed from perpetrator into victim. On May 26, 1944 a "Report on Conditions in Liberated Italy" of the Psychological Warfare office described the former Fascist troops as cannon fodder rather than cannon crews. "The political and moral conceptions of the average Italian soldier are limited; he does not look beyond his own family, his house, and the land he must cultivate; the rest does not interest him because he does not understand it."[27] After the September 8 Armistice, Mussolini's escape from prison, and the creation of the Fascist republic of Salò in northern Italy, the Italian soldiers who were fighting with Mussolini were still considered far from fanatical about the defeated regime. "The [Italian] soldier" opined a report on Italian deserters by a Fifth Army officer "has no conscience left. His sole preoccupation is to save his life. The question puzzling most of the soldiers was 'Which is the true government and whom must I obey?'"[28]

Overall, the OWI thought that Italian populace saw the Allies as protectors. There were areas of unrest and the office was concerned with the black market economy, scarcity of food, and the popularity of the Communists. Fascism, however, was a veneer easily shed. Even when the Allied powers gathered at Yalta failed to reassure Italy of the intentions of the probable victors, their headquarters in Rome reported that Romans were not alienated from the Allies, "at least not to any considerable degree." Italian public opinion just assumed that discussion of their postwar situation remained secret. The report noted that the Yugoslavs were also requesting the extradition of forty Italian military officers who had committed atrocities in the war. Italians, however, considered the request (which included General Mario Roatta and the Carabinieri general Taddeo Orlando) "absurd" and "an affront to the national honor."[29] There would be no Nuremberg accounting for Italy.

Following James Walston and Angelo del Boca a new generation of historians have unearthed the role of Italian diplomatic circles in winning this amnesty. The role of cinema in this process, however, has gone unnoticed. Neither have people noted that the notion of the innocence of the Italian soldier was in fact an Atlantic creation.[30]

The figure of the clumsy Italian soldier carried over in the first years after World War II. In Fred Sears's *El Alamein* (1953), the tank crew is initially made up by the usual ethnically varied group of two Brits (the upper-crust Captain Harbison played by Edward Ashley and the working class Sgt. Alf Law by Robin Hughes) and the all-American Joe Banning (Scott Brady), a civilian mechanic who is there to take care of the M3 tanks Americans have supplied the British Army. A mechanical mishap catches them at the tail end of Rommel's offensive and stuck behind enemy aliens. The trio are soon joined by a stranded Punjabi soldier, Cpl. Singh Das (Peter Mamakos), and, later, by several Australian soldiers. It is the usual commerce in stereotypes: the Punjabi prefers his knife to modern weapons, the Australians are rugged fellas who can't stop joking about kangaroos. Their problem is lack of water and fuel, but the Italians' inadvertent carelessness provides both. In the released film, the tank sneaks up on an Italians regiment encamped around a water hole. The Italians have an edge in numbers and equipment yet they run after just a few shots.

The script Columbia submitted to the Department of Defense to ask for cooperation (*El Alamein* was a low-cost production featuring stock film from British and American Army film archives) was even more ludicrous. In the draft, the Italians are bivouacking with trucks and heavy weapons around the water hole, seemingly oblivious to one of the biggest military confrontations of the twentieth century occurring all around them. FDR is correct: they are just opera singers in soldiers' disguises. "From the o.s. [offscreen] at a distance, comes the sound of a tenor singing in Italian (an opera selection to be chosen from those in public domain)." "An opera company?," Tom asks the British captain. "Sounds rather like it. Not a bad tenor," he answers. The battle between the real soldiers and the singing buffoons is over in a few seconds.[31]

Even if opera singing was omitted in the released film,[32] Italian soldiers were conspicuous for their inefficiency. Germans were another matter entirely. Their propaganda follows the tank crew everywhere. The crew listens to a radio taken from the Italians, and a suave female voice tells the Allies they have no chance against Rommel, the Führer, or their warriors. The film follows the narrative model of *Sahara*—though it gives no credit to the previous film—down to the ending with the motley crew defending to their death a desert ruin (this time full with ammunition and tank fuel) from overwhelming German forces till British tanks arrive. Only four of them survive including the American Banning who is alive to tell the story in the aftermath of the war. Like *Sahara*, *El Alamein* has a German Stuka strafing the tank from the sky only to be downed by the American civilian mechanic. This time around, the pilot does not survive, but he tells the Allied crew that they are doomed and guns down poor Cpl. Singh while screaming "Heil Hitler" with his last breath.

Before granting the producers access to its film and image morgue, the Department of Defense demanded assurances that the film was correct and no embarrassment for the Americans. Authenticity mattered even at the expense of American self-aggrandizement; the army objected to an early treatment of the story as the focus was on American rather than British troops (at this stage, like in *Sahara*, the tank was American and the crew picked up Brits along the way) and the main character was an American war correspondent. The head of the pictorial branch of the Office of Public Information, Lt. Col. Clair Towne, wrote the studio that "El Alamein will go down in history as a great British victory and a story about a little tank crew, predominantly American, is in no sense a fitting vehicle to carry the tile *El Alamein* . . . [and it] could be accused of borrowing glory from the British." Furthermore, a war correspondent would not be in the position to "take command of the composite tank crew." The Army's Public Information Division concurred with the Defense Department: to "portray the activities [during El Alamein] of one little tank crew, predominantly American is a most presumptuous premise."[33] At first the studio tried to defend its idea but it relented. By October 1952 the script had the tank as an M3 commanded by British troops. The American war correspondent remained, but he played second fiddle to Rick Banning, an American army sergeant. Towne was not satisfied, however, and he wrote that Banning should be more submissive toward Harbison, the British commanding officer.[34] Eager to secure US Army footage, the studio again capitulated. The third version of the script portrays Banning as a mechanic and completely in line with the British captain. The Army and the Defense Department were satisfied. "We are happy to report that no objections are interposed to the script or to any of [its] scenes," Towne wrote.[35]

As unlikely as an American tank at El Alamein was, Italians singing opera in the middle of the great battle was infinitely more dubious. The Defense Department, however, was unconcerned. No mention is made of the episode, which is present in all versions of the script. By the early 1950s Italian soldiers occupied a liminal place within Hollywood's representation of the war, as either *not there* or as mere pawns. The Academy Award–nominated screenplay of William

Wellman's *Ernie Pyle's The Story of Gi Joe* (1945) begins with a famous defeat of the American troops at the hands of Rommel's Afrika Korps and the Italian Centauro Division at Kasserine Pass in February 1943. The Italian enemies, who by all account fought well at the pass, are never mentioned. They are present in the remaining two-thirds of the film that depicts correspondent Ernie Pyle covering Company C of the Eighteenth Infantry Division in Italy. By then, however, the September 8 Armistice is in place and Italians are no longer enemies, if not yet trusted allies.

Another seminal film of the end of the war, *A Walk in the Sun* (Lewis Milestone, 1945–1946), also ignores the Italian Fascist campaigns. The film takes place in the confusing beginnings of the Salerno attack in early September 1943. An American platoon features two Italian Americans: Pvt. Rivera played by Richard Conte (introduced as "Italian American. Likes opera and would like a wife and kids, plenty of kids") and Pvt. Giorgio Tranella interpreted by Richard Benedict ("[he] speaks two languages: Italian and Brooklyn"). "Do you know who you are fighting against?" "Germans," the other answers. When the platoon encounters two Italian soldiers, one of whom has killed a German soldier with a rock, they supply comic relief: one gesticulates and the other gazes speechless into the Americans' faces.[36] After being set free by the American commanding officer they ask for cigarettes, then demand food, then try to follow the GIs. The soldiers shoo them away like a pair of stray dogs. Even when they communicate important intelligence to the Americans—the location of the German troops—their shrill voices distinguish them from the manly, American-speaking warriors. As for Italy's participation in the war, the duo argue that they had no choice. "They did not like the Germans, but they got no choice . . . Italy made a mistake," Tranella translates. Some of the other GIs are not so convinced ("always looking for a way out," one says), but Tranella defends the Italians: "They have been fighting the Germans ever since they came in and they are still fighting the Germans. What do *you* know about it?"

To Hell and Back (Jesse Hibbs 1950) was based on the autobiography of the most decorated World War II American soldier, Audie Murphy, who also interpreted himself onscreen. The film featured the African and the Sicilian campaigns, but Murphy and his comrades in arms fight only German enemies. When he makes it to continental Italy, Murphy goes on furlough to liberated Naples along with his platoon. Italians are now the defeated former enemies. Murphy lets a Neapolitan street urchin, Vincenzo, shine his shoes and offers him chocolate. Vincenzo's sister intervenes: Vincenzo is not allowed to beg, but if Audie accepts a dinner invitation, they will be permitted to take the chocolate as a respectable gift. Thus, Audie is invited into their modest Italian abode. The mother is distant and surly and prohibits English at the table. Sirens send everybody except Murphy to the bomb shelter, but the young lady returns to keep him company, and explains her mother's rude behavior: her son has been killed by the English in Africa and her husband is gone as well. Though the brother was an enemy combatant, Audie easily understands the old woman's, and especially her daughter's, plight. Her loss of a father reproduces his own, as Audie's father had also abandoned his family. The narrative of the film closes the scene with a chaste, soulful hug between the two.

It is interesting how the film version of *To Hell and Back* differs from Audie's biography by the same title. In the book Italians are not as bad or effective as the Germans, but they are not entirely victims either. Opportunism rules their interactions with the American troops. Maria, the Italian girl Audie meets, has a brother who has been killed by the English, but her father is garrulously present. Instead of anger, there is hunger, caused by war. Through the soldier's interpreter, the family asks Audie for the food he carries in his bag. The father de facto pimps his daughter to Audie, though, "as head of the family, he has dignity to maintain."[37] When the siren sounds, both father and mother go to the shelter and leave their remaining child in the company of an armed foreign soldier they just met. Audie and the woman have sex and, afterward, he asks her: "Why did you act so shy when I first came here? It is not your true nature."[38] She agrees. There is no Vincenzo in the book.

For our story the absence of the child is an important detail. The American film reproduces Roberto Rossellini's second episode of *Paisan*, written by the Anglo-American writer Alfred Hayes,[39] in which "Joe," an African American soldier (Dots Johnson), encounters a Neapolitan street urchin. Like Vincenzo (spelled Vincenti in the script) and like De Sica's Pasquale Maggi (Franco Interlenghi) in *Sciuscià* (Shoeshine, 1946), Rossellini's urchin, Pasquale (Alfonsino Pasca), is a *sciuscià*, nominally a shoeshine boy but in fact a petty thief. Joe recognizes a shared humanity with Pasquale. The kid wants the soldier's shoes, and steals them after Joe, drunk, has fallen asleep on a pile of ruins—but not before warning the soldier ("do not fall asleep or I'll steal your shoes"). Pasquale likes Joe because he has intimated that he does not have any prosperous home to go back to in America. Later apprehended by Joe, he is forced to take the soldier to his abode. "Get my shoes!," an irate Joe tells Pasquale as he is surrounded by other screaming ragged urchins. Soon, however, Joe understands the kid's situation. Rossellini shoots Dots and Pasquale in a narrative objective shot as they enter the cave where Pasquale lives together with other homeless civilians. The shot then becomes briefly subjective. Composed from Joe's point of view, the frame reveals a scene of utter poverty and degradation. The camera moves back to Joe who has now understood that, like him, Pasquale has no real home to go back to. He has decided to leave the child alone with his shoes. It is a significant camera movement, which turns the tables on the characters. As noted by Leonardo De Franceschi, Rossellini consistently uses Dots as the object of the spectators' and Pasquale's gaze.[40] Now it is the American that finally "sees" the Italian tragedy.

In *To Hell and Back*, Vincenzo plays almost the same role of Pasquale. Race is erased in Murphy's 1950s American film, but the script still stresses Vincenzo's and Audie's shared experience. Their fate is "parallel to his [Audie's] own early life" as they have been both abandoned by their fathers. As Pasquale did with Dots, Vincenzo opens the American soldier's eyes to the squalid poverty of the Italian war victims. In *Paisan*, Rossellini had used a sudden subjective shot to reveal Joe's encounter with Pasquale's reality. A similar transition was envisioned by the screenwriter of *To Hell and Back*:

> Vincenti, ad libbing in Italian, beckons for Audie to come with him. . . . Vincenti repeats his ad lib and beckoning. Intrigued Audie finally agrees and they start up the street. Vincenti trots along a few paces ahead of Audie. Another angle as Vincenti leads Audie across the street approaching the camera. As they pass, the camera pans with them to include the entrance to a dwelling, toward which they are heading. Audie holds back, but Vincenti goes to the door, still beckoning. Completely intrigued now, Audie follows. Vincenti starts to open the door. Int. House—Full shot as Vincenti and Audie enter. Included are a number of other

Atlantic Soldiers   123

younger children. Perhaps, with Vincenti, they are the same
in number, as Audie's family. They are ragged and thin and
a little fearful of Audie.[41]

The Consonance of the Celluloid Atlantic

Once again a striking consonance ruled over the Celluloid Atlantic.
It would be too simplistic to credit this to American cultural policies. The intellectual spread of neorealism consolidated the work of
the Office of War Information as neorealism directly focused on the
idea that Italy was one of the victims of the conflict. In a lecture he
gave in the late 1980s at Purdue University, neorealist director and
Communist intellectual Giuseppe De Santis argued that neorealism had no fathers, but only "a great mother, the Resistance,"[42] the
gendering of parenthood implicitly absolving neorealist practitioners
of the sins of the Fascist fathers. Thirty years earlier in 1951, the
director had suggested that neorealist cinema mirrored the anti-Fascist
mass movement of the Resistance, which was the "new phase of our
Risorgimento"[43] and was completing it.

In many Italian neorealist films the Resistance was defined as
much by the *absence* of the ordinary Italian as Fascist as by the presence
of his antithesis, the figure of the ordinary Italian as anti-Mussolini
fighter. In many aspects neorealist films were consonant with *A Bell
for Adano*: both the former and the latter assumed Italian innocence.
Differences of course existed. In postwar Italian movies American sol-
diers were accepted as liberators,[44] but the focus was often the iconic
Italian Resistance fighter, or the famished rural or urban proletarian.
Partisans and poor abounded in Giuseppe De Santis's *Caccia Tragica*
(The Tragic Hunt, 1945), Carmine Gallone's *Davanti a lui tremava
tutta Roma* (Before Him All Rome Trembled, 1946), Marcello Pagliero's
Roma città libera (1946), Carlo Lizzani's *Achtung! Banditi* (Attention!
Bandits!, 1951), or Roberto Rossellini's *Roma città aperta* (Rome, Open
City, 1945) and *Paisà* (1946).[45] Fascism was depicted as a regime
supported only by a bloodthirsty, socially well-defined minority that
had oppressed the Italian *popolo* (people). In fact, both Fascism and
anti-Fascism shared a remarkably positive notion of the Italian *popolo*.
Anna Maria Torriglia has correctly pointed out that *Open City* reset
the "national popular project" by replacing the Fascist notion of the

popolo italiano—centering on a bloody mystique of violence, subjection to the Duce, and nationalistic destiny—with a more progressive and anti-Fascist vision typified especially by Pina (Anna Magnani), the proletarian heroine of the film, "as the source of regeneration for Italian democracy."[46]

In neorealist cinema, De Santis wrote, "the streets of Italy filled with the partisans, the veterans, the homeless, the unemployed, the workers struggling for their future."[47] De Santis's long list was telling. It was both a statement of the visual goals of the director's cinema as well as an ideological and historical interpretation of Fascism and of recent Italian history. The inventory enumerated some of the staple characters of neorealist films: the people who took arms against Fascism (the partisan) as well as those who had, at some point, taken up arms to uphold its goals (the veteran). The partisan, the famished Italian, and the war veteran were placed on the same continuum of nonparticipation with the regime; all were members of a new citizenry, the *popolo*, ushered in by the Resistance.

Necessary for this reconstitution was a cavalier attitude toward the Italian past. In his acute essay on *Paisà*, American critic Robert Warshow noted that via his capacious notion of "the defeated," Rossellini obscured all differences between an Italian Fascist and an Italian partisan: both had suffered, "a view that has a special attraction for a defeated Fascist nation, and Rossellini cannot restrain himself from taking a special advantage of it." Thus, Warshow continued, *Paisà* conveyed "the fantasies of the eternally defeated as he tries anxiously to read his fate in the countenance of a new master."[48]

The Routes Not Taken

Within the narrative universe of the Celluloid Atlantic, the crimes of Italy had little place. Beginning with Vittorio de Sica's *Generale Della Rovere* (1959), from the end of the 1950s to 1962, Italian filmmakers revisited World War II and often added a comic touch to the *brava gente* myth. Italians were also allowed to be less saintly and more sassy than in the original neorealist films. Characters like Bardone Grimaldi (Vittorio De Sica), the Roman con man turned hero in *Della Rovere*, the Fascist *federale* Primo Arcovazzi (Ugo Tognazzi) in Luciano Salce's *Il federale* (The Fascist, 1961), the Italian deserter, Lieutenant

Atlantic Soldiers

Alberto Innocenzi (Alberto Sordi), in Luigi Comencini's *Tutti a casa* (1960), and the Italian tank corporal Carlo Pollini (Jean-Marc Bory) in Gianni Puccini's *Il carro armato dell'8 settembre* (1960), to name only a few, were less innocent than the victims of the early neorealist films. Yet, ultimately, the Italians all die heroically opposing Nazi Fascism, or reveal their inherent goodness—with corporal Pollini of *Il carro armato* even plotting to turn a tank into a mechanical plough for his farm.[49] In the Atlantic coproduction directed by Guy Hamilton, *Best of Enemies* (I due nemici, 1961) written by Suso Cecchi-D'amico, Age & Scarpelli, and the Briton Jack Pulman, and produced by Dino De Laurentiis with capital advanced by the Columbia studio acting as distributor of the film, Captain Blasi (Alberto Sordi) is revealed as a mirror image of the British commander Major Richardson (David Niven). They are, ahistorically enough, similar people, though Blasi is more inept at fighting a war he, of course, does not believe in. Nothing of this kind happens to the few Italian Fascists and the many beastly Germans that in all these films remain, without exception, evil.

Throughout, the Italian narrative mainstream stuck to comedy or the victimism of neorealist melodramas. Film narratives that stressed the heroism of the Italian soldier did exist, but they appealed to national or regional, not Atlantic, networks and audiences. Duilio Coletti's *La grande speranza* (Submarine Attack, 1954) told the story of an Italian submarine patrolling the Atlantic. The "Captain," interpreted by Renato Baldini, goes unnamed: "sono un marinaio" (I am just a sailor) he tells the Danish captain who wants to know whom to pray for after the Italian saves his and his men's lives. His multiaccented, multiregional crew of Italian sailors are extremely good at what they do. In the course of the film they sink three Allied ships (once using only the sub's surface cannon) and risk their lives numerous times.

In this rendition the Italians are extremely humane warriors, kind to their prisoners, even to the prisoners' pets, but they are also fiercely effective fighters. The film reversed the OWI narrative of Italian buffoonery but was also, to paraphrase Warshow's essay on *Paisan*, a fantasy of innocence and victimhood. Coletti turned a war film into a facile antiwar narrative in which all combatants, regardless of the side they are fighting on, are victims of the war whose origins rest in human nature, not politics. It is a true Hegelian night "where all cows are black." The American aging prisoner of war shouts at the British prisoner who is plotting to spoil the love fest by pursuing escape and sabotage of the ship: "We must kill!? . . . as if humanity were in need of this bloodbath . . . What would you have done in their place?" Even the man from Albion will come to respect the "Captain" and his crew.

Coletti made much hay in his postwar career out of this master narrative of Italian goodness and military prowess, repeating it in *I sette dell'Orsa Maggiore* (Hell Raiders of the Deep, 1953) and especially in *El Alamein: Divisione Folgore* (1954), which inverted *Sahara*'s version of history by erasing the Germans from the North African battle and focusing exclusively on Italian troops' heroism against the British. As impressive an action film as it is, however, *El Alamein* saw no American distribution. *La grande speranza* also never saw substantial Atlantic distribution, though it had won the Special Prize of the Senate for 1954 at the Berlin International Film Festival. Popular among segments of the audiences in the defeated nations, Coletti's was a local route that rarely crossed the Atlantic.

There were other, more truthful roads that remained scantily traveled. In the last two decades historians have unearthed the violence of Italian troops during the first three years of the Second World War, producing evidence that runs contrary to the myths that dominated the Celluloid Atlantic. But in 1960 when Dino De Laurentis produced an Atlantic film version of Ugo Pirro's novel about the Italian army in Yugoslavia, *Jovanka e le altre* (Five Branded Women, 1960), directed by Martin Ritt with Barbara Bel Geddes, Carla Gravina, Vera Miles, Jeanne Moreau, and Silvana Mangano, the story was changed and the partisans fought against the German army instead of the Italian occupiers as in Pirro's original story.[50]

It is perhaps the contrast between Atlantic mythology and the realities of the Italian invasion of Greece that supplies the best example of the suppression of truth. In April 1941, Axis-occupied Greece was divided into zones, leaving the Italians in control of about two-thirds of the nation. In the aftermath of the war the Greek factions gathered in the Hellenic National Office for War Criminals pointed out that the burning of villages, the shooting of civilians, the rapes, and the execution of *andartes* (Greek partisans) were a common feature of the twenty-nine-month-long Italian occupation.[51] In addition, Italians promoted the coercive Italianization of the Ionian Islands, created a concentration camp at Larissa in Thessaly, and encouraged ethnic violence by drafting ethnic Albanians, Slavs, and Valachians in special antipartisan units under the command of Italian officers. Interrogation techniques were often de facto torture. In the words of historian Luisa Santarelli, the result was that "thousands and thousands of pages would be needed to describe the grave infractions of international humanitarian law for which the [Italian] Royal army was responsible from 1941 to 1943."[52]

No mainstream Western film showed, for example, the fate of the Greek partisan commander Sinanoglou who, once apprehended by the Italian army, had his front teeth extracted with pliers, was dragged by a horse for three hours, beaten on the palms of his hands and his feet at regular intervals for seven days, and finally executed.[53] Nor did any such violence transpire in *Mediterraneo* (1991) by Gabriele Salvatores, one of the eleven Italian films to win the Academy Award for Best Foreign Film after the citation's official inception in 1956. *Mediterraneo* and its Atlantic fortune among critics and at the box office show the persistence of the Atlantic mythology of the good, buffoonish Italian soldier. The story of a platoon of Italians stranded on an idyllic Greek island, *Mediterraneo* shows the usual foolishness and haplessness. After the initial disorientation, Italian occupiers and the Greek population end up being friends and lovers, with some of the Italians refusing to leave the islands when the war ends.

It could have all ended up differently, at least on the screen. In the initial treatment for *Mediterraneo* by Enzo Monteleone, not all Italian soldiers were nice or harmless. Among them was Sergeant Maffei, "an all-around soldier, a true Fascist that believes in the war and who hopes to make a career out of it, a little too exuberant though, and thus not fit for the front line of combat."[54] When one of the Italian soldiers accidentally destroys the radio, Sergeant Maffei punishes him by tying him to a post under the scalding summer sun. More importantly, Sergeant Maffei is a rapist. His crime—the rape of the twelve-year-old daughter of a local prostitute—was the centerpiece of the treatment and was shown in uncompromising terms, though somewhat neutralized by the prompt reaction of the Italian commanding officer who shoots and kills Maffei.[55]

Rejecting the "bad German/nice Italian" dichotomy at the center of the Celluloid Atlantic, the initial blueprint for the film also included the image of a German U-boat arriving on the Greek island at the end of the war. Like the Italians, the Germans are tired of the war and prefer soccer to fighting. An American cruiser takes home both the Italians and Germans. Rather than a mythological, essentialist "cultural diversity"—to use Homi Bhabha's terminology—between the two peoples, the treatment enforces history, as the Germans are considered POWs and kept in the hold of the ship while the Italian troops, allies after the armistice and the 1943 Moscow conference, are allowed to remain on deck.[56] Had he reached the screen, Maffei would have been a departure from the classic *brava gente* narrative. But his character was excised, and *Mediterraneo* and its Atlantic success show the pervasive strength of the narrative choices that had become the norm of the Celluloid Atlantic forty years before *Mediterraneo* was released.

In the introduction to the published version of his screenplay for *Mediterraneo*, screenwriter Enzo Monteleone writes that when he set out to write the treatment, he drew inspiration from Renzo Biasion's 1949 autobiographical collection of novellas, entitled *Sagapò*.[57] Biasion's collection was an empathetic portrayal of the Italian troops in Greece. The author was trained as a realist painter, and his vignettes literally show soldiers in the light of neorealist victims. They are hungry and disoriented rather than cruel. If anything, Biasion makes Greek women responsible for initiating consensual sex between occupiers and occupied, portraying them as prostitutes by calling rather than necessity. In Biasion's *Sagapò*, the beautiful prostitute "Ketty" is "tormented by continuous, frenzied lust, and gave herself passionately to the [Italian] soldiers who attracted her, and they to her in turn."[58]

Salvatores's Oscar-winning film stayed close to the "Ketty" motif depicting a beautiful Greek woman, Vassilissa (Vanna Barba), who asks Italian sergeant Lorusso for his permission to practice prostitution. In *Mediterraneo* it is symptomatically and ahistorically an Italian man who comes close to being raped by a Greek woman. Amid the hilarity of the platoon, the "piccolo Farina" (diminutive Farina) (Giuseppe Cederna), a short, shy, romantic Italian confesses his desire to lose his virginity only to a woman who really loves him. Vassilissa openly courts him, even exhibiting herself to him during a soccer game and then, abruptly, kissing him. Rather than the victim of rape, the Greek woman thus becomes the temptress of the timid Italian soldier. An entire history of sexual crimes committed against the Greek civilian population by Italian troops morphs into romantic consensual sex initiated by the wily Greek woman. After falling for the kind soldier, Vassilissa willingly mends her ways and becomes an innkeeper.

The initial presence of Maffei's violence in the script, as well as its ultimate elision, point to the existence of alternative World War II narratives outside the Atlantic mainstream. As aware as he was of Biasion's short stories, Enzo Monteleone was also aware of "L'armata s'agapò," Renzo Renzi's proposal for a film on the Italian campaign in Greece that had been a cause celèbre in postwar Italian culture. Renzi, formerly an officer of the Italian army in Greece, proposed the film in an essay he wrote in February 1953 for the left-leaning magazine *Cinema nuovo*. It would be at once a rejection of the 1950s paeans to Italian military valor, a revision of neorealism, and an attempt at historical veracity in the representation of the Italian army. Renzi argued that the premises of the patriotic films à la *Carica eroica* (1952) by Francesco De Robertis about the Italian intervention in Russia in 1941 were untenable. *Carica eroica* depicted the heroism of Italian cavalry in the Russian campaign and thus missed the opportunity to tell the story of a "useless sacrifice for the wrong cause."

Renzi's project was about confirming the myth of the Italian soldiers as victims of Fascist upper echelons while revising some of its premises. Italian soldiers were disoriented fellows caught in a historical turmoil. Yet not all military deaths were equally heroic, he wrote, lest we come to embrace a "mythology of military heroism . . . as an action good per se, in all situations, regardless of the idea it serves, be that even an imperialist tyranny."[59] His treatment allowed some responsibility and accountability for the deeds the Axis committed.

Renzi's criticism of the Italian military was moderate. Stereotypes persisted: the title of the proposed movie was inspired by the British propaganda that had derided the Italian army in Greece as less interested in war than in mercenary sex with the locals (in Greek *agapein* means "to love"). Yet Renzi's treatment was a step outside the Celluloid Atlantic norm. If realized, "L'armata S'agapò" would have been "a condemnation of war and also a fraternal act toward a people, the Greeks, toward whom we have a large debt." The film would have shown ill-trained and ill-equipped Italian soldiers who traded bread for bed and sometimes did not flinch about shooting *andartes*.[60] The year 1953 was not, however, a propitious one for this kind of argument. The *brava gente* mythology was giving Italy an exemption from war trials for crimes in Ethiopia and in the Balkans. Not only did Renzi's proposal fall flat, but he and the editor of *Cinema Nuovo*, Communist film critic Guido Aristarco, were tried and sentenced, respectively, to seven and six months in a military jail for "oltraggio alle forze armate" or desecration of the armed forces.[61]

The sentences were protested by some Italian intellectuals. Even some who did not agree with Renzi's premises rightly saw it as a direct attack on freedom of expression and as evidence of the Italian military's excessive power.[62] Yet the idea for a film on Italian misbehavior was not picked up again even when it could have been much less risky to pursue. When Italian soldiers resurfaced in postwar Italian cinema, they were not likely to shoot hostages or rape women. More than anything else, Italian soldiers were nice and slightly confused fellows like Alberto Sordi and Serge Reggiani in Luigi Comencini's *Tutti a casa* (1960), a direct predecessor of *Mediterraneo*.

It was, once again, an Atlantic choice. In 1956 Dino De Laurentiis asked director Fred Zinnemann to look over Renzi's "S'agapò" as a possible prestigious and intellectually minded picture. Zinnemann was flattered by the offer and intrigued by the story. He had reservations, however, expressed in correspondence with the writer Robert E. Sherwood.

> I don't think you have a chance of getting it by the American censorship without making such profound changes that the intention and significance of the story would be lost. I believe the only way of making a good picture out this—and a very good one at that—would be to forget about the regular American market (except for the arts theaters); then with a first rate cast, you could have something to be proud of. However, if you have to start changing the prostitutes into something else, and if you have to change the nature of their relationships, the entire thing becomes, in my opinion dull and pointless.

Responding to this, the director was intrigued. "I will be very much interested to hear in regard to your further intentions with this material," he concluded.[63]

After asking around in Hollywood, however, the Austrian-born Zinnemann's doubts deepened.

> I have read SAGAPO [*sic*] again and after reading it for the second time, I have come to the conclusion that I am

Atlantic Soldiers

no longer as interested in the story as I had been when you sent it to me originally.

There is no doubt that it would offer enormously difficult censorship problems and I frankly don't believe that the material is good enough to warrant a major effort in battling the censors in the US and most other countries.[54]

Dino, then in Hollywood, promptly agreed. He told the Austrian that even an American blacklistee living in Europe, Mike Wilson, saw Zinnemann's point. "I wanted to see you to tell you that Michael Wilson too feels exactly the same way as you do about this story. We discussed it when we [met] both in Paris and in Rome, and to tell you the truth, apart from any censorship problems, he does not like the story itself."[65]

Overall, film critics and filmmakers in the Celluloid Atlantic remained silent and ambiguous about Italian responsibilities for colonialism and World War II. This "lack of internal critique," to use Neelam Srivastava's words, was pervasive across the political spectrum (as evidenced by Wilson's reaction), visible in the Italian Communist Party advocating, for example, Italian trusteeship for the former Italian colonies,[66] and in the consent and assent provided by American cinema and critics.

In Italian and Atlantic cinema there is interestingly an anti–*brava gente* critical current that attempts to build a different filmic memory of the war, only to be routinely consigned to the bin of the marginal, narrowly distributed, and rarely seen cinema, or to the contiguous one, that of the unrealized projects. And it is largely the Atlantic and strongly bipartisan purchase of the *brava gente* myth that explains this failure. It is telling that when in 1956 neorealist progressive critics Massimo Mida and Gianni Vento listed those unrealized films that, if made, would have "enriched the genre of *neorealismo*" (il filone del *neorealismo*) the critics emphasized two specific examples that centered on stories of Italian military heroism and victimhood: Renato Castelani's treatment for a possible film titled *L'eroe di Palidoro* about the martyrdom of the anti-Fascist carabineer Salvo D'Acquisto, and *La strage di Cefalonia*, a treatment by Alfredo Giannetti and Salvatore Laurani about the massacre of the Acqui Division on the Greek island of Cephalonia at the hands of the Wehrmacht following the armistice of September 8, 1943. According to Mida and Vento the treatment about Cephalonia was an example of how "to show the true face of the war and the true heroism of the Italian soldier."[67]

The solitary achievement of an anti–*brava gente* countercurrent is *Le soldatesse* (1964), an undercelebrated and largely unseen film scripted by Ugo Pirro and directed by Valerio Zurlini. One of the great screenwriters of 1960s Italian cinema, Pirro had come to Rome from the countryside around the southern small city of Battipaglia, where his father worked for the national railways. Born in 1920, Pirro was a veteran of the Greek campaign. Like Renzi, he had seen firsthand the horrors of the war. In his 1998 memoir, *Soltanto un nome nei titoli di testa*, the writer tells the story of Italians penning up Greek civilians in villages rife with typhoid fever and of an Italian platoon raping the wife of a Greek priest after beating her husband to death as the woman was compelled to look on.[68] In 1947 Pirro wrote and submitted a short story, "L'armata dell'amore," about this shameful history to a competition launched by the Communist daily *L'Unità* for the best article about real events. The paper prized the essay but declined to publish it.[69] In 1956 he went on to develop the short piece into a novella, *Le soldatesse*, which contained a slightly softened version of the story of the ordeal of the Greek Orthodox priest and his wife.[70]

Like Renzi's script and much more directly than Biasion's *Sagapò*, *Le soldatesse* clearly indicated the connection between military occupation and rape. The novella was not completely shorn of "brava gente" mythology. It was still founded on the dichotomous comparison between the bad German and the saintly Italian, and Pirro made sure to remind the reader that Germans and Italians occupiers did not get along.[71] Germans and Italian troops routinely hurl insults at each other and have fistfights at the Vaterland, the vaudeville theater commandeered by the occupiers in Athens. The context of the story was, in fact, the unpredictable behavior of Italian regular troops in opposition to the normative bloodthirstiness of the Germans and the Blackshirts. The main character, Lieutenant Gaetano Martino, falls in love with Eftickia, one of the Greek women he is escorting to serve as pleasure slaves for the Germans. He allows her to escape and join the resistance to the occupation. The erratic behavior of Italian soldiers so confuses one of the young women, Elenitza, that she complains that she never knows where they stand.[72] Eventually the lieutenant grows disheartened with his mission and with the war itself. When the radio announces that the Italians have taken Tobruk back from the English, he simply refuses to rejoice in a victory that he now knows is neither real nor moral.

Pirro's novel departs from the *brava gente* myth in important aspects. The book shows the aberrant sexual economy imposed by the occupation in which Italians raped Greek women and did not hesitate to shoot civilians in retaliation for the *andartes*'s attacks. Elenitza poignantly tells the lieutenant that in a dream she saw Greek soldiers occupying Italy and Italian women being compelled to offer sex in exchange for bread. In Elenitza's dream, the lieutenant's own sister was compelled to prostitute herself.

It took several years for Pirro's frontal attack on the "brava gente" mythology to reach the screen. Pirro's autobiography strongly identifies the state of public memory of the war as a military-imposed public amnesia: "Silence ruled over our dirty secrets. Military uniforms remained sacred parchments that could not be tainted. Not only that: nobody dared speak of what had happened in Greece during the Italian occupation, as if amnesia had been imposed on all by a military order."[73] In 1961 *nouvelle vague* French producer Raoul Lévy tried to make the film in France and commissioned a script from Pirro's trusted friend, Franco Solinas. Like Pirro, Solinas was a young man· from the rural marginal provinces of Italy. Born on the island of Sardinia, he had come to Rome after the war and tried to make it into the film industry. In 1950, the twenty-three-year-old writer had penned an important opinion piece, "Vergogna dei ricordi" (Shame of Remembrances), in the leftist daily *Paese Sera*. In the article, the young writer addressed both the horrors of recent Italian history and the difficulties Italians had in constructing the correct memory ("ricordi") of them: "I was about to end fifth grade when we went to fight [for Francisco Franco] in Spain, . . . in those years there was the war in Africa," he reminisced, but Italians were unaware of the massacres. It took Allied bombings and the death of friends to penetrate the veil and show him the depth of the German-Italian disastrous coproduction.[74]

When Pirro asked him to look at the Greek war treatment, Solinas was about to embark with director Gillo Pontecorvo on the project that was to beget *La battaglia di Algeri* (The Battle of Algiers, 1964) and *Queimada* (Burn!, 1969). Justly celebrated, these films showcase the frontal attacks on dominant discourses and memories that is typical of much of Solinas's work. When European headlines were mostly occupied by the American imperial adventure in Vietnam, Solinas made a point to show audiences the bloody imperial history of Western Europe, revealing a history of similarity, rather than alterity, to America's capitalism. It is important to note that in 1961 Pirro and Solinas were still, to use Pirro's words, young "marginal people, outside the film industry" (sprovveduti, fuori dal cinema),[75] and they especially bonded over their disgust for the Italian flawed memory with its amnesiac mythologies of undeserved innocence.

However, this effort proved unsuccessful. Solinas's work on Pirro's story remains uncredited in the final cut of the film's credits. The final film remains the product of a *bande à part* of largely marginal filmmakers. Born in Greece to a Jewish family and the survivor of an Italian concentration camp for Jews during World War II, Italo-Greek producer Moris Ergas saw the merit of Pirro's project, picked it up, and developed it in collaboration with director Valerio Zurlini. A gay man working in the Italian film industry in the 1950s and 1960s, Zurlini himself understood marginality well.[76]

Like Solinas and Pirro, Zurlini and Ergas had no patience for empty patriotism or *brava gente* victimism. Zurlini had already taken apart the myth of Italian wartime victimhood in his *Un'estate violenta* (Violent Summer, 1959), the antiheroic, and consciously anti-neorealist, story of a confused young man Carlo (Jean-Louis Trintignant), the son of a violent Fascist boss, trying to dodge all choices in the fateful summer of 1943. Zurlini eagerly embraced Pirro's project to right the wrongs of the war's public memory.

> I thought it was a rare and important opportunity to say, at least once after the grand "Please absolve us!" of *Rome, Open City* and the very humanist spectacles of neorealism: ladies and gentlemen, the massacres were not committed only by the Germans. We have equally killed, raped, wounded sensibilities, violated souls. Thus it may be high time we did some accounting of our own debts, and acknowledge our own debt toward the recent history of Europe. . . . For God's sake! Is it possible that we are so cowardly to let the other pay for all of us? And we, we did not know, really? We did not know? In Yugoslavia there were only Germans? And in Montenegro we have done horrible things, more horrible than what we did in

Greece. . . . The Italian people is notorious for avoiding blame, for this ability at subterfuge, at saving their butts, for this continuous "renversement des alliances."[77]

Zurlini's *Le soldatesse* (The Camp Followers, 1965) forcefully countered the *brava gente* story. Some of Pirro's novella's scenes are omitted: Eftikia (Marie Laforêt) is given a more openly politicized identity (she is the one who now tells the lieutenant about her dream) better befitting the mid-1960s resurrection of left-wing political activism. In addition, *Le soldatesse* ends on a curiously elegiac tone. There is no reference to the original ending of the novel with the false, official propaganda about Tobruk and Lieutenant Martino's disheartened reaction to them. Rather, the film makes a rather tentative effort to recast the story as the private memory of a love affair. After spending the night together, Lt. Gaetano Martino (Tomas Milian) and Eftikia part ways. She walks away to join the partisans while he rejoins, now fully disillusioned, the Italian army. On the soundtrack, Gaetano's offscreen voice tells us they will never meet again and ends by citing the last lines from Eugenio Montale's poem "La bufera" about the disappearance of the poet's love interest into an all-encompassing darkness. A similar fate befell the film. *Le soldatesse* was a flop in Italy and received only scant international distribution, although it won a minor award at the Moscow International Film Festival (the Special Silver Prize) in 1966.

Conclusion: The Atlantic End of Neorealism

Just as *Le soldatesse* was struggling to obtain funding and, once made, sell some tickets, *Bitter Rice*'s director Giuseppe De Santis was shooting a film that was financed by both Hollywood and Cinecittà, and was even in its title the embodiment of the Atlantic mythology of the good Italian soldier. *Italiani Brava Gente* (1964, Attack and Retreat) told the story of the Italian Expeditionary Corps to Russia from the perspective of ordinary Italian soldiers. The film begins in the summer of 1941 at the beginning of the Barbarossa operation, when the Italian Expeditionary Corps and the Wehrmacht are making a rapid advance into Russia, and ends after the battle of Stalingrad, as the defeated Axis powers are retreating out of the Soviet Union, pursued by the Red Army and the Russian winter.

Italiani reproduced the neorealist formula of Italian World War II victimhood within the context of a transatlantic coproduction that perforce denies the main pretention of neorealism, its authenticity. Italian victimhood is obviously accepted and foregrounded in almost every scene. With the exception of one dedicated Blackshirt, Ferro Maria Ferri (Arthur Kennedy), all the Italian soldiers, including their commanding officer, Colonel Sermonti (Andrea Checchi), are impeccably good-hearted. They die in a war whose reasons they do not agree with, or are unable to understand. The film depicts an improbable solidarity between Italian and Russian peasants—a woman calls a dying Italian soldier "Tovarich"—founded on a shared love and understanding of labor and soil ("If they give me a piece of land as beautiful as this one . . . I stop right here. Who gives a hoot about seeing Moscow," Private Barzocchi says),[78] and a shared animosity toward the Germans. In one central scene, the Italians come across Russian civilians penned in by German soldiers. The Russians are starving and one of the Italians, Sanna, offers a slice of his own bread to the prisoners only to be reprimanded by a German sergeant who kicks the bread to the ground shouting "Nicht schwache!!" (Don't be weak!). But the German has underestimated the meaning of bread for peasants: Sanna loses his temper and jumps on the Wehrmacht sergeant, forcing him to the ground. In the ensuing turmoil a Russian prisoner escapes.

A celebration of Italian innocence, though financially not tremendously successful, *Italiani* marked the triumph of the Celluloid Atlantic, its cohesiveness, and its political underpinnings. Its theme confirmed the tenets first proposed by OWI about the difference between Italians and Germans and the fundamental innocence of the former that was also at the center of neorealist cinema. There is, at the end of the film, a humane German soldier who dies next to Sanna during the cruel retreat, but overall the Germans are either beastly or the butt of the Italians' jokes.

The film was also financed and produced bicoastally. *Variety* was already discussing the film in 1962, possibly because, as a Soviet-American-Italian coproduction, it stood out in the production and coproduction lineup. In June, actor Nino Castelnuovo was reported to be in Moscow working on the film.[79] In September the paper announced that Cold War Soviet director Grigori Aleksandrov (*Meeting on the Elbe*) was in Rome discussing the film with De Santis.[80] In December,

Hollywood star Van Heflin was reported as one of the coproduction's stars and, one year later, American producer Joe Levine announced in *Weekly Variety* that the primary shooting of *Attack and Retreat*, with American stars Peter Falk and Arthur Kennedy, had been completed (Van Heflin had dropped out).[81]

A letter from the director of the film, Giuseppe De Santis, to "Nano" recounts the film's Atlantic intertwining. With the funds from the preproduction sale of the movie rights on the strength of its theme and its cast, Levine's Embassy Film had begun the production of *Attack and Retreat* together with an Italian company, Galatea, run by another denizen of the Celluloid Atlantic, Lionello "Nello" Santi. De Santis was well known as the director of *Bitter Rice*, and his fame had made the sale easier. In August 1964, the *New York Times* reported that *Italiani Brava Gente* was one of the new crop of films coming from one of the "Italian movie masters." "The reports on the film are excellent," the paper concluded.[82]

The film's financing and production history reproduces the Atlantic mechanism we have examined in chapter 1. Embassy shelled out the initial $350,000 in exchange for the distribution rights for the film outside the Italian Peninsula. In turn, US backing made European financing easier. After "Nello" Santi had obtained from "Jon or Jonne [*sic*] Levine" some $350,000, he went to the main source of financing for Italian movies, the Italian Banca Nazionale del Lavoro, and got a credit for 500 million liras, as the film was reputed to enhance Italian art and culture. At this point, De Santis noted, the Italian producer was financially already in the clear: the budget of the film was a moderate 300 million liras (not counting almost as much for copies, marketing, and advertising), because the Soviet contribution was not cash, but the fronting of production costs for the shooting in Russia, where most of the filming would take place. After production and marketing, everybody was going to be OK even if the film did not break box office records.[83]

Beside the coalescence of the Celluloid Atlantic in mid-1960s, *Italiani* shows how anchored the filmic West was to the politics of the West. The oddity of Russian participation underscores the Celluloid Atlantic as the cinema of the West, a West whose relationship with the Soviets were in transition after Stalin's death in 1955. According to Tony Shaw and Denise J. Youngblood, from 1953 to 1962 Hollywood producers were making the best of the relative relaxation of

138 The Celluloid Atlantic

the Cold War and even sought to recruit talent outside of the West. In 1960, the thaw made it possible for *Roman Holiday* to be shown in Moscow. From 1962 until the reprise of the harshest rhetoric in the 1980s, Hollywood rejected McCarthyism and the witch hunt; as a result, some Soviet cinema could come to America. In particular, Grigori Chukhrai's anti-Nazi World War II film *Ballad of a Soldier* (1959), an obvious influence on De Santis and *Attack and Retreat*, had been distributed in American cities, garnering critical praise. The film, a maudlin story of a Soviet teen soldier's six-day furlough before his death on the front, had been nominated for an Oscar for Best Original Screenplay and won the first award at the San Francisco Film Festival.[84]

The thaw also facilitated the collaboration between Hollywood and leftist Italian film circles. *Italiani* was, ironically, a Hollywood film by an Italian director who could not get a visa to work in Hollywood, where his work in *Bitter Rice* had been lionized.[85] It was a movie where the "Internationale" was sung and whistled and, bizarrely enough, whose production directly involved the Italian and Soviet Communist Parties. By late summer 1962, correspondence reveals that the Soviet filmmaker Grigori Chukhrai was collaborating, uncredited, on the script. In September of the same year Chukhrai sent a draft of the script to De Santis from Moscow, via the diplomatic valise of Gian Carlo Pajetta, a former partisan, a member of the Italian Parliament, and a prominent delegate on the central committee of the Italian Communist Party. Pajetta brought the script back and also confirmed that the Soviets were ready to front some of the location expenses.[86]

If the themes and the financing were Atlantic, at the level of style *Italiani* was both the continuation and the Atlantic mainstreaming of neorealism into one of the key styles of the cinema of the West. *Italiani* was, in some sense, a kitschy rendering of neorealism, or its cosmopolitan, diluted version. The neorealist pedigree of the director was augmented by nonprofessional Russian actors and by veteran neorealist actors like Andrea Checchi, who had already worked with De Santis in *Caccia Tragica*. DP Antonio Secchi did his best to shoot most of the film in exterior locations and the credits for the Italian and the American versions declared that the film was realized in the same places in Russia "where the Italian troop movements took place."[87] *Italiani* reprised the episodic structure of Rossellini's Italo-American production *Paisan*, and like that film it anchored its story to the chronology of the war and its soundtrack to Italian linguistic geography, its soldiers speaking with accents marked by their regional origin. Thus, the script begins with the words of a "soldato Veneto" (from the northeastern region of Italy) conversing with Giuseppe Sanna, whom the script identifies as "Pugliese"—just as Riccardo Cucciolla, his interpreter, who was from Bari.[88]

The Celluloid Atlantic, however, had its own structure of power and the modifications it imposed on neorealism during the making of *Italiani Brava Gente* reflected that and ended up emptying neorealism of any pretention of authenticity. Not only did the film, like *Roma città aperta*, employ professionals like Raffaele Pisu and Riccardo Cucciolla alongside nonprofessional Italian and Russian women and men, it also now had *American* professional actors in Italian roles to ensure its viability on the Atlantic market. The Atlantic, Celluloid or not, was never a covenant among members of equal standing: at the pro-filmic level, the condition that Levine had set was that *Italiani* needed to appeal to a transnational audience. The producer demanded that at least two of the leads be American, and without consulting De Santis, he shipped to Italy Arthur Kennedy and Peter Falk, who were both marketable, relatively cheap, and willing to work on a film shot in the Soviet Union. De Santis thought that the two actors were not "real enough" for their roles: the thirty-five-year-old character actor Peter Falk, who had a glass eye, was not credible as a young and dashing Italian medical officer who was to die a hero's death while attending to Soviet partisans in a hostage exchange (the Italians unwillingly execute a Russian partisan whom they have come to like). Kennedy's role (as the Fascist heavy, Ferro Maria Ferri), Carlo Lizzani reported, was instead too small. De Santis protested and even proposed to write a different role for Falk, but Levine was adamant and both actors were featured in these roles.[89]

The cosmopolitan version of neorealism that inhabited the Celluloid Atlantic was compatible with the Atlantic image of Italian soldiers, its internationalism also drawing on the warmer climate of this stage of the Cold War and the East-West confrontation. To be sure, however, some of its narrative tenets showed the dissolution of the former style. What had been a nationalistic moment of an increasing international cinema was more and more consciously anchored to an international context, its normative terms more and more diluted. Rossellini had seen the cinema of his war trilogy as a "document."

Figure 3.1. Peter Falk impersonating the myth of the good Italian soldier in Giuseppe De Santis's *Italiani Brava Gente* (1964). *Source*: PhotofestNYC.

Italian soldiers were, if possible, interpreted by Italian soldiers, Neapolitan urchins by local kids, just like Visconti had Acitrezza fishermen play themselves in *La terra trema*, the interpreters' bodies becoming evidence—albeit misleading—of the "truth" of the film. This was itself a marketing strategy (needless to say, professional actors, like Anna Magnani in *Città aperta*, were also present) and neorealist films remained theatrical performances with Atlantic roots. But in *Italiani* this theatricality increased, and authenticity turned into the kitsch version of itself. Italian heroes were played by American stars like Peter Falk and Russian actors (Lev Prygunov as Private Bazzocchi), their "Italian-ness" coded in stereotypes in physiognomy and gesticulations recognizable to the international audience that was the implicit viewer of the film. Theatricality became part of the plot. The script winked at the transnational tradition of film noir and constructed the story as a sort of flashback of dead soldiers who are commenting on the war via maudlin voiceovers. The introductory shot of the scene where the Italian troops encounter the Russian civilians imprisoned by the Germans showed, perhaps unwittingly, this theatricality. The Italians enter the scene from the woods and De Santis has the vegetation open in front of the soldiers' eyes just like a curtain would, to reveal the drama of war. Reality reveals itself as theater, an aesthetic choice, a fiction. As the Atlantic market pushed its cinema into a commerce with masks and theatricality, it is time for us to look at how racial stereotypes defined the Celluloid Atlantic.

4

Race and Atlantic Exceptionalisms

The Atlantic Journey of John Kitzmiller

> John Kitzmiller le bon nègre de *Paisà* est la suprenante vedette de ce film. Il incarne son personage come seuls, avec les enfants, savent le faire les noirs. Quelle fraîcheur, quelle simplicité de moyens, quelle âme!
>
> —*Le Monde*, review of John Kitzmiller's work in *Senza pietà* (Alberto Lattuada, 1948)

> The review mistakes Kitzmiller for Dots Johnson, one of the stars of *Paisan* (Roberto Rossellini, 1946)

❧

ONE OF THE HOSTAGES CAPTURED by the crew of the World War II Italian submarine in Duilio Coletti's *La grande speranza* (Submarine Attack, 1954) is an American, Johnny Brown, who also happens to be black. Interpreted by Earlston "Earl" Cameron, a Bermudian actor who had just had his big break in Basil Dearden's *Pool of London* (1951), Johnny shows none of the derogatory stereotypes associated with black manhood by Western culture. He comes from

144   The Celluloid Atlantic

Georgia, in the American South, speaks accent-less Italian (and thus, one would think, English), and remains cool under fire. This dignified demeanor fit well with Cameron's on- and offscreen persona, as he was then openly fighting racial discrimination in English cinema and had been one half of the first interracial romance on British screen in *Pool of London*.[1] Looking at the character of Johnny Brown in Coletti's film sixty years after its release help us see, however, different and more hidden meanings that pertain to the racial history of the Celluloid Atlantic, which is the focus of this chapter.

In *La grande speranza*, Italian racial equanimity is exalted. When Christmas comes, the Italians gather to celebrate around a makeshift Christmas tree. They even stage a *presepio* complete with the statuettes of the sacred family and three sailors masquerading as the three biblical kings who come to pay homage to the newborn God. At first, the hostages are not invited to the party but the good Italian "captain" tells *nostromo* (the boatswain) to fetch them. Of course Johnny is also invited and he gladly accepts the offer along with the other prisoners. The sole exception is the male British captive, a real snob, who refuses to join the fête organized by the Fascist sailors.

Coletti makes clear that the Italians' behavior is informed by racial tolerance, but his film shows that this tolerance should not be confused with any belief in racial equality. Johnny is included and embraced, but the film makes clear that Italians "see color" and translate it into a precise racial hierarchy. For starters, Ciccio (Carlo delle Piane), the sailor interpreting the biblical king Balthazar, appears at the Christmas party in full blackface complete with accentuated red lips and a coal-black complexion. One would expect the worst to happen, but Johnny is inexplicably pleased by the arrival of a man who is made up as a mockery of his race. Later on, after the icon of baby Jesus is placed in his small cradle, Ciccio brings in a second statuette of an infant deity, this time tinted black. He then presents the image to Johnny, who looks on with gratitude, before placing the diminutive and racialized god in a cradle next to his white Doppelganger.

Two elements of this scene stand out. The first is the obvious attempt by Coletti to ascribe tolerance to the white Caucasian crew of the Fascist submarine. Regardless of what these military men were doing when Italy was firebombing and gassing civilian populations in Ethiopia, now these Italian sailors seem to love black people and welcome all regardless of race. Steiner, the insufferable American character, chimes in that "this is the first night when different peoples understand that we can all live together in the world, like old friends." The emphasis is obviously on "different." The second, contradictory element of the scene is the Italians' blatant racism. The party celebrates segregation even in the religious sphere. The Italians, and white people in general, do not want to share their Jesus with Johnny Brown. No Canadian Jesus is passed out to the Canadian "tenente donna," Lt. Lily Donald, played by Lois Maxwell, destined to embody James Bond's misogyny as the spinster Ms. Moneypenny. Johnny, instead, needs his own colored savior.

That blackness can be used to define difference and enforce separation is a repeat ploy of *La grande speranza*. The Christmas party segregates Johnny into a different Christianity, while Coletti's use of blackface highlights an imagined racial taxonomy. The movie also recalls racial difference through Johnny's incessant gospel singing. Johnny has found protectors in the Italian crew, and a new home in their submarine, but remains othered.

An implicit hope of the film is that global audiences will acknowledge Italian racial tolerance, and Johnny's behavior is supposed to manifest this hope. When time comes for goodbyes (the submarine has made it to the Azores and the POWs are released), Johnny inquires whether he can stay onboard. The Belgian prisoners' dog makes the same demand, albeit only with pleading eyes. The puppy is allowed to stay, but the black man is sent back to his racist home. In *La grande speranza* Italian racial equanimity stood in implicit comparison with American racial unfairness. That Johnny would prefer to remain with the Italian Fascist crew rather than go back to the United States, therefore, makes perfect sense.

The film's implicit celebration of Italian "fair-mindedness" in regard to race relations, and its deployment of American racism as a way to differentiate the two sides of the Atlantic—even as it unwittingly parades Italian racism—was hardly exceptional. Rather, it was a central part of the Atlantic conversation. Europeans routinely accused the United States of being racist and ideologically inconsistent—which, to be sure, it was—while papering over Europe's own racism and colonialism. Regardless of European pretentions, this chapter argues that the ties that bound Hollywood to Cinecittà were also similarly susceptible to color and made of a similar rope to the ones that had bound human beings in many previous Atlantic crossings.

The reality of sameness and the discourse of difference coexisted in the Celluloid Atlantic. US white audiences might have objected to Coletti's references to American racism, but they would probably have agreed with Italian segregationist impulses. Shared racial hierarchies facilitated dialogue between the mostly white men in charge of the Atlantic traffic in celluloid, yet this was obscured by the theme of Atlantic difference that emphasized American racism and European racial equanimity. American racism was thus constructed as the great Euro-American difference at the very moment when other historical differences were ceasing to exist.

In the early 1930s, Antonio Gramsci posited that the Euro-American difference lay in the full-blown embrace of Fordism by the United States. Regardless of its exploitative outcome, American capitalism was a machine effectively ruling its workers through high salaries, high consumption, and sexual Puritanism. In Italy, on the other hand, corrupt parasitical classes (*questi pensionati della storia economica*) dressed as principled anti-Americanism their distaste for a capitalist modernity that they feared was bound to unseat them.[2]

But, at the end of World War II, Europe, too, was rapidly becoming Fordist. Integrated military alliances (the North Atlantic Treaty Organization signed on April 4, 1949) and economic coordination (oiled by the American financing of the European Recovery Plan launched in 1947 and put into operation from April 1948) was also thrusting the two sides of the North Atlantic closer to each other than they had ever been before.[3]

In the climate of the Cold War, Communist and leftist commentators decried Americanizing corruption. In 1948, Italian Communist leader Pietro Secchia indicted "the lowbrow ideological rubbish" produced by American trusts "that was to serve to weaken, disorient, and corrupt our people."[4] But the European left was not alone in its lament. Many conservative commentators grumbled that, to take Antonio Gramsci's terminology out of its context, Europe's "civilization of quality" was losing ground to the aggressive American "civilization of quantity,"[5] and Mario del Pero has demonstrated that even the conservative Italian Christian Democrats long saw the alliance with the Protestant and consumerist US as necessary but "uncomfortable."[6] Ironically, such a lament was echoed by cultural conservatives on the other side of the Atlantic. Visiting Hamburg in 1960, one of the architects of American foreign policy during the Cold War, George Kennan,

Race and Atlantic Exceptionalisms   147

somberly noted a disturbing—to him—novel similarity between Western Europe and the US. In the interwar period, the diplomat had fallen in love with the Old World, but he had now "nothing to say about this sturdy Hamburg . . . with its startling material success, its heavy motor traffic, its relatively egalitarian style of life, its lack of slums and great houses, its better dressed, semi-Americanized girls."[7]

European anxieties about American political and cultural contamination elicited a discursive cultural performance that shrilly stressed the opposite. The problem was, as historian Richard Pells has suggested, that Americans and Europeans had long defined themselves in opposition to each other and it was troubling to acknowledge the growing similarity: "Each needed the other for self-definition. . . . How could you identify what was 'European' without defining what was 'American'?"[8] The postwar American argument for exceptionalism was mirrored by a European reaction that underscored, if not exceptionalism, a hoped-for difference.[9]

As for American exceptionalism, as Louis Hartz suggested, it focused on the absence of class struggle and exempted America from any "Trotskyite law of combined development" that applied to other capitalist nations. In other words, the United States was "naturally liberal," because America lacked any historical experience with feudalism, in contrast to Europe.[10] "Without the feudal past," writes Daniel Rodgers, "the inner dialectical engine of history had no purchase. No Robespierre, no de Maistre, no Marx, no Goebbels, no Stalin only . . . an eternal Locke."[11]

The narrative of difference developed by Europe, instead, stressed racism. In the two decades following the end of World War II, for example, in each of the two German republics, race receded from public discourse as a category of social classification. That racist thinking existed de facto mattered little to those who argued that *Rasse* no longer applied to postwar Germany. By 1960, West German authorities were advising their citizens against letting American couples adopt racially mixed children of German women and African American GIs. American racism would have made the children's lives too hard in the United States. On the contrary, they assumed, racism was no longer a problem in Germany, and this, only a few years after the Holocaust! "In just over a decade since Hitler's defeat," Heide Fehrenbach writes, "a chastened nation appeared to have surpassed its tutor."[12] Italians were even quicker than the Germans. Publishing his travelogue *America Amara* in December 1939, at the end of the Italian bloody conquest of Ethiopia, Emilio Cecchi, the former executive of Italian film studio Cines, chastised the hypocrisy and racism of white Americans. They have "limitless love for the Ethiopian Negroes. And strangulation . . . for the anti-lynching bill, which the Negroes of America would have much appreciated."[13] Europe had produced a capitalist world untainted by what W. E. B. Du Bois termed in 1903 the "color line."[14]

Yet these discourses of difference masked bewildering similarities and historical intertwining. The United States may have not known feudalism but it had certainly experienced innumerable strikes and a blood-drenched labor history. And the slave trade and racial hierarchies have marked both sides of what Paul Gilroy calls the Black Atlantic.[15] Many European historians now situate race at the foundation of the European "république coloniale" rather than at its margins.[16] Françoise Vergès has written of the attempt to marginalize racial hierarchies and racial markings in European history. "The racism and eurocentrism of Enlightenment philosophers has been discussed, their defense or attack on slavery assessed, their support of colonization questioned, but there is a tendency to dismiss these events as occurring 'before our time,' thus deserving a chapter but certainly not becoming a central question. . . . The colonial is considered an episode in history that should not be allowed to undermine the European sense of its own superiority."[17] In the specific Italian case, Angelo del Boca has long underscored the role of Italian colonialism in shaping Italian conscience, and Alberto Burgio has shown how racial hierarchies and a strongly racialized imaginary were central to Italian culture since the Enlightenment.[18] Already present in Italian culture, according to Olindo De Napoli, racism accelerated during the Fascist *ventennio* when it also more directly emphasized biological racial destiny over historically contingent cultural underdevelopment.[19]

W. E. B. Du Bois himself pointedly cautioned against those who saw the color line as only an American problem. "The Negro problem in America is but a local phase of a world problem," he wrote in 1906, before quoting himself immediately thereafter: "The problem of the Twentieth Century is the problem of the color line."[20] In 1920 the African American political and intellectual leader discussed the "discovery of whiteness among the world's people" and connected it to modernity. "The Middle Ages regarded skin color with mild

Race and Atlantic Exceptionalisms

149

curiosity. . . . Today, we have changed all that and the world in a sudden, emotional, conversion has discovered that it is white and by that token, wonderful."[21]

This chapter explores this context of proclaimed differences while underlining its hidden similarities via the career of an African American actor who became an important, though now mostly forgotten, Atlantic star: John Kitzmiller.[22] His work serves less as a confirmation of Euro-American difference than a Rorschach test of color as an organizational principle in the North Atlantic film industry, and as evidence of the transnational cohesiveness of Western cinema in general. The actor effortlessly moved among the cinemas of Western nations, first finding work in the nationalistic Italian postwar cinema and from there moved on to make films in France, West Germany, the former Yugoslavia, the US, and England. The roles he was offered in Europe and in Hollywood were similarly constraining. Indeed, Kitzmiller's career suggests that beyond the European proclamations of its redemption from the color line, the cinema of the entire North Atlantic community was bent on its enforcement.

Kitzmiller's life also tells us about variations in racism across the North Atlantic, shedding light on how racism was conjugated according to regional and historical contingencies under the overarching supremacy of whiteness. Kitzmiller's European roles were limiting but in ways that were different from those Hollywood cinema imposed on its black performers. The actor's decision to try his luck in Italian cinema was, thus, well calculated. Like other African American performers at the time, Kitzmiller moved about the West testing these regional differences in pursuit of the maximum financial and artistic accomplishments available to him—not merely with the goal to earn a good living but also to gain a measure of fame. His resolve allowed him to do both even though, at the moment of his death in 1965, the differences that had first attracted him to European cinema had proven in no small part to be illusory.

The Beginnings of an Atlantic Career

At the time of his death, John Kitzmiller left behind no archival collections and only scant interviews. Seeking out his story we will assume similarities with other black performers who followed his route.

Economic opportunities no doubt played a role in his decision. For the sake of comparison, Woody Strode, an actor who had made his name in Westerns by John Ford, went to Europe in the early 1960s because he was unhappy with Hollywood's racist pay scale. "I moved to Rome and really started making money for the first time," Strode told the New Jersey *Record* in 1975. "Citizens of the United States do not realize the extent of the world film market."[23]

African American performers had reason to believe that the east side of the Pond offered them opportunities not available in the US. After the initial enthusiasm, however, disappointment often set in. In the early 1960s, reflecting on his European experience in the immediate postwar period, William Gardner Smith, another African American expatriate, described what he called the initial détente of the African American in Europe: "An incredible relaxation of tensions [occurs]. The black American heav[es] a sigh of relief as he arriv[es] in Europe . . . and thus immediately shed[s] the racial claustrophobia engendered by the black ghettos of America."[24] Smith's first novel, *The Last of the Conquerors*, which he wrote in 1948 after a brief stint as a GI in Germany, pits racist American MPs against friendly Germans who often welcome the black GIs with—literally—open arms. In the early sixties, after he had lived in Europe for fifteen years, Gardner Smith added that this détente was only temporary and soon the African American recognizes "the fuzzy outlines of his old enemy, racism."[25]

In the summer of 1945, when producer Carlo Ponti and director Luigi Zampa offered him a job, Kitzmiller may have been experiencing the same sense of détente. Ponti and Zampa wanted to capitalize on the renewed postwar success of "realist cinema" and wanted to make a film about the social effect of the presence of American black troops in Italy. The 92nd Buffalo Soldier Division of the Fifth Army had collaborated with the Italian partisans in several actions against the German Gothic Line in the long, blood-drenched summer months of 1944, and many of them had learned some Italian in the process.[26] The soldiers' lives radically improved after the hostilities ceased. Encamped on the Tyrrhenian coast south of Pisa, these troops were close to that city and to Livorno, a well-supplied port through which most American goods entered the peninsula. Nature too was inviting: the landscape gorgeously blended dunes, pinewoods, and sea and was relatively untouched by the heavy fighting that had wreaked havoc to the north and south. Romance with local women occurred

Figure 4.1. Giuseppe Viviani, *Le Segnorine* (1945). *Source*: Author's collection.

as suggested by this painting by local artist Giuseppe Viviani. In convincing Kitzmiller to remain in Italy and try an acting career, the languid truce offered by Tombolo's human and natural landscape may have been as important as the director's and the producer's requests.

By 1946, the Italian film industry was also undergoing an economic and cultural revolution that created opportunity for a person like Kitzmiller who was college educated, ambitious, and in no hurry to go back to the United States. The end of the Fascist regime was pushing contemporary themes to the fore. As we have seen, progressive Italian intellectuals were touting cinema as the "loudspeaker," which would reconnect them with those separated from them by the cacophony of Fascist escapism and militarism.[27] Italian cinema strove for contact with reality and African American GIs were, in film and in Italian life, a direct, albeit pliable, signifier of the perilous promises of the times. Their striding along Italian streets, entwined in the warm embrace of young Italian women, was the clearest sign of the defeat of fascism and its delirious dreams. Yet that fraternizing was also feared by a culture imbued with centuries-old racial hierarchies.[28] After all, the harbor of Livorno was dominated by the *Quattro Mori*, a bronze and marble monument featuring four Africans in chains at the feet of Ferdinand I de' Medici, the archduke of Tuscany, which commemorated the African slaves who had toiled in the construction of the harbor.

Italian cinema would bear witness both to the historical role these darker skinned warriors had in the liberation of the peninsula

Figure 4.2. Pietro Tacca, *Monument of the Four Moors* (1620–1624) in Livorno, Italy. Photo by Ingalisa Schrobsdorff. *Source*: Author's collection. Used with permission.

and to the Italians' anxieties about black soldiers' presence among them. Roberto Rossellini's *Paisá* (1946), examined in chapter 3, already showed this ambiguity. The film coupled a black GI, Joe (Dots Johnson), with a child, Pascà (Alfonso Bovino)—a narrative formula fashioned by Hollywood films (the most famous example at the time being the pairing of Shirley Temple and Bill Bojangles Robinson), and one that Italian cinema was often to emulate.[29] Rossellini infantilized and objectified Joe, who in the film is literally "sold and bought" by the street urchins, until the young coprotagonist of the story, Pascà, acquires the exclusive right to make money off the man. The neorealist filmmaker, however, also establishes the common humanity of the American black soldier and the Neapolitan ragamuffin, which entitled both to the dignity that the cruelty of racism and war had denied them.

Another way to represent these soldiers while circumscribing their postwar role was to represent African Americans as not-entirely-legitimate liberators. When Kitzmiller entered Italian cinema, this cultural strategy abounded. A former Fascist literary star, and now a member of the Communist Party, Curzio Malaparte wrote extensively about African American GIs in his 1949 bestseller, *La pelle*. Indicted by the Vatican for pornography and blasphemy, *La pelle* now reads as similar to John Horne Burns's American novel *The Gallery*, published two years earlier in 1947. Like his American model, *La pelle* dealt with the Allied occupation of Naples after the Anglo-American landing in the summer of 1943. Burns's novel is justly famous for its disenchanted look at the American occupying force, and as one of the first, honest presentations of gay life in the military. Unlike Burns's, Malaparte's imagination is deeply homophobic and racist. American gay soldiers are running amok in Naples, and Italian gay men are corrupting the left. In a relatively obvious reference to Luchino Visconti, Malaparte told the story of "Jeanlouis," a Milanese nobleman, who represented what the writer called "Marxist pederasty" that was turning "a masculine, not resigned to death, and undefeated" group of anti-Fascist intellectuals into "a generation so corrupted, so cynical and so female, so quietly and sweetly desperate."[30]

Beside homosexuality, Malaparte's other obsession was African American troops, whom he described as single-mindedly pursuing sexual intercourse with Italian white women. In *La pelle*, African American soldiers are rapists who "skid along the walls or linger on doorways to compare the price of a girl with the cost of a pack of gum or a tin of corned beef."[31] Neapolitan teenage prostitutes wear blonde wigs because black soldiers pay more when they do. When the local volcano, Vesuvio, erupts, white American, Polish, British, and French troops are among its spectators. So are black GIs, whom Malaparte describes as roaming

> around shaken and overwhelmed. . . . Negroes—almost completely naked as if they had found in the crowd their ancient jungle—wondered about with their nostrils exposed and inflamed, their white, round, eyes protruding from their dark brows, surrounded by herds of prostitutes, almost naked themselves . . . and some of [the black troops] intoned chants, others shouted mysterious words with very shrill voices, others pleaded the name of god "Oh God, my God," trying to keep afloat in that sea of heads and terrified faces, and they kept their eyes fixed to the sky as if they were spying, through the rain of fire and ashes, the slow flights of an Angel armed with a flaming sword.[32]

The book and its success were symptomatic of a larger phenomenon. In 1948 director Stefano Vanzina jotted down what he thought were the "typical characters of the neorealist film." His list was meant to be ironic, yet it fittingly posits blackness at the center of the neorealist universe while also qualifying it as criminal. The canonical "Negro," Vanzina wrote, was always "sought by the military police" (il negro ricercato dalla M.P.).[33]

John Kitzmiller's Journey through Neorealism

Italian postwar reality included nonwhite occupying troops, and a cinema that purported to document reality could not ignore this. Yet the new cinema also contained blackness via the use of long-held stereotypes that the new post-Fascist culture never questioned. It was a curious match of a novel desire for authenticity and centuries-old racist imaginary, and it marked the beginnings of John Kitzmiller's film career.

His first important film, *Vivere in pace*, was hailed as part of the luminous rebirth of Italian cinema after the Fascist dusk. Like other famous neorealist films, it rode the waves all the way to New York City, where it was released in November 1947, replacing *Rome, Open City* at the World Theater where Rossellini's film had run for ninety-one weeks.[34] In truth, the film, directed by Luigi Zampa from a script by him, Suso Cecchi D'Amico, Aldo Fabrizi, and Pietro Tellini, pointed to the blurred definition of the Italian cinematic renaissance.[35] In contrast to the severe scenography and narrative austerity of *Open City*,[36] *Vivere in Pace* employed soundstages, broad comedy, and a capable crew of professional actors. The urban and civic horizons of Rossellini's film are narrowed in *Vivere in pace* to a celebration of the "small." The opening lines of the film turn the village (*paese*) into a small village (*paesino*), the church (*chiesa*) into a small church (*chiesetta*). The scope of the story is not civic society but the family. These small places had escaped the attention of the warring factions, but in this film the familial space is intruded upon by the enormity of history. Serious social themes meet comedic flair and, in the words of film historian Peter Bondanella, the material of Rossellini's becomes a "burlesque farce."[37] Well-known thespian Aldo Fabrizi, who had just starred as the martyred Catholic priest in Rossellini's *Open City*, played Zio Tigna, the embattled patriarch who is trying to keep his family safe in the midst of the war. Kitzmiller portrayed "Joe," a black GI, who (together with a white companion, Ronald, played by one of *Paisà*'s American actors, Gar Moore) is saved and hidden by a family of Italian farmers. The story ends in tragedy when the Germans, withdrawing from Italy, shoot Tigna in retaliation for the help the village provided the American GIs.

Vivere in pace was a critical and popular success; it garnered the Italian film industry's awards for best original script and best supporting actress (Ave Ninchi) and in December 1947 Zampa's movie snagged the New York Film Critics' award for best foreign film. The script "excels in the minute description of the characters" and the directing is "neat and dry," wrote Luigi Rondi in *Il Tempo*.[38] "Very good Italian film," noted the Italian film magazine *Cine Bazar*.[39] In the *New York Times* Bosley Crowther hailed his beloved neorealism: "The revivified Italian film industry which has sent us such powerful films as *Shoeshine* and *Open City* has now sent another one along that takes a place of distinction among the fine motion pictures of our times."[40] James Agee deemed it "even more remarkable" than Rossellini's *Open City* and De Sica's *Shoeshine*, and the "wisest and most humane movie of its time."[41] In his own review Crowther cited the unknown American stars: Gar Moore and John Kitzmiller were "remarkably forthright" in embodying, respectively, an "American journalist and the Negro." "An affectionate and colorful picture of little people . . . a clear record of real people living in a real world," commented Otis Guerney in the *Herald Tribune*.[42]

Italians and Americans were to allege profound mutual differences in the deployment of racial categories. But their critical practices were actually quite homogenous. The American Bosley Crowther and the Italian Stefano Vanzina seemed confident that, just like being a newspaper reporter, "being a Negro" could define a professional identity or a state of being. Like *La grande speranza*, *Vivere in pace* separated the roles of white and black characters: Gar Moore is in charge of blandly romancing Silvia (Mirella Monti), while Kitzmiller is left alone to shoulder the comedic moments. He sings like a rooster on top of the chicken pen, drinks copiously, plays the trumpet, and even reveals his presence to the Germans, precipitating the killing of Zio Tigna.

Like most of the Americans, Italian critics were not bothered by the representation of Kitzmiller. On both the right and the left, an essentialist notion of blackness had long been dominant, and the film confirmed this. The unexplained musical ability of Kitzmiller could not surprise anyone. As he was working on *Ossessione* in 1943 Giuseppe De Santis had published an article in *Cinema* where he favorably compared the black songs of King Vidor's *Hallelujah* (1929) with the jazzy songs of Fred Astaire's *Top Hat* (Mark Sandrich, 1935). In the transition from black to white performers, De Santis wrote, jazz had become "intellectualized . . . it is no longer, the natural, the instinctual nature [*istinto*], from which jazz was born."[43] *Bianco e Nero*, the flagship film magazine issued by the Centro Nazionale di Cinematografia, praised Kitzmiller's performance as possessing "an animalesque innocence" (un animalesco candore).[44] Underlying both the transatlantic similarities and the scattershot attention to race and racism in American culture, some of the white American progressive film critics shared this view. Along with Bosley Crowther, James Agee remarked that Kitzmiller's was "the only pure presentation of a man of his race that I have seen in a movie."[45]

Race and Atlantic Exceptionalisms 157

While there is no evidence that Italian critics sensed the racial coding of the film, some American critics did doubt its progressive qualities. A few American commentators wrote of their annoyance at the film's portrayal of Joe's penchant for drunkenness: the *Hollywood Reporter* remarked that the "American Negro soldier is regrettably caricatured. The Negro is portrayed as a dimwitted jive addict with a propensity for alcohol and it is he who in a drunken stupor gives away his Italian benefactors to the Nazis."[46] Perhaps forgetting that only a few years before Disney had produced Robert Clampett's *Coal Black and De Sebben Dwarfs* (1943), the *Daily News* asserted that "the handling of the Negro is the sort of thing that you would never see in an American picture. By making him indirectly and quite innocently responsible for the ultimate death of the man who has sheltered him, a producer here would be accused of discrimination against the race. Actually the Italians use him as a symbol of the basic brotherly love which emerges when unnatural fears are removed."[47] *New York Post* critic Archer Winsten called the presentation of the African American soldier "psychologically questionable."[48]

The quality of the film aside, *Vivere in Pace* worked as a compendium of long-standing racist jokes and stereotypes in Italian culture. Upon seeing Joe, the two young children innocently ask their father, "How do Negroes know whether or not their feet are dirty?" Uncle Tigna comments that Joe is not really black, but "just a little tanned."[49] Joe's actions amount to primitive behaviors determined by simple desires: he loves wine and, of course, cannot hold it. When inebriated, he wants to dance and play the trumpet.

Yet the "marking" of the black character also assumes local and novel nuances.[50] The film uses Kitzmiller to evoke and simultaneously exorcise Italian colonialism, performing what cultural anthropologist Michel-Rolph Trouillot has called a "formula of silence." Through the character of Kitzmiller and his relation with "Granpa" (grandfather), a veteran of the Libyan campaign of 1911, the film both erases the crimes of Italian colonialism and trivializes it as a benign process performed by "Italiani brava gente" who meant no harm to the natives.[51] Repeatedly, the jovial, benevolent Granpa asks Joe whether he is an *ascaro* (a member of the colonial troops that served the Italian colonial governments in Libya and later, the Africa Orientale Italiana). The former soldier of the colonial army refers to both the conquest of Ethiopia and that of Libya and asks Joe if he has met the sovereign (*negus*) of Ethiopia and whether he has seen the war at Sciara Sciat.[52]

The cultural work that this film does in 1947 Italy, then, is more relevant than we may at first think. In the aftermath of World War II, Ethiopians and Libyans—and next to them many Serbians and Greeks—were demanding that Italy be condemned for decades of genocidal colonialist wars.[53] The performances of Kitzmiller and Ernesto Almirante have to be understood in this context. The grandfather's joviality and his persistence in identifying Joe as a former colonial servant subsumes the history of Italian colonialism—including the genocide following the defeat of Sciara Sciat—under the mythology of the "italiano brava gente." Grandpa is "nice folk," even though he is both a racist and a veteran of a cruel and protracted imperialist campaign.[54]

If Kitzmiller was dissatisfied with the role he played in *Vivere in Pace*, his next film would be an even worse disappointment. *Tombolo Paradiso Nero* (1947; Tombolo, Black Paradise) played on the fears engendered in the Atlantic community by the news that African American GIs were dating local women in the areas close to American bases in Italy and Germany.[55]

The presence of soldiers and the lure of American goods had caused makeshift settlements to spring up in the woods between Pisa and Livorno. The area became the "notorious Tombolo pinewoods" (famigerata pineta di Tombolo).[56] "A nest of debased people," wrote the cinematographer Aldo Tonti in 1964. "You would have thought that you were in Congo."[57] In May 1947 the *Washington Post* published a story about Tombolo, the "Tahiti of Italy . . . where scores of American deserters, many of them Negroes, live . . . with Italian girls."[58] For John Schillace, the author of *The Tragic Forest: Tales of the Forest of Tombolo*, the pinewoods were a "mysterious forest" peopled by GIs and deserters, girlfriends and prostitutes, whites and Negroes. One of the GIs, named Lincoln, was a notorious African American giant who, allegedly driven to insanity by the death of his two young children, had killed his Italian companion and was known to roam the woods dressed only in a blanket ("running through the forest naked with that bloody blanket, which many fanciful retellings of the story had changed into leopard skin.").[59]

The Atlantic community of the second postwar period was made up of intertwining tales, stories echoing each other across the ocean. Schillace's sordid tale of Lincoln had its roots in the *Corriere della Sera*, the Italian newspaper of record, where one of the scriptwriters for *Tombolo*, a former officer in Africa and future dean of Italian pundits, Indro Montanelli, had written about the legend in a 1947 story. Lincoln for Montanelli was "the Negro who goes about shouting in the woods . . . a giant, more than two meters tall, with huge shoulders and with bloodshot eyes with a leopard skin thrown on his naked chest."[60] Another young, soon-to-be famous journalist, Sandro De Feo, in *L'Europeo*, described black GIs going mad at the sight of the strip of "white flesh over the edge of the stocking" of the *segnorine*. "From that moment on, [African American GIs] were lost and at the women's disposal, and they would have given these women not only the tires of their automobile, but an entire tank [of gasoline], or the car itself."[61]

The Tombolo *segnorine*—Italian women dating African American servicemen—captured the country's imagination. *L'Unità*, the organ of the Communist Party, wrote with some sympathy about "Le donne di Tombolo," who begged the GIs for love and money.[62] But the frenzy De Feo described was also possessing some Italian men. The reaction of

Figure 4.3. Giorgio Casini, *Prostitutes at Tombolo*, circa 1948. *Source*: Collection of Antonio Cariello. Used with permission.

the locals to this interracial fraternization could easily become violent. In February 1947, the majority of the people living in the housing project INCIS on Viale Mameli in Livorno demanded the eviction of the *segnorine* and the purification of their apartments "with D.D.T."[63] On the night of August 3, 1947, young men from Livorno attacked several black GIs and the *segnorine* accompanying them. While the soldiers took shelter in the military barracks, twenty-three women were publicly undressed and hoisted onto a merry-go-round in the central square of Livorno.[64]

Against this backdrop, the film by Giorgio Ferroni, *Tombolo, Black Paradise*, seems almost tame. Kitzmiller plays Jack, a corrupted sergeant in the US Army who covets Anna (Adriana Benetti), the pawn of a small-time black marketeer, Alfredo (Dante Maggio). Her father is the righteous Andrea (Aldo Fabrizi), a former *carabiniere* (military policeman) in the Italian African colonial corps, who works as the custodian of a warehouse. Easily duped, Andrea lets the gangsters rob the storehouse and then is himself charged with the robbery. To convince Alfredo to pay his bail, Anna accepts "to go with the Negro" who, in return for two hours with her, agrees to allow Alfredo to plunder his military depot. Renzo (Luigi Tosi), Anna's white lover, rescues his girl from the black brute by getting him drunk. As the police and the MPs are alerted to the potential heist, Andrea dies at the hands of the corrupt Alfredo whom he pursues into a minefield. His sacrifice will buy his, and Anna's, redemption.

Kitzmiller gives a solid and sordid performance as the dyed-in-the-wool criminal soldier out to deny and defy all the good Americans have done for Italy. His lust for Anna is as evident as her repulsion toward him. Even as Anna considers going with Jack to save her dad from the gallows, she is horrified that her father may later find out that "I have gone with a Negro, that I have always gone with them." The script by Montanelli (the same writer of the Lincoln story!), Glauco Pellegrini, and Rodolfo Sonego transferred onto Jack the same stereotypes as *Vivere in Pace*, but turned the comedy into tragedy. Like John, Jack drinks too much and can't hold it. Like John, Jack is coupled with a former member of the Italian African colonial force, Andrea, who is as earnest as the black man is corrupted. Their relationship invokes a "bizarro" postwar Atlantic world in which roles are reversed: blacks have power over whites, the Ethiopians have invaded and conquered Italy.

Kitzmiller's mangled Italian grammar and lexicon also created a remarkable aural continuity between his films and what Ruth Ben-Ghiat has called the "empire cinema" of Fascist Italy. Like John in *Senza Pietà*, Jack speaks in pidgin Italian. "John Kitzmiller is a riot when he says 'where I to go? Over boat,'" noted a critic.[65] Jack's Italian is not just for comic effect. Kitzmiller's specific kind of Italian harked back to the flawed grammar that Fascist filmmakers invariably ascribed to Italy's colonial subjects in Libya or Ethiopia. In Fascist "empire cinema," this flawed Italian was "meant to facilitate a re-education of the senses that aimed to produce imperial subjects who would further Fascism's social and political agenda."[66] In post-Fascist Italy the aural dimension of Kitzmiller's characters was meant to attune Italian spectators with the new, and yet not so novel, racial order of the Mediterranean, his aural presence more evidence of what Silvana Patriarca has called the "deep continuities" between the Fascist regime and the (Italian) Republic.[67]

This time even the *New York Times*'s Crowther could not help noting the "patently biased attitude toward the American Negro soldier in uniform."[68] The scene in which Andrea visits the pinewoods was set up as a "descent into hell" soundtracked by the shrill notes of jazz and populated by scantily dressed Italian women and African American GIs who loiter, drink, and have a good time. Italian film critics were not, however, appalled: the film was well directed by Giorgio Ferroni, well interpreted by Aldo Fabrizi as the former *carabiniere*, whose idealistic portrayal could be called "the triumph of duty."[69] *Tombolo* was an "in-depth character study, and a passionate interpretation of souls," Italian magazine *Film* commented with a high degree of generosity.[70] The film effortlessly fits the neorealist genre, chimed in *L'operatore*.[71]

Kitzmiller's following role, in Alberto Lattuada's *Senza pietà* (1948, Without Pity), was intended both to correct and to cash in on Italian anxieties regarding interracial miscegenation. Once again, the story takes place in the Tombolo pinewoods. Like the previous movie, *Senza pietà* centered on Kitzmiller's obsession with white women. The "segnorina," Angela, is Carla del Poggio, then Lattuada's wife. Kitzmiller speaks the same mangled Italian as he had in his previous roles. Even his name harked back to his past movies: after John and Jack, this Kitzmiller character is called Jerry. And like *Tombolo*, *Senza pietà* is a tragedy. In the end, Angela dies at the hands of Pierluigi

(Pier Claudé), the sexually ambivalent Italian gangster who runs the black market in Livorno. Heartbroken, Angela's lifeless body next to him, Jerry drives the truck off a cliff in Marina di Pisa.

The relation between Kitzmiller's role in *Tombolo* and his new one in *Senza pietà* was hard to miss. Both films, in turn, echoed stereotypes present in other media. Vanzina was correct: Kitzmiller was becoming, and embodying, a type. In Carlo Borghesio's *Come scopersi l'America* (How I Discovered America, 1949), a present-day Cristoforo Colombo, comic star Erminio Macario, travels to the US to find better opportunities. Once in Hollywood, Macario decides to get a job as an extra in a movie. The role demands that he portray an African American. Macario knows exactly what to do. In the Celluloid Atlantic, blackness is a mask that can be donned at will. The comic applies a blackface makeup, and—voila!—he is ready to go. Asked by a priest to speak in English, Macario is in trouble, but resorts to some sort of pidgin Anglo-Italian that, for spectators in the know, features the words "Tombolo," "Senza pietà," and "segnorine"—all obvious references to Kitzmiller's career—before eventually mimicking the staccato of a machine gun. The implicit covenant between Macario and his audience reveals that Kitzmiller and his roles were by then well entrenched in Italian film culture. By 1949, he had become the quintessential black man and a social pathology.

However, *Tombolo* and *Senza pietà* catered to different obsessions and aspirations. For Italian audiences, the appeal of Kitzmiller's blackness in *Tombolo* may not have been all about fear and disgust. One wonders how the scene in the Tombolo forest and the fate of the women who live there with their black lovers may have played before starving postwar audiences. The *paradiso nero*, the "black paradise," may have appealed more as the consumerist utopia that was soon to be part of the popular appeal of the Marshall Plan in Italy. The Italian women seem to have fun and have, obviously, enough to eat and more than enough to drink.

Senza pietà appealed to moral aspirations rather than survival instincts and desires. Lattuada, and his scriptwriters Tullio Pinelli and Federico Fellini, who did uncredited work on *Tombolo*, gave the character of Jerry moral substance and ethical subtleties unexplored in Kitzmiller's previous GI roles. It is not just that Kitzmiller has more lines. This time it is Jerry who wants to save Angela from the life of a *segnorina*, and he agrees to help Pierluigi rob a military depot to keep her out of prostitution. Angela is also different than Anna. She is not repelled by Jerry: she "is fond" of him, as a friend says. The film makes clear the limits of her affection, confirming their relationship as nonsexual and emotionally uneven not so much by the images (Jerry never gets to kiss her) as by Jerry's own lines when he tells Angela that "I know. You not love Jerry. I love you. You know this. I am like brother. I not leave you no more. You will see: Jerry strong companion." (Io conosco che tu non ami Jerry. Ti voglio bene. Tu conosci questo. Sono come fratello. Non ti lascio piu'. . . . you will see Jerry è forte compagno.)[72]

That the film had a different aesthetic agenda was also evident. Lattuada, a photographer turned director, and the author of the celebrated *Il bandito* (1946), had intellectual and critical standing, and the film was part of the Italian contingent at the 1948 Venice Film Festival. Sixty years later, Lattuada still insisted that the film deserved a prize at Venice but Luigi Chiarini, a "former Fascist, former racist, former intellectual, objected."[73] Chiarini may have not been the only one to object, given the film's lukewarm critical reception. In the *Corriere della Sera*, Stefano Lanocita called the film unoriginal ("l'ennesima storia della gente di Tombolo") "the nth story about the people of Tombolo."[74] The organ of the Italian Communist Party called it a disappointment (*delusione*).[75] On the other side of the Atlantic, the *Daily Worker* concurred: the film "yields no significance, only sentimentality and melodramatic action."[76] The *New York Times* wrote that the film "lacked decision," and the *Herald Tribune* called it a "lifeless characterization."[77]

The film is tentative. It is unclear whether *Senza pietà* depicts the absence of any interracial sexual and romantic relationship as a permanent barrier or something that might be overcome. Perhaps because of this, critics had trouble placing the film into any well-defined genre. *Senza pietà* is structured as a melodrama, but it gestured toward the documentary style and fell somewhat between the two. The film "vacillates between crude melodrama and some improbable situations," wrote Crowther. "Pictorial realism which has distinguished Italian films in the past, is matched with lifeless characterization" echoed the New York *Herald Tribune*. To *Bianco e Nero*, the film oscillated between "refined calligraphy and exasperated realism."[78] For others the confusion was temporal and spatial. The film used nonprofessional actors, recognizably "real" locations, natural lighting, and a predominance of medium and long shots—but instead of a neorealist focus on contemporary and contingent Italian issues, *Senza pietà* gestured at some vague "human condition," something that was not specifically Italian and, according to the critics, not even current. Lattuada almost admitted this in a perfunctorily written prologue at the opening of *Senza pietà*: "The story takes place in Italy but could occur anywhere in the world."

Italian critics used this geographical vagueness to relocate the racism of the film to outside of Italy. "Regardless of the use of realist settings, the film does not speak to contemporary Italy but to prewar France or 1930s America," Callisto Cosulich, a Communist, tellingly wrote in 1948.[79] The film spoke to American racism, chimed in Christian Democrat Gian Luigi Rondi in *Il Tempo*. The Italian racism the film referenced had existed, but that was now in the past. The events Lattuada describes appear "positively removed into the memories of the past. . . . His characters today appear remote: they are not big enough to be part of history and they are too remote to be chronicle."[80]

The production and reception of the film marked an important moment in Italian and European cultural history. With the onset of the Cold War, the political ties that bound the Atlantic community were strained. The alliance with the United States, while de facto unquestioned, begged for qualifications. Especially on the left, a narrative of difference emerged, which displaced the color line onto America as the preeminent—and increasingly solitary—marker of regional, infra-West, difference.[81] Americans were racist, Europeans were not. American cinema was racist, European cinema did not "see color." Only thirteen years after the bloody conquest of Ethiopia, in its review of *Crossfire* (1946, Odio Implacabile) in *Bianco e Nero*, film critic Massimo Mida praised the film for its attack on anti-Semitism and noted that it also dealt with racism, "a sickness which affects America"[82] but had not touched Italy. Likewise Guido Aristarco was flabbergasted at the treatment of blacks in American cinema and the title of one of his essays shouted "Black Man, You Should Not Die!"[83]

This has become a generalized attitude. In an essay he wrote for Aristarco's magazine *Cinema Nuovo*, Rudi Berger argued that the "racial problem" had disappeared from Italian cinema because it was just part of the "artificial parenthesis imposed [on Italy] by the Fascist alliance with Nazism." Looking at "the films of Italian realism" and obviously including *Senza pietà*, *Vivere in Pace*, and *Tombolo*, Berger suggested fantastically that blacks were presented "without prejudice—just like the whites."[84] In the chapter he wrote for the 1956 Italian edition of Peter Noble's 1948 book *The Negro in Film*, Lorenzo Quaglietti argued that black characters in Italian films did not "express the terms of a racial problem."[85]

It is in this dialogue between the Italian left and American cinema that the in-betweenness of *Senza pietà* makes historical sense. In their seminal *Panorama of the American Film Noir* (1955) Raymond Borde and Etienne Chaumeton interpreted the film as an Italian homage to film noir ("echoes the noir series"), not unlike Giuseppe de Santis's *Riso amaro*.[86] Lattuada himself called it "a really American film for the way it was shot, its rhythm, its editing, and other formal solutions."[87] Yet even while referencing Hollywood genres and Hollywood style, *Senza pietà* attacked the American treatment of racial romance. The film's explicit racists are the American MPs who beat and harass Jerry and the other African American troops. The African American magazine *Our World* noted that the film "has jumped the gun on Hollywood" and feared that *Senza pietà* would be unable to crack "the nut of Southern distribution." It depicted the possibility of a relationship between a white woman and a black man and, in addition, was critical of the US.[88] *Senza pietà* asserted a notion of European difference just as it confirmed its belonging to the same milieu and filmic tradition.

Ultimately, the film fit more than it reversed the racial conventions of the Atlantic community. Positive and complex African American characters had already appeared in Hollywood postwar productions and *Our World* noted that the US distributors of Lattuada's films were building on the path opened by the successful runs of *Pinky* (1948) and *Home of the Brave* (1948).[89] The interracial liaison of the Italian film looks tame if compared to the one Joan Fontaine and Harry Belafonte would ever so "politely" gesture toward just a few years later in *Island in the Sun* (Robert Rossen, 1957). While narrowly distributed, the film was admitted to the US major markets for a subtitled foreign film, New York and Massachusetts, without significant changes.[90] Furthermore, Jerry is far from a threatening character. More consistently than Dots Johnson in the second episode of Rossellini's *Paisà*, Kitzmiller is the object rather than the subject of the story. European and American critics noted the character's "dog-like devotion to things and loved ones" ("canina devozione alle cose e alle creature care," *Corriere della Sera*) and "animal-like candor" ("animalesco candore,"

Bianco e Nero), "a kindly spirit destroyed by circumstances beyond his control" (*Herald Tribune*).[91] The French *Le Monde* praised Kitzmiller's instinctual abilities, but confused the actor with Dots Johnson (*Paisà*). "John Kitzmiller, the good negro of *Paisà*, is the surprising star of this film. He embodies his character like only Blacks, and children, can do. What freshness! What simplicity of means! What a soul!"[92] It was a common mistaken identity. American *Box Office* chimed in and remarked upon "John Kitzmiller, the American negro actor who played in *Paisan*."[93]

Who could blame these critics? In the dominant scopic regime of the Celluloid Atlantic all blacks looked the same and had the same natural characteristics. I am suggesting here that like *Riso Amaro*, another film connected with neorealism and Americanism, *Senza pietà* related to Hollywood as much in terms of rejection as incorporation. Film scholar Stefania Parigi later noted that the film was a hybrid between Hollywood genres, "the schemes and the rhythms of the *noir*," and "the will to document that is characteristic of [Italian] neorealism."[94] This illustrates the usual back and forth of the Celluloid Atlantic, in which Hollywood's mode of narration was modified in one region of the West and then sent back for further modification. In this case Lattuada and his scriptwriters devised a strategy that was to become typical of Hollywood film: the black male character was given one of the positive, central roles in the picture, but this was achieved at the cost of his desexualization.[95] His relation to Angela was childish and strongly marked as asexual—almost a love story, one in which, however, there was to be no touching or kissing, the eviscerated sexuality of Jerry enhanced by the childish vocabulary he employed in his unsophisticated division of the world between "buoni" and "cattivi." When at the end of the film he is lying wounded at Angela's feet, she calms him down by talking to him like a pet and telling him "be good, be good" (stai buono, su, stai buono). It is obvious that in their relationship, he is the junior partner—a fact that was reassuring in the strongly patriarchal postwar Italy.[96]

One Step Forward . . .

After *Senza pietà* John Kitzmiller's career sputtered on in portrait after portrait of nature untouched by the sophistication and complexities of modernity. His role in Sergio Corbucci's *La peccatrice dell'isola* (1952) serves as a good example. In the film, Kitzmiller plays Moses, a fisherman at the center of a web of misplaced passions. Dead at the beginning of the film's long flashback, Moses is suspected of having killed Carla (Silvana Pampanini), the beautiful wife of the local entrepreneur, Ingarsia (Folco Lulli), and then of having killed himself. In the end, another man, Francesco, is found to be guilty of Carla's murder. Moses, it is discovered, died trying to protect his friend, Rosario (Gianni Musy), from the clutches of the demonic woman.

Kitzmiller's Moses is a modern translation of Shakespeare's Caliban. This elemental islander is the offspring of nature who has come ashore from unknown lands: "the sea had thrown him here from who knows where," says Ingarsia. As usual, Kitzmiller's character cannot bring himself to speak in correct Italian; he drinks copiously; and can't hold his liquor. In this film, instead of playing the trumpet, he plays the mouth organ and speaks with a biblical flavor: "He always carried a Bible, which he had learnt by heart via repeated readings." Like Jerry, he is marked by his blind devotion to a white person. Faithful to his friend Rosario, he dies as he tries to protect him from the evil woman.

Nature rather than nurture marks Kitzmiller's roles. In the second film he made with Lattuada, which was also the directorial debut of Federico Fellini, who codirected and coscripted it (along with Ennio Flaiano and Tullio Pinelli), *Luci del varietà* (1952, Variety Lights), Kitzmiller was, once again, a happy-go-lucky Negro trumpeter whom Checco (Peppino de Filippo)—a vaudeville impresario on his last legs—meets one night in Rome. John (who shares both Kitzmiller's name and a past as a "chemical engineer") does not worry about his future, as opposed to the desperate Checco. He plays the trumpet, walks the city streets, and laughs his booming laughter.

Luci del varietà uses the story of Checco and his misfortunes to chronicle the changes taking place in Italy that are displacing traditions of local vaudeville troupes and revolutionizing the national mores. Like other Fellini films—the obvious example being *La Dolce Vita*—modernity was both a source of spectacle and something that remains deeply worrisome.[97] The character of Kitzmiller offers blackness as a comforting essentialism that cannot and will never change. It is what James Snead called the "metaphysical stasis" typical of Hollywood's representation of blackness.[98] Beyond the authorial interventions in

168 The Celluloid Atlantic

this early film by Fellini and Lattuada, Kitzmiller's trumpeter (in two out of the four films the actor made in Italy between 1947 and 1951 the actor brandished a trumpet, which in real life he could not play) works also as a topos of Western culture, a throwback to the use of blackness and "non-Western" art in much of European modernist art as a symbol of "a spiritual wholeness that had been obscured in an increasingly civilized and mechanized environment by layers of material development."[99] Like the theme of the African in German expressionist paintings and sculpture, Kitzmiller stands "in opposition to all aspects of bourgeois normalcy." He is a utopian simplification, in the midst of the traumas of modernization.[100] In the middle of the convulsed Italian fifties that pushed rural, provincial vaudevillians like Checco into bankruptcy, Kitzmiller's character represents the out-of-time-ness of blackness depicted through European artists' eyes.

While the clichés of blackness shaped Kitzmiller's roles, his own notion of European stereotypical difference informed his understanding of the possibilities open to him. In an interview with *Ebony* in 1951, Kitzmiller seemed entangled in Gardner Smith's détente and in what Jamaican art historian Petrine Archer-Shaw calls a "negrophiliac relation" where "both Europeans and Africans ow[n] stereotypical views about each other." The actor counted producer Carlo Ponti as his "closest friend" and while Zampa or Ponti had not required any acting "talent" from Kitzmiller beside his physical traits and his booming voice and laughter, the actor granted Italian filmmakers and Italian society a degree of fairness not warranted by reality—especially in Livorno.[101] And yet, at other times, the actor sounded more aware of the tenuousness of this presumed Italian "exceptionalism." In a late 1940s interview with journalist Aldo Santini, Kitzmiller was less optimistic than in his conversation with *Ebony*. Many black soldiers were not sure that the "victorious end of the war [was] going to bring the end of racial discrimination, and they'd rather desert than being pariahs in New York, St. Louis, or Memphis," Kitzmiller told Santini. As for the Italian Peninsula, he asserted that "sooner or later there won't be any more roles for Negroes in the Italian cinema."[102]

Kitzmiller's doubts about his future were well founded. Yet Italy was not the only European cinema willing to enlist his services, and he was willing to look elsewhere. He told *Ebony* that he wanted to become an "international actor," and in these ambitions he demonstrated an acute understanding of both the limits of Italian film culture and the increasingly internationalized structure of the Celluloid Atlantic industry. In the two decades following World War II, as Tom Bergfelder as demonstrated, the number of coproductions that involved two or more Western national cinemas increased.[103] Moving from one European film industry to another was increasingly easy.[104] More importantly, celebrities were becoming global commodities. "Cinema," Curzio Malaparte wrote in 1966, "is the nation of the nationless."[105]

And yet, just like any other commodity in the North Atlantic world, celebrities tended to fit preordained niches that were age-, race-, and gender-coded, and often followed performers across national borders—the Italian *maggiorate* rather effortlessly becoming "bombshells" when transferred and translated into English-speaking zones. In kind, Kitzmiller was offered similar roles across the Western film industry. He was a military policeman in an Italian film by Giacomo Gentilomo, *Ti ritroverò* (1949) ("wasted in the brief role," the *New York Times* commented).[106] And he had recurring roles as the African American GI in *Monastero Santa Chiara* (1949) and especially *Il grande addio* (Renato Polselli, 1954). In the latter, heavy hitting melodrama Kitzmiller was "John," an American pilot who had sired a son in Italy during the war. In the film Kitzmiller comes back to Naples to seek his son (played by Angelo Maggio, the real-life son of an African American soldier and an Italian woman) after he has given up his military career and has become a man of the cloth. Upon seeing the well-adjusted kid and considering his bleak future in America, John decides to leave him in Italy.

In and out of Italy, Kitzmiller was often cast as the servant. He was the butler, John, in the German production *The Cave of the Living Dead* (Akos Ratony, 1965). He was cast as David, the African native in *The Naked Earth* (1958), which Vincent Sherman shot for Twentieth Century Fox as an English production with an international cast while Sherman was suspected of communism,[107] and he was Kato the African slave of the Venetian nobleman Marco Venier in the made-in-Cinecittà *Due selvaggi a corte* (1958). Kitzmiller's characters often specialized in Bible thumping. He was the religious old slave in the Franco-Italo-German-Yugoslavian production of *Uncle Tom's Cabin* (Géza von Radványi, 1965) in which he also got to sing blues and gospel standards. After spouting biblical lines as Moses of *The Island Sinner*, he played another "Moses," this time the devout house

170   The Celluloid Atlantic

servant on the estate of Captain Blood, in the Errol Flynn Jr. vehicle, *The Son of Captain Blood* by the Argentinean Tullio DeMichelis (1963).

In the late fifties the actor sought better roles in the Yugoslavian film industry, and in 1957 he won the award at Cannes for best male performance for his work in *Dolina Miru* (The Valley of Peace) by Franc Stiglic. Here too, though more poignantly than in other films, Kitzmiller played an African American soldier, Jim—in this case an aviator stranded in Europe—and was paired with young children. Jim accompanies two orphans, an ethnic German girl, Lotti, and the Slovenian boy, Marko, on their journey to what they think is safety. Set in a gorgeous Slovenian summer and in a pristine alpine land-scape, *Dolina Miru* connects Kitzmiller once again to nature, children, and animals. The actor speaks pidgin German to Lotti (Wohlfeiler Ewelyne) but Marko (Štiglic Tugo), who does not speak German, instinctively understands him. When the three come upon a white horse in a meadow, the steed follows them for no apparent reason other than Jim's magnetism to children and beasts.

The film must have opened new vistas for the actor. His role is distinctly meatier than those in his previous GI films. Jim is smart and alert and saves the children several times, prompting Marko to tell him that he wants to be just like him when he grows up. Stiglic maintains some of the stereotypes of Atlantic blackness but also reverses some of them. Thus blackness is asexual and mocked (Lotti tries to wash Jims's face and feet) but in his persona is neither completely trivialized nor pathologized. The film rejects the racial separation implied by Coletti's Catholic-inflected fascism in *La grande speranza*. Like Lotti, who is an ethnic German, Jim has been discriminated against because of who he is but, as opposed to Coletti's whiteness, Jim's blackness is inclusive, a bridge rather than a separating element. When he fashions a doll for Lotti, he makes it black, and the white girl loves it immediately.

The Cannes award must have registered as an exceptional moment in the actor's career. Yet the effacement that had marked his work also accompanied the marketing of *Dolina Miru*, even after he received the award at the festival. With the exception of the US, where it was released in 1961 as *Sergeant Jim*, much of the marketing for the film featured the children Lotti and Marko, rather than Jim, as the protagonists.

In 1957, the American and European press hardly noticed him. *The New York Times* simply mentioned that he had won the prize. The young Turks of *Cahiers du Cinéma* did not mention him or the

Figure 4.4. Japanese poster for *Dolina Miru* (1957). *Source*: Author's collection.

film in their collective reportage from the festival.[108] One has the impression that the Cannes jury wanted to stake European difference vis-à-vis Hollywood, which had not yet awarded much of anything to its black stars.

172 The Celluloid Atlantic

In *Dolina Miru*, Kitzmiller (now Jim) has fewer lines than in *Senza pietà* but his performance is more complex than in most of his other films. The actor also gets to say that America is far from just. "Is America at war?" asks Lotti. "Not yet," Jim answers ambiguously, perhaps referring to the ongoing civil rights struggle or potential nuclear confrontations, his perennially smiling face suddenly pensive.

. . . And Several Backward

Kitzmiller kept traveling, but the roles repeated themselves, so that his journey through the Atlantic was becoming circular or even reversing. After his role in *Dolina Miru*, Adelchi Bianchi's *Vite perdute* (1958) must have felt like a painful step in the wrong direction. Though now largely forgotten, *Vite perdute* was not a low budget enterprise; it had a remarkable international cast comprising Kitzmiller, Sandra Milo, Virna Lisi, Glauco Mauri, and the Franco-Lithuanian star Jacques Sernas. *Vite*'s director of photography, Aldo Tonti, was a distinguished alumnus of the neorealist revolution, having worked on some of Roberto Rossellini's films (*L'amore*, 1948, and *Europa '51*, 1952) and Federico Fellini's first Oscar-winning film (*Le notti di Cabiria*, The Nights of Cabiria, 1957). Notably, Tonti was also the DP of several films by Lattuada, including the seminal neorealist gangster feature, *Il bandito* (1946), and Kitzmiller's own vehicle, *Senza pietà*. The posters of the films also gave credits to Kitzmiller, the actor occupying a central position in all of them. It was, however, a pyrrhic victory.

Vite perdute referenced with precision the real geography of the Tuscan archipelago (the iron mines of the island of Elba, the penitentiary on the island of Pianosa), which, along with the photography's sharp natural lightning and the presence of nonprofessional actors in minor roles, all suggested neorealist aspirations. Apparently, the film did not leave much of a critical trace, but the cast, as well as the film's violence and overtly sexual content, secured it distribution deals in several key markets including the US (where it was released as *Lost Souls* in August 1961), Western Europe, and Japan.

Kitzmiller played the bandit Luca, his second villain after Jack, *Tombolo*'s corrupt American GI. Luca has escaped from the penitentiary of Pianosa along with four other convicts led by the "baron" (Jacques Sernan). Their plan is to rob the offices of the iron mine on the island of Elba and then escape by boat from the island to continental Italy

Race and Atlantic Exceptionalisms 173

Figure 4.5. Italian poster for *Vite Perdute* (1958). *Source*: Author's collection.

where they plan to fly by plane to Africa. As he reminds the "baron," Luca has special skills that makes him indispensable. He is a former airplane pilot, possibly a World War II American veteran, and they need him to fly the plane to North Africa. Like *Tombolo*'s Jack, Luca is obsessed with white women, and his uncontrolled desires starkly contrast with the other escapees' emerging aspirations to redemption. Bianchi introduces Luca's otherness after the convicts have taken over the offices of the mine, taking hostage Carlo (Gabriele Tinti), the son of the mineowner, and three female friends. "Keep your temper!," the Baron barks at Luca, marking him as uniquely troublesome. "Keep your eyes and nothing else on [the hostages]!" Luca nods disingenuously, Kitzmiller distorting his face into a brutish grin.

Luca is curiously enterprising in his single-track desire to rape the white women he has under his thumb. He attacks one of them, Giulia (Sandra Milo), and kills another, Susi (Annie Alberti), when she resists him. Only death can stop him and he is finally killed by one of his own comrades, Leopoldo (Roberto Mauri), who is appalled by the man's depravity. He ultimately functions as a way for the convicts to regain their own humanity by opposing his debased desires. With the exception of Nicola (Gennaro Sebastiani), who stands guard outside and is killed by Carlo in his attempt to escape, all the other convicts confront Luca. When he sees that Luca has murdered one of the women, the Baron dresses down the brute, though to no avail. Appalled by his depravity, Leopoldo and the Baron tie him up, but Luca succeeds in escaping those restraints. When he tries to take Carlo and Giulia with him on a boat, Toni (Marco Guglielmi), one of the four convicts, tries to stop him and Luca shoots him down. He is about to make it out of the island with Giulia and Carlo as his hostages when the last surviving convict, Leopoldo, shoots him dead.

The audience's collective sigh of relief must have been sonorous. Kitzmiller's characters had always been overdetermined by racial markings, but this role went far beyond the idea of race as the historical explanation of difference—the justification for any civilizing mission—to embrace the idea of race as biological destiny, unredeemable by any contact with more civilized, white individuals. To cite Olindo De Napoli's work on the intellectual history of Italian racism, the racism that defines Luca at the end of the 1950s was formed in the Fascist *ventennio*. *Vite perdute* showed the permanence of that form of biological determinism in post-Fascist Italy. Luca is not only the result of historical circumstances, what De Napoli calls "a historical zero," his inferiority is also a biological destiny—"a future zero."[109] His cruelty is explained solely by his psyche, which, in turn, is determined by his racial identity.

The film highlights the permeability of social boundaries even as it underscores the inescapable nature of racial difference. Carlo's sister Anna (Virna Lisi), the daughter of the mineowner, falls for one of the convicts, Toni. When Toni is shot by Luca, the young man tells her that "you are the best thing that has happened to me" and Anna's smile tells the viewer that, should Toni survive, there could be room in the heart of this rich, young woman for this handsome, incarcerated proletarian. On the other hand, blackness is an impermeable wall. There is no hope that Luca may feel anything other than animalesque desire for the women or, for that matter, that the female hostages could feel anything but fear and repulsion for him. Even the asexual relationship between John and Angela in *Senza pietà* is unthinkable. Luca is sexual, violent, and dangerous. The Baron tells Carlo that nobody can make out the mind of "il negro." He is biologically different and inscrutable. "A man can explain the construction of an atom bomb or plant a satellite just using his brain, but he may not be able to control a man whose skin is of a different color than his own. Take Luca: he is a mystic, he believes in superstitions. He is afraid of black cats and the like." When he is finally shot dead, he falls into the shallow sea, thus reversing the journey that had taken Kitzmiller's Moses from the sea in *La peccatrice dell'isola*. In *Vite perdute* the camera hovers at length over the man's submerged body, as if Luca were a rock, or a sea creature, returned to its natural place.

Circularity

Vite perdute was a major role for Kitzmiller who received top billing in the marketing campaign for the film. It is likely that the Cannes prize helped him win better compensation and bigger parts in films with bigger budgets. But the roles he was offered reveal a perverse circularity. In 1962, he had a part in the James Bond installment *Dr No*. His role as Quarrel, 007's Jamaican sidekick, however, was not much of an improvement. Like his previous parts, Quarrel fits the stereotype of the uncultured man in touch with nature. His skill and usefulness to Bond (Sean Connery) came mostly from his ability to read nature's signs, like the condition of the sea, or the coming of a storm that might prevent safe passage from Jamaica to Crab Key, the isle where SPECTRE Corporation has its base. Bond and Honey

176   The Celluloid Atlantic

Ryder (Ursula Andress) may not perfectly embody Prospero and Ariel, but Quarrel would still be a serviceable Caliban.

Kitzmiller's title role as Uncle Tom in the Franco-Italo-German-Yugoslavian version of Harriet Beecher Stowe's novel builds on all the stereotypes of the preceding films. Tom sings the blues, displays evidence of a deep, mnemonic knowledge of the Bible, and is worshipped by a white child, the young Eva St Clare (Michaela May). It is possible, as William M. Slout suggested in 1973, that the film attempted "to relate old and contemporary American racial problems" but, if so, it failed to relate to both nineteenth- and twentieth-century debates about racism, and on both shores of the Atlantic.[110] The film recounted the tale of righteous slaves and monstrous slave traders (Simon Legree, an effective Herman Lom), but showed saintly slave owners as well: Saint Claire (played by former Nazi star O. W. Fischer). Its historical contribution to black liberation probably consisted in offering a few days of employment to a crew of African American and Afro-Caribbean performers (singer Olive Moorefield, Catana Cayetano, George Goodman) in Europe. Their timid onscreen actions were in stark contrast to what people of color were doing outside those theaters, in Africa, Europe, or in the United States.[111] When Legree kills Saint Claire and a mob apprehends and lynches an innocent youngster, Tom looks mournfully at the hanging corpse and asks God to forgive the mob "for they do not know what they are doing." The film does boast a thoughtful and poignant performance by Kitzmiller. Heavier and grayer, he makes Tom into a tired, broken man who lives in a world that has hurt him one time too many. Kitzmiller gifts the character with dignity and sparks of emotional authenticity. But *Cabin* was too timid in its anger, too stodgy in adhering to the genre of the historical drama, and too cynically unfaithful to the novel in its sexually explicit depiction of Legree's liaison with his slave Cassy (Moorefield). More important, the film was hopelessly dated in a Celluloid Atlantic where blackness was being redefined by the likes of James Baldwin, Angela Davis, Frantz Fanon, Malcolm X, and Martin Luther King Jr.: in this new world "Uncle Tom" was an insult.[112] The film did not find a distributor in the US until 1969. It Italy, Aldo Scaglietti wanted to sentence it directly to the dustbin of history.[113]

Kitzmiller made the most of what was available to him, giving nuanced, multilayered performances against the grain of his scripts.

At times, he seemed to be poking fun at the stereotypes shared by his producers and audiences. At the Venice Film Festival in 1948 he preempted the worn-out joke by telling Communist daily *L'Unità* that he had come "to the [famous Venice beach of the] Lido to get tanned."[114] At other times, Kitzmiller's anger shines through. For a performer whose acting talent was routinely ascribed to "nature,"[115] there is a history of resistance visible just under the surface. In *Vivere in pace*, in the scene with "Granpa," he undercuts the old man's amiable musings about Italian colonial forays. He does play the trumpet for the old timer, but he wields the instrument sullenly, with an almost palpable undertone of anger. When cast as an African native in Vincent Sherman's *Naked Earth* (1958), Kitzmiller made a point of speaking with a formal British accent.[116] "John Kitzmiller is quite formal as a native," noted the *New York Times*.[117]

Missed Opportunities

One wonders what would have happened to Kitzmiller had he not died so young in 1965. The rise to independence of former colonial powers shook the color hierarchy in European cinema and Hollywood. Black actors received more interesting roles and parts that came with more dignity, sometimes even with a larger than usual financial compensation. For example, John Ford alumnus Woody Strode played a Patrice Lumumba-like character in Valerio Zurlini's *Seduto alla mia destra* (Black Jesus, 1969), a now largely forgotten masterpiece of Western European anticolonialist cinema. The film offered Strode the opportunity to show his acting skills and deliver dialogue that, the actor told African American journalist Charlayne Hunter when the film was distributed in the US, consisted of "dignified lines."[118] Strode did the film "for free," he told *Variety*, as a favor to Zurlini whom he considered a friend. In turn, the actor considered *Black Jesus* a career milestone because he had turned himself from "cowboy actor" into a legitimate "actor."[119]

Woody Strode's late sixties roles also benefited from the new spaghetti Western sensibility that, as we will analyze in the next two chapters, was remaking the Western genre on both sides of the Atlantic. The grandson of a black Cherokee and a black Creek, Strode played a mixed-race bowman in Richard Brooks's *The Professionals* (1966) and in Edward Dmytryk's Euro-American Western *Shalako* (1968). In the latter, Strode was an Indian chief (Chato) that consistently humiliates a party of European aristocrats hunting animals and "Indians" in the American West—until he is bested by Burt Lancaster (Shalako) in the film's final duel. During the spaghetti season, Strode was a heroic Native American father in *Keoma* (1976), and, along with Bud Spencer (Hutch), Terence Hill (Cat), and George Eastman (Babydoll), was one of the four pistoleros that defeat a corrupt capitalist miner in *La collina degli stivali* (Boot Hill, 1968). Strode told *The New York Times* that it was the first time he was paid a decent salary and given adequate billing.[120] For this film Strode made seven times his salary on *The Professionals*.

Other jobs opened up for African American actors during the spaghetti Western revolution. Next to Strode's career upturn was Vonetta McGee's role in Sergio Corbucci's *Il grande silenzio* (The Great Silence, 1968), and Fred Williamson's protagonist role in *Joshua* (1976) by Larry C. Spangler. Having died in February 1965, Kitzmiller missed the spaghetti Western season, as well as the postcolonial one. The African dignitary he played in 1962 in the episodic film *Totòtruffa '62*, by Camillo Mastrocinque, was still captive to the former colonialists' paranoia. In the film, Kitzmiller played the ambassador of the "fictional" African state of Katonga (which is not really a fictional name, and should actually be spelled Katanga). When he leaves Rome on a mission, his place is taken by Italian comedian extraordinaire Totò, who dons heavy blackface to impersonate the African ambassador and cheat some businessmen who want to make deals with the newly minted, mineral-rich nation. Rather than mimicking Kitzmiller's actual body, Totò's makeup outrageously embodies all the Atlantic stereotypes of blackness made shriller by the anticolonial struggle.

In the film the ambassador of the African "banana republic" and his Italian impersonator, Totò, meet in the lobby of a hotel in the tremendous conclusion of the Kitzmiller episode. Director Mastrocinque sets the scene well. Each accompanied by a sidekick, Kitzmiller and Totò come from opposite directions in a fortuitous encounter that is reminiscent of a duel. Totò is made up in outrageous blackface, complete with huge lips and enormous nose ring. Kitzmiller glares as his eyes meet Totò's, who immediately lowers his head in an obsequious bow. As Totò visibly quakes, expecting discovery and retribution, Kitzmiller passes by him, goes a few steps further, stops, turns around, and stares at the buffoon, who slowly bows again before running away.

Figure 4.6. Totò (Antonio de Curtis) in blackface in *Tototruffa '62* (1962). *Source*: Author's collection.

Figure 4.7. The Ambassador of Katonga (John Kitzmiller) glares at Totò (Antonio de Curtis) in blackface in *Tototruffa '62* (1962). *Source*: Author's collection.

By the time the film was released in 1963, Kitzmiller was drinking heavily and his health was deteriorating. Something was taking its toll on the man. Contemporaries remember that by the middle of the 1950s Kitzmiller had changed his mind about Italy and the local possibilities for black actors. Talking to Goffredo Fofi, director Luigi Zampa remembers the actor as extremely sad, almost suicidal: "He died very badly. He died an alcoholic. He drank too much because he had so many disappointments: everybody was forgetting him."[121] That his career was stalling preoccupied the actor. In an interview with the *Battle Creek Enquirer* in 1960, Kitzmiller tried to recast his professional disappointment within a classic Cold War narrative. Radical filmmakers had at first loved him ("They used to swarm around me"), he argued, but now "they hate me" because he had refused to play along with their Communist politics. Contradicting his own previous statements for the benefit of the Midwestern paper, Kitzmiller now stated that he "never saw any race problem" in the US and that "I kept insisting [to the Communists that] I wasn't staying here because of racial discrimination in the U.S. Then they stopped writing and closed up their books."[122]

Eventually, his drinking got the better of him. According to his obituary in *Variety* (March 3, 1965), Kitzmiller died of cirrhosis of the liver in 1965 in Rome. He was only fifty-one years old. His sister, singer Sue Johnson, who traveled from Detroit to attend his funeral, was apparently unconvinced by the medical diagnosis that imputed Kitzmiller's death to natural causes.[123] At any rate, by the time of his death (or his suicide), Kitzmiller was as forgotten in Italy as he had hardly been noted in the United States. While at the American premiere of *Variety Lights* in 1965, *Village Voice* critic Andrew Sarris wrote that some colleague had asked him "facetiously" whatever happened to John Kitzmiller. Sarris did not know much. He had read somewhere that the actor was dead, he told the fellow critic.[124]

The Great Atlantic Ricochet Game

So what can we learn from this story? When Italian intellectuals constructed their version of 1950s cultural difference in relation to Hollywood's racism, they built on concrete and diverging aspects of Italian and American cinemas and societies. Italian postwar cinema de facto articulated a color line and was far from exempt from Du Bois's normative prediction, but the Italian articulation of the color line was also different from its American manifestation. The coding of blackness in Hollywood cinema reflected a social order based on the separation of black and white people that shared the same land.[125] Thus, as Michael Paul Rogin has suggested, classical American cinema

Race and Atlantic Exceptionalisms 181

is a cinema concerned with borders, and prone to a paranoia about trespassing them—a cinema that since D. W. Griffith's *Birth of a Nation* (1915) has identified the mulatto, the evidence of the porosity of these borders between races, as the deadliest of social viruses.[126]

In this period, Italian cinema was less obsessed with the evil "mulatto" and more intrigued by the typology of the childish "sambo"—a figure of racial ranking and stereotyping that supports and naturalizes Italy's attempts at hegemony in the southern Mediterranean as well as the national amnesia about Italian colonial adventures in Africa. Thus, rather than the Aryanist version of racism, which was prevalent in the United States and Nazi Germany and focused on biology and racial purity, Kitzmiller's career ran up against the hidden but still potent legacy of "Mediterraneanist racism" (razzismo mediterraneista) analyzed by Gaia Giuliani and Cristina Lombardi-Diop.[127] The Italian postwar Republic was different from Fascist Italy and Article 3 of the 1948 Constitution explicitly prohibited discrimination on the basis of "race," among other elements. The overall trajectory of Kitzmiller's remarkable career, however, shows that Mediterraneist racism was still prevalent in postwar Republican Italy focusing on cultural definitions of racial lineages (the Fascist *stirpe*) and justifying Italian domination over Africa and the southern Mediterranean Sea.

Exceptions may be found. Obsession with miscegenation and calls for racial segregation marred *Vite perdute*, but in the Italian case, racism and the markings of the color line did not directly concern a history of slavery or a nationally based *apartheid* regime, nor did they mirror an elaborate legal system designed to enforce the separation between races throughout society. While an underlying racism remained, things could be said on the east side of the Pond that could be referenced only obliquely in Hollywood. In the Italian and southern Mediterranean context, the necessity of consolidating hierarchies of races and nations was perhaps more urgent than enforcing borders between neighbors and neighborhoods. Some of Kitzmiller's roles, in *Tombolo*, for example, or in *Senza pietà*, allowed for a degree of familiarity between black men and white women even as it reinforced a racial hierarchy that marked blacks, and to an extent all Africans, as childlike and brutish.[128]

While racism made the Celluloid Atlantic coherent, the existence of regional variations created actual, if rather temporary, professional gains to be had in moving around.[129] Although the stereotype of the intellectually deficient sambo haunted Kitzmiller's film career, on European screens black manhood needed to be contained less, or in different ways, than was the case in Hollywood. In *Senza Pietà*, Kitzmiller could share space with Carla del Poggio though his pidgin Italian marked him as the intellectually inferior partner. In the landmark Hollywood film, *Guess Who's Coming to Dinner* (Stanley Kramer, 1967), Sidney Poitier's character, Dr. John Prentice, was a world-renowned medical doctor but, twenty years after *Senza pietà* and *Tombolo*, he could chastely kiss his wife, Christina Drayton (Katherine Houghton), only once, and, notoriously, solely in the reflection of a taxi cab mirror.[130] There is no role as medical doctor in Kitzmiller's long Atlantic career even though some of his neorealist roles would have stood out in late 1940s Hollywood.

In the intertwined universe of the Celluloid Atlantic regional differences allowed for cultural ricochets and recombinations. Images fashioned on either side of the Atlantic could paradoxically serve as a critique of regional articulations of racism while de facto remaining embedded in the overarching color line. In some sense, one could use Kitzmiller *versus* Poitier. It was possibly because in 1946 *Vivere in pace* had given Kitzmiller a more central role than most contemporary Hollywood film would have offered to any black actor that progressive intellectual James Agee could find the Italian film "impressive" for its "treatment of the Negro," its demeaning stereotypes notwithstanding.[131] When *Senza pietà* was released in Italy in 1948, freelance photographer Ivo Meldolesi took pictures of Kitzmiller at the Venice Film Festival joking with his costar, Carla del Poggio, and dancing with American actress Constance Dowling. It is important to note that these offscreen images represented Kitzmiller and Del Poggio physically closer than they were at any time in the actual film. And such physical contact would have hardly been possible in most of Italy—certainly in Livorno—without Del Poggio and Dowling being seen as prostitutes, or *segnorine*.[132] Despite this, it is relevant that legislation against interracial socialization was nonexistent in postwar Western Europe, with the telling exception of the colonial territories.[133]

In any case, in the Italian context Kitzmiller was often filmed or photographed dancing or dining with white Italian female actors, something that would have elicited strong reactions if represented in mainstream American press.[134] These Atlantic people and their images ricocheted across the ocean, acquiring different meanings, fueling

Figure 4.8. John Kitzmiller dancing with Constance Dowling. *Source*: *Ebony* 11 (1951), 71.

diverse agendas, and finally participating in creating the détente to which Gardner Smith refers. The photos of Kitzmiller dancing and joking with Dowling and Del Poggio made their way into the leading African-American magazine *Ebony* and the magazine noted, with excessive optimism, that Kitzmiller was a "star of Italian movies" who had "never played a stereotyped role in a film."[135]

There is one more significant example of this cultural ricocheting. Screenwriter and director Robert Rossen had become blacklisted after appearing as an unfriendly witness before the House Committee on Un-American Activities in 1951. Under pressure, Rossen changed his mind and, in 1953, he gave in to the committee's demands, naming fifty-three people as Communists. His career was saved, but Rossen decamped to Italy anyway. Once there, he accepted an offer to direct *Mambo* for Carlo Ponti and Dino De Laurentiis from a blue ribbon

Figure 4.9. John Kitzmiller joking with Carla del Poggio. *Source*: *Ebony* 11, 1951, 71.

script by Ennio de Concini (the future winner of an Academy Award for *Divorzio all'Italiana*, Divorce Italian Style, 1962), writer and journalist Guido Piovene, and the screenwriter of *Riso amaro*, Ivo Perilli. *Mambo* is the melodramatic story of an Italian dancer, Giovanna (Silvana Mangano), and the quadrangular entanglement between herself, thuggish Mario (Vittorio Gassman), Count Enrico (British star Michael Rennie), and African and Afro-Caribbean dance, especially the mambo, choreographed for the film by Jamaican American choreographer and dancer Katherine Dunham.

On the strength of Mangano's Atlantic stardom, Ponti and De Laurentiis obtained American financing from Paramount and from Joseph E. Levine, who distributed the film in the US. Several of Rossen's previous films had cast a critical look on America but they had mostly left racial relations alone. When, upon his return to Hollywood, he turned his gaze toward those, in the quasi-interracial romance *Island in the Sun* (1957) interpreted by Harry Belafonte and Joan Fontaine, the result was so bland as to be quasi-disastrous: a "movie bathed in color and filled with stars, each entitled to a big scene through which they swirled as though in a Restoration comedy."[136] "The Hollywood censors had made their pressure felt," noted *Ebony*.[137]

Before shooting *Island*, Rossen used Italy to test the waters of interracial contact. As opposed to the meek American film, the turgid melodrama Rossen shot in Cinecittà and Venice for De Laurentiis is still striking for the many scenes in which Mangano (herself a professional dancer) is shown dancing, intimately and comfortably, among Dunham's interracial troupe.[138] As important, the script by Perilli, Piovene, and De Concini repeats the usual Atlantic misconception of African dance as coming from instinctual calling rather than from talent and practice (Count Enrico calls it "savage"). The film, however, also expressed a profound admiration for the intricate skills required by a person to dance it. Rossen extensively showed how Mangano must *learn* to dance the mambo and how complicated and demanding the learning process is for her.[139] The film was not a hit in Italy though Communist *L'Unità* made much of it, calling it "spectacular, emotional, violent, dramatic and modern."[140] In the US, the *Baltimore Afro-American* was not very impressed because the film treated black performers as objects with no speaking role. The journal noted that Dunham had no line of dialogue in the film. "The best that can be said is that Dunham got a break in it," the paper remarked.[141] As the *Baltimore Afro-American* itself acknowledged, the film had both effaced the great dancer and given her a break that Hollywood had refused her. "Miss Dunham's name appears in the screen credits for special music, and lyrics of special songs. And there it ends."[142] When the film crossed the Atlantic, producer Levine had to edit twenty minutes out of it to tone down the physical, interracial intimacy the dance scenes contained. "Reportedly, it has been recut several times after Rossen finished it, and it is said to bear little resemblance to the original," *Variety* commented in its review of the film's American release."[143] *Mambo* showed Mangano in closer contact with black performers than any Caucasian actress would have been allowed to be in a Hollywood musical. In the end, however, *Mambo* excluded all the black dancers from the dialogue, and the contention for Mangano's heart is a white-man-only contest.

Ironically, if one puts together the two halves of the Celluloid Atlantic something closer to a credible humanity of these black characters would emerge. In *Mambo* Dunham is a body without a legitimate voice, in *Island in the Sun* David Boyeur (Harry Belafonte) is an articulate man without a legitimate body. The script acknowledges him as a skilled politician, granting him many important lines of dialogue but denying him any real possibility of physical intimacy with Mavis Norman (Joan Fontaine).

Despite important differences, then, racial hierarchies existed everywhere in the Atlantic. Blackness in Italian cinema referred to what pioneering Italian historian Angelo del Boca has called "the (conscious or unconscious) deletion of colonial crimes and the missing debate on Italian imperialist expansion."[144] It was meant to abet and protect the silencing and forgetting of the recent Italian past and to reconfirm the centrality of the cultural role that the coding of blacks as inferior has had in Italian culture and political aspirations for centuries.[145] Racial codes were alive and at work in Republican Italy. Fascism had been no parenthesis.

While playing a different role than its American counterpart, Italian cinema's racial code as embodied in the characters Kitzmiller played and as embedded during his twenty-year career can hardly be denied. Once put into effect, this code yielded the opportunity to obscure Italy's colonial past and, consequently, strengthened the revictimization of the former member of the Axis and former colonial power while playing a vital role in the construction of the mythology of the "Italiano brava gente."[146]

To paraphrase Amy Kaplan's suggestion that "the discourse of American exceptionalism" is based on "the denial of empire," the Italian, and perhaps European, narrative of difference stressed the denial of the "color line" in its postwar culture and society. This denial combined with downplaying racism and colonialism in Italian history and embedded itself in the *brava gente* mythology.[147] While this regional incarnation of racial markings limited Kitzmiller's career and those of other African American filmmakers in Europe, it did not jam the Hollywood/Cinecittà cultural traffic that actually intensified with the coproductions of the 1950s and the 1960s.[148]

Race and Atlantic Exceptionalisms 187

Italians' most strenuous opposition to Hollywood cinema boiled down to politics and trade, not race. It was a debate about the divisions of roles, and profits, within the Western film culture and film industry rather than a discussion about the relationship between "the West and the rest of us"—to mimic the title of Nigerian historian Chinweizu Ibekwe's pathbreaking book.[149]

Kitzmiller and other performers of color found both opportunity and its limits. As Gardner Smith wrote in 1965, "Many black Americans came alive for the first time in the ruins of Berlin, the coffeehouses of Tokyo, the homes of Frenchmen and Italians." Yet Gardner Smith almost immediately adds that "the difference between European and American racism, we all realized, was not one of kind but of degree."[150] He then goes on to describe the reaction of Jesse, another African American expat living in Paris, upon seeing an African sweeping Parisian streets: "'Job's too lowly for a Frenchman, got to import African slaves.' He shook his head again. 'Same old thing. Here or in the States. The white man rules, he's a racist, and he exploits black people. America or Europe, the whole white world, and that includes them Communist countries too.'"[151]

5

The Spaghetti Western as Atlantic Genre

It'd be a tragedy if America were to be left to the Americans.

—Sergio Leone

EFINING THE SPAGHETTI Western is notoriously difficult. The genre revolution that hides behind this term sneaked past Atlantic critics mostly unnoticed. Those critics who watched these movies upon their release on either side of the Atlantic Ocean generally saw them as a geographically limited cultural phenomenon that affected the production of a few European films. But critics mostly agreed on two things: the spaghettis were different from classical Westerns and they were an inferior product. "They were almost invariably panned by the reviewers," writes Christopher Frayling in his classic study of the spaghetti Western.[1] In *Films and Filming* critic and filmmaker David McGillivray confessed that he could not "see the appeal in this ultra-naïve approach with its putrid color and distinctly agitated cast,"[2] and his colleague Richard Davis echoed him: "We are accustomed, however imperfectly, to a sense of poetry—from John Ford via Martin Ritt to Andrew V. McLaglen—bred by an ingrained tradition. In the European Western, this tradition is non-existent, so that all the films produced in this genre are nothing more than cold blooded attempts at sterile emulation."[3] In 1980 *Sight and Sound* critic David Nicholls noted that compared with the Western of the classical Hollywood period, these films were more violent, less obsessed with morality, and more preoccupied with revenge. Others noted that next to the classical Western these movies also featured more Catholic imagery and Mexico or Mexicans in prominent roles, often in lieu of Native American characters.[4]

Contemporary critics also saw them as an Italian genre, something the moniker "spaghetti" signified. As for that particular name, apparently it was New York *Herald Tribune* critic Judith Crist who first used the term, disparagingly, in 1966 to indicate the violence of the films and their alterity to American Westerns.[5] The term became popular only a couple of years later. The *New York Times* used "spaghetti Western" for the first time in 1968 as a synonym for "Italian Westerns." The spaghetti Western, *New York Times* Renata Adler remarked, consisted of "peculiar marathons of cowboys, gore, dubbing, sadism and trompe l'oeil." Adler was confident that spaghetti Western cinema had a clear-cut beginning and "got its start" with Sergio Leone's 1964 *A Fistful of Dollars*. Many of these films, she continued, were shot in Almeria, Spain with "gypsies, unemployed for generations, now serving as Mexicans or Indians of the plains." Adler noted that several spaghettis,[6] including Leone's, had American stars like Eastwood or Eli Wallach or Henry Fonda, but this did not mitigate her conviction that the spaghettis were Italian.[7]

In the following years the *New York Times* and the majority of American critics hewed to this patchwork definition. After the end of the spaghetti revolution, some film historians tried to build a chronology of the spaghettis according to their politics. Critics argued that the spaghettis started out as apolitical with Sergio Leone's Clint Eastwood trilogy. They became more political circa Damiano Damiani's *Quien Sabe?* (A Bullet for the General, 1966), addressing anti-Americanism, the politics of decolonization, and left-wing revolutionary politics. Finally, at the end of the decade and in the early 1970s, the genre became a parody of itself, a turn exemplified by the Trinità ("Trinity") movies, and their two stars, Mario Girotti (aka Terence Hill) and Carlo Pedersoli (aka Bud Spencer). The parody began with *Dio perdona . . . io no* (God Forgives . . . I Don't, 1967) and *Lo chiamavano Trinità* (They Called Him Trinity, 1970) and went on to explode the conventions of the genre and in particular call attention to its theatrical, exaggerated violence.[8]

Overall, this chronology neither questioned the Italian-ness of the genre nor its low-brow critical categorization. To no avail did Italians filmmakers refuse to collaborate in this ghettoization. When interviewed by the *Los Angeles Times* in 1968, Leone reminded American critic Mary Blume that he was simply making "Westerns" and was thus tapping into the "great universal attraction" of the genre in its ability to recast the eternal "fables" and the "myths" onto a nineteenth-century Western landscape. The Italian reminded his interviewer that the director of *High Noon* (1950), Austrian refugee Fred Zinnemann, was not "very American" either.[9] As for his own movies, until his death Leone thought that seeing them as Italian because of the nationality of their director was as silly as deducing the Panamanian nationality of the owner of a fancy yacht from the fact that the boat was flying a Panama flag.[10]

Not much has changed in the definition of the spaghettis since the late sixties, when American film critic H. Weiler called them a "clutter of clichés . . . exceeded only by the excessive sound and fury,"[11] but such implicit moralism has subsided. In 1974, Stuart Kaminsky confessed his admiration for the spaghettis and in particular for Sergio Leone. Kaminsky's was also an early and provocative reappraisal of these films and an attempt to go beyond Leone's work and take into account the vast spaghetti archipelago. Yet for Kaminsky these films remained resolutely "Italian."[12] British film historian Austin Fisher has given a useful definition of the spaghetti Western that combines both its thematic and its productive elements. The spaghettis are "films produced or co-produced by Italian studios whose narratives are located in the USA, Mexico, or Canada and set between the Gold Rush of 1848 and the Mexican Revolution of 1910–1920."[13]

This chapter recasts the history of the spaghettis within the framework of the Celluloid Atlantic. I do not take issue with the established thematic definition of the genre. Nor do I want to suggest that the spaghetti Westerns were not a radical redefinition of this film genre. I argue, however, that the geographic origin usually ascribed to the spaghettis is limiting. Confining the spaghettis to Europe or Italy belies both their American origins, which none of their practitioners denied, and their American reverberations. The spaghettis were not born in Europe, but in the North Atlantic world, and were embedded in this world's response to what occurred outside its confines, specifically the emergence of the poscolonial global South. In this chronology Hollywood's early spaghettis preceded the European ones, and, once the spaghettis rose to prominence in Europe, their aestethics circulated back to Hollywood. In sum, rather than highlighting difference between Europe and the United States, the spaghetti Western shows the interconnectedness of what I have called the Celluloid Atlantic.

American Origins:
The Spaghettis as a Genre Revolution

While somewhat limiting, Austin Fisher's definition makes it possible for us to appreciate the rise of the spaghetti Western as a stunning moment in the history of Euro-American cinema in the second postwar era. Following Fisher's data, during the golden decade of the genre, from 1964 to 1974, 448 spaghetti Westerns were produced and released. The spaghettis started slowly with only two released in 1962, but they picked up steam, with thirty-two released in 1964 and fifty-eight in 1966. The zenith years were 1967 and 1968 when spaghettis numbered, respectively, sixty-nine and seventy-three. In 1971 Europe released forty-seven and forty-five the following year. The genre waned, like many related trends, after 1973. In 1974, there were only ten spaghettis and only one was released in 1979.[14]

UNESCO film production data for the Italian and European film industries contextualizes the spaghetti revolution in even starker profile. In 1967 Italy produced 258 films of which 69 were spaghetti Westerns. That means that that year almost 30 percent of Italian films were Westerns. Since the entire film production in Western Europe in 1967 was around 730 films, almost 10 percent of the Western European production consisted of spaghetti Westerns.[15]

Anchoring too unreflectively the origins of a film to national cinema is, of course, problematic. Many of these spaghetti Westerns were coproductions comprising several, often not solely European, nations. Leone's *A Fistful of Dollars* was the product of an Italian-German-Spanish collaboration and featured an American TV star, Clint Eastwood, in the leading role. Leone's *Once upon a Time in the West* was financed by Hollywood's Paramount and the Italian studio Rafran San Marco. To define spaghetti Westerns by their Italian or European

The Spaghetti Western as Atlantic Genre   193

cultural autochthony[16] is to fail to comprehend the nature of production process in the Celluloid Atlantic, which after 1945 was shaped by financial and cultural coproduction within the West. I argue that the spaghetti Western denotes a circular movement restructuring North Atlantic film culture, and one that complicates any simplistic acceptance of a film's nationality.

As we have seen in the previous chapters, the origins of such flawed optics lay in the discursive practices typical of the West during the Cold War. The Eastern and Western side of the Celluloid Atlantic tended to obscure similarities and highlight exceptionalisms and difference. North American critics regarded the spaghetti Western as a clumsy attempt at imitation, papering over thematic and stylistic discontinuity. The spaghettis were not related but opposed to the American genre of which they were a corruption. Leone was often "dismissed."[17] Even when they were well-disposed toward European cinema, American film critics could not help displaying a condescending tone. Regarding *Once Upon a Time in the West*, the *New Republic*'s Philip Kauffman depicted Leone as a talented child. "I almost felt that I was sitting next to little Sergio, aged ten, watching him gape wide-eyed at his own film."[18] The *New Yorker*'s Pauline Kael was more pungent in her remarks: "It was the *spaghetti* Western that first eliminated the morality-play dimension and turned the Western into pure violent reverie."[19]

Spaghettis fared little better in Europe. As *A Fistful of Dollars* was making a splash on European screens, director Ulf Michael von Mechow, implicitly referencing the success of Harald Reinl's adaptation of Karl May's novel *Der Schatz im Silbersee* (1962, The Treasure of the Silver Lake), complained to his friend John Huston that European producers were turning their attention to the Western genre with ridiculous results. "Imagine, a German Western!! German actors as American cowboys and Indians falling from Yugoslavian horses in the Yugoslavian 'Rocky Mountains.' Ridiculous!"[20]

More importantly, in Europe acknowledging the spaghettis would mean recognizing that European filmmakers were learning from American cinema. In this particular cultural and political climate, the cowboy and the Indian spectacle had developed—with some exceptions—into the American film genre par excellence, and European practitioners were at risk of being seen as the victims of American cultural power. In Italy, some critics invoked psychoanalysis to explain the violence of the spaghettis and their public appeal: "the repressed and impotent spectator" vicariously lived their vendettas onscreen or in the pages of violent comic books and dreamt of "sadist retaliations for all of the day's defeats."[21] At the Communist daily, *L'Unità*, critics were eager to see the genre wane, and repeatedly announced its demise even when, as we shall see, the genre was popular among leftist filmmakers and blue-collar workers alike.[22] In a hysterical crescendo, Roberto Alemanno linked the spaghetti Western to the Cold War imagery of James Bond films, and then to Gualtiero Iacopetti and Franco Prosperi's necrophiliac "shockumentaries" à la *Africa Addio* (1966), and finally to the cinema of Nazi Germany itself.[23]

Of course, there were exceptions. Young critic and aspiring filmmaker Dario Argento, whom Leone was to recruit to work with Bernardo Bertolucci on the script of *Once Upon a Time in the West*, wrote a glowing review pointedly shorn of any nation-based attribute of *A Fistful of Dollars* in leftist *Paese Sera*: "We were stunned [by Leone's film]. [We were] stunned because this was a Western we dreamed of seeing—the historic Western was not so inventive, not so crazy, not so stylish, not so violent."[24]

At the level of themes and violence, Leone's *A Fistful of Dollars* (1964) was more a continuation than a revolution. New York University business analysts Gino Cattani and Moritz Fliescher have noted in their case study of European creative industries that spaghettis "were originally spawned from the Hollywood classic Western genre."[25] Exotic locations, revenge, historical revisionism, and an altogether skeptical view of morals and power relations were part of the story of the American Western before the traditionally accepted beginning of the spaghetti revolution in 1964, the year marked by the release of Leone's film.

Take, for example, the career of the elusive screenwriter Philip Yordan. Chicago-born Yordan was one of the greatest and most controversial of classical Hollywood's script doctors.[26] When he died at eighty-eight years of age in 2003 many obituaries stressed his disinterest in direct political engagement, but this is misleading.[27] Condemnation of American racism and calls for racial tolerance and interracial love, a common theme in the European Western, were discernible in the Westerns Yordan worked on during his long transatlantic career. This should not be surprising. Yordan's second wife, dancer Caprice Yordan, was a member of the Ojibwe people from the Great Lakes region of the United States and Canada. In 1944 he had offered his play, *Anna Lucasta*, about the struggle of a Polish American family, to the American Negro Theater so that they could adapt it for an African American cast. Yordan was friendly with many blacklisted writers including the well-known radical screenwriter Bernard Gordon. In 1954, the same year he signed the script for Nick Ray's seminal *Johnny Guitar*, Yordan authored the story of *Broken Lance*, which was directed by a former member of the Hollywood Ten, Edward Dmytryk. The job earned him an Academy Award for screenwriting.

Broken Lance was a family melodrama that contained spaghetti themes including vendetta, interracial attraction, and sadism. Critics often compare it to *House of Strangers* (1949), a drama about an Italian American family that Yordan cowrote with Joseph Mankiewicz, who also directed it. *House* and *Lance* share plot similarities (both are about a patriarch, his possessions, and his feuding sons), but *Lance* articulates an openly antiracist message that is absent in *House*. Like its quasi-namesake *Broken Arrow* (a 1950 revisionist Western by Delmer Daves), *Broken Lance* won the Golden Globe Award as Best Film Promoting International Understanding.

Unlike *House of Strangers* but like *Broken Arrow*, which featured James Stewart (Tom Jeffords) as the husband of Sonseeahray (Debra Paget in redface), *Broken Lance* dealt with interracial love. Narrated as a flashback, the film began when half-Cheyenne Joe (Robert Wagner in light redface) was set free from prison, his lot for taking responsibility for a deadly brawl that pitted miners against his father, Matt Deveraux (Spencer Tracy), and Joe's white stepbrothers. Matt's first wife died as he was building his fortune, and the patriarch remarried, this time to an Indian woman (played by Mexican star Katy Jurado and referred to only as "Señora"), who is Joe's mother. Matt and Señora did not want Joe jailed, but his evil siblings had him convicted for the murderous brawl so they could escape the gallows and inherit their father's ranch. Matt confronted the three sons but died of a stroke before Joe could be set free. Certainly nonwhite, but suspended between "Indian red" and "Mexican brown," Señora's racial status is unclear to most. "Everyone calls her Señora. Why?," Barbara (Jean Peters) asks Joe, the good, half-breed son. "She is an Indian, after all," she adds. Joe explains to her that this way people think she is "Spanish" (i.e., Mexican), which is better than Indian because, though Matt "does not give a grip," "white men don't marry an Indian out here." According to the plot, racial mixing creates better people and the Indian spouse need not even die! Matt's chosen heir, half-breed Joe, vindicates his father, defeats his all-white crew of stepbrothers, continues the family tradition of interracial marriages by winning the hand of Barbara, and receives the blessing of his Indian mom.

Lance is important to us for its rarely noted celebration of racial mixing and its benign representation of nonwhite, or not entirely white, characters. These themes were to become central to the spaghetti revolution, and Yordan incorporated them into films on both sides of the Celluloid Atlantic. He moved to Europe in 1960; worked in Spain with Samuel Bronston; and left his mark in *Custer of the West* (1967), a revisionist Western that he produced with progressive filmmaker Irving Lerner, a former faculty member of Harry Alan Potamkin Film School. *Custer* was shot in Spain by director Robert Siodmak, who himself had a transatlantic career after going to Hollywood in exile from Nazi Germany in 1939. In 1971, Yordan signed the script for two purebred spaghettis, one shot in the US, *Captain Apache* (Alexander Singer, 1972), which he also produced together with Irving Lerner, and one shot in Spain, *Bad Man River*, directed by the Spanish spaghetti director Eugenio Martín. These films shared a transatlantic star, Lee Van Cleef, whose chiseled features and sagging Hollywood career had been revived by two chapters of Sergio Leone's trilogy with Clint Eastwood (*For a Few Dollars More*, 1965; *The Good, the Bad and the Ugly*, 1966). Both Yordan's movies contained the skeptical view of American history embedded in 1954's *Broken Lance* and the 1967 antihero tale *Custer of the West*. *Bad Man River* mocked corrupt Mexican and American elites bent on robbing the poor and one another. The leader of the Mexicans, Enrique (Sergio Fantoni), is instructed by King (Lee Van Cleef) to use his people as cannon fodder against American troops, fight bravely, and (in an ironic inversion for US audiences used to memorializing a heroic defeat) "remember the [Mexican victory at the] Alamo." But Enrique does not remember that glorious moment of Mexican history. He was not present; he does not know what King is referring to ("We won," a private tells the thick-headed officer). *Captain Apache* expands on the revisionism of *Broken Lance* by making van Cleef, in full "Indian" wig and redface, the Native American hero of the story, who fights Yankee corruption and defends Native American rights.

Yordan's life story is emblematic of the larger history of the Celluloid Atlantic. The spaghetti revolution is a story of cinematic careers crisscrossing the Atlantic, disseminating themes, and propagating film styles and discourses. Looking at neorealism's global grasp, Giuliana Muscio has noted the "labyrinthine transnational itineraries" that characterize the careers of its practitioners.[28] The same applies to the spaghetti generation. Geographic unrest mirrored normative restlessness. Yordan's *Broken Lance* is far from the only example of a Hollywood film that anticipated the spaghetti revolution. In 1955 André Bazin famously wrote that Nicholas Ray's *Johnny Guitar* (1955) marked a change in American Westerns.[29] Arthur Eckstein has explored the ways John Ford's *The Searchers* revolutionized the Western and re-created John Wayne's character, Ethan Edwards, so "that he can never be regarded as a traditional and 'clean' Western hero."[30] Many more scholars have noted that something was changing. A revolution was in the making and even its raw materials, its characters, and its settings had transnational legs.

Revising Mexico: "Budd" Boetticher's Westerns as a Model for the Spaghetti Revolution

Violence, vendetta, and interracial relations were already part of the American Western before the European studios took up the genre. So was the key element of the spaghetti, its reliance on Mexican locales and characters. In his overview of the genre, *Il Western italiano*, Italian film critic Giulio Pezzotta notes this element.[31] As the title of his book implies, Pezzotta accepts a geography that I am questioning, but *Il Western italiano* is closer than most studies at revising the mainstream narrative about the spaghettis, in part by acknowledging that Hollywood had already engaged Mexico in the 1950s. His point, however, still pivots on a Euro-American difference. In contrast to Hollywood Westerns, Pezzotta argues that in the Italian spaghettis the new Mexican presence was a stand-in for the increasing role of the Third World in global politics and discourse. Mexico had become "the metaphor of a postcolonial world that is awakening."[32]

It is this awareness of a "postcolonial Mexico" that divides Europe's and Hollywood's treatment of the southern neighbor of the

US. Hollywood's Mexico was for Pezzotta "an exotic 'other,' which is represented with a gaze that is, in the most positive cases, folkloric and aims at measuring the difference [between developing countries like Mexico] and the American civilization."[33] In the following pages I shall contend that American cinema, at least in the examples that the Europeans most often had in mind, had already seen Mexico as more than an exotic locale. In the films that mattered for the spaghetti revolutionaries, Mexico was rarely an exoticized cliché, or the junior part of the north-of-the-border neighbor. Rather, it was often the moral segment of North America and, increasingly, the trope of a postcolonial, and non–Euro-American, world.

The Second World War drew Hollywood's interest south of the border. During the conflict, the American Office of War Information had pushed Hollywood to invest in, and collaborate with, the Mexican industry. In 1943, RKO had invested money in the building of Mexico City's Churubusco studios. Relying on these new facilities, during the conflict and in its aftermath, Hollywood studios shifted the filming of Spanish-themed stories to Mexico, often at the prompting of the federal government. In the 1950s, south-of-the-border expatriation and exchanges continued. [34]

For our purposes, the relevant example here is the cinema of Oscar "Budd" Boetticher, one of the great American directors of Western films and one of the models for the 1960s European spaghetti filmmakers. An orphan adopted by an influential family from Indiana, Boetticher had played football at Ohio State before an injury dashed his professional sports hopes and he spent 1939 and 1940 in Mexico City, falling in love with the local culture and learning bullfighting.[35] Mexico and Latin America remained central in his work as a Hollywood director. For Boetticher, Mexico was not the poorer cousin of the United States, but its teacher. His early "matador" films (*The Bullfighter and the Lady*, 1951, and *The Magnificent Matador*, 1956) were both shot in the Churubusco studios in Mexico City.[36] In Boetticher's matador films Mexico was not a stand-in for America's other. Mexico and the US were, so to speak, joined at the hip and in some respects the southern nation was actually depicted as the more advanced sibling.

In both *The Bullfighter and the Lady* and *The Magnificent Matador* Boetticher and his DP, Lucien Ballard, the future collaborator of spaghetti director Sam Peckinpah, shot Mexico City without any emphasis on social melodrama, and celebrated the city's postwar modernity by representing its ample boulevards, modern highways, and fashionable apartment buildings, alongside the city's more traditional culture of bullfighting centered on the *plaza de toros*. Boetticher elided the poverty and squalor of Mexico City's slums and the street urchins, which had been filmed by Luis Buñuel in his great fresco of Mexican urban poverty, *Los Olvidados* (1950), instead turning the capital into a setting akin to the classic urban scenery of Hollywood 1950s romantic melodramas. Yet Boetticher's Mexico City was not Los Angeles either. Similar as it was to the US, the director saw Mexican culture and its metonymic partner, bullfighting, as a jolt of reality and unmediated truth that blew to the sky the veneer of the Americans' inauthentic lifeworld.[37] Mexico City was not just similar, it was morally superior to America.

This same theme of Mexico and Latin America as a place of palingenesis and liberation is at the center of Boetticher's early Westerns. In his *Cimarron Kid* (1952), World War Two hero turned actor Audie Murphy plays the title character (aka Bill Doolin) and dreams of escaping his troubles by going south of the border with his girlfriend Carrie (Beverly Tyler). Anticipating the moral nuances of Boetticher's Ranown cycle Westerns (see below), *The Cimarron Kid* is narrated from the outlaws' point of view and has the strictly interracial gang chased by cruel lawmen.[38] In contrast to the harshness of US law, Mexico and Latin America represent safety and spiritual regeneration. Rose is the Mexican girlfriend of one of the outlaws, Bitter Creek Dalton (James Best). Notably, she is herself a full-time member of the crew and prays to the Virgin of Guadalupe on behalf of the group's safety. The "kid" intends to follow the advice of another bandit who muses that, if he can make it out alive for one last heist, he will go south and give himself another chance: "Argentina. No fooling, I am going to buy me a cattle ranch there. There's a new world for a man like me. Nobody to know I was ever an outlaw. No fear somebody will take a potshot at me just to make his reputation."

In a later film by Boetticher, *Wings of the Hawk* (1953), lensed in 3D by Clifford Stine, Van Heflin is "Irish" Gallagher, an American miner-entrepreneur digging for gold in Mexico. He joins the Mexican revolutionaries after experiencing the corruption of Porfirio Díaz's *federales* and also falling in love with the beautiful Mexican guerrilla leader Rachel (Julia Adams). At the end of the film, Gallagher sacrifices his gold mine to save Rachel and allow the rebels to take Ciudad Juarez. *Wings* is a "hemispheric romance"—to use Adrián Pérez Melgosa's expression—structured around the love story between "Irish" and Rachel, and fraught with stock characters like the evil colonel Ruiz (George Dolenz) and the jilted lover of Rachel, Arturo (Rodolfo Acosta), who turns informer. Yet, contrary to most of Cold War Hollywood's "hemispheric romances" analyzed by Melgosa, where "the cure for [the American male's] condition invariably is found in the arms of an American woman from the U.S.," Gallagher finds real—and, for all we know, enduring—love with his Mexican lover.[39] Boetticher infuses the story with admiration for Mexico and its people, something that stands in direct contrast to the "derogatory stereotype" of Mexicans in much Hollywood cinema.[40] Boetticher's film neither mythicizes Mexican characters as saints nor marks them as primitive fools.[41] Instead, *Wings* presents a wide spectrum of Mexican-ness: from the sophisticated evil of Colonel Ruiz to the integrity of Rachel and the *insurrectos* with, in between, the realpolitik of the Mexican military leader, Orozco, who justifies his love for tequila and guerrillas by stating that "it takes all kinds to win the revolution, my friend: the thieves, the saints and the bandits! Not all good not all bad, but all for Mexico." Finally, *Wings* bends genre conventions with one of Boetticher's familiar themes, the conversion of the *gringo*, as Gallagher forsakes profit-seeking and gold mines for human understanding and love.

These early Westerns anticipated Boetticher's Ranown cycle that European filmmakers and critics lionized just before the spaghetti revolution. Boetticher's Ranown was a cycle of seven Westerns, all interpreted by aging star Randolph Scott and most produced by Harry Joe Brown (hence Ran-own). All—with the partial exception of *Westbound*, which was set in the Colorado territory during the Civil War—took place on the southern frontier between Mexico and the US. In one of these films, *Buchanan Rides Alone* (1958), Boetticher portrayed Tom Buchanan (Randolph Scott) crossing the US-Mexico border in California. Boetticher filmed the border at length in several scenes, including the film's climatic gunfight. This same borderland was to feature in many spaghettis. Here it serves as an implicit critique of the US social order. An unnamed Mexican village and the American Agry Town, named after the dominant Agry family, literally face each other across the borderline, making symmetry a structuring principle for the film from the initial shot.

Figure 5.1. "Budd" Boetticher's *Buchanan Rides Alone* (1958). The US and Mexico mirroring each other. *Source*: Author's collection.

Boetticher's title character is a sort of "man without a name" but, by his own admission, a man with a past in the Mexican Revolution ("ain't murder when you kill in the Revolution," he says when asked about his past). Buchanan steps in to defend a Mexican youngster, Juan de la Vega (Manuel Roja), who has killed one of the debauched plutocrats of Agry Town, Roy Agry (William Leslie), to avenge the rape of his sister.

With the telling exception of Buchanan, who works as a *trait d'union* between the two sides of the border, each of the American characters has an alter ego in Mexico. The spoiled Roy Agry is mirrored by his vanquisher, the honest and valiant Juan. Their fathers, the corrupt judge Simon Agry and the Mexican señor, Don Pedro de la Vega, also mirror each other. They are both leaders of their communities though one, the American, is a crook and the other is famously (Buchanan has heard a lot about him in his Mexican travels) a "fine man." Both men have effective aides, Simon has Abe Carbo, and de la Vega, whom the film never shows, relies on Esteban Gomez (Joe de Santis). Both leaders have sons, but Roy Agry is a drunkard and a rapist while Juan de la Vega is honest and brave.

Here Boetticher has reversed optical and ideological assumptions. The ugliness of the US border town is revealed by its opposite, the

Mexican barrio. As the plot develops, the impression of Mexican poverty and American affluence is replaced by the knowledge of American spiritual misery. The Argrys control all of their town's establishments: the saloon is the "Agry Palace," the gunsmith shop is marked by "R. Agry Prop." and is followed by the "Agry General Store," the "Agry Town Hotel," and the "Agry Saddlery." Agry Town is just a façade for American greed. After Juan kills Roy, the American villagers set up a lynching as their Mexican counterparts across the bridge look on with pain, pity, and powerlessness.[42]

Buchanan was a powerful film full of inversions and surprises. Its depiction of Mexico and Mexicans contradicts any facile assumptions about the racism of Hollywood cinema and anticipated the themes of the spaghettis. It was a marker of Boetticher's cinema. The American mimesis of the Mexican, if not the symmetry and specularity that defined *Buchanan*, is foregrounded in one of Boetticher's least-known Westerns, *The Man from the Alamo*. The historical premise of this film—the 1836 massacre of Texan patriots in a San Antonio monastery at the hands of the Mexican general Antonio López de Santa Ana—promises a collision with Boetticher's favorable attitude toward the southern republic. *Alamo*, however, surprisingly backgrounds the massacre and focuses on the cowardly raids of a gang, not of Mexican, but *American* thugs, who take advantage of the turmoil to rob the settlers' farms. The story has a telling twist as the bandits, while dressed up like Mexicans, take advantage of the settlers' animosity toward Mexico. In *The Man from the Alamo*, mimetic attempts reveal prejudice, and prejudice precludes justice. The Americans' racist ethnic assumptions prevent the settlers from realizing that the immediate danger to their communities comes not from the south, but from within.

Since André Bazin's seminal 1957 essay about one of the Ranown films, *7 Men from Now* (1956), Boetticher's reputation fared well among European cinéphiles, some of whom graduated to make Westerns. Bazin called this film a model of Western cinema ("un Western exemplaire") and "the best Western film I have seen after the end of the war." Boetticher's work, Bazin opined, was evidence that the genre was healthy and "evolving" ("en marchant").[43]

Penned by the most influential Euro-American film critic of the second postwar era, this prophecy was both correct and self-fulfilling. Spurred by Bazin's praise, European filmmakers appreciated the Hollywood director and Boetticher's films deeply marked the spaghetti

The Spaghetti Western as Atlantic Genre   203

revolution.[44] The moral ambiguity of Boetticher's Mexican general Orozco in *Wings of the Hawk* (1953)—"It takes all kinds to win the revolution, my friend: the thieves, the saints and the bandits! Not all good not all bad, but all for Mexico."—was pushed to the limit in the spaghettis. Boetticher's *Buchanan* was extensively cited by spaghettis, especially those made by influential progressive filmmakers. Carlo Lizzani explicitly referenced Boetticher's film in his 1966 Fanonist spaghetti, *Requiescant* (1966), where the titular character (Lou Castel) rides into San Antonio and encounters all the businesses owned by the evil C. B. Ferguson: the C.B. Ferguson Insurance Company, the C.B. Ferguson Copper Mining Co., the Ferguson Transport West, and the Saloon Ferguson. Sergio Leone reportedly confessed to an aging Boetticher that "Budd, I take a-everything from you."[45]

Like Yordan, Boetticher participated on both sides of the spaghetti revolution by authoring early examples in Hollywood and later coauthoring (with former blacklistee Albert Maltz) the script for *Two Mules for Sister Sara* (1970), a Mexican Revolution yarn by Don Siegel that directly built on the spaghetti credibility of Clint Eastwood, its star, who was back in Hollywood.[46]

Boetticher was not the only American director who made movies about the radical possibilities of Mexico in the 1950s. In Robert Aldrich's *Vera Cruz* (1954) two American mercenaries interpreted by Hollywood stars Gary Cooper and Burt Lancaster travel south of the border to participate in one of the many phases of the Mexican *La Reforma* (1855–1867). *Vera Cruz* was—as its credits acknowledged—"filmed entirely in Mexico" and its themes are entirely within the spaghetti tradition and chronology. Its plot takes place during the Mexican rebellion against the emperor Maximilian and his wife, Carlota, and has two American guns-for-hire, a former Confederate officer, Ben (Gary Cooper), and a bandit, Joe (Burt Lancaster), pursuing a million-dollar bounty south of the border. Ben falls for a local rebel, Nina (Spanish actress Sara Montiel), changes his mind, kills Joe, and chooses the good of the revolution over personal gain (just like Franco Nero in the 1970 spaghetti by Sergio Corbucci, *Compañeros!*). The film anticipates spaghetti tropes including torture, an unsteady moral compass, and an interest in military gadgets and contraptions like machine guns.

Critics have often invested too much in separating the American interpretation of the Western genre from the new, emerging one. For example, Mary Ann Carolan stresses that in the American Western "violence occurs primarily as a consequence of the epic struggle between good and evil, justice and injustice, while in the spaghetti western such violence, taken to the extreme, takes place outside such neat parameters."[47] Yet Gary Cooper and Burt Lancaster's characters in *Vera Cruz* are morally flawed mercenaries, and Henry King's splendid *The Bravados* (1954) was a Mexico-shot feature that had Gregory Peck roaming the US-Mexico borderland and killing people out of a misguided desire for violence and vendetta rather than justice.[48]

Sometimes the plot itself pivoted on Mexico's locales. Kirk Douglas, Dorothy Malone, and Rock Hudson carry their love triangle to Mexico in Aldrich's *The Last Sunset* (1961), which the director shot from a script by formerly blacklisted writer Dalton Trumbo, one of the original members of the Hollywood Ten. Aldrich had Kirk Douglas speak Spanish and interact with local Mexican cowboys. At other times casting choices illuminated Latino talent beyond the oft-cited Rita Hayworth and Mel Ferrer. In 1961, Marlon Brando and his production company released *One-Eyed Jacks* from a script that was signed, or worked on, by future spaghetti practitioners including the screenwriter of *Little Big Man* (1970), Calder Willingham, and the future spaghetti auteur Sam Peckinpah. Brando understood the project as a departure from Western norms. He delivered to Paramount distributors a five-hour director's cut and called the film "an attack upon a citadel of clichés" that was typical of the Western.[49] Although heavily edited by the studio, the film foreshadowed the European segment of the spaghetti revolution. A violent, heavily Freudian vendetta story, *One-Eyed Jacks* pictures a young man, Rio (Brando), who pursues and finally kills "Dad" (Karl Malden), an older man who has betrayed him. The film begins with a long prologue in Sonora before the chase moves north of the border to Monterey. Director Brando indulged in torture scenes ("the rough stuff is graphic and sickening—no biff-biff-bam," wrote the *New Yorker*) that were to find a clear echo in Sergio Corbucci's spaghetti manifesto *Django* (1966).[50] Like many spaghetti heroes to come, his flawed bandit-hero is also an unreliable protagonist. He coolly and cruelly seduces Dad's innocent stepdaughter, Luisa (Pina Pellicer), to inflict pain on his former friend. The *New Yorker* called the film a "strange new Western."[51] In *Esquire* Dwight Macdonald went further and called it "sick" and "peculiarly unpleasant . . . Everybody, including the hero, cheats and double-crosses."[52] The actor/director stressed the Mexican roots of American California via a remarkably multiethnic cast led by himself, Karl Malden, and Mexican actresses Katy Jurado and Pina Pellicer as Dad's wife and his adoptive daughter. The film's screen dialogue, devised by Brando, blew apart Hollywood's classical monolingualism by having long stretches spoken in Mexican-accented Spanish and without subtitles.[53]

A Japanese Mexico

A genuine interest in Mexico pervades some of the most influential Hollywood Westerns in the 1950s, but the power of these images lie also in their evocation of something larger than Mexico itself. Theirs is an oblique portrait of Mexico, but critics would be mistaken to read this obliquity merely as "a taste for the inauthentic" or another way to other Mexico as folkloric or exotic. Instead, this cinematic Mexico exemplified an affinity for camouflage and political masquerade, another characteristic of spaghetti aesthetics that I shall analyze in the next chapter.

In the remainder of this chapter, I explore another aspect of the Mexico of the spaghettis, one shared by the European spaghettis and their Hollywood antecedents that reveals the Celluloid Atlantic's reckoning with the larger world of the non-West. In seminal spaghettis, Mexico is larger than Mexico, its images meant to be global references. Just like Pezzotta has argued about the Italian Westerns, both in these films and in some of the 1950s Hollywood productions that preceded them, Mexico became a "metaphor of a postcolonial colonial world that is awakening": a nonwhite, non-Occidental world.

In some influential Hollywood Westerns, Mexicans were doubly racialized. Hollywood's Mexico was *two* countries, both of them outside of the old, colonizing, North Atlantic whiteness. The country on the screen was an easily recognizable celluloid Mexico, but behind it, and identifiable to most critics and filmmakers, was another country, one that was associated with the Atlantic, but increasingly imagined as part of the non-West and nonwhite claim to modernity: Japan. Japanese peasants were first turned into Mexican farmers in the seminal movie by John Sturges, *The Magnificent Seven* (1960), a remake of Akira Kurosawa's *Seven Samurai* (1954).

It is this characteristic translation from Japanese to Mexican that requires some explanation beyond the well-known popularity of Japanese cinema. Hollywood conquered Japan after Hiroshima and Nagasaki, but by the early 1950s, it was the cinema of Akira Kurosawa that captured critical discourse in America. According to Tino Balio's revealing history of highbrow foreign film distribution, Japanese cinema was next to the usual suspects (Italian, French, and British films) in the competition for American critics' attention and American art cinemas' box office. American distributors were particularly taken by samurai movies such as Hiroshi Inagaki's hit *Samurai* trilogy (1954–1956). The *New York Times* critic Bosley Crowther may have contributed more than a little to the global history of the spaghettis when in January 1956 he called Inagaki's first installment, *Samurai I* (1954), "an Oriental Western, dressed in sixteenth century get ups and costumes, but as violently melodramatic as any horse opera out of Hollywood."[54] The film received critical and popular success but, more importantly, Crowther's observation about the film's affinity with Western movies may have been the catalyst for the American remakes of Akira Kurosawa's *chanbara* (sword-and-sandal or literally "bang-bang") films.[55]

Kurosawa's success in the West predated Inagaki's. Like Rossellini did in Italy, Kurosawa began his career in the Japanese film industry during the authoritarian climate of the late 1930s and World War II. The Japanese scion of a samurai family was also quick to embrace the new postwar values and American aid. Kurosawa stumbled into international recognition with *Rashomon* (1951), drawn from a short story of murder and rape by the Japanese writer Ryūnosuke Akutagawa. Like Rossellini's early films, Kurosawa's film raised scant domestic interest before becoming a hit in the West. Thanks to Italiafilm's Giuliana Stramigioli, *Rashomon* made it to the 1951 Venice Film Festival where Kurosawa won the Golden Lion. Together with Cannes, Venice was the most important film festival in the world, and the award put Japanese cinema on the distributors' map.[56] *Variety* noted on December 11 that RKO had picked up the American distribution rights of the picture, "one of the few subtitled pictures ever handled by a major company,"[57] and by January 16 reported that the film was "doing surprisingly big biz in New York."[58] Many noted that this Japanese cinema followed on the heels of Italian neorealism's laurels.[59]

The Spaghetti Western as Atlantic Genre

Rashomon's success was followed by the *chanbara* films by Kurosawa, in particular *Seven Samurai* (1954) and *Yojimbo* (1961).

Kurosawa's rise to success among Western critics was part of the renewed interest in Europe and the United States for what was happening outside North Atlantic confines. And seminal films by the Japanese maestro were not just lionized by critics. They were also swiftly remade into Atlantic versions, which themselves became a cornerstone of the spaghetti revolution. In 1960, Walter Mirish and United Artists released John Sturges's *The Magnificent Seven*. A few years later, in 1964, Martin Ritt directed *The Outrage*, a remake of *Rashomon*. The same year, Sergio Leone directed and released the film that, nominally, was to spur the spaghetti revolution into high gear, *A Fistful of Dollars*, inspired by the Japanese director's second samurai film, *Yojimbo*.

Both American and Italian filmmakers translated the Japanese peasant class into Mexican farmers, adding a further element of racial difference to the cinema of the West's preferred trope for the global South. In translating Kurosawa's cinema into the Celluloid Atlantic, auteurs in the United States and Europe discarded Kurosawa's national lens, and foregrounded an international focus, thus confirming the spaghettis' connection to the rise of the postcolonial and nonwhite world.

The Japanese world of Kurosawa's films was ripped apart by class struggle, but reflected a national mythology of racial homogeneity. *Seven Samurai* was a "social critique of modern Japan with a debt to Russian film epics."[60] The great speech of Kikuchiyo (Toshiro Mifune) at the center of this film referenced social differences but elided racial or national markings. Kikuchiyo accused the farmers who had collectively hired the seven fighters of having no allegiance to those they hired. They considered them oppressors, only momentarily tamed by the promise of a small recompense. Were they to fall in battle, the farmers themselves would rob their corpses of their clothes and weapons. Yet, Kikuchiyo remarked, the samurais themselves were to blame for the farmers' opportunist attitude: when they needed to do so, they had not hesitated to plunder the farmers' crops and burn their villages.

Not only does the American version transform the Japanese peasants into Mexican peons, it also broadens the confines of the story's

208   The Celluloid Atlantic

conversation and expands its meaning from national to global. The character of Kikuchiyo is transformed into Chico (German actor Horst Bucholz in Mexican brownface), a young, inexperienced pistolero who is the only one of the motley crew of seven who is a thoroughbred Mexican. Marginal to the other six because of his youth and national origin and to the farmers because of his chosen profession, Chico's accusation sounds emptier. Kikuchiyo's sarcasm about the farmers' commitment was credible, but Chico's charge against the peons hardly made sense. Why should they be grateful to the mercenaries with whom they share no bonds? The two groups are, literally, foreign to one another. American guns for hire and Mexican farmers lived in different nations, their interaction was momentary and monetary, and forced upon them by circumstances.

Notably and differently from Kurosawa's painfully cynical look, Sturges's film never discounts the pistoleros' greatness. Kurosawa saw his *ronin* (samurai) through the lens of the World War II catastrophe, as human detritus from an age whose penchant for violence and obsession with honor could endanger the survival of Japan. Their obsolescence is to be welcomed, albeit melancholically. On the contrary, from the credits of the film onwards, the members of Sturges's wild bunch are not just enumerated as "seven," they are also celebrated as "magnificent"—even more so because their profession and code of honor made them obsolete in a world soon to embrace the legalistic rigor of capitalism. Rather than the attrition of two social classes brought into close quarters by the bandits' attack, Sturges's film tells the story of the encounter between the West and the non-West. The frontier world is "magnificent" *because* of its precapitalist nature. The beginning foreshadows the rest of the film, which is the story of this idealized "First World" encountering a palatable non-West threatened by rogues. Thus the film opens with some of the gunslingers defying racism north of the border, where local thugs want to prevent the honorable burial of a Native American man.[61]

In the American version of the story, Chico—the young Mexican would-be pistolero—stands for a multifaceted kind of marginality vis-à-vis the rest of the bunch, who are defined only by their impending obsoleteness. Chico compounds the marginality of his chosen profession (aspiring to be a gunfighter amid farmers, bankers, and railroad men), his inexperience (like the samurai Katsushiro [Isao Kimura] in Kurosawa's film), and his lower social status (similarly to Toshiro

The Spaghetti Western as Atlantic Genre   209

Mifune's Kikuchiyo). Like Katsushiro, Chico is young and eager to learn (from Chris [Yul Brynner]). Like Kikuchiyo, but even more so than the Japanese man, Chico is in an outsider position vis-à-vis both the pistoleros and the villagers. In Kurosawa, the characters' roles confirm the Japanese director's concern with social hierarchy in the particular context of Japan: age aside, Kikuchiyo, a farmer himself, is lower, and Katsushiro, the scion of a wealthy family, is higher than the samurai. In contrast, Sturges's world is strangely classless even for an American director. Chico's ambiguity is determined by his age, profession, and especially his non-Western origins. His ancestry becomes pivotal when his Mexican origins and proficiency in Spanish allow him to sneak into the bandits' camp and overhear their plan. Nationality, rather than social status, is also the important marking of the remaining six guns for hire, as Sturges made clear that the remaining men are all far from being aristocrats: they are similar to the farmers except for their profession and national origins (Charles Bronson is Bernardo O'Reilly, the fully assimilated Irish American gunslinger of mixed Mexican descent, representing the US capacity to be a melting pot).

John Sturges's film turned a national, class-based meditation into a conversation about international differences and obligations. The seven *ronin* became American guns-for-hire traveling south of the border to Mexico to defend a village of Mexican farmers from bandits. Sturges's film constructed a triptych unmistakably referencing the international role of the West (the gunslingers), the postcolonial emerging global South (the Mexican village), and the Soviet Union (the bandits).[62] The West–non-West dichotomy became central and embodied in the dialogue or confrontation between the United States and Mexico.

When *Rashomon* was remade in 1964 as *The Outrage*, the story was again transferred from Japan to an unnamed place on the Mexican-US frontier. The character of the bandit was given a racial marking that superseded and replaced Kurosawa's emphasis on class. The Japanese low-class bandit Tajomaru (Toshiro Mifune) became the Mexican bandit Juan Carrasco (Paul Newman), who seduces the white Tennessean played by Claire Bloom and kills her aristocratic husband, played by Laurence Harvey.

The Outrage was directed by Martin Ritt, a victim of the American blacklist. It was from a revised theatrical play by Michael Kanin, was lensed by another progressive Hollywoodian, James Wong Howe, and starred Hollywood leftist Paul Newman. This film was a politically left-of-center Atlantic translation and was made with a specific attention to the rise of the global South. Central to the marketing success of Kurosawa's film in the West, the encounter of the West with the non-West was now embedded in the story itself.

This time around, however, there is no conversation but only confrontation. The non-West is aggressive and dangerous: the Mexican bandit Carrasco attacks the Anglo couple. Carrasco is dangerous, but the film makes clear that his anger is justified, almost noble. Critics focused on Newman's preposterous rendition of the Mexican accent and on the stifled dialogue by Kanin,[63] but they mostly failed to notice what was in plain sight, that is, that the global South and decolonization were part of Martin Ritt's reinvention of the story. The decolonization process, absent in Kurosawa's version, took center stage: the trial of the Mexican bandit Carrasco resembled a lynching with Carrasco tied to a tree trunk, facing a hostile, all-white American jury. The bandit was undeterred and reminded the white settlers surrounding him that they were living in a land they stole from his ancestors.

Mexico was more and more often becoming the stand-in for the global South in the Westerns of the Celluloid Atlantic, a mechanism that occurs again when Japanese cinema is translated into Mexico by European spaghetti practitioners. In 1962, Bernardo Bertolucci, who was to write the script for Leone's *Once Upon a Time in the West*, set his first feature, a who-done-it procedural titled *La comare secca* (The Grim Reaper, 1962), among the Roman proletariat and repeated the structure of *Rashomon* with many retellings of the same story, the murder of a prostitute, from different points of view. As Bertolucci was translating the Japanese peasant class into Roman proletarians, Sergio Leone was beginning his work on what was to become *A Fistful of Dollars*, shot in Spain, but based on a story set in Mexico, with a Hollywood star, and directly drawn from Kurosawa's samurai film *Yojimbo* (1961).

Leone was interested both in the Japanese originals *and* their Hollywood translations. He often credited the influence of Hollywood "Mexican" films on his cinema. According to screenwriter Sergio Donati, the Italian director, "working only from memory, could reconstruct the scripts for both *Vera Cruz* and *The Magnificent Seven*."[64] Leone tried to get James Coburn, one of the stars of Sturges's film,

The Spaghetti Western as Atlantic Genre   211

to be the protagonist of his remake of *Yojimbo*, *A Fistful of Dollars*. He chose Clint Eastwood when Coburn proved too expensive, although Coburn wound up starring in the last of Leone's spaghettis, *Duck, You Sucker!* By that time the director had already recruited two other stars of *The Magnificent Seven*, Charles Bronson and Eli Wallach, for *Once Upon a Time in the West* and *The Good, The Bad and the Ugly*.[65] Leone was thus openly continuing a revolution of the Western genre that had begun in Hollywood. Like his American colleagues, the young filmmaker transformed Japanese farmers into Mexican peasants, the spaghettis' trope for the global South and global poor.

Having begun in Hollywood after World War II, the transatlantic revision of the classical Western reached great clarity in Leone's Eastwood trilogy, which skewered the notion that bourgeois justice was delivering the moral society that the Western Enlightenment had promised.[66] In the earliest film, *A Fistful of Dollars*, Eastwood is a gunslinger, who like Kurosawa's samurai, plays two warring factions against each other for his own enrichment. Leone turned the plot of *Yojimbo* from a story of social conflict into a meeting of nationalities and cultures, that is, the industrialized North and the global South. *Fistful* is the story of the American abroad told from the perspective of a European and in the context of the postcolonial world. Eastwood's name, "Joe," is given to him by Piripero, the carpenter/undertaker, but note that every American in Italy was a "Joe." This was the moniker given to Americans—especially American soldiers—in Italy by Italian children.

Leone is tongue-in-check reminding his audience of the present-day balance of power. "Joe" is, like America, a powerful but ultimately amoral friend, who is not fighting for any better world, only for more money for himself. This argument becomes clearer in the second chapter of the trilogy although, as screenwriter Sergio Donati remarked, Leone was never interested in making the political message of his movies obvious: "all is said obliquely" (*tutto è indiretto*) was his motto.[67] In Leone's celebrated duel at the end of *For a Few Dollars More* (1966), gun-for-hire Colonel Douglas Mortimer (Lee Van Cleef) confronts Indio (Gian Maria Volonté), the drug-addicted, deranged Mexican bandit who has raped and killed his wife. It is a peculiarly nonclassical duel as Leone casts Mortimer's ally and the main protagonist, the bounty killer "Monco" (Eastwood), in the role of judge.[68] Leone visually stresses the fate of Indio, sealed by this biased one-man jury, who, armed to the teeth, is sitting in judgment on one side of the circular arena. Leone gives each of the duelists equal and symmetrical shots beginning with two long-distance shots/countershots, and following those with symmetrical medium shots, medium close-ups, and extreme close-ups. The symmetry of this mise-en-scène echoes the equality of all points around the circle of clay that encompasses both duelists. Circle and symmetry are, however, suddenly broken by the presence of Monco. Leone's camera abruptly calls our attention to his hand, and in tandem with this visual disruption, Monco/Eastwood interrupts the circle's circumference by sitting on it. The circle is broken and the verdict is delivered before the guns are out. The Third World man has already been tried and found guilty by the Hollywood stars. Indio won't make it out of the circle of clay alive, where Leone has penned him in along with his killers.[69]

What Leone had done was certainly in a relation of continuity with the Hollywood movies by Sturges and Ritt. Like the Americans, the Italian had translated a Japanese story centered on interclass, infranational encounters into a tale of the West facing the non-West. The global, West/non-West/Soviet triptych of Sturges had been transformed by Ritt and Leone into an ironic critique of the allegedly "civilized" role of the West. As we shall see in the next chapter, this critique will become more explicit in the following years on both sides of the Atlantic. What will remain constant, however, is the masquerade, the central element of the spaghetti sensibility.

The Circular Move

In his seminal study of the spaghetti, British film critic Christopher Frayling has noted that critics are divided in their assessment of the influence of the Italian Western on the Hollywood one, some of them siding with Will Wright, who dismisses this influence, and others with John Cawelti, who sees it as crucial in the further development of the "American" Western. According to Cawelti, the spaghettis saved the Hollywood Western from both the lull and the crisis it was experiencing in the early sixties, causing "a significant resurgence in popularity of the Western film" in America.[70] Frayling suggests a middle ground. He sees the spaghetti influence in some of the Eastwood American Westerns by Don Siegel, and in the "epic qualities" of Robert Altman's *McCabe and Mrs. Miller* (1971) and in Ralph Nelson's "rhetorical effects" in films like *Duel at El Diablo* (1966), *Soldier Blue* (1970), and *The Wrath of God* (1972).[71] In particular, *Duel at El Diablo* for Frayling "proved [Nelson] to be the closest American director, in terms of technique, to Sergio Leone."[72] The influence is there, Frayling remarks, but it is in individual cases and cannot be generalized.

The critics' argument, however, is circumstantial, and the circumstances themselves seem to point to a different direction. *Duel at El Diablo* may certainly be considered as part of the spaghettis' American cohort. The story of a confrontation between Apaches and the Union army in the Southwest of the United States, *Duel at El Diablo* features American desert landscapes that recall the Spanish Almeria of Leone's films, with a similarly high body count, and extraordinary (for its time) violence.[73] It is also a "countercultural" Western that revises not just the classical Western's typical portrayal of Native Americans, but race relations in general. The Apaches are dignified, though defeated, and they fight with cruelty, but for legitimate reasons: "I wonder whether they will stay in their reservation this time," Ellen Grange (Swedish actress Bibi Andersson) comments after the Apaches' defeat at the hands of overwhelming Union troops. "Why should they?," James Remsberg (James Garner) retorts. Ellen herself has mixed feelings about the Apaches. She was their captive, had a baby with one of them, and she is not too keen to return to her dour, white husband, Willard Grange (Dennis Weaver), who has revenged her kidnapping by killing a Native woman. The film's historical revisionism, together with its emphasis on interracial relations and widespread white racism, references a changing world inside and outside of the United States. This is heightened by a far from heroic portrayal of the Union army and the US Marshals Service (the former would be overwhelmed by the Apaches, if not for the arrival of a much larger detachment of troops; the latter are all corrupt and racist), and by the presence of African American actor Sidney Poitier (Frank Toller), who shares the leading role with James Garner. Garner/Remsberg, himself, is bent on avenging—like Van Cleef in Leone's *For a Few Dollars More*—the murder of his Comanche wife who turns out to have been killed by Ellen's husband, Willard. Poitier's work onscreen is liberated enough from stereotype to allow him to kill Apaches in some scenes and beat up racist Caucasians in others.

Yet, while the emerging spaghetti sensibility is in the film, the dates hardly match. The US release of Leone's *Per un pugno di dollari* (in February 1967) occurs after the making and release, in June 1966, of Nelson's *Duel at El Diablo*. How did the former influence the latter, if Nelson had likely not seen or studied it closely?[74] A nation-based approach to the problem hinders analysis. Rather than asking which side of the Atlantic is influencing the other, films historians need to think of the increasingly integrated North Atlantic as a category of analysis. Rather than individual influences, we should look at the spaghettis as a contemporaneous revolution *in the genre of the Western that hits the Celluloid Atlantic at the same time.*

Among other things, the relation of *Duel et El Diablo* to *A Fistful of Dollars*, just like the contemporary releases of Martin Ritt's remake of *Rashomon* and Sergio Leone's remake of *Yojimbo*, point to the Atlantic dimension of what was happening to the Western. In both Europe and the US Western films were translating Japanese peasantry into Mexican bandits or peons, as a way to multiply and reimagine the encounter between the West and the emerging global South. As the spaghetti revolution continued in Europe what had begun in Hollywood, it also reverberated back into the United States.

Business analysts have sometimes done better than film scholars at understanding this circular mechanism. Looking at the relations between creative industries in Europe and the United States and focusing on the case of the spaghettis, New York University's Gino Cattani and Moritz Fliescher have argued that these films show that "processes of cross fertilization might span geographical borders—thereby promoting innovation (through the renewal of existing product categories) across countries (here Europe and the US)." They conclude that the case of the spaghettis "showed how an innovation in the movie industry in Italy not only revitalized the mature product category of Western movies in the US, but also how it changed the meaning of the existing category [i.e., the Western film genre] and stimulated innovation to take place in the existing category."[75]

By the time Leone directed his final spaghetti, *Giù la testa!* (Duck, You Sucker!) in 1971, spaghettis had circled back to Hollywood, which was now also investing in the spaghetti aesthetics. At first the change was noticed, but went unnamed, embedded in Hollywood films that the critics just found odd. For example, Englishman Sidney J. Furie's 1966 Western *The Appaloosa* (1966) was directly influenced by the spaghetti aesthetics. Marlon Brando plays Matt, a man whose prized horse is stolen by John Saxon, brownfaced as the Mexican bandit Chuy Medina.

The Spaghetti Western as Atlantic Genre 215

A spaghetti villain in the same vein as Gian Maria Volonté's Indio in Leone's second installment of the Eastwood trilogy, *For a Few Dollars More*, Chuy indiscriminately rapes, tortures, steals, and kills. Mexico is still a stand-in for the oppressed and Medina tells those who want to listen that "before his family set things straight, the 'yanquis' took everything from the place. Now the place takes everything from the world." Yet he is no saint and, opposed to this fiend, Matt stands out as righteous: he is the real friend of the Mexican poor that call him "Mateo" and help him throughout his odyssey to regain possession of his beloved steed.

In 1966 the American press was taken aback by all the protracted scenes of violence and humiliation, the slow pace of the story ("somnambulistic," according to the *Los Angeles Times*), and especially the extreme close-ups ("claustrophobic") of Brando and Saxon shot by the Oscar-winning DP Russel Metty, who was working under firm instructions from Furie.[76] With hindsight, the influence of the spaghetti revolution is clear, but at the time nobody saw it. The *New York Times* blamed this "odd sort of Western" on Furie, a Toronto-born member of the British New Wave and the director of the innovative *The Ipcress File* (1965).[77] Furie, however, explained the film as a product of "new methods originated under [Hollywood's] nose," which the American film citadel still refused to consider.[78]

Things were, however, getting clearer and clearer. In July 1965, the ABC program *Scope*, usually dedicated to political, social, and economic matters, featured interviews with Federico Fellini and producer Enrico Colombo who were asked to comment on "The 'Westerns, European Style' . . . the current big fad in European film making."[79] In July 1966, Marika Aba reported in the *Los Angeles Times* that the "Italian Westerns [are] getting the hang of it."[80]

The Western genre that had not done well in the US since the late 1950s was being revived via an injection of Atlantic content. Richard Brooks's *The Professionals* (1966) featured Italo-Franco-Tunisian star Claudia Cardinale (soon to star in Leone's *Once Upon a Time in the West*) along with new and old Hollywood stars and a plot that combined Boetticher's assertion of Mexican superior morality with Leone's interest in mercenary gunslingers. *The Professionals* shared the same locales (the Mexican-American border), time period (the aftermath of the 1913–1914 civil war in Mexico), and fascination with new, nonclassical technologies of death (dynamite and machine guns) as did other Atlantic spaghetti Westerns. Albeit with more restraint, the film also shared the politics of the spaghettis.

A popular and critical hit both in the US and in Western Europe,[81] the film told an updated version of the *Magnificent Seven* story. The gang here is reduced to four. Dolworth (Burt Lancaster), Jake (Woody Strode), Fardan (Lee Marvin), and Ehrengard (Robert Ryan) are a gang of mercenaries hired by J. W. Grant (Ralph Bellamy) to rescue his wife, Maria (Cardinale), who has allegedly been kidnapped by a Mexican revolutionary and bandit, Raza (Jack Palance). The plot is also outspokenly antiracist because of the presence in the gang of Jake (Woody Strode), an African American scout who fights with bow and arrow, and several interracial romances: Fardan had a Mexican Indian wife, and Dolworth takes up with a Mexican woman, Chiquita (Maria Gomez). The mercenaries know and respect Raza, having fought in Pancho Villa's army, but for the professional guns a contract is a contract and they aim to meet its requirements.

The confidence typical of the classical Hollywood Western is upended in *The Professionals*. It turns out that Maria and Raza are the good revolutionaries and very much in love with each other, while the Yankee Grant—as in a Boetticher movie—is an evil and corrupt capitalist. He is the real kidnapper, and, once they discover this, the professionals "fulfill" their contract by sending Maria and Raza back to Mexico.

By April 1969 things had so progressed that *Washington Post* film critic Gary Arnold, reviewing Damiano Damiani's spaghetti *Quien Sabe?* (A Bullet for the General, 1966), wrote that "the troublesome thing is that its 'style' has begun to influence American-made Westerns as well."[82]

By 1972, when George McCowan directed the fourth sequel to Sturges's *The Magnificent Seven*, *The Magnificent Seven Ride!*, the story of the seven *ronin* had detoured from a Japanese rice paddy to Mexican cornfields set up both in Hollywood and in Europe's film studios. American spaghetti star Lee Van Cleef now played the leader of the Seven to signify and embody the geography of the Celluloid Atlantic. By the early seventies, Van Cleef's costar, Clint Eastwood, had in turn starred in Hollywood Westerns deeply influenced by the spaghetti aesthetics. The *New York Times*'s Howard Thompson saw Ted Post's *Hang 'Em High* (1968), the first movie Eastwood starred in upon his return from Europe, as a direct offspring of the "masochistic exercises on foreign prairies" that had vaulted Eastwood into stardom. The only relevant difference, concluded *Newsday*'s Joseph Gelmis, was that "Leone is a better craftsman" than Post.[83]

The director of *The Magnificent Seven*, John Sturges, employed the Atlantic Western star Clint Eastwood in his *Joe Kidd* (1972). The actor reprised the role of a bounty hunter on the US-Mexico borderland. He played, or replayed, a similar role in *Two Mules for Sister Sara* (1970), which was directed by Don Siegel and scripted by former blacklistee Albert Maltz together with Budd Boetticher. The film tells the story of Sara (Shirley McLaine) and Hogan (Clint Eastwood), a fake nun and a true bounty hunter, respectively, who are looking for riches in Maximilian's Mexico while causing mischief to Napoleon the Third's colonial ambitions. It is *Vera Cruz* all over again. Football star turned television actor Burt Reynolds also traveled back from Europe, where he had starred in Sergio Corbucci's *Navajo Joe* (1966), and reentered Hollywood as "Yanqui Joe Herrera" in *100 Rifles* (Tom Grier, 1969) and Sam Whiskey in *Whiskey Sam* (Arnold Laven, 1969). Suffice it to say that "on average, more than 60 per cent of the Hollywood Westerns produced from 1965 to 1975 included at least one individual who previously was involved in making spaghetti Westerns."[84]

The American press hesitated to name the Atlantic dimension in this, the most American of film genres. But in 1967, in the British *Films and Filming*, David Austen noted that *Hang 'Em High* closely followed Romolo Guerieri's sequel of Corbucci's *Django*, *10,000 dollari per un massacro* (1967). Ted Post's film, he concluded, showed the "influence of the Italian Westerns." This phenomenon was not surprising and was to increase in speed, Austen remarked, as "producers are not slow to follow the example of box office successes" and *Hang 'Em High* was outgrossing the James Bond's films in its American release.[85] Ten years later, after the end of the spaghetti season and in the middle of the restructuring of the Celluloid Atlantic, Ignacio Ramonet acknowledged that Americans had been "imitating" the European Westerns in a series of "dirty Westerns," of which the most famous had been Peckinpah's *The Wild Bunch* (1969).[86]

Despite limited critical attention, the spaghettis had conquered America. Violence ruled and so did Mexico and the Southwestern frontier that were the locales for eighteen of the thirty-one Hollywood-produced Western films released in 1968. Even the design, by Sandy Ovore, of the screen credits of an American Western, the underexamined *The McMasters* (1970) by Alf Kjellin with Brock Peters, directly cited Iginio Lardani's seminal work in *A Fistful of Dollars* and many other spaghettis. As revealed in depth in the next chapter, the spaghetti sensibility shaped actors' performances and personae. In *The Appaloosa* John Saxon (born Carmine Orrico in Brooklyn) was made up like Volonté in *For a Few Dollars More*. In *Bandolero* Raquel Welch was to look like Sophia Loren[87] and the *Hollywood Reporter* commented that one of the key scenes of the film, which was in turn reminiscent of *The Bravados*, was "almost taken intact from an Italian Western."[88] In *Time* magazine, film critic Richard Schickel cited *Hang 'Em High* as the best of the American bunch. As for the new spaghetti sensibility embedded in American movies like Andrew McLaglen's *Bandolero* (1968), Buzz Kulik's *Villa Rides!* (1968), and Henry Hathaway's *5 Card Stud* (1968), the critic argued that they showed the "decline of a form on which a mighty industry was built."[89]

As we shall see in the next chapter the news of the Western's impending death, however, was much exaggerated. The Western was only changing to embrace the new geography of the Celluloid Atlantic.

A Cinema of Camouflage

Spaghetti Sensibility and the Postcolonial World

JESSIE (Diane Cilento): "You don't get tired, you don't get hungry, you don't get thirsty. Are you real?"

HOMBRE (Paul Newman): "More or less."

—Hombre, dir. Martin Ritt

⤚

IN 1992 RICHARD SLOTKIN wrote that the Western narrative was based on a mythology that helped spectators make sense of their historical situation, or, in Slotkin's words, understand "the place we are living." He added that this mythology needed continuous revisions because of the radical changes to "our place."[1] The spaghettis' genre revolution was a genre update dictated by history. In the previous chapter we looked at the American roots of the spaghetti Western and argued that rather than a new, European subgenre the spaghettis were a radical change *within* the Atlantic genre of the Western film. But where did this change come from? What made it necessary? In what ways was it historically contingent?

My argument is that the spaghettis were part of a sensibility that was profoundly historical and typical of the Celluloid Atlantic in the sixties and early seventies. In 1964 both Martin Ritt's *Outrage* and Sergio Leone's *A Fistful of Dollars* epitomized something akin to what, according to André Bazin, Nicholas Ray's *Johnny Guitar* (1954) had represented ten years earlier: a new way for Western cinema to reference history, or what thirty years later Slotkin called "the place we are living."[2]

In this chapter my argument hinges on three larger points. First, the spaghetti Western's transnationality reflected the increased internationalization of American capital and film personnel and its European imbrications. Contrary to Bazin's assumption, in the age of the spaghetti Hollywood was not simply an American production site, but a transnational entity powered into Europe by the European Recovery Plan of 1947 and the Smith-Mundt Act of 1948.[3] Second, although the geography of his argument is quite different from my own, I agree with Stefano della Casa's interpretation of the spaghetti as "'68 cinema *par excellence*."[4] The spaghetti Western referenced a historical and political context much larger than cinema, a way of feeling and thinking, what I call a "sensibility," that encompassed new representations of the relationship between Europe and the United States, the connection of the West to the rest of the world, and finally the linkages between postwar Europe and areas of its own past. It was a historically contingent sensibility, with its own linguistic topoi and tropes. Third, in this new age, the spaghettis updated the genre of the Western film, making it once again historically relevant and apt to converse with decolonization and the rise of the decolonizing global South.[5]

In Italian cinema, the parallel between spaghetti and neorealism helps clarify the word *sensibility*. Like the spaghetti Westerns, neorealism and its movies proved difficult to pin down. No sooner had a participant or observer created a definition than somebody else pointed to a whole group of important outliers.[6] Trying to end the impasse, Italian film historian Lino Miccichè argued that neorealism was not a well-defined filmic style, but rather a sensibility animating a generation of diverse filmmakers working in Italy immediately after World War II. Neorealism, Miccichè suggested, was most importantly a shared, ethical position "that has characterized a generation hungry for reality (to show) and of truths (to tell)."[7] In sum, neorealism's project was about recovering an authentic image of Italy after Fascist obscurantism: it was about making visible some of what fascism had tried to erase from film screens and culture.

Something similar, I shall argue, is at the center of the spaghetti sensibility. The rise of the formerly colonial possessions and "non-aligned nations" presented the so-called First World with a new panorama. As the West reencountered its former subjects, a revolution also occurred at the level of language. We know that lexicon changed as new words, like "non-aligned nations," "cultural imperialism," "Third World," or newly recoded ones like "the West," entered both the academic and common parlance.[8] As with the Western genre during the spaghetti revolution, new terms gained common usage while old ones, like the term *West*, were politically resignified.[9]

This is the cultural and political revolution that spaghettis represented. When applied to cinema this moniker shows that the historical turning point was also rendered with a linguistic and thematic revolution, one that many contemporary critics noticed, though few of them fully understood. Thus, I disagree with Ignacio Ramonet's famous contention that the "death throes of the American Western began in Bandung in 1955," though I fully agree that the famous gathering of twenty-nine African and Asian nonaligned independent and soon-to-be independent nations is an important chronological road marker for understanding the history of this genre.[10] The Atlantic Western did not die at Bandung. The spaghettis show that it kept on living, and kept transforming itself.

Proceeding from these points, this chapter will finally address the fact that the West's confrontation with colonization and the rise of the postcolonial world was destined to place many Americans and Europeans in an uncomfortable position, one fraught with feelings of complicity, guilt, and anxiety. After all, as Aimé Césaire argued in 1950, Nazi-Fascist massacres during World War II had taught Europe and the US a lesson that all colonized people already knew: racist doctrines are sooner or later bound to produce massive bloodshed. And the chickens, sometimes, come home to roost.[11]

Thus the spaghettis were not just an intellectual and aesthetic response to Euro-American colonialism, but also a recognition of the undeniable Euro-American complicity in it. At times this manifested as engaging Euro-American colonialism head-on, and at other times dodging the question and the burden in a cinema of masks and camouflage.

Spaghettis in the Midsixties

In his only completed feature film, *The Harder They Come* (1973), which he directed, wrote, and produced, Jamaican social activist, novelist, and filmmaker Perry Henzell analyzed the poverty and environmental degradation of the island via the real-life story of Ivanhoe "Ivan" Martin (Jimmy Cliff), a Jamaican gangster and musician. In this powerful statement of postcolonial radical politics and aspirations, Ivanhoe's mentor, Preacher, invites the young man to go to the movies at the Rialto Theater in Kingston. The film they go see is Sergio Corbucci's *Django*. Henzell edits Corbucci's film directly into his own movie. The screen cuts from Jamaica to the scene of the spaghetti Western where Django (Franco Nero) is besieged by dozens of thugs in the employ of racist landowner Major Jackson (Eduardo Fajardo). The gunslinger seems all but done in, and the audience, whose reactions Henzell documents almost ethnographically, reacts to his predicament with loud worry: "They are going to kill him!" someone screams out in the packed theater. Preacher knows better: "Heroes cannot die till the last reel," he shouts back. Preacher is a cinéphile, he knows how movies work and what they really mean.

The politically progressive logic of *Django*, the story of a pistolero confronting the gang led by the racist Major Jackson, is not lost on Preacher, or Henzell, and this is why both of them picked Corbucci's film for their purposes.[12] Through *Django* and other films the spaghetti sensibility afforded the two sides of the Celluloid Atlantic an opportunity to make sense of their positions within the power hierarchies of their tightly integrated world, a way of relating the "West" to the "non-West," and a specific narrative history of the contemporary world.

The Third World has been long posited as central to the history of the spaghetti Western and its chronology. Critics have argued that the Third World marks the second stage of the traditional spaghetti chronology. The chronology's first stage is constituted by the films clustered around the allegedly apolitical Leone's Westerns. In this interpretation the second stage is marked by the "Third Worldist" political spaghetti, which we will examine in this chapter, and the third by the move of the spaghetti film to becoming a parody of itself.[13]

Truthfully, there is more continuity than we usually allow in the spaghetti sensibility. As we have seen, a reappraisal of the decolonizing

A Cinema of Camouflage

world was already embodied in the "paulnewmanized" Mexican bandit of Ritts's seminal *The Outrage*, the good Latin American bandits of Boetticher, or the American south-of-the-border adventures of Gary Cooper in Robert Aldrich's *Vera Cruz*. This element remained in succeeding European Westerns like Leone's *For a Few Dollars More*, which we discussed in the previous chapter.

Things became more explicit as the decade and the genre revolution progressed. In the second half of the 1960s, in the high desert close to Tabernas in Almeria, Spain, Sergio Leone completed the most ambitious of his Westerns and the first chapter of his "Once Upon a Time" trilogy." *C'era una volta il West* (Once upon a Time in the West, 1968) was followed by *C'era una volta la rivoluzione* (Once Upon a Time in the Revolution), then renamed *Giù la testa* (Duck, You Sucker!, aka Once Upon a Time . . . a Revolution, 1971), and *C'era una volta in America* (Once Upon a Time in America, 1984). As Leone has suggested, *C'era una volta il West* worked as a genre compendium, calling it an "absolute Western" (Western assoluto) that summed up all the types and the topoi of the Western genre including the settling of the frontier, the deadly confrontation between horse and locomotive, and that between gunfighters.[14] It was, in the words of one of the film's screenwriters, Bernardo Bertolucci, "the first and only postmodern Western."[15]

Once Upon a Time in the West was also an expensive production—"two and ½ billion liras!" screamed Leone at the press conference introducing the film—mostly bankrolled by its world distributor, Paramount, producer Bino Cicogna of Euro International Film, and Leone himself. Clocking at almost three hours, the movie needed large crowds to recoup the huge budget investment. But these crowds never materialized. *Time* magazine called *Once Upon a Time* "Tedium in the Tumbleweeds." The movie flopped in the US and did only fair business (two billion liras) in Italy where critics at *Cinema Nuovo* lambasted it as "an interminable tale that tries to pass prolixity for majestic and significant narration."[16] American producers savagely shortened it, neutralizing its conscious grandiosity.[17]

The film's failure at the box office is not surprising. As both the *summa* of the conventions of the Hollywood classical Western and an anthology of the gestures that were upturning these norms, *Once Upon a Time in the West* worked in brilliant and original ways and, unbeknownst to most, showcased the highly sedimented depths of the

Celluloid Atlantic. Alongside a classical Hollywood star like Henry Fonda (the evil pistolero Frank), Leone displayed new Hollywood's Western stars like Charles Bronson (Harmonica) and Jason Robards (Cheyenne) along with European stars like Gabriele Ferzetti (Morton) and Paolo Stoppa (Sam) and the Franco-Italian-Tunisian Claudia Cardinale (Jill McBain) fresh from her star-making turn in Richard Brooks's *The Professionals* (1966).

Together with the classic themes of the American Western (the railroad, the stagecoach, the scenery of Monument Valley), Leone depicted the new spaghetti penchant for the operatic, the vindictive, and the violent. And though *Once Upon a Time in the West* seemed even less political than the dollar trilogy, the film was also a clear condemnation of capitalist greed by Leone and his screenwriters—two of whom, Bertolucci and Dario Argento, were card-carrying members of the Italian Communist Party.[18] By the time Leone completed *Once Upon a Time in the West*, ambitious spaghettis had displayed a more open kind of politics, one that went beyond Leone's or Aldrich's oblique but pointed skepticism about the gifts of capitalism.

Leone's critique, however, intensified and increasingly interacted with the forward march of the Third World. The director went back to Spanish locations and Mexican stories in his last Western film, *Duck, You Sucker!* The Celluloid Atlantic was again enshrined into the production history of the film. *Sucker* was supposed to have at its helm one of the most European directors of the Hollywood New Wave, Peter Bogdanovich. When Bogdanovich became unavailable, the directing job was assigned to one of the Hollywood practitioners of the spaghettis, Sam Peckinpah, and finally fell on Leone's shoulders when Peckinpah also backed out.[19] The resulting film clearly shows the revolutionary direction of the spaghettis. Prefaced by a belligerent phrase by Mao Tse-Tung ("The revolution is not a social dinner, a literary event, a drawing or an embroidery; it cannot be done with . . . elegance and courtesy. The revolution is an act of violence."), it whimsically opened to a close-up of bugs (an ironic citation of the opening of Peckinpah's Hollywood spaghetti, *The Wild Bunch*, 1969) climbing along a tree trunk. The irony becomes broader as urine rains on the insects. The yellow shower comes from a man figuring the Third World, Mexican Juan Miranda, played by Hollywood star in brownface Rod Steiger, an unlikely hero of the Mexican Revolution.[20]

Here Leone was directly referencing the spaghetti sensibility that embraced Mexico as a stand-in from the global South.

Leone was neither the most outspoken nor the most radical among the spaghetti practitioners. After all, his motto, "tutto è indiretto" (all is oblique), cautioned against making openly political films. But the turn in his Western cinema is indicative. As Austin Fisher argues, in the second half of the 1960s, the radical spaghetti Western "appropriated the commonplace depiction of aspirant Third World peasants and benevolent American interlopers, seeking quite literally to turn the film camera around and apply the Western's emphasis on regenerative violence to the postcolonial theses of Frantz Fanon."[21]

A New Form of Loudspeaker: Spaghettis' Intellectual Appeal

Together with Leone, by the mid-sixties many Atlantic filmmakers were becoming intrigued by the spaghettis that, although still largely despised by the critics, showed more and more purchase among intellectually astute and politically "woke" cineastes. Franco Solinas, the screenwriter we encountered in chapter 3 trying to revise the mythology of the good World War II Italian soldier, had become well established by the middle of the decade, having collaborated with director Gillo Pontecorvo on the two most famous Euro-American postcolonial manifestos, the Oscar-nominated *La battaglia di Algeri* (The Battle of Algiers, 1966) and the United Artists and Produzioni Europee Associate coproduction *Queimada* (Burn!, 1969), starring Marlon Brando. In those years, Solinas was alternating writing "blue ribbon" scripts like the one for *Algeri* with work on four spaghettis: *La resa dei conti* (The Big Gundown, 1966), *Quien Sabe?* (A Bullet for the General, 1967), *Il mercenario* (The Mercenary, 1968), and *Tepepa* (1969).

Solinas's genre and aesthetic flexibility still surprises most critics. For example, a sharp student of the writer's work like Giacomo Manzoli marvels that "the very skilled screenwriter of a world-famous masterpiece on the most fascinating anticolonial African revolution, this very man suddenly decides to spend two years of his life making four spaghetti Westerns."[22] And another one of Solinas's biographers

226   The Celluloid Atlantic

concludes that Solinas's work in the spaghetti genre was a parenthesis due more to chance than choice.[23]

Solinas's penchant for the spaghettis is, in fact, biographical. Born in the desolate poverty of the Mediterranean island of Sardinia, the scenarist saw his birthplace as an economic outlier excluded from the rest of industrialized Europe. Thus, Mexico and Sardinia could become interchangeable figurations of the non-West. Tellingly, as Solinas was drafting the idea for his first spaghetti, *La resa dei conti*, he outlined what became the chase between the Yankee bounty hunter Corbett and the Mexican bandit Cuchillo as taking place in his native Sardinia and involving an Italian cop (*carabiniere*) and a fugitive Sardinian bandit.[24]

But the attraction of the sophisticated intellectual for the genre of the spaghettis ran deeper than personal history. Rather, it was part of a long-standing quest for public relevance that had animated film intellectuals on both sides of the Atlantic. Spaghettis were popular, and Solinas argued that "political films are useful on the one hand if they contain a correct analysis of reality, and on the other, if they are made in such a way as to have that analysis reach the largest possible audience."[25] The notion of "the largest possible audience" is crucial here. It gestures toward the search for the "loudspeaker" connecting intellectuals and the masses, which was part of the democratic modernism of the 1930s intellectual Atlantic left. Solinas's interest in the Western is thus an echo of Cesare Pavese's admiration for American literature and cinema during the Fascist *ventennio*. Long after the completion of *Quien Sabe?*, the scriptwriter saw his spaghetti Westerns as set firmly between his work on *The Battle of Algiers* and the script for *Queimada* (Burn!, 1969), which Solinas cowrote with Giorgio Arlorio, who also worked with him on the story for another spaghetti, *Il mercenario* (The Mercenary, Sergio Corbucci, 1968). In *Quien Sabe?*, Solinas told film historians Goffredo Fofi and Franca Faldini, he had told the same story as in *The Battle of Algiers* and *Burn!*, the story of the oppressed confronting the imperialist oppressor. "On one side [is] Lou Castel (Bill Tate, El Niño), the 'civilized' American who respects the rules of the individualist game and not those of the game of history, and on the other side we have this sort of 'instinctive brute,' Volonté [El Chuncho]."[26] What was relevant to him, though, was that the Western could reach audiences hesitant to go see *The Battle of Algiers*.

A Cinema of Camouflage   227

The list of practitioners of politically and intellectually ambitious Westerns is, in fact, full of surprises. In Italy it comprises scenarists like Solinas and Giorgio Arlorio, sophisticated directors like Sergio Sollima, Florestano Vancini, and Carlo Lizzani, and former anti-Fascist Resistance fighter and alum of the cutting-edge intellectual magazine *Il Politecnico*, Giulio Questi. In addition, spaghettis appealed to literati like Pier Paolo Pasolini and highbrow actors like Lou Castel and Gian Maria Volonté.

In 1968 director Sollima, the author of a 1947 agile history of Hollywood cinema, may have been explaining Solinas's reasons when he told Patrick Morin, while he was editing the spaghetti Western *Corri, uomo, corri* (Run, Man, Run, 1968), that "for one thing the Western has always appealed to intellectuals and, as we know, to most Italians. Also, it gives me the possibility of using a fable, that is, a very popular story that can be understood by any public, to express myself. I can describe characters and introduce themes, dealing with the great problems of our times, and very controversial questions."[27] We need once again to stress the transatlantic nature of this intellectual attitude. Also in the United States, in this period, the Western was often visited by innovative and sophisticated filmmakers like Sam Peckinpah, Arthur Penn, Richard Brooks, Ralph Nelson, and Don Siegel, to name only a few, and actors like Paul Newman, Dustin Hoffman, Sidney Poitier, Candice Bergen, and Marlon Brando. The director of the American spaghetti *Hang 'Em High*, Ted Post, was an alumnus of the New York theater avant-garde, and he had worked with Erwin Piscator at the New School for Social Research. In 1947 he had staged a cutting-edge American Negro Theater version of *Rain* by John Colton.[28] He was by all accounts a refined student of the mise-en-scène.

Monte Hellman, the author of the cult classic *Two Lane Blacktop* (1971), signed two sophisticated, psychological Westerns in the mid-1960s, *Riding in the Whirlwind* (1966) and *The Shooting* (1966) with Jack Nicholson. Yet in *China 9, Liberty 37* (1978) Hellman embraced the transatlantic spaghetti aesthetics. The film had Sam Peckinpah in a cameo role, Warren Oates as Matthew Sebanek, the sadistic husband of Catherine Sebanek (British star Jenny Agutter), innumerable killings, and a famous sex scene between Fabio Testi (as Clayton Drumm, Catherine's lover) and Agutter. Again critics marveled: *American Film*

228 The Celluloid Atlantic

wrote that "no one who saw *Two Lane Black Top* could have envisaged that seven years later Hellman would be making a spaghetti Western with one Italian, one English, and one American star."[29]

Not unlike the work of these filmmakers, Solinas's efforts in the genre showed that he saw, in the words of the perceptive Italian critic Giacomo Manzoli,

> the Western as the terrain of the popular par excellence in the full and Gramscian interpretation of the term. [These films show] that he considered the Western as the genre whose rules determine that one was to use simple language to be understood by those who did not possess the sophisticated tools to decode [complex] messages, and yet [Solinas] did this in the conviction that it was possible to tell the history of the past, and of the present, its processes, and internal dynamics, as a Marxist teleology.[30]

The spaghetti was then the loudspeaker. But what was the message?

"I Am Reading Fanon"

Democratic modernism may have spurred some film intellectuals' investment in spaghettis, but their lasting purchase was less antifascism than Third Worldism. Like Solinas, Pontecorvo, or Brando, these filmmakers were part of a generation confronted before, during, and after the Vietnam War with the rise of the colonial world, and the spaghetti sensibility embodied a response to this epochal surge of peoples and ideas.

In 1963 director Carlo Lizzani, one of the stalwarts of the neorealist generation and a card-carrying member of the Communist Party, wrote in his diary that he was doing what many of his generation were currently doing: "I am reading Fanon."[31] Later in his diary, Lizzani acutely noted the intersection of the spaghetti Western with the debates about Italy and its Mezzogiorno, the Third World, the United States, and Hollywood genres.

> [The Western was] the most important of film genres. A repertoire of images that made it possible—just because of

the obvious temporal and spatial distance of these images from our own culture—to represent a set of emotions, of social unrests, of narrative *topoi* that had long waned because of external censorship and self-censorship. So many films had been imagined on the conflict between the [Italian industrialized] North and the [predominantly rural] Mezzogiorno; . . . the form of the Western finally allowed to perceive the weak [underclass] as victorious over the arrogant [elites]. It allowed the glorification of the poor peons and the damnation of the evil landowner. It was a tale, certainly, but a tale was better than nothing. The climate of 1968 and the upheaval of the third world did the rest.[32]

Lizzani and his cohort, most critics assume, were reading Fanon's *The Wretched of the Earth*.[33] A collection of essays written after Fanon's move from France to Algeria in 1953, *The Wretched of the Earth* was published posthumously in 1963 by *Présence Africaine* with an introduction by Jean-Paul Sartre. Confronted by the war and French repression, Fanon indicted colonialism's wounds on both its victims and the perpetrators. Among the ways out, Fanon famously suggested that the colonized should not discount violence, a tool the colonizers have used against them, but which the colonial subjects have mostly used against themselves.[34]

The radical Westerns created by Euro-American filmmakers in the second half of the sixties explicitly celebrated the right of the oppressed to rebel against their oppressors. They were a transatlantic call to action and that sentiment animated films like Corbucci's *Vamos a matar compañeros*, Brando-Solinas-Pontecorvo's *Queimada* (1967), Harold Jacob Smith and Alf Kjellin's *The McMasters* (1970), Ralph Nelson's *Soldier Blue* (1970), and Clint Eastwood's *The Outlaw Josey Wales* (1976).[35] Implicitly and sometimes explicitly these films argued that violence or active civil disobedience were the prerequisites for freedom, because the alternatives had led up to personal enslavement or the massacres of Sand Creek or My Lai.

Of course the Celluloid Atlantic was no monolith, but an interconnected zone with regional aesthetic, political, and cultural traditions. Austin Fisher remarks on this variance in the way American spaghettis dealt with liberationist violence. "While countercultural Westerns

230 The Celluloid Atlantic

in America, such as *Little Big Man* and *Soldier Blue*, expressed such political leanings through pacifism, reconciliation, and remorse, however, the political tenor of the equivalent Italian appropriations was altogether more extreme."[36] He is correct at least about the algebra of body counting. Italian spaghettis produced an exuberant numbers of corpses, but Atlantic differences, so ingrained in our culture for reasons we have examined, are easily exaggerated. *Hombre* (1967), a countercultural Western written and directed by Group Theater and Actors Studio alumni Irving Ravetch and Harriett Frank Jr. for their habitual director, Martin Ritt, opens with John "Hombre" Russell (Paul Newman) in redface makeup (Newman had been in Mexican brownface in Ritt's *The Outrage*, 1964, which we examined in chapter 5). When confronted by white racism in a saloon, Hombre and his Apache friends do not hesitate to take out their weapons and respond to white violence with their own armed response.

Less clear ideologically than *Hombre*, Clint Eastwood's revisionist Western *Josey Wales* also endorsed armed response against the state's encroachment on an individual's or population's right to self-determination. In *Josey Wales*, which Roger Ebert compared to Leone's "dollar Westerns," Comanche chief Ten Bears (Will Sampson) and Josey Wales (Clint Eastwood), a renegade Confederate soldier chased by the Union army, decide to resist the government's efforts to deny freedom to them and their people. And they succeed. Wales ultimately kills the corrupt soldier Terrill (Bill McKinney) after torturing him by firing four six-guns at him filled with blanks. Protected by his people, Wales gets away with his righteous murder.

In *The McMasters* (Alf Kjellin, 1970), well-meaning pacifist liberal Spencer (Dane Clark) is mercilessly killed by the racist thugs led by one-armed, former Confederate officer Kolby, interpreted by Jack Palance, who was back in Hollywood after interpreting heavies in many seminal spaghettis in Europe. Benjie McMasters (Brock Peters), the black man who is the righteous owner of the land coveted by the thugs, chooses another way to respond. He accepts the advice of the Native Americans, led by White Feather (David Carradine in redface) who counsel "defensive violence." And violence carries the day in this underappreciated film.

Not all acts of resistance need be violent. At the end of *Soldier Blue*, Onus (Peter Strauss) refuses to rejoin the Union army after Colonel Iverson (John Anderson), a fictionalized version of the historical architect of the Sand Creek massacre, John Chivington, perpetrates a duplicate of the 1864 massacre of mostly unarmed Cheyenne by Union troops. The female protagonist, Kathy Maribel Lee (Candice Bergen), who had been abducted by the Native Americans, also chooses sides and pays for her choice. She dons Native American garb, stays with her adoptive people, and shares their fate of deportation and imprisonment. These choices, albeit unarmed, assert the rejection of obedience, which is no longer construed as a virtue. Onus and Kathy actively defend the native people and accept the loss of their privileges and personal liberty as the consequence of their rebellion.

Whether the response was violence or overt disobedience, Fanonist Third Worldism radically shaped the spaghetti Westerns and pushed against the narrative confines of the genre. Some film-makers, like Damiano Damiani, the director of *Quien Sabe?*, even questioned whether their films could still be considered Westerns.[37] New cynicism, new locales, and new narrative strategies abandoned clear-cut moralities and happy endings. *Quien Sabe?* was a story of male bonding and train bombing set during the Mexican Revolution that featured two politically progressive Italian stars, Gian Maria Volonté and Lou Castel in the roles respectively of El Chuncho and El Niño. The Third Worldism of Solinas's script was evident in the film's focus on Mexico proper rather than the United States. Tate, aka El Niño, is an American gun trader profiting from the war. He strikes a deal with El Chuncho, a local bandit who slowly radicalizes. After he witnesses El Niño's contempt for the people of Mexico, El Chuncho becomes unwilling to collaborate with the American, nor does he want to follow him back to the United States to enjoy the fruits of their crimes. Instead, he shoots El Niño in the belly as he is boarding a US-bound train. Apprehended by the Mexican police, El Chuncho escapes, but not before tossing his bag of money to a Mexican beggar and telling him to use it to buy dynamite. Bandit though he is, El Chuncho is the hero of the story. The gringo is bad, and he is called "niño," the child, reversing the usual infantilization of America's southern neighbors at the hands of American directors and writers.

Classical Western images are present but their meaning and diegesis are often reversed. Allusions to the train robbery of *The Great Train Robbery* (Edwin Porter, 1903) and the railroad of *The Iron Horse* (John Ford, 1924) were still at the center both in *Quien Sabe?*

and in Leone's *Once Upon a Time in the West*. This time the criminals were the protagonists and the train did not bring civilization, but only *federales* to be dispatched, money to be grabbed and used for *la causa*, and an ambiguously defined capitalist modernity, in Leone's film, which demanded opposition or at least radical critique.

Regional differences did exist. The Italians exuberantly embraced violence. "Let's Go Kill, Comrades!," exploded the shrill song (music by Ennio Morricone and lyrics by Sergio Corbucci) that doubled as the title for Sergio Corbucci's 1970 film *Vamos a matar compañeros!* But who was to be killed? Corrupted local elites, of course, and the spaghettis liberally dispensed death on Mexican generals or corrupt officials north and south of the border. The genre, however, made clear that Mexican elites were often Yankee lackeys and collaborators; European elites were also cited less than American robber barons as the root cause of Mexico's poverty and mayhem. Overall, however, spaghettis were fair-minded. American countercultural spaghettis were not kind to the US Army and Italian spaghettis do feature nasty European villains—like the two French pistoleros in Sergio Sollima's *Corri, uomo, corri* (1968), a product of Napoleon III's imperialist adventures, or the sadistic German Baron von Schulenberg (Gérard Herter), the bodyguard of the American banker Brokston in *La resa dei conti*.

Revolutions and dynamite connected the two shores (Mexico and Ireland) in the second decade of the twentieth century in Leone's *Duck, You Sucker!*, which documented the Mexican exploits of an Irish separatist, John H. Mallory (James Coburn). Italian actor Franco Nero made his "*spaghetti*" name by playing an American pistolero stranded south of the border in *Django* (Sergio Corbucci, 1966). And there were well-meaning European gunmen siding with Mexican righteous rebels like the "Swede" in *Compañeros*, the Polish gun-for-hire Kowalski in *Il mercenario*, and the Russian Prince Dmitri Vassilovich Orlowsky in Duccio Tessari's *Don't Turn the Other Cheek* (1974), who was accompanied by Irish journalist and boxing champion Mary O'Donell (Lynn Redgrave).

In this chaotic universe, only a few rules were set: America was not superior to Mexico and local and Euro-American elites were likely to be corrupted, while the Mexican campesinos were almost always the victims. A Third Worldist state of mind is visible in the two spaghetti Westerns Carlo Lizzani directed in 1966 and 1967: *Un fiume di dollari* (The Hills Turn Red, 1966) and *Requiescant* (1967). Mexico is explicitly referenced in both films. As in a Budd Boetticher Western, *Un fiume di dollari* is a vendetta story that pits thieves against each other, with Mexico as the only way out of North American misery. The first shot of the film, whose plot is largely derived from Anthony Mann's *The Man from Laramie* and Brando's *One-Eyed Jacks*, makes this clear. After the credits, Lizzani frames Jerry Brewster (Thomas Hunter), a former Confederate soldier, riding a wagon by a milepost marking "three miles from the Mexican border." Mexico represents the liberation, but freedom will have to wait. Jerry has stolen government money and he does not make it to Mexico, because he is intercepted by sadistic Union troops who seem straight out of post-Reconstruction Southern redemptionist literature. Imprisoned and tortured by these thugs, Jerry is also abandoned by his partner, Ken Milton (Nando Gazzolo), who has absconded and invested their loot on a ranch just north of Austin, Texas. The rest of the story is, of course, about Jerry's rightful revenge.[38]

Third Worldism is more explicit in *Requiescant*. Reminiscing about the film, Lizzani called it "an apology" for Third World revolutions and an analysis of the relation of the Italian South ("Mezzogiorno") to those of anticolonial social movements abroad. "The problem of the peasant revolution concerned us as the 'Mezzogiorno d'Italia' was an area of conflict between land rich and land poor farmers, etc.," he told the interviewer.[39]

This note struck a chord with Italian filmmakers. Lizzani remembers that his friend Pier Paolo Pasolini, avant-garde public intellectual, queer activist, writer, and director, was immediately on board with the *Requiescant* project.[40] Critically neglected, Pasolini's participation in *Requiescant* fit the development of his sensibility and his concern for the non-West. Though already famous as a poet, novelist, journalist, screenwriter, and director, Pasolini enthusiastically gave Lizzani suggestions while playing a relatively minor character, the revolutionary priest Juan. Screenwriter Adriano Bolzoni remembers that Pasolini "took his role very seriously and tried to explain to me what revolutionary Mexico was about. To avoid the daily sermon . . . I recited to him the Plan of Ayutla [*sic*], I gave him a record [with the folk song] 'Adelita' and I guaranteed him that I [was ready to] inject the equivalent of [Emiliano] Zapata in ten more films."[41]

For Pasolini, Luca Caminati notes, "[Antonio] Gramsci's ashes, grown cold among the European proletarians and subproletarians, are blazingly hot in the rebellions of the Third World."[42] It is then logical and not "by chance" that progressive Lizzani and Pasolini participated in the spaghetti revolution.[43] To the Communist daily, *L'Unità*, which had often questioned the value of the Western genre, Pasolini opined that the spaghetti Westerns were often "good cinema" and that he loved the role of the Mexican guerrilla priest his friend Lizzani had offered him.[44]

Requiescant is a critically neglected, truly Fanonist Western. A leading member of the European film avant-garde, actor Lou Castel (Requiescant), fresh from his star-making turn in Marco Bellocchio's psychoanalytical manifesto, *I pugni in tasca* (1965), brandishes guns in defense of Mexican campesinos. He fights an evil rich man, C. B. Ferguson, a former Union officer who has massacred rebellious Mexican farmers and is interpreted by an American, Mark Damon. The peasants are led by a priest, Don Juan (Pier Paolo Pasolini), and are all interpreted by Italian actors and extras, including Pasolini's favorite thespians, Ninetto Davoli (in heavy brownface) and Sergio Citti.

Requiescant is also, front and center, a product of the Celluloid Atlantic's radical revision of the Western genre. Lizzani's hero enters San Antonio, the "border town" dominated by Ferguson, on horseback, contemplating all the establishments owned by Ferguson. It is an overt homage to a sequence in *Buchanan Rides Again*.[45] More clearly than Boetticher, however, Lizzani wanted his film to serve as a Fanonist morality tale. Spurred on by the radical preaching of Juan, the Mexican peasants rebel against their oppressor, who is executed on the same spot where he massacred many of them, including the entire family of Requiescant.

A Second Kind of Fanonism: A Cinema of Masks and Camouflage

Fanonism is not only one of the main inspirations of the spaghetti sensibility, but also a useful means to construe its more convoluted gestures. That is to say, as a theoretician of the world—both psychic and material—that the colonial process engendered, Fanon may be fruitfully used *to interpret* the very sensibility he inspired. A Fanonist lens reveals the spaghetti sensibility in ways less obvious and less overtly political than critics have allowed.

A Cinema of Camouflage

Fanon posits the inauthentic at the root of the culture created by colonialism. This culture, the mind of colonialism, he argues, was a captive of inauthentic relations. It was what another Afro-Caribbean intellectual, musician Bob Marley, invited his listeners to consider in his powerful "Redemption Song" (1979). Following Fanon, Marley urged that people need to "emancipate yourselves from mental slavery / None but ourselves can free our minds." For all its rejection of violence, the echo of Fanon is strong in Marley's words. The Fanonist call for a regeneration through violence was a call to personal authenticity, the colonial subject's regaining her or his humanity and shaking off the psychological constraints of colonization. Violence was a means to achieve clarity, emancipation from mental slavery, a way out of colonialism's straitjacket. Until liberation, for Marley and Fanon, the inauthentic was the essence of the colonized world and mind.

Alongside his rejection of any inherent superiority of the West and his novel attention to the rights of the Third World, the metaphor of makeup and masks constituted Fanon's interpretation of the colonial mindset. *Black Skins White Masks*, written ten years before *Wretched of the Earth*, while Fanon still resided in the *metropole*, describes the colonial mind and can serve as an interpretative tool of the spaghetti sensibility.

Possibly explaining its less central position than *Wretched* in contemporary debates, *Black Skins* is more about the world that colonialism made than it is about its upturning. In *Black Skins*, Fanon suggested that colonialism had created a mystified reality, an illusion where authentic experience has become impossible. Seduced by colonialism, the oppressed have embraced the mask of the oppressor: they have mimicked his or her manners, mannerisms, accent: "Out of the blackest part of my soul, through the zone of hachures, surges up this desire to be suddenly *white* [in original]. I want to be recognized not as *black* but as *white*."[46]

Fanon has been criticized as pathologizing blackness, but as Kwame Anthony Appiah has noted, *Masks* also foregrounded Fanon's doubts about any celebration of contemporary blackness that ignored its genealogy and imbrication with a history of effective injustice and violence.[47] What interests me here, however, is the theorization of masking and inauthenticity vis-à-vis the radical spaghetti. Fanon suggests that the pathology of the mask affects *all* facets of colonial and postcolonial relations: "Whatever the field we studied, we were struck by the fact that *both* the black man, slave to his inferiority, and the white man, slave to his superiority, behave along neurotic lines."[48] Colonialism pushed the colonizer, too, into inauthentic behaviors. Not only did this happen when he or she enacted superiority, it also occurred when the colonized tried to resist colonialism. Because of their tainted upbringing, these actions risked remaining performative rather than substantive.

To paraphrase and slightly extend Fanon's interpretation, I argue that at the foundation of the spaghetti is the mask worn by the West in an attempt to impersonate the non-West, the colony, and thus regain humanity and innocence. "The black man wants to be white. The white man is desperately trying to achieve the rank of [hu]man. . . . The white man is locked in his whiteness. The black man in his blackness."[49] Pushed by colonialism, some of the oppressed took up the mannerisms of their victimizers but, as importantly, some of those who were by virtue of birth in the ranks of the oppressors embraced the mask of their victims. Insofar as *blackness and whiteness are the products of the unjust colonialist system*, they both are, Fanon suggests, "alienated and mystified."[50]

In the final section of this chapter, I will examine this important component of the spaghetti sensibility. Following Fanon, I argue that spaghettis' insistence on masks and masquerade revealed a product of the West wrestling with colonialism and its legacy. Remarkably, while embracing Fanon, the spaghetti was producing images that were the opposite of real and authentic.

The two, apparently contradictory, aspects of spaghetti aesthetics—its direct and violent engagement with contemporary political issues and the distancing theatricality of its mise-en-scène—were connected because its politics was ultimately ambiguous, as they called for Third Worldist rebellion while obscuring relevant responsibilities of the "First World" in the oppression of the "Third." In the spaghettis, the exculpatory masquerade coexisted with earnest endorsements of anticolonial rebellion and anger, and this explains how spaghettis could be attractive both to the Jamaican gangsters of *The Harder They Come* and to white Euro-American intellectuals and filmmakers.

Imagining oneself as a victim has long been one way to dodge conscious or unconscious guilt. It is a cliché that during the 1960s and 1970s the scions of Euro-American bourgeoisie on their way to political extremism painted themselves as besieged communards facing death on the barricades. According to the attentive portrayal of the Italian extreme left group Potere Operaio (Workers' Power, aka PotOp) by Aldo Grandi, its members embraced both Fanon and the spaghetti Westerns. One of PotOp's leaders, Valerio Morucci, who was later to found the armed revolutionary group Brigate Rosse (Red Brigades), was especially fond of the genre. According to his friends, he even coiffed himself like Franco Nero's character in the Fanonist manifesto by Sergio Corbucci, *Vamos a matar compañeros!* (Compañeros, 1970), the story of a blond European swede, Yodlaf Peterson (Nero), who joins the Mexican peasant revolution. Morucci was not alone. Many, mostly male, PotOp leaders loved the spaghettis, sang their catchy musical themes, and fantasized about their violent crime scenes.[51] Identifying with the spaghetti heroes, real *brigatisti* were obviously embracing their violent revolutionary logic. Yet Morucci was not hoping to take over the role of the many historical Mexican rebels, but that of a fictional European fighting alongside them: an exception to colonialist cruelty. There was in this gesture, and in these films, an attempt at absolving parts of the West from the responsibility of the massacre. "There are among us, some who reject the violence of colonialist oppression!," Morucci implies. But injecting a good, anticolonialist Westerner into the story was only one of the ways through which the West attempted to dodge a blanket condemnation of itself. It was by impersonating the Third World that the First absolved itself.

This move was at times met with objections and some measure of ridicule in the cinema of the global South. The cinema of the "Third World," what Octavio Getino and Fernando Solanas called "Third Cinema" as opposed to the cinema of Hollywood and the European avant-garde, sometimes directly called out the cinema of the First for its lack of authenticity.[52] In his *Antonio das Mortes* (1969), Glauber Rocha expressed his engagement with both the spaghetti Western and those of John Ford.[53] The film relates the story of Antonio (Maurício do Valle), the hired gun of a rich, corrupt landowner, who reverses himself and sides with the people against their oppressor. Martin Scorsese notes that Rocha's film "took elements of the Italian Western, it took elements of the translation of the Westerns by Leone."[54] Mauricio do Valle is unmistakably dressed like Volonté in *Quien Sabe?* and behaves similarly, finding his truth and his redemption at the end of a gun.

Rocha's film is also different from the spaghetti of the Celluloid Atlantic. Much more than Leone, Rocha was interested in emphasizing theatricality: Antonio's story is both the plot of the movie *and* the plot of a play performed by actors on the village square in front of a modern-day audience. Antonio is both a gun-for-hire and its self-conscious enactment, a character besieged by his enemies and a representation of a gunslinger besieged by the modernity of oil rigs and the highway trucks that collide with, and deny, the mythical truth of the mise-en-scène.

The film confused critics like Roger Greenspun of the *New York Times* who saw *Antonio das Mortes* as a failed attempt at "transforming reality into theater and reading history as myth." Antonio, Greenspun noted, "combines fragments as disparate as the traditional Western hired gun, the exploitation of the masses, and the story of St. George and the dragon. And the theater, which imitates Brechtian theater, promotes the themes and rhythms of the folk by means of the methods and sophistications of the committed modern filmmaker."[55] Yet Rocha's was an important intervention as it showed, like Fanon, that the inauthentic lay at the center of the spaghetti sensibility.

Figure 6.1. A homage and a critique of the spaghetti Western: Glauber Rocha's *Antonio das Mortes* (1969). *Source*: Author's collection.

A Cinema of Camouflage

The move toward camouflage had different causes. Extending the cavalier attitude of the classical Western to historical detail, the spaghetti sensibility called attention to its inauthenticity in various ways. As is often noted, spaghetti actors and directors frequently used pseudonyms, whether in homage—in *Per un pugno di dollari*, Sergio Leone became Bob Robertson in homage to his father's pseudonym of Roberto Roberti—or to disguise one's presence in a movie of dubious quality. For his first spaghetti ("un filmetto . . . piuttosto da dimenticare"), Lizzani called himself Lee W. Beaver, while Florestano Vancini signed his *I lunghi giorni della vendetta* (Long Days of Vengeance, 1967) as Stan Vance. Anglophone impersonations may have been meant to confuse provincial spectators as to the origins of the films and their authors. The lower the budget of the film, the more it was necessary to Americanize the name of its director, or its star, in the hope that an American pedigree would lend a shred of prestige to an inferior work. But, aside from the more naïve spectators, quite a few may have seen through it. This tactic was acceptable because camouflage was the stylistic marker of the genre.

An explicitly Fanonist mask·was visible in the way the spaghetti sensibility reshaped actors' personae. Within a few months, Lou Castel, fresh from his star-making turn as a psychotic bourgeois youth in Marco Bellocchio's *I pugni in tasca* (1965), impersonated a blond, cold-blooded Yankee in *Quien Sabe?* and then played the role of a Mexican gunslinger in *Requiescant*. In Lizzani's film, Requiescant is unable to pass for white even before learning about his Mexican origins: he is called "pelle scura" (dark skin) and deemed "too swarthy" by one of Ferguson's thugs. Neither the cruel blondness of El Niño nor the swarthy Third Worldism of "pelle scura" were easy for Castel to portray. Born in Colombia to a Swedish father and an Irish mother, Castel had moved to Rome with his mother when she found work in the local film industry. The blond Castel was almost preternaturally pale-complexioned. Schooled as an actor at the prestigious Centro Sperimentale di Cinematografia in Rome, at twenty-two, his youth and delicate, fair features had made him a credible scion of the Italian bourgeoisie in *I pugni in tasca*. The same physical attributes, however, made him a rather implausible Mexican peon and too elfish to be a credible pistolero. In 1993, in the *Village Voice* review of the film's video release, Neil Strauss noted that discordance: in *Quien Sabe?*, Castel looked "as cool as Richie Cunningham in the role of the silent gringo hero."[56]

240 The Celluloid Atlantic

Castel was not the only one out of place in the Mexico of the spaghetti sensibility. During the shooting of *Requiescant*, *L'Unità* published a photo of Pasolini, ironically titled "Pasolini il guerrigliero" (Pasolini the guerrilla) in full Mexican rebel attire on the set of the film.[57] Pasolini was older and swarthier than Castel and he was possibly more credible as a Mexican. Yet the photo of the well-known, famously dapper public intellectual in rags, rifles, and guerrilla garb elicited less an impression of authenticity than a sense of carnivalesque masquerade: like many of the spaghetti Western characters, Pasolini was inhabiting a character he would love to be, but wasn't.

Those who could pushed the masking to the limit. The success of Gian Maria Volonté in Leone's first two Westerns owed much to the actor's impersonation of the stereotypes of Mexican-ness. Prior to his collaboration with Leone, Volonté had mostly worked in theater and for TV, his roles drawn from classical repertoire. He had been Romeo in a well-regarded staging of Shakespeare's tragedy and collected accolades for playing Rogozing in the Radio Televisione Italiana version of Fyodor Dostoyevsky's *The Idiot* in 1959. His film debut was as the Jewish academic Samuel Braunstein in Duilio Coletti's *Under Ten Flags* (1961), and before working for Leone he had also played the role of a young middle-class man, Piero Benotti, in Valerio Zurlini's *La ragazza con la valigia* (Girl with a Suitcase, 1961) and the role of the heroic trade unionist Salvatore Carnevale murdered by the Mafia in *Un uomo da bruciare* (A Man for Burning, 1962) by Valentino Orsini and the Taviani brothers. Immersed in the spaghetti sensibility, Volonté and Leone pushed the otherness of his screen persona to the limits. In *A Fistful of Dollars* he plays Ramon, a bourgeois criminal and Spanish creole who has adorned his home with European artifacts and armor to show his Old World pedigree. In *For a Few Dollars More*, Volonté's character was a drug-driven Mexican peasant. Indio was—almost literally—Ramon on crack cocaine. His character's name, "Indio," gestured toward a Mayan presence, even predating Mexico and the Spanish conquest.

As the spaghetti turned left, Leone's original Mexican, Volonté, became even more disguised, an iconic form of ethic stereotype. In *Quien Sabe?*, he played El Chuncho and his Mexican-ness was made even more irrepressible than in *For a Few Dollars More*. When at the end of the film, the Yankee pistolero Tate gives El Chuncho his share of the loot, Chuncho sees the possibility of trusting him: maybe it was

A Cinema of Camouflage 241

time he went north with Tate, to finally enjoy life as a rich man. "It is about time you looked like one," the impeccably appointed Yankee sarcastically tells him, as he proposes to make the Mexican bandit's appearance consonant with his new economic status.

Damiani, Castel, and Volonté made the most of this important scene. It is no longer about a simple transformation. It is the story of an impossible transubstantiation. The mask is so ingrained in the body of the character that it can no longer be separated from him. Tate first accompanies Chuncho to a barber shop to tame his curly hair. Niño looks on, satisfied, but Volonté twists Chuncho's hirsute face into a desperate stare. They then go on to a haberdashery, where Chuncho is unable to stand still. He sees the tailor as a menace. Becoming Western is a matter of learning to read the signs that distinguish threats from treats, but Chuncho fails the test. The morning after his ordeal, as Tate and Chuncho meet at the station for the last, fatal time, Chuncho is still unable to maneuver around in his fancy striped suit. His beard still shows. Once transformed by cinema into the Mexican rebel, the Italian upper-class actor cannot reclaim his Western self. He dresses like a "white" man but the clothes fit him badly. By transforming himself into a civilized man, El Chuncho has lost his gracefulness; he has become awkward. When he arrives at the station, El Niño laughs at him and sets his lapel straight. Compared to the impeccably dressed Yankee, Chuncho's body is too rough for the gentle Western fabric and he is on the verge of exploding out of his clothes and regaining his authentic, Mexican self. After killing Tate and escaping from the police, like a politicized Incredible Hulk, Chuncho tears off his clothes, his hat and jacket flying in the air like deposed shackles. The transformation, the mask, it seems, cannot be reversed.

In Sergio Sollima's *Corri, uomo, corri* (Run Man, Run, 1968) the Mexican hero, bandit Cuchillo (Tomas Milian), was given almost the same scene as El Chuncho. In *Corri*, scripted by Sollima and by a professional historian, Pompeo de Angelis, Cuchillo and Nathanael Cassidy (Franco-Irish actor Donald O'Brien) mirror *Quien Sabe?*'s El Chuncho and El Niño as unlikely allies in search of a bounty. The characters' clothes are still central to the story. Dressed in the stereotypical Mexican peasant garb as he rides across the screen right after the film's credits (splendidly designed by Igino Lardani), Cuchillo swaps his rags twice: the first time when he is enlisted by

Figure 6.2. Masks and haberdasheries. The Mexican bandit "El Chuncho" sartorially confronts the Yankee bandit "El Niño" (Lou Castel) in the finale of *Quien Sabe?* (1967). *Source*: Author's collection.

Penny Bannington (Linda Veres) as a preacher in the Christian army, and the second when Penny, revealed as the daughter of the mayor of Burton City, Texas, wants to make him respectable. Cuchillo hates both transformations because they represent ill-fitting social roles, the bluenose preacher and the bourgeois citizen. In a studiously protracted scene, he ditches his jacket and trousers as he makes up his mind to reject Penny's plans of upward social mobility and break up with her. Once again comfortable in his "authentic" Mexican ragged clothes, Cuchillo stays loyal to his low social status, rejoins the revolution, and goes back to his Mexican lover, Dolores (Chelo Alonso).

Like Gian Maria Volonté's, the screen persona of Tomas Milian was profoundly altered by the spaghetti sensibility. Although born in Cuba, it is Milian's screen persona within the Atlantic filmic discourse that is of essence here. By the time he had become Cuchillo, the Actors Studio–trained actor and US citizen was not associated with Latin American, but with Italian or American roles. Sollima recounts that there was, in fact, some studio resistance to his casting choice. In Italy, Sollima told an interviewer, Milian was famous as an Italian actor, the interpreter of sophisticated films that Sollima disparaged as "products of fake actors' studio."[58]

Milian had never wanted to play Latino roles. After training with Lee Strasberg at the Actors Studio, the actor moved to Rome to make the most of the connections offered by the Celluloid Atlantic. He had

A Cinema of Camouflage 243

already been typecast in Hollywood, playing, for example, Juan Ortega, a Puerto Rican man unjustly accused of murder, in the "Fiesta at Midnight" (1958) episode of the series *Decoy* (1957–1958). A cerebral actor, Milian wanted to work with Italian cutting-edge directors. There were not many Latinos in films that focused on Italian society in the midst of the economic boom, and the actor avoided ethnic types until he landed the role of José Gómez in Alberto Martin's Italo-American-Spanish spaghetti, *El precio de un hombre* (Bounty Killer, aka The Ugly Ones, 1966), immediately before his role in a Sollima film, *La resa dei conti*. His first Italian roles were in the privileged, upper-class mold: he was the bourgeois Moretto in *La notte brava* (Big Night, 1959) by Mauro Bolognini, the murderous English professor Thomas Premian in Lattuada's noir *L'imprevisto* (The Unforeseen, 1961), and interpreted two young, bored, upper-class men in Francesco Maselli's indictments of the Italian silver spoon set, Alberto de Matteis in *I delfini* (Silver Spoon Set, 1960) and Michele in *Gli indifferenti* (Time of Indifference, 1964) from the novel by Alberto Moravia. He was an Italian officer in Greece, Lieutenant Gaetano Martino, in Zurlini's *Le soldatesse* (The Camp Followers, 1965), and Count Ottavio in the episode "Il lavoro," directed by Luchino Visconti, of the episode film *Boccaccio '70* (1962). Just before he donned his Mexican Western clothes he interpreted one of the heavyweights of the Italian Renaissance, Raffaello Sanzio (the artist Raphael), in Carol Reed's Euro-American coproduction, *The Agony and the Ecstasy* (1965). Milian told an interviewer that it was "a great challenge to play these vulgar and loose mouthed characters [like Cuchillo]—the opposite of Antonioni and Bertolucci['s characters]."[59] It represented a huge change for an actor who was, in fact, introverted and intellectual.

When Milian entered the spaghetti territory, his makeup radically changed.[60] The screen persona of a handsome, upper-class, young, and refined Westerner became a brownface made up in sweaty canvas shirts revealing a swarthy, hairy torso that went along with dusty bandanas trying to contain his long, pitch-black hair. He became José Gómez in Alberto Martin's *El precio de un hombre* and "Cuchillo" in Sollima's *La resa dei conti* (The Big Gundown 1966), a role he reshaped and reprised in Sollima's *Corri uomo, corri* in 1968.

In Sollima's *Faccia a faccia* (Face to Face, 1967) Milian was still heavily Mexicanized as the Texas outlaw Solomon "Beauregard" Bennet. This splendid film plays, tongue in cheek, with the "colorism" and the Fanonist mask of the spaghetti sensibility. Milian squares off as a curiously moral bandit against the monstrous Professor Brad Fletcher (Gian Maria Volonté) who is, perversely, a historian from New England afflicted by tuberculosis and a paleness that is a physical manifestation of his interior "whiteness." The film plays on the recent history of both actors' screen bodies and their significance within the color codes of the spaghetti sensibility. After his role in *Quien Sabe?* Volonté is curiously "whitened," his color and upbringing doing nothing to prevent his slow metamorphosis into a cold-blooded and bloodthirsty monster. Milian, on the other hand, is in full brownface, which is visually revealed as a positive in relation to the professor's "whiteness."[61]

Milian fully understood the stereotype that lay at the foundation of makeup: "As far as the camouflage (*camuffamento*), today that I have come into my own and I am free to express my opinion, I can say that I would have liked to use a different makeup, but they set me up like that, in what was a little absurd way, but I guess at the time it worked."[62] Yet by the end of the sixties Milian had re-created himself as a socio-ethnic type, the opposite of the refined Italian he had played at the beginning of his career. By then, the association between Milian and the spaghetti sensibility was obvious, and transatlantic in nature. In his sophisticated meditation on cinema,

Figure 6.3. Gian Maria Volonté in *Faccia a facia* (1967). *Source*: Author's collection.

Figure 6.4. Tomas Milian in *Faccia a facia* (1967). *Source*: Author's collection.

The Last Movie (1971), Dennis Hopper imagined a filmmaking crew shooting a spaghetti Western in Peru. Hopper recruited Milian for the part of the local priest.

By then the spaghetti revolution was approaching its end and Milian's brownface mask was so thick that it could become a parody of itself. In Sergio Corbucci's colorist manifesto, *Il bianco, il giallo e il nero* (The White, the Yellow, and the Black, 1975), Milian became the icon of nonwhiteness, where the brownface turned into a conscious parody of itself: the actor donned a black wig, yellow powder, and a kimono to interpret Sakura, a Japanese migrant to California. This also helps complicate our understanding of the third phase of the spaghetti Western that is not separate in themes or authors from the second.

Milian's mask also made him a box office sensation. By the end of the spaghetti season, this mask was so stable that the actor could parlay it, untouched, into other genres. In 1976, the actor became a professional impersonator of proletarian gangsters in *Il trucido e lo sbirro* (Free Hand for a Tough Cop, Umberto Lenzi), where he played a thug turned police informer, "er Monnezza" (literally "garbage"), and in *Squadra antiscippo* by Bruno Corbucci (The Cop in Blue Jeans, 1976) as undercover police inspector Nico Giraldi, aka Nico "er pirata" (Nico the Pirate). The latter film begot a number of sequels, the so-called Squadre (police squad) cycle,[63] mostly directed by the

246 The Celluloid Atlantic

brother of Sergio Corbucci, Bruno. The transatlantic connection was still present because the "Squadre" cycle and both the characters of "Monnezza" and "er Pirata" were modeled after Al Pacino's head-turning role in *Serpico* (1973). Milian used the Serpico model to stress the procedure of masking, of turning oneself into someone else, which had been as at the center of the spaghetti sensibility. Like his American counterpart, Milian played an undercover cop who is famous for his ability to masquerade as a member of the Roman criminal *lumpenproletariat*.

The mask of Nico, or for that matter of "er Monnezza," were direct descendants of the spaghetti brownface. "The Monnezza and Nico er pirata are close relatives to those Westerns and to Cuchillo," Milian stated. "Er Monnezza is just a Roman Cuchillo with very little updating."[64] The movies were parading this filiation. *Il Trucido e lo sbirro* begins in a prison with er Monnezza (Milian) watching a spaghetti Western together with other inmates.

The seamless transfer from Mexican *peon* to member of the Roman lumpenproletariat is telling and has larger political and cultural implications than a solely filmic or textual reading of the spaghettis would allow. The role of the mask in the spaghetti sensibility revealed that the latter was also about infra-regional relations and the relative apportionment of responsibility in the West. "The black man wants to be white. The white man is desperately trying to achieve the rank of [hu]man," Fanon had written.[65]

Undergirding the masking of Western actors as Mexican peasants and the linkage of Monnezza and Cuchillo was the idea that Mexican and Roman underclasses were interchangeable historical personae with related filmic physiognomies. Cuchillo and Monnezza came from places that the spaghetti sensibility posited were so similar as to be interchangeable: like Sardinia and Mexico in Solinas's work, the Mexico of the early 1900s and the Italian national capital after the economic boom generated by the Marshall Plan were part of a whole. But were they really? Or was the spaghetti turning the contemporary Roman outskirts into a Third World that Rome, as the capital of the Italian state, had oppressed and colonized? The Rome of Nico Monnezza was also graced by the Axum obelisk, the Ethiopian national monument, that Fascist Italy had stolen from Ethiopia in 1937.

Italy did not return the column until the twenty-first century, in 2005, well after the spaghetti sensibility had run its course. Ethiopian

Figure 6.5. Axum obelisk in Rome in 2001. *Source*: Author's collection.

demands, bolstered by the 1947 United Nations formal support, went unheeded, even after 1948 when Italy agreed to return most of its loot. But nobody in the West had an interest in pressing Italy too hard about its colonial past. While Cinecittà produced Third Worldist films, a symbol of the unpaid debts of colonialism graced its new location in the national capital.[66]

The masking of the Western actor in the guise of the Mexican speaks to the role of the inauthentic in the spaghetti Western sensibility. In many ways it was exactly what Fanon had suggested: colonialism created a set of preordained, inauthentic behaviors. The colonized adopted the mask of the colonist. Onscreen, and elsewhere too, the colonizers masked themselves as the colonized.

It is here, then, that the spaghetti sensibility may relate to a context larger than cinema. Ten years after the creation of the "Third World," another binary term, cultural imperialism, had come to the fore. This term allowed parts of the First World to assume a colonial role, as victims of American cultural expansionism. John Tomlinson writes that the term had become popular in the West by the 1960s right when the European phase of the spaghetti began.[67] In Europe at least, the advantage of the term rested in the possibility it offered the Europeans to become part of the semantic area covered by the term *colony*.

Cultural imperialism reflected a real imbalance of power and the role that media played in the Cold War, but it was also about defining the US into a cultural and economic powerhouse and the entire world, including Europe, into its colony. In his study of French anti-Americanism, Philip Roger has suggested that the French became interested in the colonial *metaphor* in the 1950s. The interwar years had seen terms such as "invasion or conquest" used as hyperbole; in the 1950s and 1960s the colonial metaphor was, instead, meant to be descriptive. In the 1950s "the colonial metaphor triumphed."[68]

Roger's analysis can be extended to all of Western Europe. Tony Judt has written that "from Berlin to Paris a new generation of Western progressives sought solace and example outside of Europe altogether, in the aspirations and upheavals of what was not yet called the 'Third World.' "[69] British Labour's minister of defense, Emanuel "Manny" Shinwell, was wont to declare that Albion's acquiescence to American dicta within NATO made the UK an "American colony."[70] One of the leaders of the German student movement, Rudy Dutschke, theorized the role of Germany and the entire Western Europe as a "European periphery," a "colonial periphery" of the American empire.[71]

In the 1950s Italians on the left and the right saw the peninsula slowly but surely becoming an American colony. When the US pressured Italian firms to marginalize the Communist trade union, the Confederazione Generale Italiana del Lavoro, the union's secretary, Giuseppe di Vittorio, publicly accused the Italian government of transmuting the republic into a "colonia Americana."[72] Carlo Salinari, the chair of the Cultural Committee of the Italian Communist Party, used the same metaphor in 1952 at a meeting of the party Central Committee when he argued that "American dollars complete this work of destruction and reduce our culture to the rank of the culture of a colony."[73] The image of the United States as colonizers, and Western Europe as a colony, extended to the representatives of the US studios in Rome. "Americans enjoyed the comforts of living in a colony as if they were the bosses, and with greater freedom than in the controlled, moralist, and McCarthyist Hollywood of this era," novelist Oreste del Buono and film critic Lietta Tornabuoni told Goffredo Fofi and Franca Faldini.[74]

The spaghetti sensibility embodied the radical politics of Third Worldism but it also reflected its origins, not in the global South but in the West. Couched deeply in this sensibility was an attempt by part of the West to reject its role in the massacre. It was authentic anger mixed with carnival. The massacre was acknowledged; it was the question of responsibility that muddled the waters. The concept of the mask connects the two phenomena at the center of the spaghetti sensibility: on the one hand, the spaghetti Western denounced Western colonial oppression and embraced colonial subjects. The Preacher and its creator Perry Henzell were correct. On the other hand, however, it was an exculpatory impersonation that depicted European and American bodies masquerading in *brownface* or, as in the case of the US "Vietnam Westerns," *redface*. It was a process of effacement and political amnesia that fit in well with the "Italiano brava gente" mythology analyzed in chapter 3 while shifting the burden of imperialism squarely onto the shoulder of Yankee elites.

This gesture was also larger than cinema and encompassed political and cultural movements that emphasized the mask and the masquerade. Contemporary to the spaghettis, Guy Debord, a French film theorist and an opponent of the Algerian War, theorized the "society of the spectacle." His script for a film by the same title suggested that "in societies dominated by modern conditions of production, life is presented as an immense accumulation of *spectacles*. Everything that was directly lived has receded into a representation."[75] Masking oneself was part of the political work of the German *Indianer* or the Italian *Indiani metropolitani*, important Western political formations that emerged in the sixties and seventies and clearly embraced the spaghetti sensibility. In Germany, a radical leftist group that seceded from the youth section of the Socialist Democratic Party called itself Viva Maria Gruppe, borrowing its name from the French spaghetti Western of the same name that had Brigitte Bardot and Jeanne Moreau embracing the Mexican Revolution. The mask produced more masks.[76]

Third World incarnations and impersonations emerged throughout the West. In his controversial 1967 Pulitzer Prize–winning *The Confessions of Nat Turner*, William Styron remade the leader of the most important slave rebellion in the continental United States into "an authentic Third World revolutionary."[77] More ominously, Asa

250 The Celluloid Atlantic

Carter, the Ku Klux Klan member and George Wallace segregationist speech writer, "played Indian" or at least half Indian, as Forest Carter, the author of the fake environmentalist autobiography, *The Education of Little Tree* and, as we have seen, his novel, *The Outlaw Josey Wales*, served as the foundation for the critically applauded homonymous spaghetti by Clint Eastwood.[78]

In fact, Americans masked themselves as effectively and as passionately as their mates on the east side of the Pond. Just like the spaghetti mise-en-scène made the Mexicans reference the entire Third World, progressive Hollywood was smuggling the Vietnamese under Native American war paints and tepees. After the credits designed by Sandy Ovore and modeled after those by Igidio Lardani, *The McMasters* (Alf Kjellin, 1970) depicts Benjie McMasters (black actor Brock Peters) riding into a Southern village in a Union army uniform. Benjie soon faces his racist adversaries, led by a one-armed former Confederate officer, Kolby (Jack Palance, back in Hollywood in a role identical to his Curly in Corbucci's *The Mercenary* and his "Wooden Hand" John in Corbucci's *Vamos a matar compañeros*). Both Benjie and Kolby act in character until the latter is killed by the Native Americans who save the former's life in an act of racial cooperation. Neil McMasters, the older white man who bestows his land to his adoptive son Benjie, was interpreted by folk singer Burl Ives, a radical performer temporarily blacklisted in 1953, and the film was scripted by Academy Award winner and Hollywood radical writer Harold Jacob Smith, who had won an Oscar for his integrationist script for *The Defiant Ones* (1958). The film's "Indians" used spurious Marxist slogans about the inequity of private property and recalled Vietnamese guerrillas. To make matters muddier, or actually clearer, Benjie's supposedly Indian wife Robin was impersonated by Anglo-Chinese actress Nancy Kwan. On his way to Shaolin and *Kung Fu* fame, racial impersonator par excellence David Carradine effortlessly wore the *redface* mask as the Indian leader White Feather. Carradine's clothes and makeup solidly linked American Indians and Southeast Asians within the tradition of Western impersonation of minorities that the spaghetti sensibility was both building on and reshaping.

In *The McMasters* and other, better-known films like *Little Big Man* (Arthur Penn, 1970), *Soldier Blue* (Ralph Nelson, 1970), or *A Man Called Horse* (Elliot Silverstein, 1970), the 1864 Sand Creek Massacre was recalled and referenced as an obvious stand-in for the My Lai slaughter and progressive Caucasian stars like Candice Bergen, Dustin Hoffman, and Richard Harris appeared in skimpy clothes wearing versions of *redface* masking. In *Hombre* (Martin Ritt, 1967), Paul Newman's character John "Hombre" Russell is not really an Indian. He is white but was kidnapped as a child by the Apaches. Now that he is grown up, he has no intention of going back to Caucasianland. The film opens with a long close-up of Newman in redface makeup that in its length recalls Sergio Leone's famous close-ups of Clint Eastwood's face. Even after he cuts his long hair to rejoin temporarily the white man's world to cash in on the inheritance his adoptive white father left him, his skin remains red. Hombre has learned Apache skills, which he uses to defend a stagecoach from the attack of a violent gang of Anglo and Mexican bandits. *Hombre* continues the exercise in stereotyping seen in Newman's interpretation of the Mexican bandit Carrasco in *The Outrage*. Just like Newman/Carrasco was a collection of clichés about Mexican clothes, temperament, and accent, Newman/Hombre perfectly fits the stereotypes of the "white man's Indian." His arms permanently folded across his chest or behind his back, Hombre is noble, laconic, and a ruthless fighter if provoked. In the end he will die to save the passengers, saying that "we all die, it is just a question of when." The film seems aware of the impersonation game that Newman/Hombre is playing. "You don't get tired, you don't get hungry, you don't get thirsty. Are you real?," Jessie (Diane Cilento), one of the stagecoach passengers, asks him. "More or less," Hombre responds. In fact, he is so nonwhite that the corrupt Indian Bureau agent Doctor Favor (Fredric March) tells him that "you have learned something about white people. They stick together." To which Hombre retorts by embracing his Native American-ness, while othering himself from whiteness (and its crimes): "*They*'d better" (my emphasis).

Critic Roger Ebert was not impressed, noting the inauthenticity of the American films:

> Like *A Man Called Horse*, another so-called pro-Indian film [*Soldier Blue*] doesn't have the courage to be about real Indians. The hero in these films somehow has a way of turning out to be white. In *A Man Called Horse*, Richard Harris was your average English aristocrat, but damned if he couldn't out-hunt, out-fight, out-shoot and out-lead all those Sioux, who made him their chief out of pure

The Celluloid Atlantic

gratitude. And now in *Soldier Blue*, Candice Bergen is the white girl from New York who "understands" Indians and makes liberal speeches and goes back to warn the tribe when the Cavalry is coming.[79]

Conclusion

It is a truism that what is radically new is also often unwelcome. Like the early spaghettis, Nick Ray's classic *Johnny Guitar* was not a critical hit upon its release, and its scenarist, Philip Yordan, remembered that in 1954 critics "broke its back." According to Michael Wilmington it was Bazin and his followers that committed *Johnny Guitar* to cinema's history and glory.[80] Furthermore, the French critic understood that the film was deeply in dialogue with the history of "its place," America, then tainted by McCarthyism. "Other Westerns have contemporary references and parallels," Wilmington wrote in 1974, paraphrasing Bazin. "But the probing outspokenness of *Johnny Guitar* sets it apart."[81]

In 1955 Bazin famously wrote that Ray's film marked a change in the American genre of Western films. It was not the first of such epochal genre developments. *Stage Coach* (1939) had been the perfect classical Western fifteen years earlier, "a wheel so perfect as to be able to balance on its axis in any position one places it." But according to Bazin the Second World War had radically changed America and opened the gates for a "super-Western" ("sur Western") able to incorporate "the influence of the war on the evolution of the Western after 1944." The Western was the American cinema "par excellence," he had written in 1953. It was the genre that, like Russian cinema of the prewar Soviet Union, directly referenced the birth of that other "new civilization," competing with the Soviet one, which was America. Via the same mechanism, he argued, the postwar "super-Western" was followed in the 1950s by a "novelistic," more psychological, more intimate, and more character-driven kind of Western, best exemplified by *Johnny Guitar*, a change that was also connected to the fertile soil of Hollywood and a broadly defined American society.[82]

Bazin's method is still relevant though his untimely death at forty years of age, in 1958, did not make it possible for him to mull over the changes in the film industry that underpinned the rise of the Celluloid Atlantic and the spaghettis. Both *Johnny Guitar* and *A*

Fistful of Dollars redefined the Western. Both films updated the genre to make it converse with their new historical moment and the altered geography of cinema, politics, and culture.[83] Both films also faced almost unanimous critical scorn.

To paraphrase and slightly push further Fanon's interpretation, in the age of the Vietnam War and what Philip Roger and Monique Selim have called the *métaphore coloniale*, masking oneself as a colonial subject was an eminently political gesture that was both liberating and exculpating.[84] Europeans inhabiting Mexican stereotypical bodies and Hollywood liberals donning Indian masks were all taking their distance from the bloody past and present of the West. Similar to what Philip Deloria has suggested about American culture's propensity for "playing Indian," in the Atlantic cinema non-West types and masks both comment on and reflect the marginalization and trivialization of the so-called Third World. In the US context Deloria has defined the "have-the-cake-and-eat-it-too dialectic of simultaneous desire and repulsion [for the Indian]";[85] Deloria examines several moments, from British settlers donning Indian garb during the Boston Tea Party to 1960s white American communalism and New Left politics, where

Figure 6.6. Boy Scouts Order of the Arrow Shenshawpotoo Lodge #276 meeting, summer 2018. *Source*: Author's collection.

white Americans used Indian-ness as a way to expand American identity and, sometimes, critique it. It was, he cautions, an ambiguous move that prevented clarity and presented "a double vision of the world, on the one hand anarchic possibility, on the other affirmation of the status quo."[86] After all, "playing Indian" encompassed both opposition to American imperialism and dressing like an Indian in the Boy Scouts' Order of the Arrow.

As ambiguously, Euro-American filmmakers donned a blackened, or browned, Boston Tea Party costume to embrace the cause of the Third World while ignoring the profits of colonialism. The spaghetti sensibility is fraught with this ambivalence: the contemporaneous idealization of the non-West coexisting with its brutal stereotyping and a growing amnesia about European colonial crimes. To go back to Deloria's reading of the famous initial episode of the American rebellion against the British Empire, spaghettis' practitioners righteously throw the tea in the harbor, but without questioning their own colonialist and racialized relations to East Asia, or the rest of the once colonized, and now postcolonial, world.

7

The Last Dance of the Celluloid Atlantic

PAUL BENETTI (Bernard Fresson): Go to America: It is the real homeland of serial killers.

—*Six-Pack*, dir. Alain Berbérian

∽

IN ALAIN BERBÉRIAN'S *Six-Pack* (2000) Paris has the same problem as many American cities, at least according to the urban sociology of American thrillers. A bloodthirsty serial killer haunts the metropolis, murdering young women. Detective Nathan (Richard Anconina) is in charge of the investigation. He resembles the usual weary and slightly-out-of-control cop that Mel Gibson and Clint Eastwood have made famous (or notorious). His sidekick, Philippe (Frédéric Diefenthal), is young, innocent, and computer savvy. Even with their skills combined, Nathan and Philippe are unable to stop the monster. Enter the legitimate authority on serial killers: crime writer Paul Benetti (Bernard Fresson). His advice to Nathan is simple: he is just looking in the wrong place. There are no serial killers in France or, better said, there are no *French* serial killers, because all serial killers come from the United States, which is, for reasons that remain unexplained, the "real homeland of serial killers." If the two detectives want to find their perp, they must look among the American community in Paris. The duo follows the advice, find the American monster, and Philippe kills him.

What is striking here is that this utterance of European difference and anti-Americanism is displayed in the most American of cinematic vehicles: a cop movie about male bonding and serial killers. The model of American cinema is embedded in a French film by a director who allegedly "made all his artistic and narrative choices so as to avoid producing a Hollywood clone."[1]

Six Pack obeys all the rules of its genre. Blade (Jonathan Firth), the unimaginatively named villain, kills women *and*, of course, pines for them. Blade stalks his first victim, Hèléne Moulinier (Carole Richert), at an amusement park, longingly gazing at her from a distance, before wooing her, denuding her, and stabbing her. He does the same with his second victim with whom he flirts on the metro. *Six Pack* is a romance, though a perverse and pedestrian one—the latest in a long history of films in which men have killed women they were attracted to.

For our argument in this chapter, *Six Pack* also resembles a remake of Bernardo Bertolucci's *L'ultimo tango a Parigi* (Last Tango in Paris, 1972), another film about a relationship consummated in Paris by an American man and a French woman. Like *Six Pack*, which, pace Berbérian, remained a derivative "Hollywood clone," *Last Tango in Paris* consciously referenced European *and* American cinemas. Both films and directors built on the history of Euro-American cinema though Bertolucci was much more deliberate than his later French colleague about his constant citations from the rich Euro-American cinematic tradition, and more conscious of their meaning. Like *Six Pack*, *Last Tango* was a perverse and homicidal love story that possibly featured an American expat as a serial killer.

Thirty years separated the two films and in that span of time the Celluloid Atlantic had largely dried up. While Hollywood still made movies in and about Europe, the runaway productions were no longer running away from Southern California into Europe but rather from Los Angeles to other states of the union, like Texas, New York, and Arizona. In 1971, *Variety* reported that Hollywood on the Tiber was no longer thriving and "the American community in Rome has been steadily shrinking during the past year."[2] By 2000

The Last Dance of the Celluloid Atlantic 257

international audiences were still important for Hollywood, but in China more so than in Italy or France.[3] The North Atlantic Treaty Organization was still viable, but France had built its own *force de frappe* and the Atlantic spirit had been eroded by Suez, Vietnam, and other confrontations that exacerbated European anti-Americanism and American anti-Europeanism. According to Frank Costigliola, the Franco-American alliance had grown cold in the sixties, with French president Charles De Gaulle often worrying aloud about American foreign policy. *Six Pack* is strongly infused with this chill toward what Philip Roger has called "the American enemy."[4]

In many ways the release of *Last Tango* marked the beginning of this process, its deadly romance between an American man and a European woman initiating the descent of the Euro-American romance that will wind up in the banality of *Six Pack*'s evil. Brando's character, Paul, a man who rapes a woman onscreen, and may have murdered another, is the original Blade. In this chapter I shall analyze Bertolucci's deadly love story as a filmic echo of the dissolution of the Celluloid Atlantic.

I began this book with a look at the Marshall Plan and the Smith-Mundt Act and their role in fostering Euro-American cinematic integration. Similarly, I begin this chapter by illustrating the financial and fiscal crises of the Celluloid Atlantic mainly generated by Richard Nixon's Tax Revenue Act of 1971. In cultural or intellectual matters the presence of an obvious "smoking gun" is infrequent. The connection between Nixon's policies and the changes in film resemble more the interlocking steps of two dancing partners than a simple and linear process of cause and effect. The passing of this legislation, however, was a key, and often neglected, moment in the histories of both American and European cinemas, and one important reason for the contemporary rebirth of American domestic production and the nosedive of Cinecittà and other European film centers as film production hubs. I tell the story of their financial changes in the first part of this last chapter, largely based on my reading of American trade papers.

The Atlantic, however, was not just about the economy. It was also a political structure, what we called the "West," that underwent a profound transformation in those same years for reasons larger than Nixon's fiscal policy. The West itself was becoming untenable because of Vietnam, Algeria, and the rise of the postcolonial and decolonized world that we have seen, in part, reflected in the spaghetti sensibility.

258 | The Celluloid Atlantic

The crisis of the Celluloid Atlantic that this chapter depicts was doubly a tango, a pas de deux between America and Europe and between politics and culture. Not only do *The Last Tango in Paris* and its denouement document the intertwining and disentangling of cinemas, they also adumbrate the crisis of the West, a crisis with which this book ends.

Untangling the Atlantic Economy

Unions had never been entirely happy with the Celluloid Atlantic's reorganization of labor. As we have seen, Italian film labor at all levels, with the exception of the exhibition sector, had frowned upon Hollywood's "invasion" even with Italian bottom lines in the black. Their American counterparts also saw the Atlanticization of Hollywood as a problem, perhaps with even more reason than the Europeans.[5] American and European unions' shared concerns, an Atlantic pas de deux, were one more trace of the transnational nature of the moment. To be sure unions' opposition was never completely coordinated and usually the Hollywood talent unions, representing the so-called above-the-line employees of the studios, had been relatively happy to stay in the Atlantic framework, content to jet back and forth across the ocean and, until 1962, avoid any federal income tax for up to eighteen months of employment while residing abroad.[6]

More in tune with Cold War cries of cultural imperialism, representatives of Italian above-the-line talent had basked in steady employment in the Cinecittà ateliers, but they also participated in rallies to protect Italian national cinema like the large one that took place in Piazza del Popolo, in Rome, on February 20, 1949, and saw the participation of Vittorio de Sica and Anna Magnani among others.[7] The rally showed "a perfect agreement—a rare thing—between capital and labor and between manual and intellectual workers," director Alberto Lattuada then commented.[8] The American Screen Actors Guild had also expressed doubts in the congressional hearings of 1961 about unemployment in the film industry. Its president, Charlton Heston, had tried to make his union a sort of middle ground between producers and below-the-line Hollywood employees. The actor testified in Congress that there were fewer pictures shot in Southern California, echoing the concerns of his Hollywood working-class colleagues. Represented at the hearings in Washington by H. O. Neil Shanks, the executive

The Last Dance of the Celluloid Atlantic 259

director of the Screen Extras Guild and chairman of the Foreign Committee of the AFL Film Committee, the International Alliance of Theatrical and Stage Employees Steve Inzillo (of the East Coast Motion Picture Council), and John W. Lehners (of IATSE's screen editors union), and the Screen Extras Guild's legal counsel, Robert Gilbert, the below-the-line unions all considered runaway productions a threat to American employment.[9]

Heston, however, was careful not to contradict Hollywood brass. MPAA president Eric Johnson, vice president Charles S. Boren, and Griffith Johnson, the executive in charge of the European and African desks of the Motion Picture Export Association, had all defended the industry's decision to make movies in Europe.[10] Heston's testimony was largely in agreement with the producers and often directly contradicted those of the other union leaders. The actor argued that he had tried to pursue the "villains" of the story as he habitually did onscreen. "Unfortunately I can't honestly say that I can find any," he told the committee, then chaired by New York representative Adam Clayton Powell.[11] The actor agreed with the producers' rejection of any governmental control over the film industry and allowed that, because the films' themes or the size of their budgets demanded large capital, "these films would not have been made at all if it had, for any reason, been impossible to make them overseas."[12] Congress took no meaningful action. The Celluloid Atlantic was still the norm. For another decade or so, the Atlantic film exchange kept drawing strength from a simple triptych: the necessity to rebuild fully a prosperous, democratic Western Europe, the American film producers' resolve to do away with their bulky studio system, and the capacity of film culture to cross national borders easily and appeal to international audiences.

It took the revolutionary Republican presidency of Richard Nixon to make the labor critique of the Celluloid Atlantic viable again. Elected by a slim majority in 1968, by 1970's midterm elections Nixon had decided to appeal to working-class unionized voters who had traditionally voted Democratic. On November 3, 1969, in a televised speech, Nixon famously launched the term *silent majority*; by mid-1970, the media was adding a geographical moniker and labeling Nixon's approach the Southern strategy, as the president aimed to capture the southern senatorial seats up for grabs that November.[13]

The president's silent majority turned vociferous and bellicose and wore a hard hat during the riots in May 1970 in New York and other cities. During these noisy, all-white, and only partially working-class rallies, mobs attacked students and anti–Vietnam War demonstrators. It was a momentous change in American conservative politics whose results are still with us.[14] Nixon's strategy also had direct repercussions in Hollywood. With the midterm elections yielding unsatisfactory results, the Nixon administration felt queasy about the incumbent's prospects in the 1972 presidential reelections. Former Alabama governor George Wallace was going to compete for the vote of the white working class and the traditionally Democratic South,[15] and Southern California was also in the balance, struggling with a film industry recession that began in 1969 largely because of the studios' overproduction in the previous five years.[16] Nixon could take it all by revising the constituting rules of the Celluloid Atlantic. There was not much to lose in this. After World War II, the restructured film industry had not performed any good deed for the Republicans. Hollywood was shorn of the Communists and their sympathizers, and two of its denizens, George Murphy and Ronald Reagan, respectively, were elected to the Senate in 1964 and to the California governor's mansion in 1966. They were key figures in the conservative revolution that was to carry one of them to the White House. Yet Hollywood was still to the left of Nixon and many of its stars vocally opposed the president and the Vietnam War.[17] Hollywood's European imports had also worried some of the tradition-minded constituencies on whose votes Nixon had set his sights, while Democrats in the state were unwilling to sacrifice it all for the sake of Hollywood's investment in Italy and, more generally, the Atlantic world.

On November 30, 1970, the situation came to a public and bipartisan display, in a rally in Los Angeles. Newly reelected Republican governor Ronald Reagan was joined on the dais by the newly elected Democratic senator John V. Tunney, who had just unseated the first Hollywood star to become a senator, the staunch conservative Republican George Murphy. The writing was on the wall and both men agreed that something had to be done to support workers in the film industry. Their demands did not differ much from those vented by Roy Brewer twenty years earlier. American movies were made abroad to the detriment of American workers and even of American audiences, who did not know that they were assisting in the demise of their own country's economy. As a conservative, Reagan confessed that he should have felt uneasy about demands for governmental intervention, but the situation was dire and America needed a "counterattack."[18] Both

The Last Dance of the Celluloid Atlantic 261

politicians agreed that American film employees should be protected both from foreign movies and from foreign-made "American" movies that, according to Reagan, accounted for 70 percent of "playing time on American screens." He proposed to make 20 percent of the profits earned by an "American made" film exempt from taxation, a proposal that Democratic California representative James Corman also sponsored.[19]

Testifying before the same committee in 1971, Charlton Heston conveyed a different message from the cautious one of ten years earlier. Hollywood was in shambles, the actor said, its condition "disastrous." We were looking at nothing less than the "the collapse of the American film industry," he said. It was Moses in front of the Red Sea all over again, with the Egyptians in hot pursuit. Heston prayed for divine intervention, the government's, to be specific. As opposed to ten years earlier, the Screen Actors Guild president was eager to embrace Washington and its fiscal powers as protectors. "Historically this country has refrained from government sponsorship of the arts," the conservative thespian noted, but now we recognize that "this is an important area of government responsibility."[20] This time around, the producers agreed, with Charles Boren, the vice president of the MPAA, demanding government intervention as protection in the form of tax shelters and aid to those who withdrew from abroad and invested in America. The Celluloid Atlantic was treading water.

A bipartisan wind in Congress blended together long-standing union concerns about the Celluloid Atlantic with new cultural preoccupations about the diminishing power of America and the cultural causes of this decline. The problem was not merely the dwindling unemployment in Southern California's film industry. In the early 1970s the "foreignness" of American film was viewed through lenses tinted by paranoia. In 1957, writing a report for the Hollywood labor unions, labor scholar Irving Bernstein had already noted that the "growing internationalization of the audience [of American movies is], leading to the making of pictures of more universal appeal."[21] Fifteen years later the tone was shriller. The Celluloid Atlantic, Reagan argued at the December 1970 rally, had brought about bad exploitation pictures and a taste for the "pornographic" that the future president deemed alien to the American mind. "While most of these suggestions for Government help drew torrid audience mitting," *Variety* noted that "one of the largest roars of approval went to Reagan's condemnation of 'vulgarity, and pornography' in contemporary pix."[22] Runaways were allegedly making it easier to smuggle in un-American content in the form of sexually explicit films. Under attack, America retrenched to parochialism and suspicion of anything foreign. Some mourned that even the names of theaters were succumbing to the foreign "epidemic." No longer "theaters," American entertainment centers were becoming—imagine that!—"cinemas": "Very British it is. And very confusing," concluded *Variety*.[23] Many in the 92nd Congress complained that movies were a particular culprit for the corruption of America.[24]

The old cry for protectionism acquired a new anticosmopolitan shrillness in the age of Nixon. As the economy slowed down, the administration rode to the polls the twin steeds of American Puritanism and self-righteousness, and appealed to working-class voters. In 1970 two Democratic members of Congress, both of them steadfast labor supporters, Representative James A. Burke (D-MA) and Senator R. Vance Hardtke (D-IN) led the charge. The Burke-Hardtke Bill, as it became known, included protectionist import restrictions and a radical expansion of mandatory import quotas. It also featured an attempt at regulating the foreign deployment of American capital and included incentives for domestic reinvestment.

Hollywood unions fell hard for the bill. In May 1972 the AFL bought a page on *Variety* to announce that it had created a task force to spur the passage of the Burke-Hardtke bill and "to halt exportation of jobs."[25] In July, the New York chapter of the AFL-affiliated International Alliance of Theatrical and Stage Employees announced its decision to start a campaign to lobby "for the inclusion of films in the Burke Hardtke bill on import quotas, and a government subsidy for filmmaking."[26] The national echelons of the union and of the AFL were receptive, and at the AFL national convention in Milwaukee, they endorsed a plank "to combat runaway and non-union production; mobilize support for the Burke Hardtke Bill to include protection of the American motion picture industry."[27] IATSE members rallied on Manhattan's Madison Avenue in October 1972 in support of the bill.[28]

Burke-Hardtke ultimately did not pass. The bill was simply too protectionist and worried many export-oriented American businesses. More importantly, many American firms, even more than Hollywood, had become multinationals and stood to lose from the new economic nationalism embodied in the bill. American businesspeople assured

The Last Dance of the Celluloid Atlantic 263

their European partners of their opposition to the legislation.[29] The powerful New York Chamber of Commerce rejected it.[30] And a major source of film financing, California's Wells Fargo Bank, called the measure akin to "cutting one's head to cure a cold."[31]

But the battle was far from over. The Revenue Tax Act of 1971 contained many of the ideas that undermined the Celluloid Atlantic. The negotiation for this revenue bill had not begun auspiciously. Nixon met with an industry delegation in April 1971 that included Jack Valenti and IATSE president Richard Walsh and aimed among other things at securing a 20 percent tax-free gross on domestic production. Nixon was receptive and met the industry reps for longer than scheduled, but no concrete promises were made either on support for the Burke-Hardtke Bill, which was then being discussed, or any explicit fiscal policy. *Variety* concluded that while the president was "'sympathetic' . . . no tax help for Hollywood" was coming.[32]

They were wrong, and things rapidly changed in the following months. In May 1972 Thomas Pryor wrote a substantial essay in *Variety* summing up the gains Southern California had achieved with the Tax Revenue Act the Congress had passed the past December. Over the previous twenty years, Pryor argued, Hollywood had "dispers[ed] from its home base," among other things to profit from the subsidies that foreign countries had offered in exchange for producing "American" films abroad. In the process, Hollywood had built or revitalized other "native filmmaking at the ultimate expense of the American worker." In the last few months, however, Hollywood had come back home and was "far better grounded." The April conference had "set in motion a series of historic US government aids." It was a complex policy, but Pryor noted that the revised Revenue Act of 1971 allowed Hollywood to completely amortize the costs of a film during its first period of release (not waiting for TV or other revenue) and it also allowed a 7 percent investment credit against taxes for domestic productions (a film costing $2,000,000 would then generate $140,000 in tax credits and excesses could be carried over to the following fiscal years). The most important concession was the creation of the Domestic International Sales Corporation, which allowed a deferment on the tax on earnings from exports when such earnings were plowed back into domestic production. This was, Pryor concluded, "an incentive to domestic film production, which could be translated into more jobs for American workers."[33]

264   The Celluloid Atlantic

The revision of the fiscal policies that had undergirded the Celluloid Atlantic had bipartisan support. Protectionism and anticosmopolitanism were broadly in fashion in the early 1970s. When the Democrats were able to elect their own candidate to the White House, they elected a proud son of the South, Georgia governor Jimmy Carter, a politically savvy and deeply religious peanut farmer who, among other things, had helped wrestle Hollywood capital away from Europe and into Georgia with the slogan "Georgia. We'll do anything to be in show business."[34] Representative Wilbur D. Mills (D-Arkansas), the chair of the Ways and Means Committee from 1958 to 1974 and "the most powerful man in Washington," was reported in *Variety* as "ready to do anything he can to assist Hollywood" and fully committed to bringing film production back to Southern California. Hollywood honchos, including MPAA leader Jack Valenti, lavishly feted Mills in Hollywood after the congressman made sure that the 7 percent tax credit for domestic investments and the creation of the Domestic International Sales Corporation were passed by a large bipartisan majority. The celebration was justified as both measures benefited Southern California film production enormously, concluded *Variety*.[35]

In 1976 some in Congress tried to revisit the issue of the generous tax shelters Hollywood had won for itself. Senator Ted Kennedy—from the non-film-producing commonwealth of Massachusetts—openly sneered at these shelters in August 1976. By revoking them, Kennedy noted, the government would have gained $30 million in 1977 and $40 million in 1981. Kennedy was on board with any attempt to stimulate domestic employment in the US. The problem was not the intention of the law, but the implicit, invidious comparison between Hollywood and other industries. Why was Hollywood to be coddled for producing in America? "The problems of unemployment in movies . . . are no greater than they are in real estate and many other industries."[36] In the middle of the seventies and the Cold War, Kennedy's point found few sympathetic ears. California senator John Tunney reversed his argument. Why should we abandon Hollywood after all it had done for America after the end of World War II? "Why single out the movie industry as the whipping boy?," he asked. "It is so obvious to me that some people who do not understand the industry believe that all the screen technicians in Hollywood somehow live the life of Riley, sitting by their swimming pools drinking Martinis

The Last Dance of the Celluloid Atlantic   265

all day. . . . These are hard-working people, God-fearing people."[37] Kennedy's proposal was rejected, 49–33.[38]

And so it happened that the financial policy that undergirded the Celluloid Atlantic was changed and parts of the Celluloid Atlantic were disentangled from one another. Without American capital, European production rapidly deflated. It was impossible for this not to happen. In 1967, Eitel Monaco, president of the Italian Associazione Nazionale Industrie Cinematografiche Audiovisive, remarked that in the previous ten years the United States had invested an average of $35 million a year in Italy "for the purchase and the co-production of Italian films and the production of USA movies in our context."[39]

Basing his work on this quote, British historian Christopher Wagstaff has approximated that $35 million translates into 21 billion liras at the 1965 exchange rate, when the total investment in Italian film was about 30 billion. In other words, since an average Italian films cost around 160 million liras (a coproduction about three times that figure), American investments covered the total production costs of 130 Italian films or 42 coproductions, that is, more than two-thirds of the total Italian film production of 185 features in 1965.[40]

By the end of the 1960s, everybody in Cinecittà knew that Italian and American film production were intertwined. When, in 1968, in the midst of a recession, Hollywood threatened to pull capital out of Europe, the Italian film industry panicked and Jack Valenti had personally to reassure Eitel Monaco that all was good and stable.[41] Yet in 1971, the cat was out of the bag. The Nixon White House was calling back capital to stimulate domestic investments and employment. In 1972 Thomas Pryor noted in *Variety* that Europe was experiencing a recession, "due to withdrawal of Yank production funding."[42] The largest of Western Europe's film industries, Italian cinema, did not immediately enter a crisis, and "the numbers of films produced started diminishing drastically only in the mid-seventies." By the end of the decade, however, the number of feature films had decreased by 38 percent.[43] In 1967 Italy produced 258 features,[44] in 1978 the figure was ninety-eight.[45] By the early 1980s, writes film historian Peter Bondanella, "the crisis of the Italian film industry had become prime-time television news, and such embarrassing bits of information as the enormous indebtedness of Cinecittà and that institution's difficulty in meeting employee payrolls became common knowledge."[46]

We can quibble about whether or not the crisis of the Italian film industry was entirely due to the radical slowdown of traffic on the Atlantic routes. In her *Con qualche dollar in meno*, Italian economic historian Barbara Corsi is slightly more cautious than Wagstaff in casting American withdrawal and the Italian film industry's crisis in a tight cause-effect nexus. Corsi concurs that "the tightening of American investments is surely one of the causes of the crisis of European cinema,"[47] but she adds more endogenous factors (like the Italian film industry's general financial weakness and lack of capital) and sociological reasons (the growth of the Italian TV audience and the diffusion of cars and mopeds that gave Italians more mobility and more entertainment opportunities and hit Italy later than the US).

The Celluloid Atlantic was not solely about capital and investments, however. An intermingling of cultural and political choices motivated the financial ones. As the West was untangling its film finances, its political and cultural ties were also loosened. The demise of the Celluloid Atlantic was curiously present in a movie that celebrates the infraregional similarities of the West.

Last Tango in Paris as a Euro-American Romance

Film scholar Adrián Pérez Melgosa has written about the many films produced both in the United States and in Latin America that center on a romantic relation between a citizen of the United States and a Latin American man or woman, what he terms the "hemispheric romance at the cinematic contact zone." Melgosa argues that "the cinematic romance between a character from the U.S. and another one from a Latin American country has been a common and recurrent theme in Hollywood film production across genres. . . . These Anglo-Latin love stories imply a correspondence between erotic and political desires, thus using commonly held notions of romantic love—understood as the result of a spontaneous inter-personal attraction—into a trope to explain the history of the U.S. Latin American relations."[48] Similar romances, which I call Euro-American, were represented in the Celluloid Atlantic and were, as well, used as metaphors of international relations and their contemporary state. This practice built on a long tradition that coded relations between nations or infranational social groups as mostly heteronormative romantic liaisons.[49] In 1901 German

The Last Dance of the Celluloid Atlantic   267

chancellor Bernhard von Bülow famously equated Italy's opening to France, a nation hostile to the German-Austro-Italian Triple Alliance, to a wife that is innocently dancing with a man who is not her husband. In his *The Birth of a Nation*, D. W. Griffith used both consensual love and its opposite, rape, to symbolize what he saw as the irreconcilable differences between whites and blacks and his reconciliationist desires to find common ground between whites in the North and South. The notorious attempted rape of Mae Marsh's Flora by the African American soldier Gus led to his lynching by the Ku Klux Klan, while the film ends with the double marriage between the white North and white South (the northerners Elsie and Phil Stoneman, Lilian Gish and Elmer Clifton, to the southerners Ben and Margaret Cameron, Henry B. Walthall and Miriam Cooper).[50] Griffith proposed a version of the same story in the World War I drama *Hearts of the World* (1918), where the American "Girl" (Lilian Gish) is threatened with rape at the hands of the German Von Strohm (George Siegmann).[51]

The Celluloid Atlantic increased international romances, and since these represented a love story and a hierarchy of power within international alliances, their narratives were tellingly gendered. The "motif of the US Don Juan" romancing the Latin *senõrita*, which Melgosa notes in Hollywood's "hemispheric romances," is present in the Atlantic zone as well. When made in Hollywood by male American directors, the Euro-American romances were stories of European women falling for American men—often older, sometimes much older, American men. Thus, for example, in *It Started in Naples* (Melville Shavelson, 1960), Lucia Curcio, played by twenty-six-year-old Sophia Loren, falls for the aging American Michael Hamilton, played by Clark Gable, then fifty-nine years old. Like Melgosa's hemispheric romances, these films were sophisticated in representing Atlantic relations since they were meant to appeal to both sides of the Pond. In Fred Zinnemann's *Teresa* (1951), the love between Phil Cass (John Ericson) and Pier Angeli (in the title role) survives all kind of travails, signifying the relationship between the US and Italy immediately after the war. Loren's vehicle, *It Started in Naples*, was a Euro-American romance that mirrored the contradictions of the Atlantic alliance. Hardly linear or unidirectional in its representation of such a liaison, the film noted Italians' unease about American influence in Italy while highlighting its ultimately benign effects. For example, director Melville Shavelson has Loren dance to the tune of Renato Carosone's "Tu vo fa' l'ammericano"

(1956), a song that makes fun of the Americanized Italians who pretend to be "American." The style and rhythm of the song, however, pointed to a hybrid of jazz and swing, and Carosone's performance was itself embedded in a Euro-American cultural coproduction (Paramount and Capri Production). "Tu vo fa' l'ammericano" was thus doing what its title castigates within one of the cultural goods whose malign influence it was supposed to ridicule.

When Europeans remade Euro-American heteronormative romances, however, as Jean-Luc Godard did in his famous film debut, *À bout de souffle* (Breathless, 1960), the opposite was tellingly the norm. Godard had the American character, the American student Patricia Franchini (Jean Seberg), gendered female, and the French character, small-time gangster and car thief Michel Poiccard, aka Laszlo Kovacs (Jean-Paul Belmondo), as male. Even more tellingly, in the Hollywood remake of *À bout de souffle*, *Breathless* (1981) by Jim McBride, the story remained the same, but was relocated to Southern California and the gender of the characters was again inverted. The American character is Jessie Lujack (Richard Gere) as the hypermasculine thug who romances the middle-class French graduate student, appropriately surnamed Monica Poiccard, interpreted by Valerie Kaprisky.[52]

When the cinephiliac Bernardo Bertolucci decided to make *Last Tango in Paris* about the relationship between a middle age American man in France and a young Parisian woman, he obviously had this tradition of Euro-American romance in mind. He had paid homage to Godard in his second film, *Prima della rivoluzione* (Before the Revolution, 1964), where he confessed his love for *À bout de souffle* and *Une femme est une femme* (Jean Luc Godard, 1961) and for the French director's wife, actress Anna Karina. Like the Hollywood-obsessed Godard, who at the time of *À bout de souffle* had just authored a series of perceptive essays on classical Hollywood cinema, Bertolucci was a creature of the Celluloid Atlantic, even when his films seemed to resist this context. In *Prima della rivoluzione*, a *Bildungsroman* about Fabrizio (Francesco Barilli), a young and committed Marxist intellectual who falls in love with his aunt, Gina (Adriana Asti), the twenty-two-year-old director had paid tribute to Godard but also to all the Hollywood films by Alfred Hitchcock and to Howard Hawks's *Red River*. Yet in *Tango* Bertolucci also wanted to go further than Godard.

The son of the celebrated poet Attilio Bertolucci, Bernardo was ambitious, well connected, and hard-working. Only twenty years old,

The Last Dance of the Celluloid Atlantic   269

he had won a prestigious literary prize, the Viareggio, for his first book, the poetry collection *In cerca del mistero* (1962). Talented and extremely well read, he understood the value of networks. His father had helped Pier Paolo Pasolini publish his first novel, *Ragazzi di vita* (1955), and Bertolucci celebrated the poet/filmmaker/novelist in one of the poems of *In cerca del mistero*, "A Pasolini." Bernardo made no secret of his love for cinema and, not surprisingly, Pasolini kept him in mind. He hired the young man to be his assistant director on *Accattone* (Beggar, 1960) and facilitated Bertolucci's directorial debut in 1962 for *La comare secca* by writing the original story and helping him and Franco Citti with the script's dialogue. As we have seen in chapter 5, the film, the story of the murder of a prostitute retold from five different viewpoints, was indebted to Kurosawa's *Rashomon* and steeped in the Celluloid Atlantic's interest in Japanese cinema that was at the core of the spaghetti sensibility.

While deeply concerned with European and Italian topics in his early films, in fact Bertolucci was not afraid of going transnational. He collaborated on the script of Leone's Paramount-financed *Once Upon a Time in the West*, and in *La comare secca* he employed an American actor, the elfish blond Allen Midgette, to play a young Italian soldier. He used Midgette again in *Prima della rivoluzione*, before the actor went back to New York to become a member of Andy Warhol's entourage.[53] By the time he made *L'ultimo tango a Parigi* the director was fully part of the Celluloid Atlantic. The film Bertolucci directed prior to *Tango*, *Il conformista* (The Conformist, 1970), a dark story about an antifascist turncoat (Jean-Louis Trintignant) who murders his former mentor, Professor Quadri (Enzo Tarascio), in Paris at the behest of the regime, had been largely funded by its American distributor, Paramount.[54] Presented at the New York Film Festival on September 23, 1970, the film had elicited what *Variety* termed an "electric" reaction.[55] Paramount put its might behind the distribution of the film and by March 1971 *Il conformista* was recording "the biggest opening" in the history of the prestigious Carnegie Hall in New York.[56] The film won the National Board of Review award and was a runner up for Best Picture Award from the National Society of Film Critics.[57]

Now world-famous and with a taste for the colossal, Bertolucci had a deal with Paramount to make one more movie after *Il conformista*. He chose a script he had written with Franco "Kim" Arcalli, the editor on *Il conformista* and many other 1960s Italian films.[58] By mid-

1971 *Tango* was already in preproduction. In September, United Artists replaced Paramount as the source of funds[59] and the Americans were flanked by Alberto Grimaldi's Produzioni Europee Associate. *Tango*'s acting cast and stars reflected its Atlantic nature. Invited to collaborate on the project from the beginning, Marlon Brando had been eager to participate. In early August 1971, *Variety* spotted the director and his star at the Beverly Hills Hotel "confabbing—in French—on *The Conformist* writer director pic-plan for Brando in his yet untitled contemporary love story."[60] The trade paper reported that the actor read and approved the script [61] and accepted a modest $250,000 salary to keep the budget under $2 million (plus 10 percent of the gross above $3 million). It was a wise choice given the film's eventual gross of around $60 million.[62] French actress Dominique Sanda was initially to star but, when she became pregnant, she was replaced by a relatively unknown nineteen-year-old French actress, Maria Schneider.[63] François Truffaut's and Jean Luc Godard's alum and cinematic alter-ego, Jean-Pierre Léaud, was also cast as Jeanne's cuckolded fiancée. The lone female director of the *nouvelle vague*, Agnes Varda, collaborated on the dialogues along with actor Jean-Luis Trintignant, who had been briefly considered for the leading male role.

A Celebrated "Bad Romance"

Tango had its world premiere on October 14, 1972 in New York rather than Italy, at the New York Film Festival. Grimaldi had negotiated an Italian premiere anteceding the American one and the film was commercially released in Italy on December 13, 1972, and in America on January 27, 1973. By then *Tango* had already touched off a controversy about censorship because of the raw sexual nature of some of the scenes between Paul (Brando) and Jeanne (Schneider) and, in particular, of Jeanne's rape by Paul, the American man she has met in an apartment they both want to rent. The rape scene is still stunning for its violence and misogyny. Both Schneider and Brando have stated that all the sex acts in the film were simulated, notwithstanding Bertolucci's invitation "to do it." But the production history of the film is still horrifying given the long-neglected fact that Schneider had not been informed by Bertolucci and her costar of the explicit nature and sheer physical violence of the sequence.[64]

Figure 7.1. Bertolucci and Brando on the set of *Last Tango in Paris* (1972). *Source*: PhotofestNYC.

As with the racism of the Celluloid Atlantic, the patriarchal order and the misogyny in many of its films, notably this one, went—and sometimes still go—unremarked upon by its mostly male critics.[65] On both sides of the Atlantic critics applauded *Last Tango*, the shrillest criticisms coming from conservative Christians who saw the film as the embodiment of both obscenity and Marxism.[66] The film was finally deemed "obscene" by the Corte di Cassazione in 1976, taken out of circulation, and all copies (but the three that were given to the Cineteca nazionale) existing on Italian soil sentenced to be burnt. It was a bizarre prohibition, as copies continued to circulate, and the film cooperative Missione Impossibile defiantly projected the director's own 35 mm copy in 1982 to reopen the case. It became legal again to show *Tango* in Italy only in 1987 when Judge Paolo Colella acknowledged that the film is a "work of art."[67]

Conservative American Christians also attacked the film and some of them besieged the theaters that showed it.[68] As in Italy, the problem that these conservative Christians had with the film was not its misogyny but its explicit sexual scenes. The editor of the *Christian Century*, James M. Wall, blasted *Tango* and accused the "triple crown" press (*Time*, *Newsweek*, and the *New York Times*) of promoting it "out of all proportion to the film's intrinsic merits."[69] *Variety* reported that "local yahoos" and churchgoers had protested the film in Montclair, New Jersey and in other areas. The liaison between church and state is more tenuous in the US than in Italy, and United Artists played it safe. The studio was ready to organize advance showing of the film upon request of "local police and municipal officials."[70] When the *Los Angeles Times* relegated the film to the company of only X-rated movies, United Artists shrewdly defended it and withheld any advertisement for the film from the paper.[71]

While conservative Christians rioted, critics mostly concurred that the film was special. Those who were more tepid about it, like novelist Norman Mailer, or *New York Times* film critic Vincent Canby, seemed unsure about their reasons, taking issue with the film almost out of pique, as a way to stand out from the hoi polloi who stood in line. Brando, Mailer argued, had given us "a greater sense of improvisation out of the lines of a script than any other professional actor," yet the film was not "authentic" enough.[72] *Tango* had "superlative production" by Bertolucci and an "extraordinary performance by Brando," Canby wrote, but it is also "so overpraised that it will disappoint you. *Tango* is so perfectly on target about the modern issues concerning relationships, sex, and masculinity, that its way of dealing with these will soon become a cliché." "You'd better see it quickly," the critic counseled, "so that nobody will spoil the surprise for you—even though the price of the ticket, at $5, is itself revolutionary for its cost."[73]

At least the logic of Pauline Kael was linear. In her *New Yorker* review (October 28, 1972), she called *Tango* "the most powerfully erotic movie ever made" and "the most liberating movie ever made." The date of *Tango*'s premiere at the New York Film Festival (October 14, 1972) "should become a landmark in movie history comparable to May 29 1913—the night *Le sacre du Printemps* was first performed—in music history."[74] There were some cogent critiques, like that of art critic Grace Glueck, who pointed to the film's machismo. In the *New York Times*, Glueck upended the discourse of authenticity that many had attached to the physicality and the emotions portrayed in the films. What *Tango* authentically represented was a male fantasy of domination, and the problem was that Bertolucci embraced it.

Tango de facto glorified women's inferior status in the patriarchy. And spectators were deceived into feeling preposterously sorry for Paul, when Jeanne kills the man who has raped her in many different ways during the film and who may have killed his own wife.[75]

Tango "comes closer than any 'romantic' film I have seen to exposing woman's real sexual status,"[76] Glueck ironically concluded. It was not praise, and she was not in the majority. Following her essay, the *New York Times* published an entire section of readers' letters (mainly from women) who mostly defended the film.[77] The general audience was also ready to forgive the largely uninterrogated misogyny of the script. The box office of the film was nothing short of stupendous. After opening in ninety-two cities and seventeen countries in February 1973, by July *Tango* was the top-grossing film for United Artists for the year and had netted more than $32 million.[78]

The Celluloid Atlantic and Last Tango in Paris

In her *New Yorker* essay, Kael pointed out what Vito Zagarrio has called Bertolucci's "strategia citazionista" (citationist strategy),[79] that is, his obsession with citations from other films and other cinemas, his awareness of the history of cinema, and his eagerness to make of his films an opportunity to reflect upon its meaning. "Movies are a past we share," Kael wrote, "and, whether we recognize them or not, the copious associations are at work in [*Tango*] and we feel them."[80] Bertolucci's passion for referencing other films and other kinds of intellectual intervention also turned *Last Tango* into a summa of the Celluloid Atlantic. The film explored the very nature of the Atlantic, both as a cinema and as a political construction, and wound up undermining its premises and implicitly calling for its dissolution.

The first element that Kael highlighted was the film's realism. This had to do with what she saw as the honest representation of the sexual element of the plot: "this unexpected sexuality and the new realism it requires of the actors." But it was not the only kind of realism that the film evoked. There was the film's reliance on exterior shots and real, recognizable Parisian locales, something that made *Tango* redolent of the neorealist lesson. But Kael pointed out immediately that "much of the movie is American in spirit," because it drew from what we have recognized as one of the earliest concerns of European observers of American culture: the realism of important segments of American literature. The frank representation of sex and death in the film makes Kael think of the same authors that forty years before had intrigued Cesare Pavese: "[Paul's] profane humor and self-loathing self-centeredness and street 'wisdom' are in the style of the American hardboiled fiction aimed at the masculine-fantasy market, sometimes by writers (often good ones, too) who believe in more than a little of it." Paul's hard-boiled demeanor and dialogue pointed to James Cain's *The Postman Always Rings Twice* but not so much in its original American literary version. Kael saw the spirit of *The Postman* referenced in the film via the presence of Massimo Girotti (Paul's wife's lover), who was the main character in Luchino Visconti's screen rendition of Cain's novel, *Ossessione*, one of the founding texts of the Celluloid Atlantic that we analyzed in chapter 2.

> In substance this is [Bertolucci's] most American film, yet the shadow of Michel Simon seems to hover over Brando, and the ambience is a tribute to the early crime of passion films of Jean Renoir, esp. *La Chienne* and *La Bête Humaine*. . . . Bertolucci's soft focus recalls the thirties films, with their lyrically kind eye for every variety of passion: Marcel Carné comes to mind. . . . He uses the other actors for their associations too—Girotti, of course, the star of so many Italian films, including *Senso* and *Ossessione*, Visconti's version of *The Postman Always Rings Twice*, and, as Paul's mother-in-law, Maria Michi, the young girl who betrays her lover in *Open City*.[81]

In its evocation of its Atlantic nature, *Last Tango* is explicit, almost pedestrian. The insistent reliance on real locales and the presence of *Ossessione*'s star Massimo Girotti (more on this below) point to Italian neorealism.[82] The French *nouvelle vague* is blatant in the character of Jeanne's fiancé, the *cinéma verité*–obsessed cuckolded filmmaker Tom, who is played by Jean-Pierre Léaud, one of the favorite actors of François Truffaut and Jean-Luc Godard. A much-noted reference to Jean Vigo's *L'Atalante* (Jeanne and Tom throw a life preserver in the Canal de Saint Martin where they are shooting—the location of the scene itself a reference to Marcel Carné's 1938 film *Hôtel du Nord*) completes Bertolucci's obvious gestures to the *nouvelle vague*.

The Last Dance of the Celluloid Atlantic   275

Tango also celebrates the hybridity embedded in the Celluloid Atlantic. The Actors Studio techniques are as prominent as its polemical debts to neorealism and *nouvelle vague*. The script asked Brando, Stella Adler's most famous alumnus, to demonstrate his teacher's technique. At one point the script has Paul talk about his own childhood onscreen: "My father was a . . . a drunk, whore-fucker, bar fighter, super masculine, and he was tough. . . . My mother was . . . very poetic, also drunk . . ." Paul/Brando recalls while lying on a mattress in the apartment in front of Jeanne, who has temporarily become both Stella Adler and the actor's therapist. The dialogue are Paul's words, but they also overlap with Brando's recounting of his own childhood in Omaha, Nebraska, and Chicago, Illinois, and of his troubled relationship with his parents, who both struggled with alcohol addiction.[83]

Many currents of the Atlantic flow into this film, including Italian, French, and American actors, European and American acting styles, and several concepts of realism. Via these centripetal streams of Atlantic film cultures, *Tango*'s story, and *Tango*'s mode of telling it, find a powerful cohesion and a sense of authenticity: the film is the chronicle of "an authentic American abroad [told] in a way that an Italian writer-director simply couldn't do without the [American] actor's help," Kael concluded, somewhat imprecisely.[84]

Tango is, however, far from celebrating the Atlantic liaison and it was more than the sum of its filmic and literary citations.[85] Its repeated reliance on exterior shots that identified real Parisian places was a sign of Bertolucci's continuing conversation with neorealism. Yet the use of exterior shooting in specific locations may reveal what other scenes of the film confirm: a concern that Kael and most contemporary critics missed. *Tango* is a polemical engagement with the history of the West and its colonialism.

The Last Tango of the West

The film's neorealist penchant for location shooting is revealing. *Last Tango* opens on an overpass on a bulky iron bridge that was called pont du Passy till 1949. Paul is capping his ears and shouting curses at God. Jeanne comes from behind him, looks at the man with curiosity, and keeps walking on the overpass. They will meet later but the bridge is an interesting location. In 1949 it was renamed to honor the

World War II battle of Bir Hakeim, which marked both the beginning of Rommel's defeat at el Alamein and the Franco-Anglo-American reconquest of the French colonies in North Africa. It was a Western victory but not a significant one for those under the talon of Western colonialism. Pont de bir-Hakeim is close to the Tour Eiffel, and at the center of a district that, like the battle it memorializes, glorifies Atlantic unity. From the bridge one can see the quarter-scale replica of the Statue of Liberty on the Ile aux Cignes donated to Paris in 1889 by the community of American expatriates for the centennial of the French Revolution.

Figure 7.2. The places of *Last Tango in Paris* (1971). Île aux Cignes, Pont de bir-Hakeim, Avenue du Président Kennedy. *Source*: Author's collection.

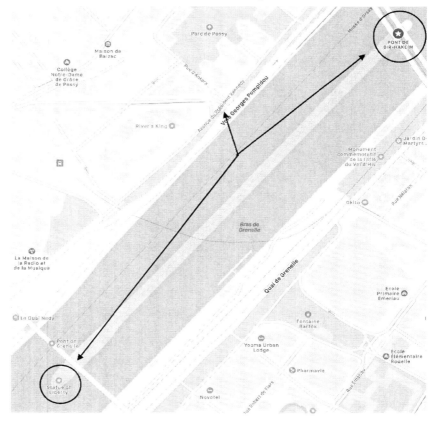

Figure 7.3. The Statue of Liberty of Paris (on the Île aux Cignes). Photo by Stefano Chessa Altieri. *Source*: Author's collection. Used with permission.

When Jeanne negotiates the car traffic to get to the fateful apartment building, she crosses Avenue du Président Kennedy (till 1964 named quay de Passy), celebrating the slain American president. The bar from which Jeanne calls her mother before entering the building where she meets Paul for the first time was, and still is, called Kennedy-Eiffel Bar. Even the real name of the famous street of the notorious apartment has an Atlantic echo. In *Tango*, it is called Rue Jules Verne, but it is easily recognizable as Rue de l'Alboni, and it too hints at an American-European connection. Marietta Alboni was the Italian nineteenth-century opera singer that American poet Walt Whitman famously celebrated in his *Leaves of Grass* poem "To a

Certain Cantarice" after seeing her perform during her only American tour in 1852–1853.[86]

I am tempted to see the toponymy of *Tango* as by no means casual but, rather, as a riddle encoding a conglomerate of signifiers of the Atlantic union. Bertolucci had already encased the meaning of one of his previous films, *La Strategia del ragno* (The Spider's Stratagem, 1970), in the name of streets and squares of a northern Italian village, introduced at the beginning of the film. The end of *Strategia del ragno* revealed the lie behind those names. The streets are named after a false anti-Fascist hero who, in fact, was a collaborator. The alliance celebrated in the Pont bir-Hakeim and on the Isle aux Cignes may also be less than it appears. And the "bad romance" of *Last Tango* may be larger than Jeanne and Paul's.

For starter, the film does a curious job with Marlon Brando's persona. The actor had been involved with the critique of American and European colonialism for a long time. His affair with anticolonial causes dated from his work in *The Teahouse of the August Moon* (1956), the earnest effort by progressive Hollywood director Daniel Mann to describe the problems of the postwar American occupation of Japan. Brando had played—in yellow-face—a local Japanese man, Sakini, to Glenn Ford's—straight-faced—impersonation of a good-hearted American foreign aid official, Captain Fisby. According to the actor's autobiography, he had signed on to finance film work on the United Nations' technical assistance in Asia. But the film had raised his colonial conscience:

> En route to Tokyo for the filming in the Spring of 1956, I had made a detour to South East Asia to look for story ideas and visited the Philippines, Thailand, Indonesia and several other countries. From afar I had admired the efforts of industrialized countries to help poorer nations improve their economies, and thought that this was the way the world ought to work. But I found something quite different: even though colonialism was dying, the industrialized countries were still exploiting the economies of these former colonies. . . . Apparently because the United States had more television sets and automobiles, [American foreign aid officials] were convinced that our system was infallible and that they had a God-given mission to impose our way of life on others.[87]

The Last Dance of the Celluloid Atlantic 279

A famous and vocal supporter of Native Americans' struggle for justice in the US, just before he began working on *Tango* Brando had declined to accept an Oscar for his work on Francis Ford Coppola's *The Godfather Part I* (1972) and had sent a Native American activist, Sasheen Littlefeather, to reject publicly the award at the Academy Award ceremony in Los Angeles.

The actor's activism on behalf of the colonized world had been as tenacious as it had been consistently cinematic. Brando had participated in the Atlantic beginnings of the spaghetti revolution and, as we have seen in chapter 5, in his 1961 Western, *One-Eyed Jacks*, he had made one of the most attentive and sympathetic portrayals of native Mexican women Hollywood had produced to that date. Before working on *Tango*, he had participated in Gillo Pontecorvo's anticolonialist *Queimada* (Burn! 1969) written by another master of the Third Worldist spaghetti, Franco Solinas. The actor loved Pontecorvo's directorial skills: "Aside from [Elia] Kazan and Bernardo Bertolucci, [Pontecorvo is] the best director I worked with . . . even though we nearly killed each other." He saw in *Queimada* "a lot of parallels to Vietnam."[88] Till his death Brando considered his work on this film "the best acting I have ever done."[89]

Given Brando's personal investment in *Tango*, the actor's notorious ability to control his dialogue, and his political investment in anticolonialism (alongside Bertolucci's and Arcalli's own investment in leftist politics), it is surprising that Bertolucci's film makes no mention of the infamous colonial war that was setting ablaze Parisian streets all around the set and the American intervention that was coming to its bloody conclusion in Vietnam during those months.

One would almost expect Brando's character, Paul, to reveal some personal connection to the conflict. There are opportunities in *Tango* to emphasize this part of Brando's life, and the film had already referenced elements of his real biography in the Actors Studio exercise we examined earlier in this chapter. Even before that scene, which mined Brando's troubled childhood, Paul, the character, has appropriated segments from the life of Brando, the actor.

At the beginning of the film, after Paul and Jeanne have just had their first tryst, the young woman has gone to meet her boyfriend, Tom. Bertolucci uses these early scenes to set up the equivalence between Paul and Jeanne. Upon meeting Tom at the railroad station, Jeanne promptly lies to him, telling the young man that while he was gone she has "thought of [him] day and night." It is a justifiable slip as Tom is obnoxiously filming their encounter for his TV *cinèma verité* "Portrait of a Girl," and Jeanne is encouraged to perform. Paul's crime, referenced afterward almost in a cross-edited montage, may be darker than Jeanne's lie. After his encounter with Jeanne, we see him back to the little hotel he used to run with his wife Rosalie, aka Rosa (Veronica Lazar), before the woman's suicide. The maid (Catherine Allégret) tells him that the police have been investigating his past, unconvinced by the cause of his wife's death. The scene is directly out of a horror movie, the camera framing the young woman squeezing a red-soaked rag in what is literally a bucket of blood. "They didn't believe in suicide," the maid tells Paul, as she cleans a blood-stained curtain. "Too much blood all over. . . . [they asked] if you fought, if you hit her. . . .' 'Nervous type your boss!' . . ."

The police have revealed to the maid details of Paul's life that she now recounts to him, and the spectators. The maid's story is over-determined, both playful and consciously meaningful. It is a mixture of Brando's own life and that of a character from a hardboiled novel, but there is no hint of Vietnam, antiwar activities, or any current military conflict: "He used to be a boxer . . . but he didn't do well. He was an actor and then a bongo player. Revolutionary in South America. Journalist in Japan. One day he debarks in Tahiti. Wanders around. Learns French. Then he arrives in Paris and here meets a woman with money. Marries her and he's kept [by her]." There are references to both the actor's biography ("an actor," the reference to Tahiti, and so forth) and filmography here (the anticolonialist film *Queimada*—"revolutionary in South America"—or his role in Terry Malloy, the "contender" of *On the Waterfront*, perhaps to Brando's modeling his Kowalski on Rocky Graziano in *A Streetcar Named Desire*, and so forth). The list mixes life and professional roles. It is the ultimate Actors Studio exercise, but it is also incomplete and misleading. Pointedly, there is no reference to his participation in the antiwar movement, his daughter Cheyenne, or his fight for Native American rights. It is almost as if, like Paul's name, all these are too obvious, pleonastic, excessive, or just too well known to be mentioned. We all know about what America is doing in Vietnam. One just needs to open the newspaper and read the headlines.

Explicit throughout the film, instead, is a more forgotten conflict and colonial past. If *Tango* silences the Vietnam tragedy, the film shouts about the Algerian catastrophe. Relics of the conflict dominate

Jeanne's apartment. "It is a little old, but full of memories now," Paul says after breaking in, in the film's tragic final scene.⁹⁰ In a previous scene Jeanne has paraded her father's colonial past before her own mother. Dad was a French colonial officer in Algeria and the walls are covered with what he has stolen in North Africa. Bertolucci's accusations are insistent, his irony mordant. He frames Jeanne's mother (Gitt Magrini) cleaning one of her husband's uniforms on the terrace over Paris while Jeanne is visiting, literally washing in public her family's dirty laundry. In the same scene, Jeanne dresses up in another of the father's uniforms. She parades it in front of her mother, points her dad's colonial army gun at a mirror, reminiscing about the time when he taught her how to shoot. Finally, she finds in the jacket pocket a photo of a half-naked black woman. She does not look Arab or Berber, her complexion actually hinting at sub-Saharan Africa. "This was his orderly?," she asks her mother with a cruel smile. "A fine example of a Berber," the older woman replies.

It is not the first time Jeanne has drawn attention to her father's racism. Earlier in the film, she and Tom have shot scenes of their *cinéma-verité* film exercise in her country house. She has shown him her family's past, the ornate tombstone of a German shepherd to which her dad had given an Arab name, "Moustapha, Oran 1950—Paris 1958." Moustapha was Jeanne's "childhood friend" and he "could

Figure 7.4. The memory of European colonialism in *Last Tango in Paris* (1972). *Source*: Author's collection.

always tell the rich from the poor. He never made a mistake. . . . If a beggar showed up, you should have seen him. What a dog! The colonel, Jeanne's father, trained him to recognize Arabs by their odor," Olympia (Luce Marquand), the family maid, tells Tom and his crew.

Olympia is, in Jeanne's words, an "anthology of domestic virtues—faithful, admiring, and racist." The problem is that Tom does not get the irony. He wants to name their son Fidel (Castro) and their daughter Rosa (Luxemburg), but he does not comment on the French racism on display. He loves it all: "It's you. It's marvelous, it's your childhood, it's everything I've been looking to find . . ." Even when Jeanne shows her colonial artifacts he does not demur: "It's Papa . . . there," she tells him. "You take off . . . and find your childhood again!" he incites.

JEANNE: [He is] in full dress uniform.

TOM: Don't be afraid. Overcome the obstacles.

JEANNE: Papa in Algiers . . .

TOM: You are fifteen, fourteen, thirteen, twelve, eleven, ten, nine . . .

JEANNE: My favorite, at eight years old . . .

It is a pungently ironic scene. Tom is unaware of the meaning of what his fiancé is telling him, inviting Jeanne to regress into amnesia while madly operating the lightweight camera typical of *nouvelle vague* directors in rooms whose walls are almost literally drenched in the blood of the victims of French imperialism.

Tango ventures two definitions of union: one romantic (Tom and Jeanne, Paul and Jeanne, Paul and his wife Rosa), one political and cultural, referencing the West and the Celluloid Atlantic. As we have seen, a romance referencing a political alliance was not new, but here the film departs from the norm. The Euro-American romances were mostly love stories although some of them, like the two versions of *Breathless*, have more than a trace of amour fou in them. But the union in *Tango*, both political and romantic, is problematic at best, criminal at worst. No liaison had ever been as bad as *Tango*, where

The Last Dance of the Celluloid Atlantic   283

the American male rapes his European mate who then kills him. Paul and Jeanne are the epitome of the dangerously dysfunctional couple and, in Bertolucci's misogynist universe, they are mirror images of each other.

Bertolucci prefaces this equivalency in failure in the credits of the film—again obviously—where the spectator is treated to Francis Bacon's left panel of *Double Portrait of Lucian Freud and Frank Auerbach* (representing only Freud) and *Study for Portrait of Isabel Rawsthorne* (1969). Bertolucci took both the DP of the film, Vittorio Storaro, and Marlon Brando (but not Maria Schneider!) to see these specific canvases at the Tate Gallery, asking them both to draw inspiration from them.[91] Such inspiration was hardly conducive to sympathetic and warm portrayals, as Bacon's technique casts the figures in a stark light, their features contorted, their bodies decaying, what film scholar Gabriele Anaclerio has called a form of "tragic and disassociated body-ness" (*una corporeità tragica, dissociata*).[92] From the beginning, Bertolucci casts aspersions on both Jeanne and Paul.

The identification and condemnation of Jeanne and Paul and of Europe and America is part of the film diegesis. *Tango* makes the identity of Europe and America obvious. It is a political identification but, for Bertolucci, it also involves the regions' supposedly separated cinemas, which the director sees as imbricated with each other. This equivalency is plain in the encounter between the contemporary American star, Marlon Brando, and the star of Italian cinema of yesteryear, Massimo Girotti. Girotti, who was *Ossessione's* implausible Atlantic "hobo," plays Marcello (like Mastroianni!), the Italian lover of Rosa. The scene, between a sad husband and the sad lover of his suicidal wife, is shorn of confrontation. At the beginning Paul is slightly aggressive: he does not want Marcello's compassion. But Marcello is composed and calm. He remains sitting, working at his table ("it helps distract me," he tells Paul) and he notes the obvious. He and Paul are wearing identical robes: "We have lots of things in common," Marcello tells the other man.[93] Rosa remained elusive and they both abandoned her to her pain, neither of them able to save her. The men talk about minor details: a fever blister or their health regimens ("how do you keep in shape?" the slightly paunchy Brando asks the fit Girotti: "my problem is the belly"). Mostly they remark upon what they have in common: the robe, the bourbon that Paul favors, and which Rosa also gave to Marcello, and the memory of a woman neither of them could really love, or help. Bathed in natural light and captured by Storaro's extraordinary photography, the scene is about shared sadness rather than anger. Their disappointment is at themselves and their inability to save Rosa. It is a sad sameness of two unworthy people.

Conclusion: Chewing Gum

The juxtaposition of Europe and America is again part of the climax of the film, when Brando pursues Jeanne to her family apartment. I am not convinced by Esther Rashkin's provocative but undersubstantiated reading of this scene that decodes Brando's irruption as signifying Paul's "becom[ing] Algeria itself," the mad Arab terrorist who is now supposedly threatening the colonizer, who responds by killing the intruder.[94] The connection between Brando and Algeria, even metaphorically, is tenuous. Brando is first and foremost a Hollywood star. As such, he can never leave America. He violently breaks in and surveys the macabre décor of the place, the walls covered by the memorabilia of French colonialism. "How do you like your hero? Over easy or sunny [side] up?" The line seems incoherent, and one almost gives in to the impression that Paul has lost his mind. Yet what follows makes sense, if one keeps in mind that the Paul-Jeanne relation adumbrates a larger political context. He now talks to her like America, relating not to Jeanne, but to France itself. Donning her father's hat from the Algerian War, he addresses Jeanne directly. "You ran through Africa, and Asia, and Indonesia. And now I found you. And I love you. I want to know your name." His line shows Paul's discovery of her past, which makes his request for her name almost superfluous. But it is too much to say and to ask. Jeanne fires her pistol at him, in his groin and at close range. Paul stumbles to the balcony murmuring "our children, our children, our children. Will remember . . ."

It is a scene clear, like most of Bertolucci's cinema, in its literalness. Paul and Jeanne are the United States and Europe and theirs is a deadly, bloodstained relationship that appropriately comes to its conclusion in rooms adorned with a legacy of blood. Possibly their progeny will remember their sins and won't forgive them. Brando's final gesture, before he crumples dead on the balcony, is meaningful in this context: he takes a piece of chewing gum out of his mouth, and sticks it to the underfold of the ornate balcony. It is a political gesture and, like too much in this film, also a cinematic reference. Gum had long marked American culture in Europe. It was first a romantic MacGuffin in King Vidor's 1924 *The Big Parade* (Jim and Melisande bond over her discovery of American candy) and became the symbol of American corruption of Europe's youth in the second postwar period, and the commonplace signifier of the allegedly irreconcilable difference between the Atlantic partners. Is Brando's gum the same that marked Silvana's and Walter's perdition in *Riso Amaro?* Maybe. But Paul sticks it there to remind the spectators of what he really represents, and to taint and taunt Europe and the West one more time. As they well deserve.

Conclusion

Reprovincializing Western Cinema

LIKE NATURE, HISTORY *non facit saltus*, and the Celluloid Atlantic did not end on that Parisian balcony. Bertolucci went on to direct *1900* (1976), a political colossal generously funded by Paramount. This time around, however, the studio came to regret its support for the film. *1900* told the interconnected lives of two Italian boys, Olmo Dalcò (Gérard Depardieu) and Alfredo Berlinghieri (Robert de Niro) from birth to old age. Olmo's and Alfredo's story is a ploy to recount the entire first half of the Italian twentieth century. The boys are born on the same day in 1901 (on January 27, 1901 the day composer Giuseppe Verdi died) to families on opposite sides of the social tracks. The son of sharecroppers toiling on the land that belonged to Alfredo's father, Olmo befriends Alfredo in the early scenes of the film. Their friendship endures against all odds, crisscrossing the bloodiest part of the past century. Bertolucci frames his story in intimate familial terms, but, like D. W. Griffith in *The Birth of a Nation* (1915)—a clear inspiration—the director's filmmaking ascribes epic meaning to individuals' stories. Accompanying Olmo and Alfredo on their journey through the past century, the film tells of two world wars, the rise and fall of Italian fascism, and the possibility of a benign kind of national-popular communism that in the first half of the 1970s seemed still within grasp and logics.

American cinema has always recast historical and social problems as conundrums in an individual's life. We even have a word for this narrative strategy. It is called *burbankization* and takes its name from

Warner Brothers' old studios in Burbank, California. Bertolucci added to the Hollywood recipe paeans to communism and a penchant for aestheticizing the struggle of the proletariat. This burbankization of history and the social movements that inhabit it owed more to classical Hollywood's narrative traditions than to Italian political and aesthetic avant-gardes. With its story of male bonding, rural landscapes, violence, railroads, and brothels, *1900* revealed Bertolucci's debt to his former mentor, Sergio Leone, and would serve well as a fourth component of Leone's "Once Upon a Time" trilogy, maybe entitled *Once Upon a Time in Communism*.[1]

Still, the Italian peasants singing the "Internazionale" and parading a multipatched red flag that seems to cover the entire earth was too much for an American studio. Paramount demanded that Bertolucci's directorial cut of 317 minutes be edited down to the contractual 195 minutes. That version was deemed unwatchable both by Bertolucci and by American audiences who stayed away en masse, the American fame of the director notwithstanding. Eventually the film was released in Italy in two separate installments totaling 305 minutes. In the US, the studio released a 247-minute version—*sans* red flag. The director's cut became available in America only in 1987.[2] By that time Bertolucci had found new, non-Atlantic ways to continue his filmmaking project. He stuck to big budget filmmaking and obsessive cinephiliac homages and citations to create meditations on politics, communism, and power.[3] His *The Last Emperor* (1987), with a $25 million budget, was independently produced by Briton Jeremy Thomas and directly or indirectly financed by several European banks and the People's Republic of China.[4]

Bertolucci was not the only one to exit the Celluloid Atlantic. By that time many of the producers who had sustained it were retiring, or choosing sides. In 1973, six years after his production company Embassy joined the giant conglomerate AVCO, Joe Levine left the corporation. The producer's career entered a decline. He did work his magic on one last, great coproduction, *A Bridge Too Far* (Richard Attenborough, 1977), partly financed by United Artists. But the World War II epic disappointed on the American market and did only fair business in Europe. In 1978 Peter Dunn wrote in the *Sunday Times* that after "creat[ing] Hercules or Mike Nichols or Sophia Loren or Mel Brooks or Dustin Hoffman or Julie Christie or Marcello Mastroianni . . . [and] tower[ing] over the lesser moguls of filmdom like a

Conclusion 289

short, bespectacled, colossus," Levine was "in the closing sequences of a melodramatic career."[5] He produced one more film, the exploitation film *Tattoo* (1981), and died in 1987.

Other denizens of the Atlantic settled on one side of the pond, and it is not surprising that, given the crisis of the Italian cinema, those who could migrate favored the American coast. In the aftermath of the Revenue Act of 1971, Dino de Laurentiis closed his Italian studio, Dinocittà, which he had opened with great fanfare in 1964 to accommodate coproductions with American studios.[6] "The most American of Italian producers and the most Italian of American producers"[7] resettled his business in the United States, becoming, to all effects, a Hollywood producer. A resourceful man, De Laurentiis continued to make big budget films in the aftermath of his move across the Atlantic. His career had ups (*U-571* in 2000, *Hannibal* in 2001) and downs (*Dune* in 1984) and "in betweens" (*King Kong* in 1976), but became indistinguishable from that of an American-born, big-time producer. In 1977 Carlo Ponti closed his offices in Rome, retired from film production, and moved to Los Angeles with his wife, Sophia Loren.[8]

California supporters of Burke-Hardtke and the Revenue Act of 1971 were also not entirely happy with some outcomes of this legislation. The Revenue Act called back American capital from Western Europe but did not necessarily redirect it into Southern California. After the end of the studio system in the 1950s, more and more producers were working independently on the California studio facilities, free to move their productions wherever costs were cheaper. Jimmy Carter successfully lured Warners to shoot John Boorman's *Deliverance* (1972) in Georgia. Many other states followed suit and successfully competed with California for movie money. In October 1983 the California Assembly's Committee on Economic Development and New Technologies held hearings at the Museum of Science and Industry in Los Angeles about the "Flight of the Motion Picture Industry from California." In 1957 labor economist Irving Bernstein had worried about investments and technical jobs leaving California for Western Europe, but almost thirty years later, the state committee mostly heard complaints about other American states' grabbing California film business.

The industry was still important for California. Filmmaking was a "nonpolluting" business and "at present employs 77,000 employees and generates over \$100 million in state and local tax revenues."[9] Its relevance to the state's economy was, however, jeopardized by other states' competition.[10] Some foreign nations were getting crumbs of the cake, like the UK for *Chariots of Fire* (Hugh Hudson, 1981) and India for *Gandhi* (Richard Attenborough, 1982), but the strongest competition came from inside the union.[11] "Forty-nine [American] states have set up film development programs," reported *Daily Variety*.[12] To lure productions from California, states like New York were cutting the red tape and made obtaining permits a "one step process." Other states were even wilier. Sy Salkowitz, president of Los Angeles–based Viacom Productions, was made a colonel of Kentucky's National Guard.[13] Even Tom Hayden, the state assemblymember from Santa Monica and progressive star politician, advocated making the bureaucracy easier to navigate and advised local unions "to make concessions."[14]

The following year the California legislature passed the California Motion Pictures Television and Commercial Industries Act with the goal of streamlining the bureaucracy and keeping the manufacturing of moving images in the state. In 1985, at a hearing of the California Assembly's Committee on Economic Development and New Technologies in Monterey, the California Film Office reported that out of the 156 films made in the United States the previous year only fifty-six had been shot entirely in the state. Twenty more had been shot in part in California, but the majority (eighty) had been entirely shot in other states. At this hearing UCLA professor Susan Christopherson noted that 1973 had been the watershed year when the runaways ceased to be shot abroad but were predominantly shot in other US states.[15] Some of the non-California-made movies were also among the most successful movies of these decades. Film historian Richard Koszarski notes that between 1968 and 1980 sixteen films made in New York were nominated for an Academy Award for Best Picture and several of them (*Midnight Cowboy* by John Schlesinger in 1969, *The French Connection* by William Friedkin in 1971, *The Godfather Part I* by Francis Ford Coppola in 1972, and *Annie Hall* by Woody Allen in 1977), won the ultimate film industry's nod.[16]

Film also retrenched into more national themes and traditions. What Diane Jacobs called the "Hollywood Renaissance"[17] of the 1970s produced a generation of "movie brats" that used the lesson of the *nouvelle vague* and French criticism to fall in love, again, with classical Hollywood cinema. Ideas traveled back and forth on the routes of the Celluloid Atlantic and the French New Wave admiration

Conclusion 291

for American cinema had circled back to American film criticism in the 1960s especially via the influential work of *Village Voice* film critic Andrew Sarris. Out was what Thom Andersen has called the "anti-Hollywood consensus," the contempt for Hollywood typical of the American intellectuals of the 1950s.[18] In was, instead, the love for Hollywood genres and auteurs. The new generation of American filmmakers, many of them the product of film schools and film criticism in Los Angeles and New York, had learned, ironically from Jean-Luc Godard and François Truffaut, to love American locales, Hollywood genres, and Hollywood studio authors. *The Last Picture Show* (1971), film critic Peter Bogdanovich's first feature film, was a proclamation of love for Texas landscapes and for Cybill Shepherd. His second, *What's Up Doc?* (1972), was an update of the American screwball comedy with Barbara Streisand and Ryan O'Neal replacing Katherine Hepburn and Cary Grant. In the 1970s NYU graduate Martin Scorsese and UCLA graduate Francis Ford Coppola shot some of the most influential gangster films in the history of the genre (respectively, *Mean Streets* in 1973, and *The Godfather* part I and part II in 1972 and 1974) and USC graduate George Lucas ticked off an American nostalgia operation with *American Graffiti* (1973). In Robert Sklar's words: "For guidance the new generation looked backward, toward the studio era. They proved as interested in reviving [classical Hollywood] genres as in revising them. They were memorably called 'movie brats' not just because they were young (in earlier periods many directors started in their twenties) but because they were crazy about old [American] movies."[19]

Italian cinema looked inward too. In her classic 1984 panorama of Italian cinema, Maria Liehm anointed Nanni Moretti as the "only enfant terrible of Italian cinema of the Seventies" and the "spokesman for his generation."[20] The assessment held. In 2004, Ewa Mazierska and Laura Rascaroli called the filmmaker, born in 1953, "the most important Italian filmmaker of the last thirty years."[21] Disclaimers notwithstanding, Moretti has often been seen as representative of Italian cinema of the late 1970s. For Divo Cavicchioli, Moretti's second feature film *Ecce Bombo* (1978) is like Fellini's *La dolce vita* (1960). *Ecce Bombo* was one of the few Italian films that represent the complexity of Italian sociology.[22]

Connecting these two films is helpful, though Moretti's cinema, or a close analysis of *La dolce vita*, is outside the purview of this book. The comparison between Fellini's portrayal of the "Hollywood on the Tiber" and Moretti's representation of young Roman intellectuals in the aftermath of '68 shows how the cinematic landscape had narrowed. Almost reluctantly, Fellini's lenses captured a transnational world inhabited by characters that, like those of Rossellini's *Paisan*, could not help producing a soundtrack where Italian and English cohabited, clashed, and intermingled (Marcello Mastroianni's character Marcello is addressed by a prostitute as "Aggregorypeccke" in reference to Gregory Peck's American-in-Rome reporter Joe Bradley in William Wyler's *Roman Holiday*, 1953). In Robert Gordon's words *La dolce vita* reflected "the entire subculture" of Hollywood on the Tiber and "recodified Rome . . . in the light of the new Americanized glamour and decadence. Here, Rome was the playground of Hollywood, which brought new prosperity but also a new strangeness, a moral vacuum in its wake."[23]

Twenty years later, Nanni Moretti's *Ecce Bombo* looks and sounds almost claustrophobic, circumscribed by Roman middle-class accents and by a geography that does not extend beyond Rome and its beach town, Ostia. In the movies that followed *Ecce Bombo* in the 1980s, Moretti's cinema became even more narrowly focused. In *Sogni d'oro* (Golden Dreams, 1981), *Bianca* (1984), *La messa è finita* (The Mass Is Ended, 1985), and *Palombella rossa* (Red Wood Pigeon, 1989), almost every frame is dominated by Moretti himself, via his onscreen alter ego Michele Apicella.

Like Francis Ford Coppola's rediscovery of classical Hollywood genres, Moretti's work serves well to mark the end of the Celluloid Atlantic. His cinema was a fortunate confluence of personal tastes, a political project, and an adherence to contextual sociological mutations. Moretti is doing what Fellini was unable to put into effect. *La dolce vita*, after all, was all about the Celluloid Atlantic, which was happening all around Fellini's set. Twenty years later, in a Rome devoid of Hollywood capital and Hollywood players, Moretti could make a point of speaking to specific, almost parochial, Italian issues. He easily succeeded in walling off the rest of the world. Like *Ecce Bombo*, his films of the late seventies and early eighties are pungent, monolingual portrayals of Italian post-1968 slackers. They are terrific films, but they are part of a new phenomenon described by Tiziana Ferrero-Regis as "the emergence of the intimate space film, in which memory and autobiography substituted for grand historical events."[24] "My films are very personal," Moretti wrote. "I never bother to think whether the Italian public will understand them, never mind worrying about what North Americans might think."[25] The words of this important post–Celluloid Atlantic filmmaker may well serve as an ending to the story this book has told.

Notes

Introduction

1. *Economist*, July 7, 2018. For nineteenth-century uses of the term *Pond* to connote the North Atlantic, see for example, Donald McLeod, ed., *Good Words for 1885* (London: Isbister and Co., 1885), 562. Accessed July 7, 2019. https://books.google.com/books?id=CskhAQAAIAAJ&printsec=frontcover&hl=en#v=onepage&q=%22across%20the%20pond%22&f=false.

2. Robert Kagan, "Power and Weakness," *Policy Review* 113 (June–July 2002). See also his book *Of Paradise and Power: America and Europe in the New World Order* (New York: Alfred A. Knopf, 2003).

3. Leader, "Transatlantic Riff," *Economist*, July 7, 2018. Accessed July 7, 2019. https://www.economist.com/leaders/2018/07/05/the-western-alliance-is-in-trouble.

4. Edward W. Chester, *Europe Views America: A Critical Evaluation* (Washington, DC: Public Affairs Press, 1962), 128.

5. Harold Laski, *The American Democracy* (London: Allen and Unwin, 1949), 680–81.

6. Theodor Adorno, "*Kultur* and Culture," trans. Mark Kalbus, *Social Text* 27, no. 2 (Summer 2009): 145–58, citation from 158. On the lecture, see also Claus Offe, *Reflections on America: Tocqueville, Weber and Adorno in the United States*, trans. Patrick Camiller (Cambridge: Polity, 2009), 89.

7. On the American side of the question, see Kariann Akemi Yokota, *Unbecoming British: How Revolutionary America Became a Postcolonial Nation* (New York: Oxford University Press, 2010), and Elisa Tamarkin, *Anglophilia: Deference, Devotion, and Antebellum America* (Chicago: University of Chicago Press, 2008). On the European side there is a plethora of works. Notable among them are Philippe Roger, *L'ennemi americain* (Paris: Seuil, 2002), English translation, *The American Enemy: A Story of French Anti-Americanism* (Chicago: University of Chicago Press, 2005).

295

Notes to Introduction

8. Alexis de Tocqueville, *Democracy in America*, ed. J. P. Mayer and trans. George Lawrence (New York: HarperCollins, 1988), 465–68.

9. Russell cited in Richard Pells, *Not Like Us: How the Europeans Have Loved, Hated, and Transformed American Culture since World War II* (New York: Basic Books, 1997), 67.

10. Angelo D'Orsi, *Gramsci: Una nuova biografia* (Milan: Feltrinelli, 2017), 429. My translation from the Italian. All translations are mine unless directly specified otherwise.

11. Serge Regourd, *L'exception culturelle* (Paris: Presse Universitaire de France, 2004).

12. Adorno, *"Kultur* and Culture," 146–47.

13. Adorno, *"Kultur* and Culture," 156.

14. Antonio Gramsci, "Americanism and Fordism," in Gramsci, *Selections from the Prison Notebooks*, selected and ed. Quentin Hoare and Geoffrey Nowell Smith (London: Lawrence and Wishart, 1971), 605–7. On the intellectual success of Fordism in Europe, see Mary Nolan, *Visions of Modernity* (New York: Oxford University Press, 1994).

15. On radio and the political culture of the 1930s, see Wolfgang Schivelbush, *Three New Deals: Reflections on Roosevelt's America, Mussolini's Italy, and Hitler's Germany, 1933–1939* (New York: Picador, 2007), 73–102.

16. See, for example, George H. Roeder, *The Censored War: American Visual Experience during World War Two* (New Haven, CT: Yale University Press, 1993), and Clayton R. Koppes and Gregory D. Black, *Hollywood Goes to War: How Politics, Profits, and Propaganda Shaped Hollywood Movies* (Berkeley: University of California Press, 1990).

17. See, for example, Fabrice Montebello, "Hollywood Films in a French Working Class Milieu: Longwy 1945–1960," in *Hollywood in Europe: Experiences of a Cultural Hegemony*, ed. David Ellwood and Rob Kroes (Amsterdam: VU University of Amsterdam Press, 1994), 213–46.

18. See Stephen Gundle, "Il Pci e la campagna contro Hollywood," in *Hollywood in Europa: Industria politica publico del cinema (1945–1960)*, ed. David Ellwood and Gian Piero Brunetta (Florence: La Casa Usher, 1991), 113–32.

19. Cited in Fabrice Montebello, "Hollywood Films in a French Working Class Milieu: Longwy 1945–1960," in *Hollywood in Europe: Experiences of a Cultural Hegemony*, ed. David Ellwood and Rob Kroes (Amsterdam: VU University of Amsterdam Press, 1994), 234.

20. Theodor Adorno and Max Horkheimer, *Dialectic of Enlightenment: Philosophical Fragments* (Stanford: Stanford University Press, 2002).

21. The turn of phrase is by Thomas Mann. See Detlev Claussen, *Theodor W. Adorno: One Last Genius* (Cambridge, MA: Harvard University Press, 2008), 116. For Adorno's critique of America, see Claus Offe, *Reflections on America: Tocqueville, Weber and Adorno in the United States*, trans. Patrick Camiller (Cambridge: Polity, 2009), 69–92.

Notes to Introduction

22. Theodor Adorno and Max Horkheimer, *Dialectic of Enlightenment: Philosophical Fragments* (Stanford: Stanford University Press, 2002), 115.

23. John Tomlinson, *Cultural Imperialism: A Critical Introduction* (Baltimore: Johns Hopkins University Press, 1991), 2.

24. See Mary Nolan, *The Transatlantic Century* (Cambridge: Cambridge University Press, 2012); Kristin Thompson, *Exporting Entertainment: America in the World Film Market 1907–34* (London: British Film Institute Books, 1985); David Ellwood and Rob Kroes, eds., *Hollywood in Europe: Experiences of Cultural Hegemony* (Amsterdam: VU University of Amsterdam Press, 1994); Andrew Higson and Richard Maltby, eds., *Film Europe and Film America: Cinema Commerce and Cultural Exchange* (Exeter, UK: University of Exeter Press, 1999); Toby Miller, Nitin Govil, John McMurria, and Richard Maxwell, *Global Hollywood* (London: BFI, 2001); Geoffrey Nowell-Smith and Steven Ricci, *Hollywood and Europe: Economics, Culture, National Identity* (London: British Film Institute, 1998); Daniela Treveri Gennari, *Post-War Italian Cinema: American Intervention, Vatican Interests* (London: Routledge, 2009). For two early correctives to the cultural imperialism thesis, see Miriam Bratu Hansen, "Fallen Women, Rising Stars, New Horizons: Shanghai Silent Film as Vernacular Modernism," *Film Quarterly* 54, no. 1 (Fall 2000), and Victoria De Grazia, *Irresistible Empire: America's Advance through Twentieth-Century Europe* (Cambridge, MA: Harvard University Press, 2006).

25. Cesare Zavattini, "Some Ideas on the Cinema," *Sight and Sound* 23, no. 2 (October–December 1953): 65.

26. As far as the colonized are concerned, wrote Aimé Césaire in his 1955 *Discourse on Colonialism*, the Dutch oil company Shell or American Standard Oil are the same and their wealth "will never console me [for the loss] of the Aztecs and Incas." Aimé Césaire, *Discourse on Colonialism* (1955; New York: Monthly Review Press, 2001), 42. Chinweizu Ibekwe, *The West and the Rest of Us: White Predators, Black Slavers, and the African Elite* (New York: Vintage, 1975).

27. Glauber Rocha, "Cinema Novo v. Cultural Imperialism," in *The Cineaste Interviews: The Art and Politics of the Cinema*, ed. Dan Georgakas and Lenny Rubenstein (Chicago: Lake View Press, 1983), 10–24; citation on 19.

28. Rocha, "Cinema Novo v. Cultural Imperialism," 17.

29. Françoise Pfaff, "The Uniqueness of Ousmane Sembène's Cinema," in *Ousmane Sembène: Dialogues with Critics and Writers*, ed. Samba Gadjigo, Ralph H. Faulkingham, Thomas Cassirer, and Reinhard Sander (Amherst, MA: University of Massachusetts Press, 1993), 14–21, 19.

30. "The Creation of an African Film Aesthetic/Language for Representing African Realities," in *A Call for Action: The Films of Ousmane Sembène*, ed. Sheila Petty (Westport, CT: Greenwood Press, 1996), 105–17.

31. "The Creation of an African Film Aesthetic/Language," 109.

32. Fernando Solanas and Octavio Getino, "Towards a Third Cinema," *Afterimage* 3 (Summer 1971): 16–35.

298 Notes to Introduction

33. Glauber Rocha, "Cinema Novo v. Cultural Imperialism," in *The Cineaste Interviews: The Art and Politics of the Cinema*, ed. Dan Georgakas and Lenny Rubenstein (Chicago: Lake View Press, 1983), 17.

34. Mary Harrod, Mariana Liz, and Alissa Timoshkina, eds., *The Europeanness of European Cinema: Identity, Meaning Globalization* (London: I.B. Tauris, 2015).

35. Harrod, Liz, and Timoshkina, *The Europeanness of European Cinema*, 2.

36. Giuliana Muscio, *Napoli/New York/Hollywood: Film between Italy and the United States* (New York: Fordham University Press, 2019), 258.

37. Saverio Giovacchini and Robert Sklar, eds., *Global Neorealism: The Transnational History of a Film Style* (Jackson: University Press of Mississippi, 2012), and Karl Schoonover, *Brutal Vision: The Neorealist Body in Postwar Italian Cinema* (Minneapolis: University of Minnesota Press, 2012), 183; Muscio, *Napoli/New York/Hollywood*, 253–96.

38. Cited in Andrew Spicer, *European Film Noir* (Manchester, UK: Manchester University Press, 2007), 2.

39. See Raymond Borde and Etienne Chaumeton, *A Panorama of American Film Noir 1941–1953*, trans. Paul Hammond (1955; San Francisco: City Lights, 2002). See the insightful work of James Naremore, *More Than Night: Film Noir in Its Contexts* (Berkeley: University of California Press, 2008), 9–36.

40. Andrew Spicer, *European Film Noir* (Manchester, UK: Manchester University Press, 2007), 17.

41. Theodor Adorno, "The Essay as Form," *New German Critique* 32 (Spring–Summer 1984): 165.

42. See Vanessa Schwartz, *It's So French! Hollywood, Paris, and the Making of Cosmopolitan Film Culture* (Chicago: Chicago University Press, 2007). See also also Alexander Walker, *Hollywood UK: The British Film Industry in the Sixties* (London: Stein and Day, 1974).

43. Adorno, "*Kultur* and Culture," 149.

44. Vanessa Schwartz, *It's So French! Hollywood, Paris, and the Making of Cosmopolitan Film Culture* (Chicago: Chicago University Press, 2007).

45. See Gian Piero Brunetta, *Il ruggito del leone: Hollywood alla Conquista dell'impero dei sogni nell'Italia di Mussolini* (Venice: Marsilio, 2013), 15. See also his *Buio in Sala: Cent'anni di passioni dello spettatore cinematografico* (Venice: Marsilio, 1989).

46. Mary Ann McDonald Carolan, *The Transatlantic Gaze: Italian Cinema, American Film* (Albany: State University of New York Press, 2014), 1.

47. Giorgio Bertellini, *Italy in Early American Cinema: Race, Landscape, and the Picturesque* (Bloomington: Indiana University Press, 2010), and Muscio, *Napoli/New York/Hollywood*. See also Carolan, *The Transatlantic Gaze*.

48. David Ellwood, "Italy, Europe, and the Cold War: Politics and Economics," in *Italy in the Cold War: Politics, Culture and Society 1948–58*, ed.

Christopher Duggan and Christopher Wagstaff (Oxford: Berg, 1995), 34. See also Ellwood, *Rebuilding Western Europe: America and Postwar Reconstruction* (London: Longman, 1992), and Nicola White, *Reconstructing Italian Fashion: America and the Development of Italian Fashion History* (Oxford: Berg, 2000), esp. 9–34.

49. See Thomas Elsaesser, "European Cinema in the Twenty-First Century: Enlarging the Context?," in *The Europeanness of European Cinema*, ed. Mary Harrod, Mariana Liz, and Alissa Timoshkina (London: I.B. Tauris, 2014),17–32.

50. Jacques Aumont, "L'histoire du cinema n'existe pas," *Cinémas* 21, nos. 2–3 (2011): 153–68, 168.

51. Aumont, "L'histoire du cinema n'existe pas," 166.

52. Pascale Ory, "L'histoire culturelle de la France contemporaine question et questionnement," *Vingtième Siècle. Revue d'histoire*, no. 16 (October–December 1987): 67–82, 68.

53. See Daniel Rodgers, "Exceptionalism," in Anthony Molho and Gordon S. Wood, eds., *Imagined Histories* (Princeton: Princeton University Press, 1998), 21–40. On American exceptionalism, see also Byron Shafer, ed., *Is America Different?* (Oxford: Clarendon Press, 1991). See also the recent critique of the concept as applied to the alleged absence of American empire in A. G. Hopkins, *American Empire: A Global History* (Princeton: Princeton University Press, 2018).

54. See the pioneering work by Shelleen Greene, "*Buffalo Soldiers on Film:* Il soldato Americano nel cinema neorealista e postbellico italiano," in *L'Africa in Italia*, ed. Leonardo De Franceschi (Rome: Aracne, 2013), 93–107.

Chapter 1

1. In 1978 Peter Dunn reported that Levine's voice was still "blurred with anger" when the film was mentioned in his presence. "Those Maysles brothers . . . they put one over me." Peter Dunn, "The Last Movie Mogul," *Sunday Times*, February 5, 1978, 40–43.

2. See, for example, Richard Abel, *The Red Rooster Scare: Making Cinema American, 1900–1910* (Berkeley: University of California Press, 1999). On early Italian-American interaction, see Muscio, *Napoli/New York/Hollywood*, and Bertellini, *Italy in Early American Cinema*.

3. On studios' talent hunts in the 1920s, see Graham Petrie, *Hollywood Destinies, European Directors in America, 1922–1931* (1985; rev. ed., Detroit: Wayne State University Press, 2002); Kristin Thompson, *Exporting Entertainment: America in the World Film Market, 1907–1934* (London: BFI, 1985); Ruth Vasey, *The World according to Hollywood, 1918–1939* (Madison: University of

300 Notes to Chapter 1

Wisconsin Press, 1997). On German-speaking refugee filmmakers in Hollywood, see Jan-Christopher Horak, *Fluchtpunkt Hollywood: Eine Dokumentation zur Filmemigration nach 1933* (Münster: Maks Publikationen, 1986), and my own "Reconsidering the Hollywood Exiles" in *The Anatomy of Exile*, ed. Peter Rose (Amherst, MA: University of Massachusetts Press, 2005). Spanish translation: "Inmigración alemana y antifascismo en la comunidad hollywoodiense de los años treinta," *Historia Mundial del Cine* (Madrid: Akal, 2011), 771–89.

4. Vasey, *The World according to Hollywood*, 7.

5. Thomas Schatz, *Boom and Bust: American Cinema in the 1940s*, vol. 6 of *History of the American Cinema* (Berkeley: University of California Press, 1999), 303.

6. Official transcript of testimony of Susan Christopherson at Joint Hearings on "Runaway Film Production and Film Production in Non-Metropolitan Areas," California Assembly Committee on Economic Development and Technology and California Assembly Subcommittee on Sports and Entertainment, Monterey, California, December 9, 1985. Sacramento, California State Library, 3–6.

7. "Il cinema italiano potrà sopravvivere?," *Star*, March 17, 1945, 1 and 2.

8. Tim Bergfelder, *International Adventures: German Popular Cinema and European Co-Productions in the 1960s* (New York: Berghahn Books, 2005), 53.

9. Carlo Ponti cited in Michael Dost, Florian Hopf, and Alexander Kluge, *Filmwirtschaft in der BRD und in Europa: Götterdämmerung in Raten* (Munich: Carl Hanser Verlag, 1973), 21–22.

10. Tino Balio, *The Foreign Film Renaissance on American Screens 1946–1973* (Madison: University of Wisconsin Press, 2010).

11. Peter Decherney, *Hollywood: A Very Short Introduction* (New York: Oxford University Press, 2016), 86.

12. Schatz, *Boom and Bust*, 323.

13. Schatz, *Boom and Bust*, 290.

14. Tino Balio, ed., *The American Film Industry*, rev. ed. (Madison: University of Wisconsin Pres, 1985), 401.

15. See Gallup data in Gene Brown, *Movie Time: A Chronology of Hollywood from Its Beginnings to the Present* (New York: Macmillan, 1995), 193.

16. A. T. McKenna, *Showman of the Screen: Joseph E. Levine and His Revolutions in Film Promotion* (Lexington: University Press of Kentucky, 2016), loc. 640.

17. Thomas Schatz, *The Genius of the System: Hollywood Filmmaking in the Studio Era* (1988; New York: Metropolitan Books, 1996), loc. 210. On the studio system, see also Ronny Regev, *Working in Hollywood: How the Studio System Turned Creativity into Labor* (Chapel Hill: University of North Carolina Press, 2018).

Notes to Chapter 1   301

18. Leo C. Rosten, *Hollywood: The Movie Colony, the Movie Makers* (1941; reprint ed. New York: Arno Press, 1970), 230–80. Directors, writers, and actors get a chapter of about twenty-four pages each.

19. Rosten, *Hollywood*, 267–69.

20. It was a long-standing assumption that Robert Sklar traced to the early movie producers' moniker, "Moguls," which highlighted their otherness, "part splendid emperors, part barbarian invaders," vis-à-vis white Americans' imagined community Robert Sklar, *Movie-Made America: A Cultural History of American Movies* (New York: Vintage Books, 2010), 46.

21. Rosten, *Hollywood*, 275.

22. Rosten, *Hollywood*, 275.

23. At the end of *Sunset Boulevard*, unwilling to let him go, Norma shoots Joe Gillis three times in the back and this tragic denouement explains the film's famous incipit that has Gillis's corpse floating in Norma's pool.

24. The other is Alex Seagal, *Harlow* (1965), and features Carol Lynley in the titular role.

25. The producer told Wilder that he should be "tarred and feathered and run out of Hollywood," to which the usually wittier director answered with a plain "Fuck you." See Robert Sklar, "Hollywood about Hollywood: Genre as Historiography," in *Hollywood and the American Historical Film*, ed. J. E. Smyth (New York: Palgrave, 2011), 71–93.

26. *New York Times*, September 5, 1953, 7.

27. Cited in Sklar, "Hollywood about Hollywood," 81.

28. Paul Buhle and Patrick McGilligan, *Tender Comrade: A Backstory of the Hollywood Blacklist* (Minneapolis: University of Minnesota Press, 2012), 497 and 712.

29. On Scott, see Jennifer Langdon-Teclaw, "The Progressive Producer in the Studio System: Adrian Scott at RKO, 1937–1947," in *Un-American Hollywood: Politics and Film in the Blacklist Era*, ed. Frank Kutrick, Steve Neele, Brian Neve, and Peter Stanfield (New Brunswick, NJ: Rutgers University Press, 2007), 152–69.

30. On Zanuck and the blacklist, see George F. Custen, *Twentieth Century's Fox: Daryl F. Zanuck and the Culture of Hollywood* (New York: Basic Books, 1997), 314–16. Custen reports that the mogul had been "hardly courageous" though "better than almost all other power brokers" (316). He had tried to protect both Ring Lardner Jr. in 1947 and Abraham Polonski in 1951 but he had eventually fired both of them. He was more successful with shielding Samuel Fuller. See Haden Guest, "Hollywood at the Margins. Samuel Fuller, Phil Karlson and Joseph H. Lewis," in *The Wiley Blackwell History of American Film*, vol. 3, *1946–1975*, ed. Cynthia Lucia, Roy Grundmann, and Art Simon (Oxford: Wiley Blackwell, 2012), 158–76.

302   Notes to Chapter 1

31. *Los Angeles Times*, October 30, 1947, 1 and 2.

32. Dore Schary, *Heyday: An Autobiography* (Boston: Little Brown, 1979), 166–67.

33. *New York Times*, November 26, 1947, 1 and 27.

34. Matthew Bernstein, *Walter Wanger, Hollywood Independent* (Minneapolis: University of Minnesota Press, 2000), 227–28; citation, 228.

35. See Daniel Spoto, *Stanley Kramer, Film Maker* (Hollywood: Samuel French, 1990), 75–76. See also Stanley Kramer, with Thomas M. Coffey, *A Mad, Mad, Mad, Mad World: A Life in Hollywood* (New York: Harcourt Brace, 1997), 86–87.

36. Steven Ricci, *Cinema and Fascism: Italian Film and Society, 1922–1943* (Berkeley: University of California Press, 2008), 127, and Gian Piero Brunetta, *Il ruggito del leone: Hollywood alla conquista dell'impero dei sogni nell'Italia di Mussolini* (Venice: Marsilio, 2013), 154.

37. Ricci, *Cinema and Fascism*, 167–68.

38. Marina Nicoli cites the episode in her *The Rise and Fall of the Italian Film Industry* (New York: Routledge, 2017), 139. Her source is Lorenzo Quaglietti, *Storia economica-politica del cinema italiano* (Rome: Editori Riuniti, 1980), 37–38. Quaglietti, however, does not reference any source for his anecdote about Stone's words.

39. Franca Faldini and Goffredo Fofi, *L'avventurosa storia del cinema italiano raccontata dai suoi protagonisti, 1935–1959* (Milan: Feltrinelli, 1979), 95 ("*Città Aperta* che sembra il film capostipite del rinnovamento delle strutture e' in fondo la continuazione dei film precedenti").

40. Barbara Corsi, *Con qualche dollaro in meno: Storia economica del cinema italiano* (Rome: Editori Riuniti, 2001), 64.

41. *Variety*, May 14, 1952, 18. See also *New York Times*, May 9, 1952, 20.

42. Stefano Della Casa, ed., *Capitani coraggiosi: Produttori italiani 1945–1975* (Milan: Electa, 2003).

43. John Izod, *Hollywood and the Box Office, 1895–1986* (New York: Columbia University Press, 1988), 159.

44. Bergfelder, *International Adventures*, 53.

45. The first coproduction agreement was signed between Italy and France in 1946 and renegotiated in 1949 and 1953. See Nicoli, *The Rise and Fall of the Italian Film Industry*, 150–54.

46. Kevin Heffernan, *Ghouls, Gimmicks, and Gold: Horror Films and the American Movie Business 1953–1968* (Durham, NC: Duke University Press, 2004), 115. On the success of foreign films in the United States, see Tino Balio, *The Foreign Film Renaissance on American Screens 1946–1973* (Madison: University of Wisconsin Press, 2010).

47. Stephen Gundle, *Glamour: A History* (Oxford: Oxford University Press, 2009), 72–197.

Notes to Chapter 1 303

48. *Variety*, January 23, 1957, 1.

49. Izod, *Hollywood and the Box Office*, 158.

50. Miriam Bratu Hansen, "Fallen Women, Rising Stars, New Horizons: Shanghai Silent Film as Vernacular Modernism," *Film Quarterly* 54, no. 1 (Fall 2000): 10.

51. Dorothy B. Jones, "Foreign Sensibilities Are Even More Unpredictable Than Foreign Quota and Currency Restrictions," *Films in Review* 6, no. 9 (1955): 449–51. See also Thomas H. Guback, *The International Film Industry: Western Europe and America since 1945* (Bloomington, Indiana University Press, 1969), 4.

52. *Variety*, November 16, 1955, 7.

53. *Variety*, March 14, 1956, 4.

54. Tullio Kezich and Alessandra Levantesi, *Dino De Laurentiis, la vita e i film* (Milan: Feltrinelli, 2001), 98.

55. See Roeder, *The Censored War*.

56. See Roeder, *The Censored War*, and the classic Black and Koppes, *Hollywood Goes to War*.

57. M. Todd Bennett, *One World, Big Screen: Hollywood, the Allies, and World War II* (Chapel Hill: University of North Carolina Press, 2012), 16–17.

58. *New York Times*, January 2, 1942, 25.

59. Cited in Jan Jarvie, "The Postwar Economic Foreign Policy of the American Film Industry, Europe 1945–1950," in *Film History* 4 (1990): 279.

60. Schatz, *Boom and Bust*, 289.

61. David Ellwood, *The Shock of America: Europe and the Challenge of the Century* (Oxford: Oxford University Press, 2012).

62. Cited in Jan Jarvie, "The Postwar Economic Foreign Policy of the American Film Industry, Europe 1945–1950," in *Film History* 4 (1990): 280.

63. The irony does not escape Thomas Schatz. See his *Boom and Bust*, 289.

64. The figure of the ERP moneys going to Europe is from Tony Judt in his *Postwar: A History of Europe since 1945* (New York: Penguin, 2005), 91.

65. *Variety*, April 7, 1948, 23.

66. Christopher Wagstaff, "Italy in the Post-War International Cinema Market," in *Italy in the Cold War: Politics, Culture, and Society 1948–1958*, ed. Christopher Duggan and Christopher Wagstaff (Oxford: Berg, 1995), 95.

67. Law 408, 80th Congress, 1948, accessed December 10, 2017, https://www.state.gov/documents/organization/177574.pdf.

68. *Variety*, April 7, 1948, 3 and 23.

69. *New York Times*, January 17, 1948, 1. On the Smith-Mundt Act, see also Pells, *Not Like Us*, 62–63.

70. The currency issue was crucial as foreign governments often objected to the repatriation of studios' profits abroad as it denuded their dollar reserves.

71. Tomlinson, *Cultural Imperialism*, 2.

304   Notes to Chapter 1

72. The cultural imperialism thesis informed the influential book by Guback, *International Film Industry*. More than thirty years ago, in his provocative study of the "Euro-American art film," Peter Lev argued that the notion of American cultural domination over Europe at the center of Thomas Guback's influential work "needs to be modified to suggest a more complex and subtle relationship." Peter Lev, *The Euro-American Cinema* (Austin: University of Texas Press, 1993), xi and xii.

73. Stefano Cambi, *Diplomazia di celluloide? Hollywood dalla seconda Guerra mondiale alla guerra fredda* (Milan: Angeli, 2016), 160.

74. Giuseppe De Santis, "Il comizio del cinema," *L'Unità*, February 22, 1949, 1.

75. Giaime Pintor, "La lotta verso gli idoli," in *Il sangue d'Europa (1939–1943)*, ed. Valentino Giarratana (Turin: Einaudi, 1950), 216.

76. Carlo Salinari, "La lotta dei comunisti per una cultura libera, moderna e nazionale," in *Per la costituzione democratica e per una libera cultura: Rapporti alla sessione del CC del PCI del 10–12 novembre 1952*, ed. Palmiro Togliatti, Luigi Longo, and Carlo Salinari (Rome, 1953), 112.

77. Judt, *Postwar*, 86–90.

78. Christopher Wagstaff, "Italy in the Post-War International Cinema Market," in Duggan and Wagstaff, *Italy in the Cold War*, 95.

79. Schatz, *Boom and Bust*, 299–300.

80. Similarly to the French, Italian and US negotiators agreed that twenty days out of each quarter in the fall, winter, and spring (the summer months were not considered as they traditionally produced a very low box office) were devoted to Italian productions. Christopher Wagstaff, "Italy in the Post-War International Cinema Market," in Duggan and Wagstaff, *Italy in the Cold War*, 89–115.

81. The best account of this economic negotiation is Corsi, *Con qualche dollaro in meno*.

82. Jean-Pierre Jeancolas, "From the Blum-Byrnes Agreement to the GATT Affair," in *Hollywood and Europe: Economics, Culture, National Identity, 1946–1996*, ed. Geoffrey Nowell-Smith and Steven Ricci (London: BFI, 1998), 47–59.

83. French Communist leader Maurice Thorez cited in Jeancolas, "From the Blum-Byrnes Agreement to the GATT Affair," 51.

84. *Fortune*, March 1964, 130.

85. Robert S. Gordon, "Hollywood and Italy: Industries and Fantasies," in *The Italian Cinema Book*, ed. Peter Bondanella (London: Palgrave Macmillan, 2014), 125.

86. *Los Angeles Times*, June 3, 1946, A1.

87. Daniel Steinhart, *Runaway Hollywood: Internationalizing Postwar Production and Location Shooting* (Berkeley: University of California Press, 2019), loc. 202. On IATSE's objection to overseas production, see Camille

Johnson-Yale, *A History of Hollywood's Outsourcing Debate: Runaway Production* (Lanham, MD: Lexington Books, 2017), 18–45.

88. *Variety*, April 19, 1950, 2. The figures are from Irving Bernstein, *Hollywood at the Crossroads* (Los Angeles: AFL Film Council, December 1957), 31.

89. Johnson-Yale, *History of Hollywood's Outsourcing Debate*, 39.

90. Toby Miller, Nitin Govil, John McMurria, and Richard Maxwell, *Global Hollywood* (London: BFI, 2001), 3.

91. *Variety*, October 29, 1969, 1 and 29.

92. See Wallis's concise description of the process in "Hal Wallis" in George Stevens Jr., *Conversations with the Great Moviemakers of Hollywood's Golden Age at the American Film Institute* (New York: Alfred A. Knopf, 2006), 590. See also Hal Wallis, with Charles Higham, *Starmaker: The Autobiography of Hal Wallis* (New York: Macmillan, 1980).

93. Quaglietti, *Storia economica-politica del cinema italiano*, 229.

94. See Nicoli, *Rise and Fall of the Italian Film Industry*, 137.

95. Angelo D'Orsi, "Introduzione," in Riccardo Gualino, *Frammenti di Vita* (Turin: Aragno, 2007), 8; citation on 71.

96. "Nulla è più pericoloso del volersi occupare di un prodotto dall'origine al consumo . . . Interessante a questo proposito l'esempio di Ford che continuamente facilita la produzione presso altri dei pezzi che gli occorrono per le sue automobile." Gualino, *Frammenti di Vita*, 72.

97. Alberto Farassino, "Roma Via Po': Storia e sistema della Lux Film," in Alberto Farassino, Tatti Sanguineti, and Jean A. Gili, *Lux film: Esthétique et système d'un studio italien* (Locarno: Editions du Festival international du film de Locarno, 1984), 21.

98. Farassino, "Roma Via Po'," 24.

99. Kezich and Levantesi, *Dino*, 84.

100. Kezich and Levantesi, *Dino*, 102–4.

101. Kezich and Levantesi, *Dino*, 106.

102. *Variety*, March 28, 1956, 18.

103. Cited in Kezich and Levantesi, *Dino*, 89.

104. Kezich and Levantesi, *Dino*, 164.

105. Giuseppe Meucci, *la città dei sogni* (Pisa: Pacini editore, 2005).

106. Della Casa, *Capitani coraggiosi*, 15.

107. Irving Bernstein, *Hollywood at the Crossroads: An Economic Study of the Motion Picture Industry* (Hollywood: Hollywood AFL Film Council, 1957), 55. Daniel Steinhart has rightly noted that Bernstein's figures are good for identifying "the growing trend" though not complete. See Steinhart, *Runaway Hollywood*, Kindle loc. 311.

108. Rebecca Prime, *Hollywood Exiles in Europe: The Blacklist and Cold War Film Culture* (New Brunswick, NJ: Rutgers University Press, 2014), Loc. 1416.

109. *Congressional Record*, 83rd Congress, House, August 3, 1953, 1154.

110. On Wallis's work in *Rose Tattoo* and *Wild Is the Wind* (George Cukor, 1957), the second film he made with Magnani, see Wallis, *Starmaker*, 127–35.

111. Gil Kurland Collection, Folder *The Rose Tattoo*, Herrick Library, AMPAS.

112. Gil Kurland Collection, Folder *The Rose Tattoo*, Herrick Library, AMPAS.

113. Paramount Pictures Production Records, Folder Post Production, Herrick Library, AMPAS.

114. Cristina Vaccarella and Luigi Vaccarella, *Anna Magnani: Quattro storie americane* (Rome: Nuova Arnica editrice, 2003), 47.

115. Jane Cianfarra, "The Lioness of Italy's Screen," *New York Times Sunday Magazine*, October 16, 1949, 28–33. *Life*, February 13, 1950.

116. Alberto Anile and M. Gabriella Giannice, *La Guerra dei vulcani* (Rome: Le Mani, 2010).

117. Howard Thompson, "Magnani: Testament of a Tamed Tempest," *New York Times*, April 19, 1953, X5.

118. Paramount Pictures Press Sheets Collection, Folder *The Rose Tattoo*, Herrick Library, AMPAS.

119. Giorgio N. Fenin, "Anna in America," *Cinema Nuovo* 6, no. 73 (December 25, 1955), 456. My translation.

120. See *New York Times*, September 29, 1968, D 17.

121. *Variety*, March 28, 1956, 2.

122. *New York Times*, April 15, 1960, accessed January 2, 2018, http://www.nytimes.com/movie/review?res=9F00EEDF153EEF3ABC4D52DFB266 838B679EDE.

123. Mark Shivas, "In the Beginning There Was Magnani. Then Came Loren. 'Ecco!,' " *New York Times*, September 29, 1968, D17.

124. Kramer to Abe Fogel, November 20, 1967, Box 217, Folder Magnani, Stanley Kramer Papers, UCLA Special Collections.

125. *Santa Vittoria* Production Files, Stanley Kramer Papers, UCLA, Special Collections.

126. On Kramer's first contract at UA, see Tino Balio, *United Artists*, vol. 2, *1951–1978: The Company That Changed the Film Industry* (Madison: University of Wisconsin Press, 2009), 141–43.

127. On Bronston's career in Spain, see Neal Moses Rosendorff, "Hollywood in Madrid: American Film Producers and Franco's Spain, 1950–1970," in *Historical Journal of Film, Radio, and Television* 27, no. 1 (March 2007): 77–109. See also Mel Martin, *The Magnificent Showman: The Epic Films of Samuel Bronston* (Albany, GA: BearManor Media, 2007). On Hollywood productions in Spain after Bronston's fall from grace, see *Variety*, May 19, 1965, 7.

Notes to Chapter 1

128. "Stanley Kramer," in George Stevens Jr., *Conversations with the Great Moviemakers of Hollywood's Golden Age at the American Film Institute* (New York: Alfred A. Knopf, 2006), 573.

129. Katharine Hamill, "The Supercolossal—Well, Pretty Good—World of Joe Levine," *Fortune*, April 1964, 130. By Hamill, who was hired by Fortune as a research assistant in 1931, see also "Women as Bosses," *Fortune* 1956, accessed December 4, 2103, http://0-features.blogs.fortune.cnn.com.library. ccbcmd.edu/2012/09/23/women-as-bosses-fortune-1956/. Tino Balio, "New Producers for Old: United Artists and the Shift to Independent Production," in *Hollywood in the Age of Television*, ed. Tino Balio (Cambridge: Unwyn, 1990), 165. See also his *United Artists* vol. 2, *1951–1978*.

130. *Variety*, February 22, 1956, 18. See also Peter H. Brothers, *Mushroom Clouds and Mushroom Men: The Fantastic Cinema of Ishiro Honda* (Seattle, WA: CreateSpace Books, 2013), 72.

131. *Variety*, April 4, 1956, 21, and April 18, 1956, 13. On saturation opening, see Justin Wyatt, *High Concept: Movies and Marketing in Hollywood* (Austin: University of Texas Press, 1994).

132. *Variety*, June 17 1956, 4. *Variety's* review was more telling: they noted that the film was going to net the usual "box-office excitement in houses geared to bally product" but *Godzilla* was also going to gather some attention among "deluxers harassed by the current product shortage." *Variety*, April 25, 1956, 6. See Bosley Crowther review in *the New York Times*, April 28, 1956, 11.

133. *Variety*, December 10, 1958, 7. Gay Talese, "Joe Levine Unchained: A Candid Portrait of a Spectacular Showman," *Esquire* 55 (January 1961), 65–68.

134. The figure comes from *Fortune*, March 1964, 131. In 1977 *Hercules* was still among *Variety's* "All Time Film Rentals Champs." *Variety*, January 5, 1977, 16.

135. *New Yorker*, September 16, 1967, 58.

136. Balio, *United Artists*, vol. 2, *1951–1978*, 1.

137. See Tino Balio, "New Producers for Old: United Artists and the Shift to Independent Production," in *Hollywood in the Age of Television*, ed. Tino Balio (Cambridge: Unwyn, 1990), 168.

138. Balio, "Introduction to Part I," 7. See also Balio, *Foreign Film Renaissance*. See Corsi, *Con qualche dollaro in meno*, 91–92.

139. UNESCO, *Statistics on Film and Cinema 1955–1977* (Paris: Division of Statistics on Culture and Communication, 1981), 34–35.

140. But Godard makes him the butt of the joke (and the quintessential American producer) in *Le mépris* (Contempt, 1963).

141. *Variety*, March 28, 1956, 18.

142. Greg Elmer and Mike Gasher, eds., *Contracting Out Hollywood: Runaway Productions and Foreign Location Shooting* (Lanham, MD: Rowman & Littlefield, 2005), 15.

143. *L'Unità*, February 23, 1963, 7.

144. Calvin Tomkins, "The Very Rich Hours of Joseph Levine," *New Yorker*, September 16, 1967, 55–57.

145. See A. T. McKenna, "Joseph E. Levine: Showmanship, Reputation, and Industrial Practice, 1945–1975," PhD diss., University of Nottingham, UK, 2008, 56–57.

146. Abel Green, "Top Heavy Film Studios Fade, "*Variety*, October 29, 1969, 1 and 29.

147. Cited in Gian Piero Brunetta, *Buio in sala: Cent'anni di passioni dello spettatore cinematografico* (Venice: Marsilio, 1989), 163.

148. Tino Balio, "New Producers for Old: United Artists and the Shift to Independent Production," in *Hollywood in the Age of Television*, ed. Tino Balio (Cambridge: Unwyn, 1990), 165.

149. Ronny Regev, *Working in Hollywood: How the Studio System Turned Creativity into Labor* (Chapel Hill: University of North Carolina Press, 2018).

150. Interview of De Laurentiss with Mauritz de Hadeln in Della Casa, *Capitani coraggiosi*, 33–36 and 56–60; citations from 56.

151. Katharine Hamill, "The Supercolossal—Well Pretty Good—World of Joe Levine," *Fortune*, March 1964, 130–32 and 178–85; quotation, 130.

152. McKenna, *Showman of the Screen*, loc. 1647.

153. Oriana Fallaci, "Dietro le luci di Cinecittà: VI. Non sono in casa per De Mille," *L'Europeo*, November 23, 1958, 16–21; citations on 16 and 20.

154. Kezich and Levantesi, *Dino*, 60.

155. Della Casa, *Capitani coraggiosi*, 77.

156. Faldini and Fofi, *L'avventurosa storia del cinema italiano*, 97.

157. Interview of Marina Cicogna with Della Casa in Della Casa, *Capitani coraggiosi*, 33–36; citations on 35 and 36.

158. William Murray, *The Fugitive Romans* (New York: Vanguard, 1955).

159. Neal Moses Rosendorff, "Hollywood in Madrid: American Film Producers and Franco's Spain, 1950–1970," in *Historical Journal of Film, Radio, and Television* 27, no. 1 (March 2007): 96.

160. Oriana Fallaci, "Dietro le luci di Cinecittà. Part 1," *L'Europeo*, October 12, 1958, 30–37; citation on 35.

161. See Wheeler Winston Dixon, *Death of the Moguls: The End of Classical Hollywood* (New Brunswick, NJ: Rutgers University Press, 2012).

162. On the sale of the TCF lots to William Zeckendorf, the developer of Century City in Los Angeles, see *Los Angeles Times*, December 16, 1958, 21. On the sale of part of the MGM lot to James Thomas Aubrey and Culver City, see *Los Angeles Times*, June 5, 1970, 12.

163. "Cinecittà è come Hollywood, un modo di dire." Oriana Fallaci, "Dietro le luci di Cinecittà. Part 1," 35.

Notes to Chapter 2   309

164. Ivan Volkman to Earl Kramer, June 17, 1967, Box 217, Folder Santa Vittoria Locations, Stanley Kramer Papers, UCLA Special Collections.

165. Interview with Valentina Knox by the author, Los Angeles, June 12, 2013.

Chapter 2

1. Robert Kroes, R. W. Rydell, and D. F. J. Bosscher, eds., *Cultural Transmissions and Receptions: American Mass Culture in Europe* (Amsterdam: VU University Press, 1993), 322.

2. See Saverio Giovacchini, "Reconsidering the Hollywood Exiles," in *The Anatomy of Exile*, ed. Peter Rose (Amherst: University of Massachusetts Press, 2005). And "Immigrazione tedesca e antifascismo nella comunità di Hollywood degli anni Trenta," in *Storia del cinema mondiale*, vol. 2, ed. Gian Piero Brunetta (Turin: Einaudi, 1999). Spanish translation, "Inmigración alemana y antifascismo en la comunidad hollywoodiense de los años treinta," *Historia Mundial del Cine* (Madrid: Akal, 2011), 771–89.

3. Arnaldo Fraccaroli, *Hollywood: Paese d'avventura* (Milan: Fratelli Treves, 1929), 10. My translation from the Italian.

4. Blaise Cendrars, *Hollywood la mecca del cinema*, trans. Emanuela Stella (1936; Italian trans., Rome: Lucarini, 1989), 49.

5. Cedric Belfrage, "Teas Feature Social Life of Hollywood," *Herald Tribune*, August 7, 1927, n. p. Cedric Belfrage Papers, Tamiment Library, New York University, Box 10, Folder 27.

6. Cited in Hans Pensel, *Seastrom and Stiller in Hollywood* (New York: Vantage Press, 1969), 264.

7. David Roediger, *The Wages of Whiteness: Race and the Making of American Working Class* (1991; London: Verso, 2022).

8. *L'Humanité*, April 15, 2001.

9. "Il passaggio barbarico dell'orda hollywoodiana." Gian Piero Brunetta, *Storia del cinema italiano*, vol. 3, *Dal neorealismo al miracolo economico* (1982; 2nd rev. ed., Rome: Editori Riuniti, 1993), 13.

10. *UNESCO Statistics on Film and Cinema 1955–1977* (Paris: Division of Statistics on Culture and Communication, 1981).

11. My thinking about this has been influenced by what Seth Fein has written about Mexican cinema in its so-called Golden Age. See Seth Fein, "Transnationalization and Cultural Collaboration: 'Mexican' Cinema and the Second World War," *Latin American Studies in Popular Culture* 17 (1998). Or Seth Fein, "From Collaboration to Containment: Hollywood and the International Political Economy of Mexican Cinema after the Second

310   Notes to Chapter 2

World War," in *Mexico's Cinema: A Century of Film and Filmmakers*, ed. Joanne Herschfield and David R. Maciel (Wilmington, DE: SR Books, 1999), 123.

12. Schivelbusch, *Three New Deals*, 189.

13. Robert W. Rydell and Rob Kroes, *Buffalo Bill in Bologna: The Americanization of the World, 1869–1922* (Chicago: University of Chicago Press, 2013).

14. Ellwood, *Shock of America*, 73.

15. See Michela Nacci, "La barbarie del comfort: L'antiamericanismo in Italia e in Francia negli anni '30," in *Nemici per la pelle*, ed. Pier Paolo D'Attorre (Milan: Angeli, 1991), 81–108; Michela Nacci, *L'antiamericanismo in Italia negli anni Trenta: Con otto fotografie di Berenice Abbott* (Turin: Bollati Boringhieri, 1989).

16. Emilio Gentile, "Impending Modernity: Fascism and the Ambivalent Image of the United States," *Journal of Contemporary History* 28, no. 1 (January 1993): 15.

17. Cited in Ellwood, *Shock of America*, 159.

18. Corsi, *Con qualche dollaro in meno*, 24. See also Ruth Ben-Ghiat, *La cultura fascista* (Bologna: Il Mulino, 2004), 142–48.

19. Thomas Doherty, *Hollywood and Hitler, 1933–1939* (New York: Columbia University Press, 2013), chap. 5.

20. Steven Ricci has argued that they were "the largest production facilities in Europe." See Ricci, *Cinema and Fascism*, 68 and 158.

21. Michela Nacci, *L'antiamericanismo in Italia negli anni Trenta*, 149–50. Joe Breen to the American Association of Motion Pictures Producers, October 31, 1935, *The Merry Widow* PCA File, Margaret Herrick Library, AMPAS.

22. Vittorio Foa, *Questo novecento* (Turin: Einaudi, 1997), 155.

23. Mark Rudman, introduction to Cesare Pavese, *The Moon and the Bonfires*, trans. R. W. Flint (New York: New York Review Books, 2002), v.

24. "Per la famosa rinascita" in *Archivio Pavese* (AP) November 22–23, 1927. Report in Cesare Pavese, *Il serpente e la colomba: Scritti e soggetti cinematografici*, ed. Mariarosa Masoero (Turin: Einaudi, 2009), 8–15.

25. "You've got to predominate in this century all over the civilized world as before did Greece, and Italy, and France. What in their little sphere have American movies done in Old Europe—and I have always abused those who maintained it was their financial organization and advertisement which brought them up: I say it is, not even their artistic value, but their surpassing strength of vital energy, don't mind whether pessimistic or joyful—what I say have done Movies will do the whole of your art and thought. Each of your worthy writers finds out a new field of existence, a new world, and writes about it with such a downrightness and immediateness of spirit it's useless for us to match." Pavese to Chiuminatto, April 5, 1930. My editing

Notes to Chapter 2   311

of Pavese's English. In Cesare Pavese, *Vita attraverso le lettere*, ed. Lorenzo Mondo (1966; Turin: Einaudi, 2004), 82–85; citation from 84.

26. Cesare Pavese, "Di un novo tipo d'esteta," December 3, 1930, 29–31. It was republished "due inediti di Pavese" by Massimo Mila in *Cinema Nuovo* 134, no. 7 (July–August 1958): 20–21.

27. Pavese, "Di un novo tipo d'esteta."

28. "ben distinte e ambedue legittime . . . : divertimento e distrazione serale o il punto di contatto fra popolo e idee." *Domus*, September 1939.

29. *Filmcritica*, May 1954, 87–90.

30. The first president of the Motion Pictures Producers Association of America, who was responsible for inventing the self-censorship production code.

31. *Filmcritica*, May 1954, 90.

32. Cited in Piero Berengo Gandin, "Alberto Lattuada. Interno. Giorno," in Alberto Lattuada, *Alberto Lattuada Fotografo: Dieci anni di Occhio Quadrato*, ed. Piero Berengo Gandin (Florence: Alinari, 1982), 9.

33. Umberto Eco cited in Brunetta, *Il ruggito del leone: Hollywood alla conquista dell'impero dei sogni nell'Italia di Mussolini* (Venice: Marsilio, 2013), 19.

34. Clipping from the *New York Sun*, dated November 12, 1927, Box 10, Folder 26, Cedric Belfrage Papers, Tamiment Library, New York University, New York.

35. John Howard Lawson, *Processional: A Jazz Symphony of American Life in Four Acts* (New York: Thomas Seltzer, 1925). Cited in Saverio Giovacchini, *Hollywood Modernism* (Philadelphia: Temple University Press, 2001), 22.

36. Giovacchini, *Hollywood* Modernism, 21.

37. John Dos Passos, foreword to John Howard Lawson, *Roger Bloomer: A Play in Three Acts* (New York: Thomas Seltzer, 1925), viii.

38. Lattuada, preface to *Occhio Quadrato* (Milan: Edizioni di Corrente,1941).

39. But Gian Piero Brunetta remarks that Italian critics were still reviewing Hollywood films after 1938. See Brunetta, *Il ruggito del leone*, 282–86. On Hollywood films in Italy during the *ventennio*, see also Ricci, *Cinema and Fascism*, 125, and Ruth Ben-Ghiat, *Italian Fascism's Empire Cinema* (Bloomington: Indiana University Press, 2015), 48–50.

40. Emilio Cecchi, *America amara* (1939), in Emilio Cecchi, *Saggi e viaggi*, ed. Margerita Ghilardi (Milan, Italy: Mondadori, 1997), 1277.

41. Cecchi, *Saggi e viaggi*, 1277.

42. Cecchi, *America amara*, 1246.

43. Cecchi, *America amara*, 1239.

44. Cecchi, *America amara*, 1235.

45. Cecchi, *America amara*, 1235.

46. Cecchi, *America amara*, 1353.

47. Cecchi, *America amara*, 1209.

48. Cecchi, *America amara*, 1209.

49. I owe the information about the original ending to Italian documentary filmmaker and journalist Luca Martera.

50. De Santis, *Harlem* in *Cinema*, no. 165, May 10, 1943, now in Giuseppe De Santis, *Verso il neorealismo: Un critico italiano degli anni quaranta*, ed. Callisto Cosulich (Rome: Bulzoni, 1982), 195–98; citation from 196.

51. *Bianco e Nero*, June 1, 1943. Cited from http://it.wikipedia.org/wiki/Harlem_(film), accessed July 30, 2013. On Carmine Gallone, see Pasquale Iaccio, ed., *Non solo Scipione: Il cinema di Carmine Gallone* (Naples: Liguori, 2003).

52. Gianni Rondolino, *Luchino Visconti* (1981; Turin: UTET, 2006), 59 and 77–78.

53. To my knowledge the Visconti Papers at the Fondo Visconti at the Istituto Gramsci in Rome offer scant traces of these travels, perhaps because the bulk of the papers refer to later years in the director's life and career.

54. Rondolino, *Luchino Visconti*, 100.

55. Cited in Rondolino, *Luchino Visconti*, 136.

56. James M. Cain, *The Postman Always Rings Twice* (1934; New York: Vintage, 1992), 67.

57. Cain's novella *Double Indemnity* (published in eight installments in *Liberty* magazine in 1936) was the basis of Billy Wilder and Raymond Chandler's script for the 1944 movie by the same title. On the film's obsession with insurance and corporate America, see Jonathan Auerbach, *Dark Borders: Film Noir and American Citizenship* (Durham, NC: Duke University Press, 2011), 57–89.

58. Alan Williams, *Republic of Images: A History of French Filmmaking* (Cambridge, MA: Harvard University Press, 1992), 240–42.

59. Giuseppe De Santis, "E con *Ossessione* osai il primo giro di manovella," *Cinema Nuovo*, no. 289 (June 1984) and nos. 290–91 (August–October 1984). Reprinted in *Rosso Fuoco: Il cinema di Giuseppe De Santis*, ed. Sergio Toffetti (Turin: Lindau, 1996), 255–66; Paola Bassani, *Se avessi una piccola casa mia: Giorgio Bassani, il racconto di una figlia* (Milan: La nave di Teseo, 2016), 91.

60. Harold Strauss, "Six Minute Egg," *New York Times*, February 18, 1934, BR8.

61. See Stephen Gundle, "Neorealism and Left-Wing Culture," in *The Italian Cinema Book*, ed. Peter Bondanella (London: Palgrave Macmillan, 2014), 81.

62. Giuseppe De Santis and Mario Alicata, "Verga e il cinema italiano," *Cinema* 10 (October 1941), now in Giuseppe De Santis, *Verso il neorealismo: Un critico italiano degli anni quaranta*, ed. Callisto Cosulich (Rome: Bulzoni, 1982), 44–50.

Notes to Chapter 2   313

63. On Bassani's political views, see Alessandro Roveri, *Giorgio Bassani e l'antifascismo (1936–1943)* (Ferrara: 2 G Editrice, 2002).

64. Giorgio Bassani, "Chiacchiere," *Corriere Padano*, November 26, 1936. Now in Rita Castaldi, "Bassani tra letteratura e cinema," in Rita Castaldi, *Scritti su Bassani: Articoli, Testimonianze e Interviste tra Storia, Letteratura e Cinema* (Bologna: Diogene, 2016), 91–95.

65. Bassani's note is entirely reproduced in Federica Villa, *Il cinema che serve: Giorgio Bassani cinematografico* (Turin: Edizioni Kaplan, 2010), 81.

66. Giuseppe De Santis, "Confessioni di un regista," *Rivista del cinema italiano*, nos. 1–2 (January–February 1953), reprinted in *Rosso Fuoco: Il cinema di Giuseppe De Santis*, ed. Sergio Toffetti (Turin: Lindau, 1996), 227–46.

67. Giuseppe De Santis, "Per un paesaggio italiano," *Cinema* no. 25 (April 1941), in De Santis, *Verso il neorealismo*, 42–44.

68. Rob Kroes, "American Empire and Cultural Imperialism," in *Rethinking American History in a Global Age*, ed. Thomas Bender (Berkeley: University of California Press, 2002), 296.

69. When the film was released in the United States, Vincent Canby noted that the film followed the novel "with remarkable fidelity." *New York Times*, June 4, 1977, 12.

70. The 1946 film has him getting out of a car after getting a lift. In the novel, Frank is detected and thrown off a hay truck next in the vicinity of Twin Oaks.

71. Because the film was shot in Fascist Italy during the war, Visconti did not worry about copyright issues although the film was to be released in the US only in 1977 after premiering in 1976 at the New York Film Festival. MGM had blocked it until then to make the most of its expensive property title.

72. Luchino Visconti, "Il cinema antropomorfico," *Cinema* 8, nos. 173–74 (October 25, 1943), 108–9.

73. Giuseppe De Santis, "E con *Ossessione* osai il primo giro di mano-vella," *Cinema Nuovo*, no. 289 (June 1984) and nos. 290–291 (August–October 1984), reprinted in *Rosso Fuoco: Il cinema di Giuseppe De Santis*, ed. Sergio Toffetti (Turin: Lindau, 1996), 255–66, 257.

74. "Qui giunto finisce in un caffè, passa le sue giornate a giocare a biliardo, in attesa di trovare un imbarco per le colonie." Fondo Visconti, "Palude" (C10–003043), marked as "soggeto cinematografico di" . . . no names and n.d.

75. Cain, *The Postman*, 83.

76. Cain, *The Postman*, 106.

77. The "Frank" of the first American film version of the novel, inter-preted with great insight by James Garfield, is made of some of the same cloth as Gino. As opposed to the novella's character, Gino and Frank both have dreams and ideals. The conversation Frank/Garfield has been having

314   Notes to Chapter 2

with Kyle Sackett in the car before the latter drops him in front of Twin Oaks Tavern must have been intense, perhaps highfalutin. "Thanks for not laughing at my theories on life," he tells Sackett. While not revealing his identity as the DA, the lawman seems impressed. He wants to know more: you stopped in the middle of it, he tells Frank, and you did not explain why "you keep looking for new places, new people, new ideas." Frank tells him that he has not found anything worth settling down for yet, but maybe he will. In the meantime, what is left is the quest, the search. Maybe he will achieve it right here, he tells Sackett, pointing at the "Man Wanted" sign posted on the door of Twin Oaks.

78. A secret hidden in plain sight that, nonetheless, took critics more than twenty years to discuss.

79. "Il denaro ha le gambe e deve camminare. Se resta nelle tasche prende la muffa. E invece tu ne prendi un morso poi lo passi a un altro che anche lui ci campa. Con le lire che si fanno a Roma ci si campa a Torino, a Palermo."

80. Cristina della Colletta, "Myths in the Mirror of History: The Rules of Fate and the Responsibilities of Choice in Visconti's *Ossessione*," in Cristina della Colletta, *When Stories Travel: Cross-Cultural Encounters between Fiction and Film* (Baltimore: Johns Hopkins University Press, 2012), 44–66.

81. "Sei mai stato a Genova? A Genova si può camminare per ore intere sulla banchina. È come una strada. Ci si incotrano tanti amici. Perché a Genova ci vanno tutti."

82. Istituto Gramsci, Rome, Fondo Visconti, Folder C10–003043. The treatment has neither date nor author as it lacks its frontispiece.

83. See Adriano Baracco's review of *Ossessione* in *Film Roma*, June 5, 1943. Istituto Gramsci, Rome, Fondo Visconti, *Ossessione* Clippings.

84. *Popolo di Romagna*, June 19, 1943, in Istituto Gramsci, Rome, Fondo Visconti, *Ossessione* Clippings.

85. Adriano Baracco, *Film Roma*, June 5, 1943, in Istituto Gramsci, Rome, Fondo Visconti, *Ossessione* Clippings.

86. Treatment for "Palude," marked "Sig. De Matteis. Folder C10–003043, Istituto Gramsci, Rome, Fondo Visconti.

87. Mara Liehm, *Passion and Desire: Film in Italy from 1942 to the Present* (Berkeley: University of California Press, 1984), 57.

88. Interview with Carlo Lizzani in Pasquale Iaccio, *Cinema e storia: Percorsi immagini testimonianze* (Naples: Liguori, 2000), 277.

89. *Fiamma di Parma*, June 14, 1943, Istituto Gramsci, Rome, Fondo Visconti, *Ossessione* Clippings.

90. *Brennero*, July 8, 1943, Istituto Gramsci, Rome, Fondo Visconti, *Ossessione* Clippings.

Notes to Chapter 2 315

91. *Corriere Padano*, June 27, 1943, Istituto Gramsci, Rome, Fondo Visconti, *Ossessione* Clippings.

92. *Il Veneto* (Padua), May 21, 1943, Istituto Gramsci, Rome, Fondo Visconti, *Ossessione* Clippings.

93. *L'Avvenire d'Italia* (Bologna), June 15, 1943, Istituto Gramsci, Rome, Fondo Visconti, *Ossessione* Clippings.

94. *Italia Giovane* (Novara), June 19, 1943, Istituto Gramsci, Rome, Fondo Visconti, *Ossessione* Clippings.

95. *Resto del Carlino*, June 18, 1943, Istituto Gramsci, Rome, Fondo Visconti, *Ossessione* Clippings.

96. *Cine Illustrato*, June 13, 1943, Istituto Gramsci, Rome, Fondo Visconti, *Ossessione* Clippings.

97. *Corriere Padano*, June 27, 1943, Istituto Gramsci, Rome, Fondo Visconti, *Ossessione* Clippings.

98. Guido Aristarco to Giuseppe De Santis, August 2, 1943. Correspondence, Giuseppe De Santis Papers, Cinecittà, Rome.

99. Commissariato di Pubblica Sicurezza presso la Direzione Compartamentale delle Ferrovie dello Stato di Bologna to Questura of Ferrara, April 18, 1941. The document is published in Rita Castaldi and Antonietta Molinari, "Documenti dell'Archivio di Stato di Ferrara," in Rita Castaldi, with Antonietta Molinari, *Scritti su Bassani*, ed. Maurizio Villani (Bologna: Diogene, 2016), 73–74.

100. See Elena Filanti, "Is the Politics of Resistance (Un)Translatable? Translating James M. Cain in Fascist Italy," in *Rereading Schleiermacher: Translation, Cognition, and Culture*, ed. Teresa Seruyo and José Miranda Justo (Berlin: Springer, 2016), 255–65.

101. Filanti, "Is the Politics of Resistance (Un)Translatable?," 260.

102. Filanti, "Is the Politics of Resistance (Un)Translatable?," 264.

103. Sergio Toffetti, ed., *Rosso Fuoco: Il cinema di Giuseppe De Santis* (Turin: Lindau, 1996), 257.

104. Diego Gabutti, *C'era una volta in America: Un'avventura al saloon con Sergio Leone* (1984, Milan: Rizzoli; repr., Milan: Milieu Edizioni, 2015), 122.

105. Giuseppe De Santis, "Cinema and Narrative," in *Film d'Oggi* 21 (June 1945): 1–16, cited in Antonio Vitti, *Giuseppe De Santis and Postwar Italian Cinema* (Toronto: University of Toronto Press, 1996), 38.

106. Lattuada, "Cinema italiano," *Il Mondo*, July 1945.

107. James Naremore, *More Than Night: Film Noir in Its Contexts* (Berkeley: University of California Press, 2008), 5.

108. Naremore, *More Than Night*, 221.

109. Stefano Masi, "L'hardware del neorealismo," in *Neorealismo: Cinema italiano 1945–49*, ed. Alberto Farassino (Turin: E.D.T., 1989), 49–52.

110. Alberto Farassino, "Neorealismo storia e geografia," in Farassino, *Neorealismo*.

111. Peter Bondanella and Federico Pacchioni, *A History of Italian Cinema* (London: Bloomsbury, 2017), 115.

112. See Lino Micciché, "Per una verifica del neorealismo," in *Il neorealismo cinematografico italiano*, 2nd ed., ed. Lino Micciché (1977; Milan: Marsilio, 1999), 7–28. Vittorini's article that Micciché refers to is Elio Vittorini, "Una nuova cultura," *Politecnico* 1 (September 29, 1945). A definitive critique of the myth of neorealism's technical difference from commercial and American cinema can be found in Stefano Masi, "L'hardware del neorealismo," in *Neorealismo: Cinema italiano 1945–49*, ed. Alberto Farassino (Turin: E.D.T., 1989), 49–52.

113. Cesare Zavattini, "Some Ideas on the Cinema," *Sight and Sound* 23, no. 2 (October–December 1953), 64–69. Edited from a recorded interview published in *La rivista del cinema italiano* 2 (December 1952). Translated by Pier Luigi Lanza.

114. See Farassino, *Neorealismo*, table, 60.

115. *Hollywood Quarterly* 2, no. 1 (October 1946): 91.

116. James Agee, *Agee on Cinema* (Boston: Beacon Press, 1958), 192 and 194–96. See also Edward Murray, *Nine American Film Critics: A Study of Theory and Practice* (New York: Ungar, 1975), 5–22.

117. Agee, *Agee on Film*, 236.

118. *New York Times*, March 3, 1946, X 1.

119. *Aufbau*, 1946, Billy Rose Collection, New York Public Library, *Rome Open City* Clipping File, n.d., n.p.

120. Alfred Hayes, "Author's Note on the Birth of *Paisan*," *New York Times*, March 7, 1948, X5. On Geiger, see Balio, *Foreign Film Renaissance on American Screens*, 47.

121. See Stefano Masi, "L'hardware del neorealismo," in *Neorealismo: Cinema italiano 1945–49*, ed. Alberto Farassino (Turin: E.D.T., 1989), 50.

122. *New York Times*, March 30, 1948. http://www.nytimes.com/movie/review?res=9F0CE1DD123EE03BBC4850DFB5668383659EDE.

123. *Time*, April 24, 1948. He repeated the accusation of sycophancy in his review for the *Nation*, April 24, 1948, now in Agee, *Agee on Film*, 348.

124. Schoonover, *Brutal Vision*, 183.

125. Gian Piero Brunetta, "Parabola del mito Americano: Hollywood 1930–1960," in *Il mito americano: Origini e crisi di un modello culturale*, ed. Saveria Chemotti (Padua: Cleup, 1980), 21.

126. Carlo Lizzani, "Apologia del mestiere," *Cinema*, May 10, 1943, now in Carlo Lizzani, *Attraverso il Novecento* (Turin: Lindau, 1998), 27–29.

127. Carlo Lizzani to Giuseppe De Santis, August 19 1947, De Santis Papers, Cinecittà, Rome. Correspondence File.

Notes to Chapter 2 317

128. Stuart Schulberg, "A Letter about Billy Wilder," *Quarterly of Film, Radio, and Television* 7, no. 4 (Summer 1953): 434–36.

129. Herbert G. Luft, "A Matter of Decadence," *Quarterly of Film, Radio, and Television* 7, no. 1 (Autumn 1952): 58–66.

130. *Aufbau*, 1946, Billy Rose Collection, New York Public Library, *Rome Open City* Clipping File, n.d., n.p.

131. Gianni Puccini, "Il venticinque luglio del cinema italiano," *Cinema Nuovo* 2, no. 24 (December 1, 1953): 340–42.

132. Zavattini, "Some Ideas on the Cinema," 11.

133. M. V. in *Bianco e Nero* no. 3, 65.

134. Vinicio Marinucci, "Appunti sul realismo del film americano," *Bianco e nero* 9, no. 4 (February 1948): 36–41.

135. Vinicio Marinucci, "Appunti sul realismo del film americano," *Bianco e nero* 9, no. 4 (February 1948): 36–41.

136. *Cinema Nuovo* 14, July 1, 1953, 18–20.

137. Enrico Emanuelli to Giuseppe De Santis, December 7, 1947, De Santis Papers, Cinecittà, Rome. Correspondence File.

138. The building had caved in when a crowd of unemployed women applying for a single, low-paying position as typist had besieged it. The collapse caused one death and several injuries. Vitti, *Giuseppe De Santis*, 30 and 62.

139. See, for instance, Gian Piero Brunetta, *Il cinema neorealista italiano: Da "Roma città aperta" a "I soliti ignoti"* (Bari: Laterza, 2009), 21.

140. Brunetta, *Il cinema neorealista italiano*, 21.

141. Faldini and Fofi, *L'avventurosa storia del cinema italiano*, 154.

142. Archer Winstein, *Post*, September 19, 1950, n.p. in *Bitter Rice/ Riso Amaro* file, Production Code Administration Records, American Motion Pictures Arts And Science, Margaret Herrick Library, Los Angeles, California.

143. Antonio Vitti, "Riso Amaro," in *The Cinema of Italy*, ed. Giorgio Bertellini (London: Wallflower, 2005), 53–60.

144. Cited in Pier Francesco Gasparetto, *Sogni e soldi: Vita di Riccardo Gualino* (Turin: Nino Aragno, 2007), 260.

145. *Variety*, February 8, 1950, 15.

146. *Variety*, July 8, 1950, 18.

147. On Dowling's success after *The Lost Weekend*, see Frank Chapman, "Bad Girl, but Good," *Post-Standard* (Syracuse, NY), January 20, 1946, 49.

148. See Lux to Doris Dowling, May 4, 1948. The contract is in *Rosso Fuoco: Il cinema di Giuseppe De Santis*, ed. Sergio Toffetti (Turin: Lindau, 1996), 166–68.

149. Faldini and Fofi, *L'avventurosa storia*, 155.

150. Sergio Toffetti, ed., *Rosso Fuoco: Il cinema di Giuseppe De Santis* (Turin: Lindau, 1996), 169.

318   Notes to Chapter 2

151. *Daily News*, September 19, 1950, n.p., in *Bitter Rice* Ampas Clipping File and *New York Times*, September 19, 1950.

152. Cited in Silvia Pagni, "Riso Amaro, di Giuseppe De Santis" (Rome: Associazione Nazionale Archivistica Italiana, 2014), *Il mondo degli archivi*, February 28, 2014.

153. *L'Unità*, September 9, 1949, 3.

154. Fofi and Faldini, *L'avventurosa storia del cinema italiano*, 155.

155. Antonello Trombadori, "*Riso Amaro* di De Santis e il problema della realtà nell'arte," in *Vie Nuove*, September 25, 1948, 14–15.

156. Trombadori, "*Riso Amaro* di De Santis."

157. Carlo Muscetta, "L'arte e la critica," *Vie Nuove*, October 9, 1949, and Unberto Barbaro, "L'arte di tendenze," *Vie Nuove*, October 24, 1949.

158. Pietro Secchia, "Il Partito Comunista e gli intellettuali," *L'Unità*, February 5, 1948, 3.

159. Joseph Breen to Gordon S. White, October 5, 1950, *Bitter Rice* PCA File.

160. Memo from Gordon S. White to Breen, October 9, 1950, *Bitter Rice* PCA File.

161. Breen to Sidney Schreibner, March 5, 1951, *Bitter Rice* PCA File.

162. Gordon White to Sidney Schreibner, March 15, 1951, *Bitter Rice* PCA File.

163. Bernard Kreisler to Geoffrey Shurlock, July 15, 1951.

164. The PCA file for *Bitter Rice* documents several censorial requests by individual states. These are mostly concerned with shots of Silvana's breasts. See the sheet for Ohio, October 21, 1950; Pennsylvania, November 30, 1950; Massachusetts, February 2, 1951; Maryland, April 30, 1951. Most of these states acquiesced after the cuts were implemented, although Massachusetts demanded further elisions on June 6, 1952. New York approved the film without cuts on March 31, 1950. *Bitter Rice* PCA File. Notably the film had no censorship problems in Italy where it was granted the government *nulla osta* #5894 on August 22, 1949. See Pagni, *Riso Amaro*.

165. *Variety*, December 27, 1950, 18; *Variety*, November 15, 1950, 9.

166. Franco Solinas, "I dieci di Hollywood," *Paese Sera*, April 29, 1950, in Solinas, *Squarciò e altri scritti*, with a preface by Ugo Pirro (Nuoro: Ilisso Edizioni, 2001), 130–32.

167. It was in many ways a situation similar to the one Seth Fein has brilliantly described for Mexican cinema during its Golden Age when the post–World War Two resurgence of Mexican cinema was couched in what Fein called a "pseudonationalist discourse." Mexican films stressed national, Mexican themes while deeply embedded in a very intense transnational collaboration with the Hollywood studios. Seth Fein, "From Collaboration to Containment: Hollywood and the International Political Economy of Mexican

Notes to Chapter 3   319

Cinema after the Second World War," in *Mexico's Cinema: A Century of Film and Filmmakers*, ed. Joanne Hershfield and David R. Maciel (Wilmington, DE: Scholarly Resources, 1999), 127.

Chapter 3

1. Cesare Zavattini, *Un Paese*, with photographs by Paul Strand (Turin: Einaudi, 1955).

2. Ironically on its way to be renovated and made safe for present-day wealthy consumers of Lincoln Center operas, Whole Foods Market goods, and Trump Hotel political fantasies.

3. Eugene Archer, "Wise 'Story' Direction," *New York Times*, October 15, 1961, X7.

4. Schoonover, *Brutal Vision*, 73.

5. Alberto Moravia, "Il film conformista," *Cinema Nuovo* 2, no. 13 (June 15, 1953), 361. "I film di coproduzione, con registi italiani e attori stranieri o viceversa [like *Stazione Termini*]. Il carattere nazionale, in un film, come del resto in qualsiasi opera d'arte, è della massima importanza. Questi film ibridi non possono aspirare che a un dignitoso livello commerciale. Un regista italiano che lavori con attori stranieri equivale a uno scrittore che scrivesse parte dei suoi libri in francese o in inglese."

6. James T. Sparrow, *Warfare State: World War II Americans and the Age of Big Government* (New York: Oxford University Press, 2013), 13–14.

7. See Marco Battini, *Peccati di memoria: La mancata Norimberga italiana* (Bari: Laterza, 2003), ix. On Italian racism, anti-Semitism, and the *brava gente* myth, see David Bidussa, *Il mito del bravo italiano* (Milan: Il Saggiatore, 1994). On Italian crimes in the Balkans, see Enzo Collotti, "Sulla politica di repressione italiana nei Balcani," in *La memoria del Nazismo nell'Europa di oggi*, ed. Leonardo Paggi (Florence: La Nuova Italia, 1997). See also Filippo Focardi and Lutz Klinkhammer, "The Question of Fascist Italy's War Crimes: The Construction of a Self-Acquitting Myth," *Journal of Modern Italian Studies* 9, no. 3 (2004); Filippo Focardi, "I mancati processi ai criminali di guerra italiani," in *Giudicare e punire: I processi per crimini di guerra tra diritto e politica*, ed. Luca Baldisseri and Paolo Pezzino (Naples: L'ancora del Mediterraneo, 2005). On Italian crimes in Africa, see Nicola Labanca, "Colonial Rule, Colonial Repression, and War Crimes in the Italian Colonies," *Journal of Modern Italian Studies* 9, no. 3 (2004): 308–9, as well as the earlier pathbreaking historiographical interventions of Angelo del Boca and Giorgio Rochat. See Giorgio Rochat, *Il Colonialismo Italiano* (Turin: Loescher, 1973), and *Le guerre italiane: 1935–1943: Dall'impero d'Etiopia alla disfatta* (Turin: Einaudi, 2005), and Angelo Del Boca, *I gas di Mussolini: Il Fascismo e la guerra*

320 Notes to Chapter 3

d'Etiopia (Rome: Editori Riuniti, 1996). See also Nicola Labanca, "La tardiva decolonizzazione degli studi storici coloniali italiani," in Labanca, *Oltremare* (Bologna, Italy: Mulino, 2002), 440–48.

8. See my "Soccer with the Dead: Mediterraneo and the Myth of Italiani Brava Gente," in *Re-picturing the Second World War: Representations in Film and Television*, ed. Mike Paris (London: Palgrave Macmillan, 2007).

9. U.S. 77th Congress, *Congressional Record. Senate* (Washington, DC: Government Printing Office, 1942), vol. 87, 9758–59.

10. See Greg Robinson, *By Order of the President: FDR and the Internment of Japanese Americans* (Cambridge: Harvard University Press, 2001). See also Richard Polenberg, *War and Society: The United States, 1941–1945* (Philadelphia: J.B. Lippincott, 1972), 61.

11. Geoffrey Perrett, *Days of Sadness, Years of Triumph: The American People 1939–1945* (New York: Coward, McCann, and Geoghegan, 1973), 218. On the reaction of the German-speaking refugee committee, see Ralph M. Nunberg, "Wir klagen nicht an," in *Aufbau*, April 3, 1942, 15.

12. Henry Koster, *Henry Koster*, interviewed by Irene Kahn Atkins (Metuchen, NJ: Scarecrow Press, 1987), 77.

13. Francis Biddle, *In Brief Authority* (1962; rev. ed., New York: Praeger, 1976), 207.

14. On the largely unsuccessful Fascist efforts to recruit Italian American communities to the Italian war effort, see Stefano Luconi and Guido Tintori, *L'ombra lunga del fascio: Canali di propaganda fascista per gli 'italiani d'America'* (Milan: M & B Publishing, 2004).

15. Peg Fenwick review, RG 208, May 7, 1943. Box 3516, Folder *Five Graves to Cairo* Nara College Park.

16. Ulric Bell to Luigi Luraschi, May 12, 1943, Box 3516, Folder *Five Graves to Cairo*, Nara College Park.

17. On *The Thirteen*, see the *New York Times*, June 27, 1937, 139.

18. Richard Slotkin, "Unit Pride: Ethnic Platoons and the Myths of American Nationality," *American Literary History* 13, no. 3 (September 2001): 469–98.

19. See February 1, 1943 script review in folder *Sahara* in National Archives, OWI Papers, RG 208, Box 3524.

20. OWI staff review of *Sahara*, July 8, 1943, in folder *Sahara* in National Archives, OWI Papers, RG 208, Box 3524.

21. Watterson Rothacker and Ulric Bell, July 8, 1943, in folder *Sahara* in National Archives, OWI Papers, RG 208, Box 3524. Bell repeated this to Columbia Pictures' B. B. Kahane on November 1, 1943, telling the producer that OWI was recommending *Sahara* for Italian and overseas distribution. "We think [*Sahara*] it is one of the best," Bell wrote. Bell to Kahane, November 1,

Notes to Chapter 3   321

1943, in folder *Sahara* in National Archives, OWI Papers, RG 208, Box 3524.

22. Peg Fenwick review of feature film *Lifeboat*, December 21, 1943, folder "Lifeboat" in National Archives, OWI Papers, RG 208, Box 3520.

23. *New York Times*, July 6, 1945, 8. The italics are mine.

24. See initial script review by Sandy Roth and Dorothy Jones, Feature Script Review of *A Bell for Adano*, January 21, 1944, the feature film review dated June 16, 1945 by Virginia Richardson, and final decision for overseas distribution, dated September 18, 1945 in RG 208, OWI Box 3516, Folder "A Bell for Adano."

25. Ben Kagan "The Nature of the Enemy Script," May 17, 1943. RG 208, Box 3, Folder "Nature of the Enemy Exhibition."

26. See "The Enemy Strikes" Chronology; "Quote Suggestions for Signs or Posters to Use in Tableau-Ramas"; "Remarks by Henry Smith Leiper on Desecration of Religion," in RG 208, Box 3, Folder "Nature of the Enemy Exhibition."

27. Allied Forces Headquarters, Information and Censorship Section, Psychological Warfare Branch, "Report on Conditions in Liberated Italy," May 26, 1944, Folder Report on Conditions in Liberated Italy, Rg 208, Bureau of Overseas Operations Branch, Bureau of Overseas Intelligence Regional Analysis Division, All Regions, Box 238.

28. Memo by F. A. McCulloch, December 18, 1944, Rg 208, Bureau of Overseas Operations Branch, Bureau of Overseas Intelligence Regional Analysis Division, Central Files Europe, 1941–45, Box 326, Folder Interrogation of Deserters.

29. Report by Captain Bruno Gori, February 18, 1945, Rg 208, Bureau of Overseas Operations Branch, Bureau of Overseas Intelligence Regional Analysis Division, All Regions, Box 238, Folder JICA/A.F.H.Q. Rome Italy, Estimate of Situation Report.

30. See, among their many publications, James Walston, "History and Memory of Italian Concentration Camps," *Historical Journal* 40 (March 1997): 169–83; Angelo Del Boca, *Italiani, brava gente?* (Venice: Neri Pozza, 2005).

31. Draft of Script for *El Alamein!*, Department of Defense Film Collection, Georgetown University, Box 4, Folder 17.

32. The version of the film I examined was the DVD version released by Alpha Video in 2015.

33. Lt. Col. Clair E. Towne to Robert Cohn, July 23, 1952. Memo to the DoD Pictorial Branch of Col. Patrick Welch, Chief, Public Information Division, U.S. Army, July 22, 1952. Both in Department of Defense Film Collection, Georgetown University, Box 4, Folder 16.

34. Robert Cohn to Clair Towne, July 29, 1952; Clair Towne to Raymond Bell, October 31, 1952.

Notes to Chapter 3

35. Clair Towne to Raymond Bell, May 15, 1953.

36. Director Sam Fuller, a former GI, was famously "keenly disappointed" with Milestone's film. See his letter cited in full in Nicholas J. Cull, "Samuel Fuller on Lewis Milestone's *A Walk in the Sun* (1946): The Legacy of *All Quiet on the Western Front* (1930)," *Historical Journal of Film, Radio and Television* 20, no. 1 (2000): 79–87.

37. Cull, "Samuel Fuller on Lewis Milestone's *A Walk in the Sun*," 73.

38. Cull, "Samuel Fuller on Lewis Milestone's *A Walk in the Sun*," 77.

39. Alfred Hayes, "Author's Note on Paisan," *New York Times*, March, 7 1948, X5.

40. Leonardo De Franceschi, "Fra teatro e storia, la doppia scena del reale: Il secondo episodio," in *Paisà: Analisi del film*, ed. Stefania Parigi (Venice: Marsilio, 2005), 57–63.

41. *To Hell and Back*, final script dated June 14, 1954, Department of Defense Film Collection, Box 11, Folder 19, Georgetown University.

42. Giuseppe De Santis, untitled notes for lecture at Purdue University, October 7, 1989, De Santis Archive, Scuola Nazionale di Cinematografia, Rome. Now published as "La genesi di *Riso Amaro*," in Antonio Vitti, *Peppe De Santis secondo se stesso* (Pesaro: Metauro, 2006), 37–58.

43. Giuseppe De Santis, "È in crisi il neorealismo?," *Filmcritica* 1, no. 4 (March 1951): 109–12.

44. Notable exceptions may be the two films by Luigi Zampa, *Vivere in Pace* (To Live in Peace, 1947) and *Un americano in vacanza* (A Yank in Rome, 1945), which both have American GIs at their center. I shall deal with the former in the following chapter. In *Un americano in vacanza*, Dick (Leo Dale), an American soldier, romances Maria (Valentina Cortese), a poor but very prudish Italian teacher who is in Rome to campaign for funds for rebuilding her village destroyed by bombings.

45. Interestingly, however, Rossellini showed no German Resistance fighter in the third installment of his war triptych, *Germania anno zero* (Germany, Year Zero, 1947), where Germans, even those who spent the Nazi years abroad, are struggling with their own material and moral decay.

46. Anna Maria Torriglia, *Broken Time, Fragmented Space: A Cultural Map for Postwar Italy* (Toronto: University of Toronto Press, 2002), 12–13 and 183, note 76.

47. Torriglia, *Broken Time, Fragmented Space*, 110.

48. Robert Warshow, "Paisan" (1948), in Robert Warshow, *The Immediate Experience*, with an introduction by Lionel Trilling (New York: Atheneum, 1970), 221–29, quotation from 229.

49. The Fascist Arcovazzi has a change of mind while conman Bardone chooses to die a hero's death as the anti-Fascist general he is impersonating and Lt. Innocenzi die fighting the Nazis and screaming that "one cannot

Notes to Chapter 3   323

always be a spectator" (non si può star sempre a guardare). On the new crop of Italian Resistance films, see Maurizio Viano, *A Certain Realism: Making Use of Pasolini's Film Theory and Practice* (Berkeley: University of California Press, 1993), 85–86.

50. Pirro writes that it was the Italian government that pushed for the change while De Laurentiis denied this charge and argued that it was his own decision, as "the Italians conducted a war where humanity still mattered while the Germans practiced excessive cruelty everywhere." Cited in Kezich and Levantesi, *Dino De Laurentiis*, 145. See Ugo Pirro, *Soltanto un nome nei titoli di testa: I felici anni sessanta del cinema italiano* (Turin: Einaudi, 1998) 161.

51. See Office National Hellenique des Criminels de Guerre, *Les atrocités des quattres envahisseurs de la Grèce: Allemandes, Italiens, Bulgares, Albanais* (Athens: ONHCG, 1946), 78–124.

52. Lidia Santarelli, "Muted Violence: Italian War Crimes in Occupied Greece," *Journal of Modern Italian Studies* 9, no. 3 (2004): 280. See also Hagen Fleisher, *Im Kreuzschatten der Machte: Griechenland 1941–1944* (Frankfurt am Main: Lang, 1986).

53. Office National Hellenique des Criminels de Guerre, *Les atrocités des quattres envahisseurs de la Grèce*, 100–101, referring to Acte d'accusation no. 206/52. The Greeks indicated 151 Italians as war criminals. *Les atrocités des quattres envahisseurs de la Grèce*, 4.

54. Enzo Monteleone, "Soggetto," in Monteleone, *Mediterraneo* (Milan: Baldini and Castoldi, 1992), 16.

55. Monteleone, "Soggetto," 31–33.

56. See Homi K. Bhabha, *The Location of Culture* (London: Routledge, 1994). Bhaba's notions of "cultural diversity" as a system of pregiven, unchanging knowledge about a culture, and of "cultural difference" as a process of signification about a culture that is, on the contrary, open to change, is employed by Dimitris Eleftheriotis in his stimulating discussion of *Mediterraneo*, Emir Kusturica's *Underground* (1995), and Gurinder Chadha's *Bhaiji on the Beach* (1993) in his *Popular Cinemas of Europe: Studies of Texts, Contexts, and Frameworks* (New York: Continuum, 2001), 47–67.

57. Enzo Monteleone, *Mediterraneo* (Milan: Baldini and Castoldi, 1992), 8. "We researched that period in depth," Salvatores told historian Pasquale Iaccio. "We read [Renzi's] 'L'armata s'agapò,' novellas and historical novels." See Iaccio, *Cinema e storia*, 461–63.

58. Elio Vittorini introduced the Einaudi edition of Biasion's novel in 1953. Renzo Biasion, *Sagapò* (1953; Turin: Einaudi, 1991). I am quoting the English translation of the novel by Archibald Colquhoun and Antonia Cowan. See Renzo Biasion, Mario Tobino, and Mario Rigoni Stern, *The Lost Legions: Three Italian War Novels*, trans. Archibald Colquhoun and Antonia Cowan (London: McGibbon and Kee, 1967), 37. On the drawings that Biasion

324 Notes to Chapter 3

realized while in Greece, see *Ricordi di guerra e di prigionia: I disegni di Renzo Biasion della Fondazione Giorgio Cini* (Venice: Marsilio, 2004).

59. See Renzi, "L'armata s'agapò," 74.

60. See Renzi, "L'armata s'agapò," 73–75.

61. On this largely forgotten episode, see Paolo Calamandrei and Renzo Renzi, eds., *Il Processo s'agapò: Dall'Arcadia a Peschiera* (Bari: Laterza, 1954). Part of the documents relative to the controversy have been republished as "Dossier s'agapò" in *Il Nuovo Spettatore* 9 (December 2005): 41–90.

62. See Calamandrei and Ranzi, *Il Processo s'agapò*, 61–98.

63. Zinnemann to De Laurentiis, October 19, 1956, Zinnemann Papers, Correspondence Files, AMPAS.

64. Zinnemann to De Laurentiis, April 14, 1958, Zinnemann Papers, Correspondence Files, AMPAS.

65. Dino to Zinnemann, April 17, 1958, Zinnemann Papers, Correspondence Files, AMPAS.

66. Neelam Srivastava, "Anti-Colonialism and the Italian Left: Resistances to the Fascist Invasion of Ethiopia," *Interventions: International Journal of Postcolonial Studies* 8, no. 3 (2006): 413–29.

67. See Massimo Mida and Giovanni Vento, "Storie Italiane," *Cinema Nuovo* 74 (January 10, 1956), 13–20; citation from 16.

68. Ugo Pirro, *Soltanto un nome nei titoli di testa* (Turin: Einaudi, 1998), 59–60.

69. Pirro, *Soltanto un nome nei titoli di testa*, 57–60.

70. Ugo Pirro, *Le soldatesse* (Milan: Bompiani, 1965).

71. On this dichotomy, see Filippo Focardi, "Antifascism and the Resistance: Public Debate and Politics of Memory in Italy from the 1990s to the Present," in *Rethinking Antifascism: History, Memory and Politics, 1922 to the Present*, ed. Hugo García Mercedes Yusta, Xavier Tàbet, and Cristina Clímaco (New York: Berghahn Books, 2016), 258–75, especially 260.

72. Pirro, *Le soldatesse*, 36.

73. Pirro, *Soltanto un nome nei titoli di testa*, 62.

74. Franco Solinas, "Vergogna dei ricordi," elzeviro for *Paese sera* 1950. Reprinted in Solinas, *Squarciò e altri scritti*, 142–44.

75. Pirro, *Soltanto un nome nei titoli di testa*, 23.

76. Gay filmmakers were often ferociously disparaged by a heteronormative macho culture that often ridiculed queer cinema masters like Pier Paolo Pasolini and Mauro Bolognini. For example, see Elio Petri to Giuseppe De Santis, April 13, 1958, in Correspondence, Giuseppe De Santis Papers, Centro Sperimentale di Cinematografia, Cinecittà, Rome.

77. Cited in Gianluca Minotti, *Valerio Zurlini* (Milan: Il Castoro, 2001), 62 and 63.

Notes to Chapter 4   325

78. "A me se mi danno un pezzo di terra come questa . . . mi fermo qui. Chi se ne fotte di vedere Mosca." 17.

79. *Variety*, June 6, 1962, 62.

80. *Variety*, September 27, 1962, 3.

81. *Variety*, December 4, 1962, 2, and *Variety*, October 2, 1963, 19.

82. *New York Times*, August 30, 1964, X9.

83. De Santis to "Nano" [no last name], no date [1962?], Giuseppe De Santis Papers, Folder 16 (*Italiani Brava Gente*), Centro Sperimentale di Cinematografia, Cinecittà, Rome.

84. Tony Shaw and Denise J. Youngblood, *Cinematic Cold War: The American and Soviet Struggle for Hearts and Minds* (Lawrence: University Press of Kansas, 2010).

85. On the rejection of De Santis's visa application, see L. N. Coswell to De Santis, March 3, 1954, Giuseppe De Santis Papers, General correspondence, Centro Sperimentale di Cinematografia, Cinecittà, Rome.

86. Grigori Ciukhrai to De Santis, September 5, 1962, Giuseppe De Santis Papers, Folder 16 (*Italiani Brava Gente*), Centro Sperimentale di Cinematografia, Cinecittà, Rome.

87. *Daily Variety*, October 6, 1965, 2.

88. "Italiano Brave Gente" sceneggiatura di Ennio de Concini, Giuseppe De Santis, Augusto Frasinetti, Giandomenico Giagni, Serghiei S. Sminov in Giuseppe De Santis Collection, Z. Smith Reynolds Research Library, Wake Forest University.

89. De Santis to unspecified "Cari amici," May 1963, in folder *Italiani Brava Gente*, De Santis Papers, Cineteca Nazionale, Rome. See also Pirro, *Soltanto un nome nei titoli di testa*, 188–89; Carlo Lizzani, diary entry, July 19, 1963, in Carlo Lizzani, *Attraverso il novecento* (Turin: Lindau, 1998), 95. The Russians asked for script modification as well, and demanded that the film avoid showing Russian soldiers as prisoners of war. De Santis agreed. The final version of the film turns the Russian POWs into captive civilians.

Chapter 4

1. *The Telegraph*, July 12, 2017, https://www.telegraph.co.uk/films/classic-british/earl-cameron-on-breaking-racial-boundaries/.

2. See Antonio Gramsci, "Quaderno 22: Americanismo e fordismo" (1934), in Antonio Gramsci, *Quaderni del carcere*, critical edition of the dell'Istituto Gramsci, ed. Valentino Giarratana (1975; Turin: Einaudi, 2001), 2139–81.

3. See De Grazia, *Irresistible Empire*; Marie-Laure Djelic, *Exporting the American Model: The Post-War Transformation of European Business* (New

326 Notes to Chapter 4

York: Oxford University Press, 2001). There's a very balanced description of how this process worked in the Italian economic context in David W. Ellwood, "The Politics and Economics of Limited Sovereignty," in Duggan and Wagstaff, *Italy in the Cold War*.

4. Pietro Secchia, "Il Partito Comunista e gli Intellettuali," *L'Unità*, February 5, 1948, 3.

5. Gramsci, "Quaderno 22: Americanismo e fordismo."

6. Mario del Pero, *L'alleato scomodo: Gli USA e la DC negli anni del centrismo (1948–1955)* (Rome: Carocci, 2001).

7. Cited in John Lamberton Harper, *American Visions of Europe* (Cambridge: Cambridge University Press, 1994), 231.

8. Richard Pells, *Not Like Us*, 154.

9. Daniel Rodgers acutely suggests that the term was a "Stalinist coinage of the 1920s which unexpectedly found its way into the core vocabulary of American historical writing after the Second World War." See Daniel Rodgers, "Exceptionalism," in *Imagined Histories*, ed. Anthony Molho and Gordon S. Wood (Princeton: Princeton University Press, 1998), 21–40; citation on 23. See also Ian Tyrrell. "American Exceptionalism in an Age of International History," *American Historical Review* 96, no. 4 (October 1991): 1031–56. For the role of American racism in the French perception of America, see also Richard F. Kuisel, *Seducing the French: The Dilemma of Americanization* (Berkeley: University of California Press, 1997), and in particular 12–13, 28, 50. For a revisionist, statistics-based take on the Euro-American relationship and alleged differences, see Peter Baldwin, *The Narcissism of Minor Differences: How America and Europe Are Alike, an Essay in Numbers* (New York: Oxford University Press, 2009).

10. Louis Hartz, *The Liberal Tradition in America: An Interpretation of American Political Thought since the Revolution* (New York: Harcourt and Brace, 1955), 3–7.

11. Rodgers, "Exceptionalism," 29.

12. Heide Fehrenbach, *Race after Hitler: Black Occupation Children in Postwar Germany and America* (Princeton, NJ: Princeton University Press, 2005), 167. See also Fehrenbach, "Learning from America: Reconstructing 'Race' in Postwar Germany," in *Americanization and Anti-Americanism: The German Encounter with American Culture after 1945*, ed. Alexander Stephan (New York: Berghahn Books, 2005), 107–25.

13. Emilio Cecchi, *America amara* (1939), in Emilio Cecchi, *Saggi e viaggi*, ed. Margerita Ghilardi (Milan: Mondadori, 1997), 1209. My translation. French intellectuals had long chastened the US for its treatment of African Americans. In the second postwar period, the tones became somewhat shriller. In his 1946 bestseller, *I Spit on Your Tomb*, Boris Vian adopted the persona of an African American writer, Vernon Jordan, to write of the lynching of a black man guilty of murdering two white sisters to exact revenge for the lynching

Notes to Chapter 4   327

of his little brother. Boris Vian, *I Spit on Your Grave* (1946; San Francisco: Tam Tam Books, 1998). *J'irai cracher sur vos tombes* sold 125,000 copies in three months. It had sold 500,000 by 1950. See Christopher M. Jones, *Boris Vian Transatlantic: Sources, Myths, and Dreams* (New York: Peter Lang, 1998). Simone de Beauvoir's decision to dedicate her American memoir to black expatriate Richard Wright and Jean Genet's later support of the Black Panthers and black separatism were in the vein of many French commentaries on the US that had stressed American racism for most of the nineteenth and twentieth centuries. In the second postwar period, not only were the French more racially tolerant than the Americans, but they had almost morphed into "honorary slaves," courtesy of American business expansion in Europe and what Philippe Roger calls the "métaphore coloniale." Frenchmen, wrote *La Nouvelle Critique*, were becoming "slaves to the modern slave owners that are the sovereign of the dollars." For the themes of French anti-Americanism, see Roger, *The American Enemy*, citation on 332. On the European concern about racial relations in the United States, see also Mary L. Dudziak, *Cold War Civil Rights: Race and the Image of American Democracy* (Princeton NJ: Princeton University Press, 2011).

14. W. E. B. Du Bois, "Forethought," in *The Souls of Black Folk*, ed. Henry Louis Gates Jr. and Terry Hume Lewis (1903; New York: W. W. Norton, 1999).

15. See Paul Gilroy, *The Black Atlantic: Modernity and Double Consciousness* (Cambridge: Harvard University Press, 1993). The Atlantic has been long used as a conceptual framework in the history of Africa, Africans, African Americans, and Blackness. John Thornton has investigated the role of people of African descent in the Atlantic in his *Africa and Africans in the Making of the Atlantic World* (Cambridge: Cambridge University Press, 1992). See also the conceptualization of "Atlantic Creole" in Ira Berlin, *Many Thousands Gone: The First Two Centuries of Slavery in North America* (Cambridge: Harvard University Press, 1998). See Toyin Falola and Kevin D. Roberts, eds., *The Atlantic World, 1450–2000: Blacks in the Diaspora* (Bloomington: Indiana University Press, 2008).

16. Nicolas Bancel, Pascal Blanchard, Sandrine Lemaire, and Françoise Vergès, *La République coloniale: Essai sur une utopie* (Paris: Bibliothèque Albin Michel Idées, 2003).

17. "Françoise Vergès: Postcolonial Challenges," in Nicholas Gane, *The Future of Social Theory* (London: Continuum, 2004), 187.

18. Angelo del Boca, *L'Africa nella coscienza degli Italiani: Miti, memorie, errori, sconfitte* (Milan: Mondadori, 2002); Alberto Burgio, *Nel nome della razza: Il razzismo nella storia d'Italia 1870–1945* (Bologna: Il Mulino, 2000).

19. See Olindo De Napoli, "Race and Empire: The Legitimation of Italian Colonialism in Juridical Thought," *Journal of Modern History* 85

(December 2013): 801–32, and Olindo De Napoli, "The Origins of Racial Laws under Fascism: A Problem of Historiography," *Journal of Modern Italian Studies* 17, no. 1 (2012): 106–22.

20. W. E. B. Du Bois, "The Color Line Belts the World," *Collier's Weekly*, October 20, 1906, 30; repr., David Levering Lewis, ed., *W.E.B. Du Bois: A Reader* (New York: Holt, 1995), 42–43. Marilyn Lake and Henry Reynolds have made the case for a "global colour line" in their important *Drawing the Global Colour Line: White Men's Countries and the International Challenge of Racial Equality* (Cambridge: Cambridge University Press, 2008). The title notwithstanding, however, Lake and Reynolds are mostly interested in the English-speaking world.

21. W. E. B. Du Bois, "The Souls of White Folk," in Du Bois, *Darkwaters: Voices from within the Veil* (New York: Harcourt & Brace, 1920). Repr. in Lewis, ed., *W.E.B. Du Bois: A Reader* (New York: Henery Holt and Co., 1995), 453.

22. Kitzmiller has received almost no attention from critics. The only exception is my essay "Living in Peace after the Massacre" in *Global Neorealism: The Transnational History of a Film Style*, ed. Saverio Giovacchini and Robert Sklar (Jackson: University Press of Mississippi, 2012), and "John Kitzmiller, Euro-American Difference, and the Cinema of the West," *Black Camera* 6, no. 2 (Spring 2015), and the important work by Shelleen Greene, "*Buffalo Soldiers on Film*: Il soldato Americano nel cinema neorealista e postbellico italiano," in *L'Africa in Italia*, ed. Leonardo De Franceschi (Rome: Aracne, 2013), 93–107, and her *Equivocal Subjects: Between Italy and Africa—Constructions of Racial and National Identity in the Italian Cinema* (London: Bloomsbury Academic, 2014).

23. New Jersey *Record*, January 27, 1975, Woody Strode, Clipping File, NYPL, Schomburg Center. On Strode's economic reasons for his decision to work in Italy, see also "Just a Hardworking Western Actor," *Variety*, February 17, 1971, 34.

24. William Gardner Smith, *Return to Black America* (Englewood Cliffs, NJ: Prentice-Hall, 1970), 63.

25. Gardner Smith, *Return to Black America*, 65.

26. Hondon B. Hargrove, *Buffalo Soldiers in Italy: Black Americans in World War II* (Jefferson, NC: McFarland and Company, 1985).

27. Alberto Lattuada defined cinema as the intellectuals' loudspeaker in an essay he published in *Filmcritica* in 1954. *Filmcritica*, May 1954, 87–90.

28. An early and important mapping of racism in Italian history is in Burgio, *Nel nome della razza*.

29. See, for example, the ending of *Ovosodo* (Hard Boiled Egg, 1997) by Paolo Virzì that couples a young, mentally handicapped Italian man with Senegalese immigrants. "Nobody understands what they are saying to one

Notes to Chapter 4   329

another," the protagonist, Piero (Edoardo Gabriellini), says in the offscreen comment, "but they obviously have a lot of fun together."

30. Curzio Malaparte, *La pelle*, in Curzio Malaparte, *Opere Scelte* (Milan: Mondadori, 1997), 1062 and 1067.

31. Malaparte, *La pelle*, 1039.

32. Malaparte, *La pelle*, 1248.

33. Steno, "Personaggi inevitabili del film neorealista," *Star*, August 24, 1948; repr., Farassino, *Neorealismo*, 130.

34. Otis Guernsey Jr., *Herald Tribune*, November 25, 1947, n.p., NYPL Billy Rose Collection, *To Live in Peace* Clipping File.

35. The debate about neorealism and its meaning exceeds the limit of this book. On the debate about what constitutes neorealism, see Peter Bondanella, *Italian Cinema: From Neorealism to the Present* (1983; New York: Continuum, 2001), 31–47. See also Millicent Marcus, *Italian Film in the Light of Neorealism* (Princeton, NJ: Princeton University Press, 1986), 33–127; Tag Gallagher, *The Adventures of Roberto Rossellini: His Life and Films* (New York: Da Capo, 1998); Christopher Wagstaff, *Italian Neorealist Cinema: An Aesthetic Approach* (Toronto: University of Toronto Press, 2007), 7–35. In Italian, see Farassino, *Neorealismo*; Miccichè, *Cinematografico italiano*; Gian Piero Brunetta, *Storia del cinema italiano*, vol. 3, *Dal Neorealismo al miracolo economico* (1982; 2nd ed., Rome: Editori Riuniti, 1993).

36. Many acute commentators have pointed out how constructed was the reality of *Open City*. See Wagstaff, *Italian Neorealist Cinema*, 31–40.

37. Bondanella, *Italian Cinema: From Neorealism to the Present*, 77.

38. *Il Tempo*, March 20, 1947.

39. *Cine Bazar*, March 25, 1947, 12.

40. *New York Times*, November 25, 1947, 37.

41. *Nation*, December 13, 1947. Repr. in James Agee, *Agee on Film* (New York: McDowell, Obolensky, 1960), 285.

42. Otis Guernsey Jr., *New York Herald Tribune*, November 25, 1947, n.p. *To Live in Peace* Clipping File, Billy Rose Collection, NYPL.

43. De Santis, "Il Jazz e le sue danze nel cinema," *Cinema*, no. 164 (April 25, 1943), in Giuseppe De Santis, *Verso il Neorealismo: Un critico cinematografico degli anni quaranta*, ed. Callisto Cosulich (Rome: Bulzoni, 1982), 65–68, citation on 68.

44. *Bianco e Nero* 2, no. 10 (1948), 73.

45. James Agee, *Agee on Film* (New York: McDowell, Obolensky 1960), 285.

46. *Hollywood Reporter*, November 13, 1947.

47. *Daily News*, May 14, 1948.

48. *Agee on Film*, 285.

330 Notes to Chapter 4

49. Remarkably, this is a comment that has been echoed by Italian prime minister Silvio Berlusconi apropos of American president Barack Hussein Obama. See "Berlusconi: Obama Is Young, Handsome, Tan," *New York Post*, November 6, 2008.

50. On "marking," see James Snead, *White Screens/Black Images: Hollywood from the Dark Side*, ed. Colin MacCabe and Cornel West (New York: Routledge, 1994).

51. Michel-Rolph Trouillot, *Silencing the Past: Power and the Production of History* (Boston: Beacon Press, 1995), 96. See also Emmanuelle Saada, "L'Empire," in *Dictionnaire Critique de la République*, ed. Vincent Duclert and Christophe Prochasson (Paris: Flammarion, 2002), 481. On the formation of the mythology of "Italiani brava gente," see my ""Soccer with the Dead: Mediterraneo, the Legacy of Neorealismo, and the Myth of Italiani Brava Gente," in Paris, *Repicturing the Second World War*. See also del Boca, *Italiani brave gente?*; Filippo Focardi, *La Guerra della memoria* (Bari: Laterza, 2005); Filippo Focardi, "La memoria della Guerra e il mito del 'bravo italiano,'" *Italia Contemporanea*, nos. 220–221 (September–December 2000).

52. In late October 1911 Italian colonial troops were attacked at Sciara Sciat, an outskirt of Tripoli, with about 500 killed. Italian troops responded by executing 3,000 of the 30,000 inhabitants of the city and deporting several thousand to work in concentration camps in southern Italy. See Nicola Labanca, *Oltremare* (Bologna: Il Mulino, 2002), 115.

53. Battini, *Peccati di memoria*. See also Filippo Focardi and Lutz Klinkhammer, "The Question of Fascist Italy's War Crimes: The Construction of a Self-Acquitting Myth," *Journal of Modern Italian Studies* 9, no. 3 (2004); Filippo Focardi, "I mancati processi ai criminali di guerra italiani," in *Giudicare e punire: I processi per crimini di guerra tra diritto e politica*, ed. Luca Baldisseri and Paolo Pezzino (Naples: L'ancora del Mediterraneo, 2005); Lidia Santarelli, "Muted Violence: Italian War Crimes in Occupied Greece," *Journal of Modern Italian Studies* 9, no. 3 (2004).

54. Nicola Labanca suggests that *genocide* is the appropriate term to describe the Italian colonialists' reaction to Sciara Sciat, in Labanca, *Oltremare: Storia dell'espansione coloniale italiana* (Bologna: Il Mulino, 2002), 422–23.

55. The German case has attracted quite a bit of historical attention. See Maria Höhn, *GIs and Fräuleins: The German-American Encounter in 1950s West Germany* (Chapel Hill: University of North Carolina Press, 2002). On the mixed race children who were often the offspring of these relations, see Fehrenbach, *Race after Hitler*. Uta G. Poiger has looked at the way American culture entered Germany via these troops in her *Jazz, Rock, and Rebels: Cold War Politics and American Culture in a Divided Germany* (Berkeley: University of California Press, 2000).

56. *Il Telegrafo*, January 16, 1947, 1.

Notes to Chapter 4   331

57. Aldo Tonti, *Odore di cinema* (Firenze: Vallecchi, 1964), 119.

58. "Tin Cans, Tombolo and Reconstruction," *Washington Post*, May 25, 1947, B 2.

59. John A. Schillace, *The Tragic Forest: Tales of the Forest of Tombolo* (New York: Exposition Press, 1951), 32–34; citation on 34.

60. Indro Montanelli. "C'è un negro pazzo che urla nella pineta," *Corriere della sera*, March 30, 1947, 3.

61. *L'Europeo*, March 28, 1948.

62. "Le abbiamo viste ai margini della pineta di Tombolo, sugli autocarri addossate ai 'Tommies' lungo le strade a chiedere l'elemosina d'amore e di quattrini." *L'Unità*, June 12, 1947, 4.

63. *Il Telegrafo*, February 20, 1947, 2.

64. The episode is recounted by Aldo Santini in his *Tombolo* (Milan: Rizzoli, 1990), 68.

65. "Kitzmiller è un poema quando dice 'Dove andare? Sopra barcone.' " F. Grassi, *Hollywood*, no. 125 (1947), 42–43. My translation.

66. Ruth Ben-Ghiat, *Italian Fascism's Empire Cinema* (Bloomington: Indiana University Press, 2015), 51.

67. See Silvana Patriarca, *Race in Post-Fascist Italy: "War Children" and the Color of the Nation* (Cambridge: Cambridge University Press, 2022), 12.

68. *New York Times*, December 31, 1950. New York Public Library, Billy Rose Collection, *Tombolo* Clipping File.

69. *Corriere della Sera*, October 26, 1947, 2.

70. *Film*, October 18, 1947, 3.

71. "Intermezzo," *L'Operatore*, November 21 and 22, 1947.

72. Stefania Parigi calls the Angela-Jerry liaison "a relation shorn of sensuality," and the film "a dialectic of love (without eroticism) and death." Stefania Parigi, "Senza Pietà," in *Alberto Lattuada: Il cinema e i film*, ed. Adriano Aprà (Venice: Marsilio, 2009), 152–56.

73. Lattuada's interview is in Pasquale Iaccio, *Cinema e storia: Percorsi immagini testimonianze* (Naples: Liguori, 2000), 288–94.

74. *Corriere della Sera*, October 3 1948, 2.

75. *L'Unità*, August 31, 1948, 2.

76. *Daily Worker*, March 16, 1950, n.p. *Senza pietà* Clipping File, Schomburg Collection, NYPL.

77. *New York Times*, March 16, 1950; *Herald Tribune*, March 16, 1950.

78. *Bianco e nero* 9, no. 19 (December 1948), 72–3.

79. Callisto Cosulich, ed., *Verso il neorealismo: Un critico italiano degli anni quaranta* (Rome: Bulzoni, 1982), 42.

80. *Il Tempo*, August 30, 1948.

81. For America's racism as a theme of Fascist anti-Americanism, see Nacci, *L'antiamericanismo in Italia negli anni trenta*.

332 Notes to Chapter 4

82. "Un male di cui soffre l'America," *Bianco e Nero* 9. no. 1 (March 1948), 650.

83. "Uomo nero non devi morire!," *Cinema Nuovo* 2, no. 11 (May 15, 1953).

84. "il problema razziale" was part of the "artificiosa parentesi imposta dall'alleanza col nazzismo," "nei film del realismo italiano i negri sono presentati senza pregiudizi, alla stessa stregua dei bianchi." Rudi Berger, "Italia: Vivere in pace," *Cinema Nuovo* 2, no. 11 (May 15, 1953), 312.

85. Lorenzo Quaglietti, "Aggiornamento," in Peter Noble, *Il Negro nel film* (Rome: Bocca, 1956), 193.

86. Raymond Borde and Etienne Chaumeton, *A Panorama of American Film Noir 1941–1953*, trans. Paul Hammond (1955; San Francisco: City Lights, 2002), 125.

87. Iaccio, *Cinema e storia*, 288–94.

88. *Our World*, May 1950, 37. When the film came out *Ebony* remarked that the young authors of *Senza pietà* "have stolen the play not only from veteran picture producers on the Continent but also from Hollywood." *Ebony*, November 1948, 62.

89. *Ebony*, November 1948, 62.

90. See *Senza pietà* (Without Pity), Production Code Administration File, Margaret Herrick Library of the Academy of the Motion Picture Art and Sciences.

91. According to Lanocita, Jerry "does not own anything, but wants to be owned by somebody, for example by a white woman" (egli non possiede nulla, ma vuole appartenere a qualcuno: per esempio a una ragazza bianca). *Corriere della Sera*, October 3, 1948, 2. *Bianco e nero* 9, no. 19 (December 1948), 72–3. *Herald Tribune*, March 16, 1950, n.p. *Senza Pietà* (Without Pity) Clipping File, Billy Rose Collection, NYPL.

92. "John Kitzmiller le bon nègre de *Paisà* est la suprenante vedette de ce film. Il incarne son personage come seuls, avec les enfants, savent le faire les noirs. Quelle fraîcheur, quelle simplicité de moyens, quelle âme!" *Le Monde*, July 22, 1949, n.p. *Senza pietà* Clipping File, Bibliotheque du Film, Paris.

93. Box Office, April 15, 1950, *Senza pietà* (Without Pity) Clipping File, Billy Rose Collection, NYPL.

94. Stefania Parigi, "*Senza pietà*," 153.

95. In his classic study Bogle describes the early characters of Sidney Poitier, the Afro-Caribbean actor whose rise to stardom chronologically parallels Kitzmiller's career, as "almost sexless and sterile." See Donald Bogle, *Toms, Coons, Mulattoes, Mammies, and Bucks* (4th ed., New York: Continuum: 2002) 176.

96. Sexual and racial anxieties encroached on the film production itself: a brawl broke out when Angela (Carla Del Poggio) was mistaken for a "segnorina" and harassed by a local young man, and Kitzmiller was often arrested

Notes to Chapter 4   333

by the MPs who mistook him for a deserter. Faldini and Fofi, *L'avventurosa storia del cinema italiano*, 129.

97. See Stephen Gundle, "*La Dolce Vita*," in David W. Ellwood, *Movies as History: Visions of the Twentieth Century* (Stroud, UK: Sutton, 2000), 132–40.

98. Snead, *White Screens/Black Images*, 3.

99. Petrine Archer-Straw, *Negrophilia: Avant-Garde Paris and Black Culture in the 1920s* (New York: Thames and Hudson, 2000), 18. See also Jost Hermand, "Artificial Atavism: German Expressionism and Blacks," in *Blacks and German Culture*, ed. Jost Hermand and Reinhold Grimm (Madison: University of Wisconsin Press, 1986), 68–72.

100. Jost Hermand, "Artificial Atavism."

101. Archer-Straw, *Negrophilia*, 14; *Ebony*, November 1951, 73.

102. *Il Telegrafo*, May 15, 1949, 2.

103. Bergfelder, *International Adventures*.

104. See the figures in UNESCO *Statistics on Film and Cinema 1955–1977* (Paris: Division of Statistics on Culture and Communication, 1981). In Italy by 1954 a quarter of all the films in production were coproductions. See David Forgacs and Stephen Gundle, *Mass Culture and Italian Society from Fascism to the Cold War* (Bloomington: Indiana University Press, 2007), 142. See also Jane Cianfarra, "Americans in Rome," *New York Times*, May 14, 1950, 14.

105. See de Grazia, *Irresistible Empire*, 363; Curzio Malaparte, *Diario di uno straniero a Parigi* (Florence: Vallecchi, 1966), 12.

106. *New York Times*, May 19, 1951, 9.

107. Vincent Sherman, *Studio Affairs: My Life as a Film Director* (Lexington: University Press of Kentucky, 1996), 246–66.

108. *New York Times*, May 18, 1957, 22; *Cahiers du Cinéma* 12, no. 72 (June 1957).

109. Olindo De Napoli, "Race and Empire: The Legitimation of Italian Colonialism in Juridical Thought," *Journal of Modern History* 85 (December 2013): 832.

110. William M. Slout, "Uncle Tom's Cabin in American Film History," *Journal of Popular Film* 2, no. 2 (Spring 1973): 137–53.

111. Phyllis Klottman calls the film a "throwback to the early film versions, with the faithful and self-sacrificing Uncle Tom." See Phyllis Klottman, "John Kitzmiller: Actor Abroad," in Phyllis Klottman, *Project Director, African Americans in Cinema: The First Half Century*, CD-ROM (Urbana: University of Illinois Press, 2003).

112. See Baldwin's scathing assessment of the novel in his essay "Everybody's Protest Novel," in James Baldwin, *Notes of a Native Son* (1955; Boston: Beacon Press, 1984), 13–23.

113. "Uncle Tom Cabin in American Film History," *Journal of Popular Film* 2, no. 2 (Spring 1973): 150. *Bianco e Nero* 26, nos. 10–11 (October–November 1965): 115.

114. See *L'Unità*, August 31, 1948, 2.

115. Luigi Zampa stressed his "istinto eccezionale" (exceptional instinct), in Faldini and Fofi, *L'avventurosa storia del cinema italiano*, 124.

116. See *Battle Creek Enquirer*, January 3, 1960, 2.

117. *New York Times*, August 29, 1958.

118. Charlayne Hunter, "Woody Strode? He Wasn't the Star but He Stole the Movie," *New York Times*, September 19, 1971, D5.

119. *Variety*, December 8, 1971, 2 and 47.

120. *Variety*, December 8, 1971, 2 and 47.

121. Faldini and Fofi, *L'avventurosa storia del cinema italiano*, 124.

122. *Battle Creek Enquirer*, January 3, 1960, 1 and 2.

123. The sister's doubts—she calls her brother's death "mysterious"—are reported in the obituary of the *Battle Creek Enquirer*, March 1, 1965.

124. *Village Voice*, May 6, 1965.

125. Snead, *White Screens/Black Images*, 5.

126. See Paul Michael Rogin, "'The Sword Became Flashing Vision': D. W. Griffith's Birth of a Nation," *Representations* 9 (Winter 1985): 150–95.

127. Gaia Giuliani and Cristina Lombardi-Diop, *Bianco e nero: Storia dell'identità raziale degli italiani* (Florence: Le Monnier, 2013), 1–19.

128. This was noted in "Without Pity: Italian Film Stars John Kitzmiller in Negro-White Love Story," *Our World*, May 1950, 37. See also the review of *Senza pietà* in *Bianco e nero*, where Giulio Cesare Castello calls Kitzmiller's work in the film "an elementary sincerity, an animalesque candor." *Bianco e nero* 9, no. 19 (December 1948): 72–73.

129. Woody Strode with Sam Young, *Goal Dust: An Autobiography* (New York: Madison Books, 1990), 234.

130. And, of course, this was not the only MD Poitier played. His debut role in a feature film had been as Dr. Luther Brooks, MD, in the Joseph L. Mankiewicz 1950 thriller *No Way Out* (1950). On the controversy over the kiss in *Guess Who's Coming to Dinner*, see Ed Guerrero, *Framing Blackness: The African American Image in Film* (Philadelphia: Temple University Press, 1993), 75–78.

131. *Agee on Film*, 285.

132. DP Aldo Tonti remembered the "tornado of fistfights" (turbine di cazzotti) accompanying the interracial crew of the film wherever they went. Tonti, *Odore di cinema*, 117.

133. Fascism had institutionalized a regime of apartheid in the colonies before the 1938 racial laws. Nicola Labanca analyzes what he calls the "institutionalized racism" (razzismo istituzionalizzato) that Italy enacted in 1937 with the goal of enacting "separation between whites and blacks." See Labanca, *Oltremare*, 414. See also Gianluca Gabrielli, "Africani in Italia negli

Notes to Chapter 4 335

anni del razzismo di stato," in Burgio, *Nel nome della razza*, 201–12; Riccardo Bonavita, "L'amore ai tempi del razzismo. Discriminazione di razza e di genere nella narrativa fascista," in Burgio, *Nel nome della razza*, 491–502. For a more general interpretive framework for the relation between segregated colonies and nonsegregated metropoles, see Bancel et al., *La République coloniale*. In a richly argued text that focuses on France but whose theoretical implications go further, Bancel, Blanchard, Lemaire, and Vergés argue that the republican liberty enjoyed at home is actually founded on the denial of liberty in the colonial territories. "Égalité ici, inégalité là-bas, extension des droit ici, restriction des droits là-bas" (93).

134. See "Nel mondo del cinema: Serata al Grande Hotel di Roma," *La settimana Incom*, February 16, 1949, https://www.youtube.com/watch?v=i-HApkc4CPU4&t=79s, accessed July 9, 2024. But also "John Kitzmiller in un locale con una donna" ("John Kitzmiller sitting at a lounge with a woman"), April 1959. Archivio Luce, Fondo Dial, Photo identifying code D295-27.

135. *Ebony*, November 1951, 71.

136. Thomas Cripps, *Making Movies Black: The Hollywood Message Movie from World War II to the Civil Rights Era* (New York: Oxford University Press, 1993), 264.

137. Cited in Cripps, *Making Movies Black*, 264.

138. See Alan Casty, *Robert Rossen: The Films and Politics of a Blacklisted Idealist* (Jeferson, NC: McFarland and Co., 2013), 175–81 and 194–210.

139. See Dorothea Fischer-Hornung, "The Body Possessed: Katherine Dunham Dance Techniques in Mambo," in *Embodying Liberation: The Black Body in American Dance*, ed. Dorothea Fischer-Hornung and Alison D. Goellker (Berlin: LIT Verlag, 2001), 91–112.

140. *L'Unità*, November 7, 1954, 6. See also April 19, 1954, 8, and June 11, 1954, 6.

141. *Baltimore African American*, April 2, 1955, 7. Dunham herself, however, maintained a pleasant memory of the film, and fifty years later, in 2002, wrote De Laurentiis that she had "fond memories of working with you in Italy in the 1950s." Katherine Dunham to Dino De Laurentiis, June 11, 2002. Katherine Dunham Papers, Box 10, Folder 15, Library of Congress, Manuscript Division.

142. *Baltimore African American*, April 2, 1955, 7.

143. *Variety*, November 24, 1954, 6.

144. Del Boca, *L'Africa nella coscienza degli italiani*, xi. See also his "Il mancato dibattito sul colonialismo," in Del Boca, *L'Africa nella coscienza degli italiani*, 111–28.

145. See, for example, Alessandro Verri, "Dialogo tra il Pedante e l'Ottentotto" (1765), http://www.cromohs.unifi.it/9_2004/abbattista_ottassab.

html. Alberto Mario Banti has analyzed the racial overtones of the Italian nation-building moment in his *La nazione del Risorgimento: Parentela, santità e onore alle origini dell'Italia Unita* (Turin: Einaudi, 2000).

146. This, I would argue, has led, in part at least, to a generalized understatement of the role of racism and the color line in Italian history and to what Neil MacMaster has termed "a strong resurgence of racism" in the last quarter of the twentieth century. Neil MacMaster, *Racism in Europe, 1870–2000* (New York: Palgrave, 2001), 190. This racism is revealed not just in the slogans of the extreme right, but in some of the policies enacted by mainstream government parties toward extra–European Union immigration or in the nonchalance with which Premier Silvio Berlusconi extolled the superiority of Judeo-Christian civilization in the aftermath of 9/11. This omission, and the lack of debate about it, left Italian cinema, even that part of it which was supposed to be progressive, somewhat unprepared to deal with the non-European and racially different migrants who arrived in Italy en masse beginning in the late 1980s and early 1990s. To give only a telling example, in Paolo Virzì's *Ovosodo* (Hard-Boiled Egg, 1997), an homage to neorealist cinema and a sympathetic portrait of Livorno's Communist working class, not only is the century-long racial history of the city papered over, but the new generation of black migrants are also compared—with outstanding, and largely undetected, nonchalance—to the mentally disabled.

147. Amy Kaplan, *The Anarchy of Empire in the Making of U.S. Culture* (Cambridge, MA: Harvard University Press, 2005), 16, 17.

148. A lucid and succinct analysis of this is Christopher Wagstaff, "Italy in the Post-War International Cinema Market," in Duggan and Wagstaff, *Italy in the Cold War*, 89–115. See also Corsi, *Per qualche dollaro in più*.

149. Ibekwe, *The West and the Rest of Us*.

150. Smith, *Return to Black America*, 42.

151. Smith, *Return to Black America*, 94. On Smith and his late-in-life appreciation of Ghana, where he helped organize Ghana Television upon Shirley Graham Du Bois's invitation before his untimely death from cancer in 1974, see David Peterson del Mar, *African, American: From Tarzan to Dreams from My Father—Africa in the US Imagination* (London: Zed Books, 2017), 162–63.

Chapter 5

1. Chistopher Frayling, *Spaghetti Western: Cowboys and Europeans from Karl May to Sergio Leone* (1981; London: I.B. Tauris, 2006), 121.

2. David McGillivray's review of *One Silver Dollar* (Giorgio Ferroni, 1965) in *Films and Filming* 13, no. 10 (July 1967): 26.

Notes to Chapter 5 337

3. Richard Davis review of *A Fistful of Dollars* (Sergio Leone, 1964) in *Films and Filming* 13, no. 12 (September 1967): 26.

4. David Nicholls, "Once Upon a Time in Italy," *Sight and Sound* 50, no. 1 (Winter 1980–1981): 46–49. See also the classic Frayling, *Spaghetti Western*. In Italy the most recent and notable addition to the literature on the spaghetti Western is the succinct but important volume by Alberto Pezzotta, *Il western italiano* (Milan: Il Castoro, 2013).

5. Crist's origins and use of the term is cited in Louise Sweeney, "TV and Films Move to Mop Up Violence," *Christian Science Monitor*, June 21, 1968, 1 and 12. Crist is cited on 12.

6. I have decided to deploy the expression "spaghetti" as it defines most specifically the terms of the revolution that I am describing in this chapter. I thus use it in that sense and without italics.

7. Renata Adler, "Film Studios All over Italy Feasting on 'Spaghetti Westerns,'" *New York Times*, September 13, 1968, 41.

8. Most of these views are summarized in the documentary by David Gregory, *The Spaghetti West* (Blue Underground, 2005).

9. Mary Blume, "Connoisseur of Italian Westerns," *Los Angeles Times*, April 7, 1968, D24.

10. Talking to Sergio Gabutti, Leone noted that his Westerns may have "had an Italian passport the same way millionaires' boats fly a Panama flag. *Un pugno di dollari* was a film about the United States and about my youth as a cinemagoer." Gabutti, *C'era una volta in America*, 124.

11. *New York Times*, July 10, 1969, 28.

12. Stuart Kaminski, "Once Upon a Time in Italy: The Italian Western beyond Sergio Leone," *Velvet Light Trap* 12 (April 1974): 31–33.

13. Austin Fisher, *Radical Frontiers in the Spaghetti Western: Politics, Violence and Popular Italian Cinema* (London: I.B. Tauris, 2014), 258.

14. The data are from Fisher, *Radical Frontiers*, 224. Fisher's data are not substantially different from those offered by the very comprehensive reference book by Ulrich Bruckner, *Für ein paar Leichen mehr: Der Italo Western von seinen Anfängen bis heute* (Berlin: Schwartzkopf und Schwartzkopf, 2002).

15. UNESCO *Statistics on Film and Cinema 1955–1977* (Paris: Division of Statistics on Culture and Communication, 1981), 9 and 30–35. The rise in European-based Western production mirrored the decline in Hollywood-produced Westerns. In 1967 John Cawelti calculates that Hollywood "turned out approximately 37 major Western features." John G. Cawelti, *The Six-Gun Mystique Sequel* (Bowling Green, OH: Bowling Green State University Popular Press, 1999), 2.

16. Stefano della Casa uses the latter and writes of a "European Western" or "Eurowestern" within which he feels necessary to identify a "Western

italiano." See della Casa, "Un fenomeno complesso," *Bianco e Nero* 58, no. 3 (1997): 5–8.

17. Simon Melzer, "We're Taking Leone Too Lightly," *Audience* no. 46 (April 1972): 6.

18. Philip Kaufman review in the *New Republic* 160, no. 25 (June 29, 1969), 22.

19. Pauline Kael, "Killing Time," *New Yorker*, January 14, 1974.

20. von Mechow to Huston, September 11, 1964, Huston Papers, Box 8, Folder 85, Academy of Motion Picture Arts and Sciences, Los Angeles, California.

21. Pierluigi Gandi, "Terrore e miseria del fumetto nero," *L'Unità*, February 5, 1967, 12.

22. See "È finita l'epoca del Western all'italiana," *L'Unità*, April 22, 1969, 7.

23. Roberto Alemanno, "Gli eredi del cinema di Hitler," *L'Unità*, March 30, 1966, 9.

24. Cited by Christopher Frayling, *Sergio Leone: Something to Do with Death* (London: Faber and Faber, 2001), 163.

25. Gino Cattani and Moritz B. Fliescher, "Product Category Dynamics in Cultural Industries: Spaghetti Westerns' Renewal of the Hollywood Western Movie Genre," in *Creative Industries and Innovation In Europe: Concepts, Measures and Comparative Case Studies*, ed. Luciana Lazzeretti (New York: Routledge, 2013), 213.

26. On Yordan, see Patrick McGilligan, "The Script Men," *American Film: A Journal of the Film and Television Arts* 15 (August 1990): 21–25.

27. *Guardian*, April 8, 2003, https://www.theguardian.com/news/2003/apr/09/guardianobituaries.film. Accessed April 10 2019.

28. Muscio, *Napoli/New York/Hollywood*, 258.

29. André Bazin, "The Evolution of the Western," in Bazin, *What Is Cinema? Volume II* (Berkeley: University of California Press, 2004), 149–57. Bazin explicitly rooted his analysis of the Western in the neo-historicism of J.-L. Rieupeyrout, *Le Western ou le cinéma Américain par excellence* (Paris: Editions du Cerfs, 1953), for which he had written the preface. See Bazin, "The Western, or the American Film *Par Excellence*," in *What Is Cinema? Volume II*, 140–48.

30. Arthur M. Eckstein, introduction to *The Searchers: Essays and Reflections on John Ford's Classic Westerns*, ed. Arthur M. Eckstein and Peter Lehman (Detroit: Wayne State University Press, 2004), 4.

31. Pezzotta, *Il western italiano*, 44–48.

32. "la metafora di un mondo postcolonialista che si risveglia." Pezzotta, *Il western italiano*, 48.

Notes to Chapter 5   339

33. "Un altrove esotico un luogo che viene descritto con uno sguardo che nel migliore dei casi è folklorico e di cui si misura esplicitamente la differenza rispetto alla civiltà americana." Pezzotta, *Il western italiano*, 47.

34. See Seth Fein, "Myths of Cultural Imperialism and Nationalism in Golden Age Mexican Cinema," in *Fragments of a Golden Age: The Politics of Culture in Mexico since 1940*, ed. Gilbert M. Joseph, Anne Rubenstein, and Eric Zolov (Durham, NC: Duke University Press, 2001), 159–98. Also, Saverio Giovacchini, "In the Foucauldian Mirror: Budd Boetticher's Mexico and the United States in the 1950s," in *Projecting the World: Representing the "Foreign" in Classical Hollywood*, ed. Anna Cooper and Russell Meeuf (Detroit: Wayne State University Press, 2017).

35. See Budd Boetticher, *When in Disgrace* (Santa Barbara, CA: Neville, 1989), esp. 8–38.

36. Giovacchini, "In the Foucauldian Mirror."

37. Giovacchini, "In the Foucauldian Mirror," 196–97.

38. Black actor and civil rights activist Frank Silvera played one of the bandits. A Mexican woman, Rose Cimarron (Yvette Duguay), is also part of the cohort.

39. Adrian Pérez Melgosa, *Cinema and Inter-American Relations: Tracking Transnational Affect* (New York: Routledge, 2014), 76–105; citation from 93. Notably, Boetticher films a similar narrative choice in *Cimarron Kid*. Mexican Rose and the Yankee bandit "Bitter Creek" Dalton are separated only by his murder at the hands of sadistic white vigilantes, one of whom steals the Guadalupe icon from Dalton's inanimate body, because "it will look good on my little girl."

40. Camilla Fojas, *Border Bandits: Hollywood and the Southern Frontier* (Austin: University of Texas Press, 2008), 19.

41. On Hollywood narrative devices of mythification, marking, and omission see Snead, *White Screen/Black Images*.

42. Lynching parties and kangaroo courts manned by white Americans occur, or are about to occur, in several Boetticher's films: in *Horizons West* a mob tries to kill Dan Hammond (Robert Ryan), a Confederate soldier turned bandit; John Straub (Glenn Ford) is almost lynched by the white folks of Franklin in *The Man from Alamo*; in *Seminole*, Lance Caldwell (Rock Hudson) and Chief Aceola (Anthony Quinn) are, respectively, condemned to death after a flawed trial and tortured almost to death by white American troops; Boetticher's last Western film, *A Time for Dying* (1969), features a toothless and deranged Judge Roy Bean (Victor Jory) ruling the city of Vinegaroon on the Mexican-US borderland along the Pecos River in a reign of madness masquerading for justice.

340 Notes to Chapter 5

43. André Bazin's review of 7 *Men from Now* ("Un Western exemplaire") in *Cahier du Cinéma* 74 (August–September 1957), available in English in Jim Hillier, ed., *Cahiers du Cinéma: The 1950s. Neo-Realism, Hollywood, New Wave* (Cambridge: Harvard University Press, 1986), 169–72.

44. See Antoine de Baecque, *La cinéphilie: Invention d'un regard, histoire d'une culture, 1944–1968* (Paris: Éditions Fayard, 2004). See also Antoine de Baecque, *Cahiers du Cinéma: Histoire d'une revue 2* (Paris: Editions Cahiers di Cinéma, 1991), 2:73 and 2:337.

45. Sergio Leone cited by Lee Server in "Blood, Sand, and Bullets," in *Daily News*, December 23, 2001, 14.

46. *Two Mules for Sister Sara* too is directed by Don Siegel with Clint Eastwood and scripted by Budd Boetticher and Albert Maltz. At the time of its release everybody noted the linkages with the European work of Eastwood. See *Two Mules for Sister Sara* clipping file at NYPL BR.

47. Carolan, *Transatlantic Gaze*, 61.

48. *The Bravados* was later cited as one of the inspirations for the first of the American spaghettis starring Clint Eastwood, *Hang 'Em High* (Ted Post, 1968). See David Austen review of *Hang 'Em High* in *Films and Filming* (November 1968), n.p., *Hang 'Em High* Clipping File, NYPL, Billy Rose Collection.

49. David Cairns, "I Ain't Hung Yet," video essay in *One-Eyed Jacks* (Criterion Edition, 2016).

50. In both cases the bones in the hero's hands are crushed by his enemies to impair his ability to shoot. Corbucci employs the same narrative device in his later *Il grande silenzio* (The Great Silence, 1968).

51. *New Yorker* ca. 1961, no date, no page, *One Eyed Jacks* Clipping File, Billy Rose Collection, New York Public Library, New York City.

52. Dwight Macdonald, "Three Years, Six Million, One Film," *Esquire*, October 1961, n.p., *One Eyed Jacks* Clipping File, NYPL-BR.

53. Cairns, "I Ain't Hung Yet."

54. Cited in Balio, *Foreign Film Renaissance*, 125.

55. Balio, *Foreign Film Renaissance*, 121–27.

56. Steven Okazaki, *Mifune: The Last Samurai* (Strand Releasing, 2015).

57. *Variety*, December 11, 1951, 4.

58. *Variety*, January16, 1952, 5.

59. *Variety*, January 23, 1952, 7 and 20.

60. Dolores P. Martinez, *Remaking Kurosawa: Translations and Permutations in Global Cinema* (New York: Palgrave Macmillan, 2009), 114.

61. Noted by reviewers, see, for instance, *Daily News*'s Dorothy Masters in *Daily News*, November 9, 1960, n.p., in *The Magnificent Seven* Clipping File, NYPL.

Notes to Chapter 5 341

62. Christopher Frayling has noted that like other Hollywood films of the period that dealt with Mexico, *The Magnificent Seven* "enact[s] President Kennedy's famous promise of technical and military assistance as part of the new frontier 'to those people in the huts and the villages of the globe struggling to break the bonds of mass misery.'" Frayling, "The Italian Western and the Mexican Revolution," in *Critical Perspectives on the Western: From 'A Fistful of Dollars' to 'Django Unchained*,' ed. Lee Broughton (Lanham, MD: Rowan and Littlefield, 2016), 1–26.

63. Even the *New York Times*'s A. H. Weiler noted it and called Paul Newman's acting "too broad" and Carrasco "a parody of the Mexican villains of the old movies." *New York Times*, October 8, 1964, 48.

64. Sergio Donati cited in Marco Giusti, *Dizionario del western all'italiana* (Milan: Mondadori, 2007), 196.

65. Gabutti, *C'era una volta in America*, 27.

66. For a discussion from a non-Western perspective of the Enlightenment and its promises of reason and justice, see Pankaj Mishra, *Age of Anger: A History of the Present* (New York: Farrar, Straus and Giroux, 2017.

67. Donato interviewed in David Gregory, *The Spaghetti West*, directed and written by David Gregory and produced by Blue Underground, Netflix, and Independent Film Channel (IFC), 2005.40:14.

68. Eastwood apparently resented what was only a supporting role in the climactic scene of the story. See Gabutti, *C'era una volta in America*, 142.

69. The scene of the duel and the biased judge—with the important absence of the circle—is cited by Sollima at the end of two of his Fanonist Westerns. In *La Resa dei conti* (The Big Gundown 1966), based on a story by Franco Solinas, the Mexican peon Cuchillo (Tomas Milian) kills the capitalist rapist Chet Miller (Àngel del Pozo) as Corbett (Lee Van Cleef) looks on and play the "judge." In *Corri uomo corri* (Run, Man, Run, 1968), Cuchillo (Tomas Milian) kills Jean Paul (Luciano Rossi) as Nathaniel Cassidy (Donald O'Brien) makes sure that all is fair and watches them from a distance—his rifle at the ready.

70. Cawelti, *The Six Gun Mystique*, 31.

71. Frayling, *Spaghetti Western*, 281–86; Will Wright, *Sixguns and Society: A Structural Study of the Western* (Berkeley: University of California Press, 1977); Cawelti, *The Six Gun Mystique*.

72. Frayling, *Spaghetti Western*, 283.

73. The film was "grim, tough, and taut. There is barely a moment in it that is not a moment of violence," wrote Robert Alden in the *New York Times* in his review of *Duel* (June 16, 1966, 53).

74. For the release date of Leone's film, see Fisher, *Radical Frontiers*, 68. For the release of Nelson's film, see the *New York Times*, June 16, 1966, 53.

75. Gino Cattani and Moritz B. Fliescher, "Product Category Dynamics in Cultural Industries: Spaghetti Westerns' Renewal of the Hollywood Western Movie Genre," in *Creative Industries and Innovation In Europe: Concepts, Measures and Comparative Case Studies*, ed. Luciana Lazzeretti (New York: Routledge, 2013), 228.

76. *Los Angeles Times*, October 29, 1966, B6.

77. October 28, 1964, http://www.nytimes.com/movie/review?res=9902E7D91E3FEE32A2575BC2A9669D946591D6CF, accessed February 28, 2017.

78. Sidney J. Furie, "Hollywood Misses Its Cue," *Los Angeles Times*, October 9, 1966, B11.

79. *Los Angeles Times*, July 28, 1965, C12.

80. *Los Angeles Times*, July 3, 1966, I 10.

81. The film was nominated to three Academy Awards (Best Director, Best Screenplay, and Best Cinematography) and won a Golden Screen Award in Germany. It was a *Variety*'s "All Time Film Rentals Champs" (January 7, 1977, 44) and was ninth at the box office in France in 1966. https://en.wikipedia.org/wiki/The_Professionals_(1966_film).

82. *Washington Post*, April 25, 1969, B13.

83. *New York Times*, August 8, 1968, 27; *Newsday*, August 8, 1968, n.p., *Hang 'Em High* Clipping File, Billy Rose Collection, NYPL.

84. Gino Cattani and Moritz B. Fliescher, "Product Category Dynamics in Cultural Industries: Spaghetti Westerns' Renewal of the Hollywood Western Movie Genre," in *Creative Industries and Innovation In Europe: Concepts, Measures and Comparative Case Studies*, ed. Luciana Lazzeretti (New York: Routledge, 2013), 224.

85. *Films and Filming*, November 1968, n.p., *Hang 'Em High* Clipping File, NYPL, Billy Rose Collection.

86. Ignacio Ramonet, "Italian Western as Political Parables," *Cineaste* 15, no. 1 (1986): 31.

87. *Variety*, July 5, 1968, n.p. *Hang 'Em High* Clipping File, NYPL, Billy Rose Collection.

88. *Hollywood Reporter*, June 3, 1968, 3.

89. Richard Schickel, "The Cowboy Sinks Slowly in the West," *Life*, September 20, 1968, n.p., *Hang 'Em High* Clipping File, NYPL, Billy Rose Collection.

Chapter 6

1. Richard Slotkin, *Gunfighter Nation: The Myth of the Frontier in Twentieth-Century America* (New York: Athenaeum, 1998), 655.

Notes to Chapter 6 343

2. André Bazin, "The Evolution of the Western," in Bazin, *What Is Cinema? Volume II* (Berkeley: University of California Press, 1972), 149–57.

3. Laura Belmonte, *Selling the American Way: US Propaganda and the Cold War* (Philadelphia: University of Pennsylvania Press, 2008).

4. See Della Casa, "Un fenomento complesso," 8.

5. See the synthesis by Prashad, *The Darker Nations*.

6. See Saverio Giovacchini and Robert Sklar, introduction to *Global Neorealism: The Transnational History of a Film Style* (Jacksonville: University of Mississippi Press, 2012).

7. Lino Miccichè, "De Santis e il verosimile," in *Non c'è pace tra gli ulivi: Un neorealismo postmoderno*, ed. Vito Zagarrio (Rome: Scuola Nazionale di Cinematografia, 2002), 7.

8. See Prashad, *The Darker Nations*, 6–7. By 1964, writing his book *The Third World*, British anthropologist and sociologist Peter Worsely confessed that he "saw no need to define it any more precisely than that it was the world made up of the ex-colonial, newly-independent, non-aligned countries." Worsely cited in B. R. Tomlinson, "What Was the Third World?," *Journal of Contemporary History* 38, no. 2 (2003): 307.

9. For a politically liberal and a politically conservative rebirth and resignification of the term, see, respectively, William McNeill, *The Rise of the West* (Chicago: University of Chicago Press, 1963), and James Burnham, *Suicide of the West* (New York: John Day, 1964).

10. Ignacio Ramonet, "Italian Western as Political Parables," *Cineaste* 15, no. 1 (1986): 31.

11. Aimé Césaire, *Discours sur le colonialisme* (Paris: Réclame, 1950), 21. English ed., *Discourse on Colonialism*, trans. Joan Pinkham, with a new introduction by Robin D. G. Kelley (New York: Monthly Review Press, 2001).

12. And this logic was not lost on Quentin Tarantino either when he cited Corbucci's film in his antiracist spaghetti manifesto, *Django Unchained* (2012), where Franco Nero, the original Django, shares a drink of tequila with the new Django, played by African American actor Jamie Foxx: "How do you spell your name?," Nero asks, "The 'd' is silent," Foxx replies.

13. Among the many interventions that make this point about the spaghetti triptych like chronology and evolution, see the documentary by David Gregory, *The Spaghetti West* (2005), written, edited, and directed by Gregory and produced by Blue Underground, Netflix, and the Independent Film Channel.

14. Gabutti, *C'era una volta in America*, 54.

15. Cited in Marco Giusti, *Dizionario del Western all'Italiana* (Milan: Mondadori, 2007), 81.

16. Cited in Giusti, *Dizionario*, 86.

344   Notes to Chapter 6

17. Frayling, *Sergio Leone*. 291. Box office figures from Roberto Poppi and Marco Pecorari, *Dizionario del cinema italiano*, vol. 3, *I films: 1960–1969* (Rome: Gremese, 1992).

18. Leone cast Morton (Gabriele Ferzetti), the railroad baron, as the capitalist villain of the story. *Once Upon a Time in the West* makes clear that the settling of the West was a war fought by ordinary people for the benefit of a few rich men. The train, allegedly the bearer of civilization, is actually "a vehicle for greed and vengeance that brings destruction and degradation instead of progress." See Catalan, *Transatlantic Gaze*, 64.

19. "Sergio Leone Talks," *Take One* 3, no. 9 (January–February 1972): 26–32, 26.

20. "Sergio Leone Talks," 27.

21. Fisher, *Radical Frontiers in the Spaghetti Western*, 5.

22. Giacomo Manzoli, "Solinas e il Western: Un gioco gramsciano fra industria e ideologia," in *Franco Solinas: Il cinema, la letteratura, la memoria*, ed. Lucia Cardone (Pisa: ETS, 2010), 56.

23. Gianni Olla, *Franco Solinas: Uno scrittore al cinema* (Cagliari: CUEC, 1997), 78–80.

24. Chistopher Frayling, "The Wretched of the Earth," *Sight and Sound* (June 1, 1993), 3. Sollima cited in Giusti, *Dizionario del western all'italiana*, 424.

25. Frayling, *Spaghetti Western*, 239–42.

26. Cited in Giusti, *Dizionario*, 412.

27. Patrick Morin, *Western Italian Style*, WKW Productions 1968. Sergio Sollima started his career as a critic and historian of cinema. His *Il Cinema in USA* (Rome: Veritas, 1947) was so critical of American cinema that, according to historian Daniela Treveri Gennari, it was pulled out of circulation by direct intervention of the Vatican, which was, then, increasingly shifting toward supporting American cinema as an ally in the struggle against Communism. And yet Sollima, too, had embraced the spaghetti Western by the mid-1960s. Daniela Treveri Gennari, *Post-War Italian Cinema* (New York: Routledge, 2009), 81–83.

28. Ted Post Clipping File, NYPL Billy Rose Collection See Scully Scrapbook, n.d., n.p.

29. *American Film*, March 1979, n.p. *China 9 Liberty 37* Clipping File, NYPL, Billy Rose Collection.

30. Manzoli, "Solinas e il Western: Un gioco gramsciano fra industria e ideologia," in *Franco Solinas: Il cinema, la letteratura, la memoria*, ed. Lucia Cardone (Pisa: ETS, 2010), 63–64.

31. Carlo Lizzani, *Il mio lungo viaggio nel secolo breve* (Turin: Einaudi, 2007), 182.

32. Lizzani, *Il mio lungo viaggio nel secolo breve*, 198–99.

Notes to Chapter 6   345

33. Fisher, *Radical Frontiers*, 73.

34. Prashad, *The Darker Nations*, 121–22.

35. The similarity of Penn's and Nelson's work to the European Western was noted in *Cineaste* by Ignacio Ramonet in the essay "Italian Western as Political Parables," *Cineaste* 15, no. 1 (1986): 30–35.

36. Fisher, *Radical Frontiers*, 69.

37. Interview with Damiano Damiani in *Quien Sabe?* (A Bullet for the General) DVD (Florence: Editoria Elettronica, 1994).

38. A brief summary and analysis of the two Westerns by Lizzani is in Luca Pallanchi, "Nelle vene della terra: Il Western," in *Carlo Lizzani: Un lungo viaggio nel cinema*, ed. Vito Zagarrio (Venice: Marsilio, 2010), 212–19.

39. Lizzani interview in the NoShame DVD edition of the collective episodic film *Amore e Rabbia* (1969).

40. Lizzani interview in the NoShame DVD edition of the collective episodic film *Amore e Rabbia* (1969).

41. Bolzoni cited in Pallanchi, "Nelle vene della terra," 217; Bolzoni, "Il buono, il brutto, il bugiardo," *Il Borghese*, November, 26, 1978, 825–26, now in F. Grattarola, *Pasolini, una vita violentata: Pestaggi fisici e linciaggi morali: Cronaca di una Via Crucis laica attraverso la stampa dell'epoca* (Rome: Coniglio Editore, 2005), 220. On Pasolini and the Third World, see Luca Caminati, *Orientalismo eretico: Pier Paolo Pasolini e il cinema del terzo mondo* (Milan: Bruno Mondadori, 2007).

42. Caminati, *Orientalismo eretico*, 47.

43. Following the general critical neglect for these films, for Pallanchi, Lizzani arrived at the spaghetti Western "per caso" (by chance). See Pallanchi, "Nelle vene della terra," 213.

44. *L'Unità*, December 28, 1966, 9. And *L'Unità*, January 5, 1967, 9.

45. See André Bazin, "Un Western exemplaire," in *Cahier du Cinéma* 74 (August–September 1957), available in English in Hillier, *Cahiers du Cinéma, the 1950s*, 169–72. See de Baecque, *La cinéphilie*. See also the heavily Bazinian essay by Jim Kitses, "Budd Boetticher: The Rules of the Game," in Jim Kitses, *Horizons West: Anthony Mann, Budd Boetticher, and Sam Peckinpah; Studies in Authorship within the Western* (Bloomington: Indiana University Press, 1969), 89–130.

46. Frantz Fanon, *Black Skins, White Masks*, introduction by Kwame Anthony Appiah, trans. Richard Philcox (1952; New York: Grove Press, 2008), 45.

47. Kwame Anthony Appiah, introduction to Fanon, *Black Skins, White Masks*.

48. Appiah, introduction to Fanon, *Black Skins, White Masks*, 41–42.

49. Fanon, *Black Skins, White Masks*, xiii.

Notes to Chapter 6

50. Fanon, *Black Skins, White Masks*, 12.

51. Aldo Grandi, *La generazione degli anni perduti: Storia di potere operaio* (Turin: Einaudi, 2003), 137–39. Frayling reports that the German Baader-Meinhoff Group was a fan of Sergio Corbucci's *Il grande silenzio* (The Big Silence, 1968). Frayling, "The Italian Western and the Mexican Revolution," in Broughton, *Critical Perspectives on the Western*, 9. Luisa Passerini has also documented the influence of action films on the way Prima Linea female members constructed or reconstructed their experiences by referencing "stereotipi cinematografici o televisivi." See Passerini, "Ferite della memoria: Immaginario e ideologia in una storia recente," in *Rivista di storia contemporanea* 17, no. 2 (1988): 173–217, esp. 186.

52. Fernando Solanas and Octavio Getino, "Towards a Third Cinema," in *Movies and Methods: An Anthology*, ed. Bill Nichols (Berkeley: University of California Press, 1976), 44–64.

53. On Rocha and the Western, see Ismail Xavier, "Black God, White Devil: Allegory and Prophecy," in his *Allegories of Underdevelopment: Aesthetics and Politics in Modern Brazilian Cinema* (Minneapolis: University of Minnesota Press, 1997), 40–41.

54. Interview with Martin Scorsese on Glauber Rocha's *Antonio Das Mortes*, https://www.youtube.com/watch?v=Lw4eT1vhrcw, accessed July 31, 2017.

55. *New York Times*, April 3, 1970, 42.

56. *Village Voice*, April 20, 1993, n.p. *Quien Sabe?* Clipping File, NYPL, Billy Rose Collection.

57. *L'Unità*, January 5, 1967, 9.

58. Sergio Sollima interview in David Gregory, *The Spaghetti West* DVD (Los Angeles, IFC, 2005).

59. "Tomás Milian el épico," Frabel (blog), December 16, 2010, http://frabel45.blogspot.com/2010/12/tomas-milian.html.

60. And possibly more than his makeup. It is interesting that the acting of Tomas Milian had an Actors Studio pedigree as he had trained with Lee Strasberg in New York City. In Volonté's case, there was no formal Actors Studio's training. Both actors, however, were renowned for their histrionic capacities, their skill at transforming themselves into the characters they played.

61. For Marco Giusti the character of Milian was not "exactly Cuchillo, but a kind of hairy, mustachioed relative" of that character. See Giusti, *Dizionario del Western all'Italiana*, 195. Milian was then Tepepa in the homonymous film Giulio Petroni, shot from the script by Franco Solinas in 1968. In Sergio Corbucci's *Vamos a Matar Compañeros* (Compañeros, 1970), Milian went Mexican again as Chato aka El Blasco, sporting a Guevaresque Basque hat and a *brownface* that grew darker in relation to the blond Yodlaf Peterson (Franco Nero), the Swedish gun trader who turns revolutionary.

Notes to Chapter 6 347

62. Cited in Giusti, *Dizionario del Western all'Italiana*, 425.

63. To cite a few, all directed by Bruno Corbucci: *Squadra antimafia* (1976), *Squadra antitruffa* (1977), *Squadra antifurto* (1978), *Squadra antigangster* (1979).

64. Milian to Fofi and Faldini, *L'avventurosa storia del cinema italiano*, 303. Sergio Sollima made the same point, but in the opposite direction. When he cast Milian as Cuchillo, he told David Gregory in the early 2000s, the director was trying to make him into a Neapolitan urchin as "the character of Cuchillo is a Neapolitan street urchin" (il personaggio di Cuchillo è uno scugnizzo napoletano). David Gregory, *The Spaghetti West*, at 38:04.

65. Fanon, *Black Skins, White Masks*, xiii.

66. "No Return for Ethiopian Treasure," BBC News, June 22, 2001, http://news.bbc.co.uk/1/hi/world/africa/1402354.stm.

67. John Tomlinson, *Cultural Imperialism: A Critical Introduction* (London: Pinter 1991), 2.

68. Philippe Roger, *L'ennemi américain* (Paris: Seuil, 2002), trans. as Roger, *The American Enemy* (Chicago: University of Chicago Press, 2005), 331–32.

69. Judt, *Postwar*, 322.

70. See one of the rare approving commentaries of the PCI about the British Labour Party in *L'Unità*, May 25, 1955, 5.

71. Martin Klimke, *The Other Alliance: Student Protest in West Germany and the United States in the Global Sixties* (Princeton, NJ: Princeton University Press, 2010), 66.

72. *L'Unità*, February 17, 1952, 5. The term appears at least thirty times in the Communist daily from January 1950 to December 1960.

73. Carlo Salinari, "La lotta dei comunisti per una cultura libera, moderna e nazionale," in Togliatti, Longo, Salinari, *Per la costituzione democratica e per una libera cultura. Rapporti alla sessione del CC del PCI del 10–12 novembre 1952*, 112 (Rome: Istituto Gramsci, Commissione Cultura).

74. Oreste del Buono and Lietta Tornabuoni, eds., *Era Cinecittà: Vita, morte e miracoli di una fabbrica di film* (Milan: Bompiani, 1979), 23.

75. Guy Debord, *Complete Cinematic Works: Scripts, Stills, Documents* (Oakland, CA: AK Press, 1994), 43.

76. Klimke, *The Other Alliance*, 63–65.

77. See J. Hoberman, *The Dream Life: Movies, Media and the Mythology of the Sixties* (New York: New Press, 2005), 182.

78. See Mark McGurl, "Learning from *Little Tree*: The Political Education of the Counterculture," *Yale Journal of Literary Criticism* 18, no. 2 (Fall 2005): 243–67.

79. *Chicago Sun*, January 1, 1970, http://www.rogerebert.com/reviews/soldier-blue-1970.

348 Notes to Chapter 7

80. Michael Wilmington, "The Western: Nicholas Ray's *Johnny Guitar*," *Velvet Light Trap* 12 (April 1974): 20–24; Yordan citation at 20.

81. Wilmington, "The Western," 21.

82. Bazin, "The Evolution of the Western," in Bazin, *What Is Cinema? Volume II*. Bazin explicitly rooted his analysis of the Western in the neo-historicism of Rieupeyrout, *Le Western ou le cinéma Américain par excellence*, for which he had written the preface. See Bazin, "The Western, or the American Film *par excellence*," *What Is Cinema? Volume II*, 140–48.

83. Bazin, "The Western or the American Film *par excellence*," in Bazin, *What Is Cinema? Volume II*, 148.

84. Roger, *The American Enemy*, 331–32; Monique Selim, "De la globalisation des métaphores colonials," *L'Homme et la Société* 4, no. 174 (2009): 15–26.

85. See Philip Deloria, *Playing Indian* (New Haven, CT: Yale University Press, 1998), 3.

86. Deloria, *Playing Indian*, 17.

Chapter 7

1. *Variety*, May 8, 2000, https://variety.com/2000/film/reviews/six-pack-1200462390/.

2. *Variety*, February 17, 1971, 34.

3. See Erich Schwartzel, *Red Carpet: Hollywood, China, and the Global Battle for Cultural Supremacy* (New York: Penguin, 2022).

4. Frank Costigliola, *France and the United States: The Cold Alliance since World War II* (New York: Twayne, 1992), 120–47; Thomas Allan Schwartz, *Lyndon Johnson and Europe: In the Shadow of Vietnam* (Cambridge: Harvard University Press, 2003), 91–139; Philippe Roger, *L'ennemi americain* (Paris: Seuil, 2002).

5. Johnson-Yale, *A History of Hollywood's Outsourcing Debate*, 18–45.

6. It was only with the Revenue Act of 1962 that such exemption was lowered to a maximum of $20,000. *The Revenue Act of 1962. Brief Summary of Provisions in HR 10650* (Washington, DC: US Government Printing Office, 1962), 7. See also Prime, *Hollywood Exiles in Europe*, loc. 1425 of Kindle edition.

7. On the rally, see Quaglietti, *Storia economica e politica del cinema italiano*, 59–61, and Forgacs and Gundle, *Mass Culture and Italian Society*, 136.

8. Lattuada translated by, and cited in, Nicoli, *The Rise and Fall of the Italian Film Industry*, 144.

9. US Congress, Hearings held in Washington, DC, November 27–30, 1961, December 1–5, 1961, and January 5, 1962 before the Sub-Committee of the Committee on Education and Labor on the Influence of Imports

and Exports on American Employment, 87th Congress, First and Second Sessions, Part 8 (Washington, DC: US Government Printing Office, 1962).

10. US Congress, Hearings, 463.

11. US Congress, Hearings, 621.

12. US Congress, Hearings, 621.

13. Rick Perlstein, *Nixonland: The Rise of a President and the Fracturing of America* (New York: Scribner, 2008), 464.

14. Perlstein, *Nixonland*, 495, and Joshua Freeman, "Construction Workers, Manliness, and the 1970's Pro War Demonstrations," *Journal of Social History* 26, no. 4 (Summer 1993): 725–44.

15. Perlstein, *Nixonland*, 535.

16. A. D. Murphy, "Film Trade Sanity Asserts itself," *Variety*, April 12, 1972, 3.

17. On Regan and Murphy and the conservative revolution, see Steven Ross, *Hollywood Left and Right: How Movie Stars Shaped American Politics* (New York: Oxford University Press, 2011), 131–83.

18. *Daily Variety*, December 1, 1970, 8.

19. *Daily Variety*, December 1, 1970, 8. About James Corman, see *Variety*, December 15, 1970, 3 and 20.

20. US Congress, Hearings held in Los Angeles, California, October 29 and 30, 1971, before the General Sub-Committee on Labor of the Committee on Education and Labor on Unemployment Problems in the American Film Industry, 92nd Congress, First Session (Washington, DC: US Government Printing Office, 1972), 76.

21. Bernstein, *Hollywood at the Crossroads*, 65.

22. Bernstein, *Hollywood at the Crossroads*, 65.

23. A. D. Murphy, "'Cinema' Handle Now Epidemic," *Daily Variety*, September 19, 1972, 1 and 8.

24. Elizabeth Donaho, "The Obscenity Issue and the 92nd Congress," February 7, 1972. American Law Division.

25. *Daily Variety*, May 6, 1972, 5.

26. *Daily Variety*, July 25, 1972, 2.

27. *Daily Variety*, August 7, 1972, 3.

28. *Daily Variety*, October 24, 1972, 13.

29. *New York Times*, March 3, 1972, 55.

30. *New York Times*, April 10, 1972, 52.

31. *Los Angeles Times*, March 27, 1972, 9.

32. *Daily Variety*, April 6, 1971, 1 and 12.

33. *Daily Variety*, May 15, 1972, 1 and 14.

34. On Jimmy Carter's efforts as Georgia governor, see Johnson-Yale, *History of Hollywood Outsourcing Debate*, 91–92.

35. *Variety*, October 11, 1972, 4.

350   Notes to Chapter 7

36. *Congressional Record*, Senate, 94th Congress, 2nd session, vol. 122, part 20 (August 4, 1976), 25610–11.

37. *Congressional Record*, August 4, 1976, 25613.

38. *Congressional Record*, August 4, 1976, 25614.

39. Eitel Monaco cited in Quaglietti, *Storia economica e politica del cinema italiano*, 228.

40. Christopher Wagstaff, "Il nuovo mercato del cinema," in *Storia del cinema mondiale*, vol. 2, *L'Europa: Miti, luoghi, divi*, ed. Gian Piero Brunetta (Turin: Einaudi, 1999), 860.

41. Quaglietti, *Storia economica e politica del cinema italiano*, 229. See David A. Loehwing, "It's the Reel Thing," *Barron's*, January 24, 1972, 3 and 8.

42. *Daily Variety*, May 15, 1972, 14.

43. Liehm, *Passion and Desire*, 250.

44. UNESCO, *Statistics on Film and Cinema 1955–1977* (Paris: Division of Statistics on Culture and Communication, 1981), 9.

45. Quaglietti, *Storia economica del cinema italiano*, 246.

46. Bondanella, *Italian Cinema*, 319.

47. Corsi, *Con qualche dollaro in meno*, 80.

48. Pérez Melgosa, *Cinema and Interamerican Relations*, 76.

49. See Luisa Passerini, *Love and the Idea of Europe* (Oxford: Berghan Books 2009), and Passerini, *Europe in Love, Love in Europe: Imagination and Politics between the Wars* (New York: New York University Press, 1999).

50. On the political triumph of sectional reconciliationism and its cultural ramification, see David W. Blight, *Race and Reunion: The Civil War in American Memory* (Cambridge: Harvard University Press, 2001).

51. Conversely, in his *The Big Parade* (1924), King Vidor had the wounded American World War I veteran, Jim Apperson (John Gilbert), wind up in the nurturing arms of a French country girl, Melisande (Renée Adorée).

52. Notably, French director Julie Delpy cast a heterosexual Euro-American romance, as Godard did, in her *Two Days in Paris* (2002), but she tellingly inverted the genders. The female character, Marion (Delpy), is a French self-assured woman, while the male character, tellingly named Adam (Adam Goldberg), is a fragile American male abroad.

53. Gary Comenas, "Allen Midgette Interview," at Warholstars.org, accessed July 1, 2018, http://www.warholstars.org/andywarhol/interview/midgette/allen_midgette.html.

54. *Variety*, October 15, 1969, 32.

55. Eric Spilker, "A Hit at New York Fest, Bertolucci Wins a Sandwich and Paramount," *Variety*, September 23, 1970, 5.

56. *Variety*, March 31, 1971, 19.

57. *Variety*, January 12, 1972, 24.

58. Including Valerio Zurlini's *Le soldatesse* and *Seduto alla sua destra* (Black Jesus, 1968), Giulio Questi's standout spaghetti, *Se sei vivo spara* (Django

Kill, 1967), and the documentary film by Alessandro Perrone, *Vietnam: Guerra senza fronte* (Vietnam: War without Frontline, 1967).

59. *Daily Variety*, September 23, 1971, 8.

60. *Daily Variety*, August 11, 1971, 2.

61. *Variety*, August 25, 1971, 41.

62. *Daily Variety*, February 1, 1972, 2.

63. *Daily Variety*, February 1, 1972, 2.

64. Mariana Fonseca, "Maria Schneider Already Called *Last Tango in Paris* Scene Rape: Why Did We Only Listen When Bernardo Bertolucci Admitted It,?" *Independent*, December 4, 2016, https://www.independent.co.uk/voices/last-tango-in-paris-maria-schneider-marlon-brando-bertolucci-director-butter-anal-rape-scene-male-a7455166.html#gallery.

65. For a learned, recent essay published five years after Schneider's statement about the rape that deals with the erotic dimension of the film and its relation to Georges Bataille without ever engaging Schneider's accusation, see Gabriele Anaclerio, "Ultimo Tango a Parigi," in *Bernardo Bertolucci*, ed. Giorgio De Vincenti (Venice: Marsilio, 2012). On p. 74, Anaclerio writes that the apartment in the film "is the place where Jeanne learned how to live, thanks to Paul-Brando." On Schneider, see Lina Das, "I Felt Raped by Brando: Interview with Maria Schneider," *Daily Mail*, July 19, 2007, http://www.dailymail.co.uk/tvshowbiz/article-469646/I-felt-raped-Brando.html. Brando's 1994 autobiography references the rape rather obliquely. See Marlon Brando, *Songs My Mother Taught Me* (New York: Random House, 1994), loc. 5111–5122.

66. *Variety*, March 21, 1973, 30.

67. Stefano Socci, *Bernardo Bertolucci* (Milan: Il Castoro, 1996), 59–60; Ornella Magrini, *Una scomoda ossessione: Ultimo Tango a Parigi, Memorie da un film proibito* (Arezzo: Zona, 2006), 5–7.

68. "UA Shows Tango if Official Want," *Variety*, May 23, 1973, 35.

69. "March Mag Blames Tango," *Variety*, March 7, 1973, 6 and 30.

70. "UA Shows Tango if Official Want," *Variety*, May 23, 1973, 35.

71. *Daily Variety*, April 25, 1973, 5.

72. Norman Mailer, "A Transit to Narcissus," in Bernardo Bertolucci and Franco Arcalli, *Bernardo Bertolucci's Last Tango in Paris*, the screenplay with critical essays by Pauline Kael and Norman Mailer (New York: Delacorte Press, 1973), 199–224; citation from 223.

73. See Canby first review of the film in *New York Times*, October 16, 1972, 46, and *New York Times*, January 28, 1973, 107.

74. Kael's essay in the *New Yorker* is reproduced at https://www.criterion.com/current/posts/834-last-tango-in-paris and was immediately reprinted in Bertolucci and Arcalli, *Bernardo Bertolucci's Last Tango in Paris*, 9–22.

75. Schneider said so explicitly in her interview with Lina Das. See Das, "I Felt Raped by Brando."

352 Notes to Chapter 7

76. Grace Glueck, "I Won't Tango Don't Ask Me," *New York Times*, March 18, 1973, 127.

77. "They Will Tango: Just Ask Them," *New York Times*, April 18, 1973, 143.

78. *Daily Variety*, July 12, 1973, 8.

79. Vito Zagarrio, "Respiro, suspense e storia: Appunti sulla regia di Bertolucci," in *Bernardo Bertolucci: Il cinema e i film*, ed. Adriano Aprà (Venice: Marsilio, 2011), 133.

80. Zagarrio, "Respiro, suspense e storia," 17.

81. Kael, "Introduction" in Bertolucci and Arcalli, *Bernardo Bertolucci's Last Tango in Paris*, 16.

82. Giuseppe Bertolucci remembers that before Paramount, and then United Artists, embraced the project, they were thinking of shooting the film in Milan using nonprofessional actors. See Marco Giusti and Enrico Ghezzi, eds., "Interview with Giuseppe Bertolucci," in *Kim Arcalli: Montare il cinema* (Venice: Marsilio, 1980), 80.

83. See Brando, *Songs My Mother Taught Me*, loc. 5101.

84. Kael, "Introduction" in Bertolucci and Arcalli, *Bernardo Bertolucci's Last Tango in Paris*, 15.

85. Vito Zagarrio, "Respiro, suspense e storia: Appunti sulla regia di Bertolucci," in Aprà, *Bernardo Bertolucci*, 133.

86. Whitman, "To a Certain Cantatrice," in *Leaves of Grass* (Philadelphia: Rees Welsh and Co. 1882), 16. Whitman wrote that he "heard Alboni every time she sang in New York and vicinity." Walt Whitman, *Prose Works 1892*, vol. 1, *Specimen Days*, edited by Floyd Stovall (New York: New York University Press, 1963). 20.

87. Brando, *Songs My Mother Taught Me*, loc. 2780.

88. Brando, *Songs My Mother Taught Me*, loc. 5650.

89. Brando, *Songs My Mother Taught Me*, loc. 5650.

90. On the film's iteration of the Algerian theme, see Esther Rashkin, *Unspeakable Secrets and the Psychoanalysis of Torture* (Albany: State University of New York Press, 2008), 74–82.

91. "Bernardo Bertolucci," in Laurent Tirard, *Moviemakers' Master Classes: Private Lessons from the World's Foremost Directors* (New York: Farrar, Straus and Giroux, 2003), 47–56.

92. Gabriele Anaclerio, "Ultimo Tango a Parigi," in de Vincenti, *Bernardo Bertolucci*, 64. On Bertolucci's interest for art history, see Kolker, *Giuseppe Bertolucci*. Beside Bacon in *Last Tango*, among others, Kolker notes Bertolucci's use of René Magritte's work in *Spider's Stratagem* and Pelizza da Volpedo in his *1900*.

93. Kolker calls Marcello "an almost literal double" of Paul. Kolker, *Bertolucci*, 136.

94. Rashkin, *Unspeakable Secrets*, 73–74.

Conclusion

1. Umberto Bruno did note this irony in *Filmcritica* and wrote that the film was "at the level of style, a homage to the grand spectacles by [Douglas] Sirk and [Vincent] Minnelli." Edoardo Bruno, cited in Elio Girlanda, *Stefania Sandrelli* (Rome: Gremese, 2002), 48.

2. See Robert Phillip Kolker, *Bernardo Bertolucci* (London: British Film Institute, 1985).

3. For a Gramscian interpretation of some of Bertolucci's cinema, see Millicent Marcus, "Bernardo Bertolucci's *The Last Emperor*," in Marcus, *After Fellini: National Cinema in the Postmodern Age* (Baltimore: Johns Hopkins University Press, 2002), 61–75.

4. See "Making *Emperor* in China: An Epic Job of Financing," *Los Angeles Times*, February 1, 1988, http://articles.latimes.com/1988-02-01/business/fi-26783_1_modern-china.

5. Peter Dunn, "The Last Movie Mogul," *Sunday Times* (London), February 5, 1978, 40–44.

6. Kezich and Levantesi, *Dino De Laurentiis*, 169.

7. Corsi, *Con qualche dollaro in meno*, 168.

8. Alberto Crespi, "Ponti: Cinema, amore e fantasia," *L'Unità*, January 11, 2007, 19.

9. California, Assembly Committee on Economic Development and New Technologies, *Hearing Summary* of the Hearing on "The Flight of the Motion Picture Industry from California," October 11, 1983, Museum of Science and Industry, 2, California State Library, Sacramento, California.

10. California Assembly hearing, "The Flight of the Motion Picture Industry from California," 3.

11. California Assembly hearing, "The Flight of the Motion Picture Industry from California," 4.

12. October 13, 1983, n.p. California Assembly Committee on Economic Development and New Technologies, Hearing on "The Flight of the Motion Picture Industry from California," October 11, 1983, Museum of Science and Industry, Clipping File, California State Library, Sacramento, California.

13. *Hollywood Reporter*, October 12, 1983, n.p. California Assembly Committee on Economic Development and New Technologies, Hearing on "The Flight of the Motion Picture Industry from California," October 11, 1983, Museum of Science and Industry, Clipping File, California State Library, Sacramento, California.

14. *Sacramento Bee*, October 17, 1983, n.p. California Assembly Committee on Economic Development and New Technologies, Hearing on "The Flight of the Motion Picture Industry from California," October 11, 1983, Museum of Science and Industry, Clipping File, California State Library, Sacramento, California.

354 Notes to Conclusion

15. Joint Hearing of the California Assembly Committee on Economic Development and New Technologies and the California Sub Committee on Sport and Entertainment on "The Flight of the Motion Picture Industry from California," December 7, 1985, Monterey, California, California State Archive.

16. Richard Koszarski, *Hollywood on the Hudson: Film and Television in New York from Griffith to Sarnoff* (New Brunswick, NJ: Rutgers University Press, 2008), 7.

17. Diane Jacobs, *Hollywood Renaissance* (New York: Dell, 1980).

18. See Thom Andersen, "Red Hollywood," in *Literature and the Visual Arts in Contemporary Society*, ed. Suzanne Ferguson and Barbara Groseclose (Columbus: Ohio State University Press, 1985), 176–89.

19. Sklar, *Movie-Made America*, loc. 6660–6663 of Kindle ed.

20. Liehm, *Passion and Desire*, 266.

21. Ewa Mazierska and Laura Rascaroli, *The Cinema of Nanni Moretti: Dreams and Diaries* (London: Wallflower Press, 2004), 1.

22. Cavicchioli cited in Flavio De Bernardinis, *Nanni Moretti* (Milan: Castoro Editore, 2001), 54.

23. Robert S. Gordon, "Hollywood and Italy: Industries and Fantasies," in Bondanella, *The Italian Cinema Book*, 123.

24. Tiziana Ferrero-Regis, "From Cinecittà to the Small Screen, Italian Cinema after the Mid 1970s Crisis," in *A Companion to Italian Cinema*, ed. Frank Burke (Oxford: Wiley, 2017), 284–303.

25. Angela Baldassarre, "Nanni Moretti Talks about His Career," in Baldassarre, *The Great Dictators: Interviews with Filmmakers of Italian Descent* (Buffalo, NY: Guernica, 1999), 66.

Bibliography

Books

Abel, Richard. *The Red Rooster Scare: Making Cinema American, 1900–1910.* Berkeley: University of California Press, 1999.

Adorno, Theodor. "*Kultur* and Culture." Translated by Mark Kalbus. *Social Text* 27, no. 2 (Summer 2009): 145–58.

Agee, James. *Agee on Cinema.* Boston: Beacon Press, 1958.

Aprà, Adriano. *Alberto Lattuada: Il cinema e i film.* Venice: Marsilio, 2009.

Aprà, Adriano, ed. *Bernardo Bertolucci: Il cinema e i film.* Venice: Marsilio, 2011.

Archer-Straw, Petrine. *Negrophilia: Avant-Garde Paris and Black Culture in the 1920s.* New York: Thames and Hudson, 2000.

Auerbach, Jonathan. *Dark Borders: Film Noir and American Citizenship.* Durham, NC: Duke University Press, 2011.

Baldassarre, Angela. *The Great Dictators: Interviews with Filmmakers of Italian Descent.* Buffalo, NY: Guernica, 1999.

Baldissara, Luca, and Paolo Pezzino, eds. *Giudicare e punire: I processi per crimini di guerra tra diritto e politica.* Naples: L'ancora del Mediterraneo, 2005.

Baldwin, James. *Notes of a Native Son.* 1955; Boston: Beacon Press, 1984.

Balio, Tino, ed. *The American Film Industry.* Madison: University of Wisconsin Press, 1985.

Balio, Tino. *The Foreign Film Renaissance on American Screens, 1946–1973.* Madison: University of Wisconsin Press, 2010.

Balio, Tino, ed. *Hollywood in the Age of Television.* Boston: Unwin Hyman, 1990.

Balio, Tino. *United Artists,* vol. 2, *1951–1978: The Company That Changed the Film Industry.* Madison: University of Wisconsin Press, 2009.

Bancel, Nicolas, Pascal Blanchard, Sandrine Lemaire, and Dominic Richard David Thomas, eds. *Histoire globale de la France coloniale.* Paris: Philippe Rey, 2022.

356 Bibliography

Banti, Alberto Mario. *La nazione del Risorgimento: Parentela, santità e onore alle origini dell'Italia Unita*. Turin: Einaudi, 2000.

Battini, Marco. *Peccati di memoria: La mancata Norimberga italiana*. Bari: Laterza, 2003.

Bazin, André. *What Is Cinema? Volume II*. Translated by Hugh Gray. Berkeley: University of California Press, 2004.

Belmonte, Laura A. *Selling the American Way: U.S. Propaganda and the Cold War*. Philadelphia: University of Pennsylvania Press, 2010.

Bender, Thomas, ed. *Rethinking American History in a Global Age*. Berkeley: University of California Press, 2002.

Ben-Ghiat, Ruth. *Italian Fascism's Empire Cinema*. Bloomington: Indiana University Press, 2015.

Ben-Ghiat, Ruth. *La cultura fascista*. Bologna: Il Mulino, 2004.

Bennett, M. Todd. *One World, Big Screen: Hollywood, the Allies, and World War II*. Chapel Hill: University of North Carolina Press, 2012.

Bergfelder, Tim. *International Adventures: German Popular Cinema and European Co-Productions in the 1960s*. New York: Berghahn Books, 2005.

Berlin, Ira. *Many Thousands Gone: The First Two Centuries of Slavery in North America*. Cambridge, MA: Harvard University Press, 1998.

Bernstein, Irving. *Hollywood at the Crossroads: An Economic Study of the Motion Picture Industry*. Hollywood: Hollywood AFL Film Council, 1957.

Bernstein, Matthew. *Walter Wanger, Hollywood Independent*. Minneapolis: University of Minnesota Press, 2000.

Bertellini, Giorgio, ed. *The Cinema of Italy*. London: Wallflower Press, 2005.

Bertellini, Giorgio. *Italy in Early American Cinema: Race, Landscape, and the Picturesque*. Bloomington: Indiana University Press, 2010.

Bertolucci, Bernardo, and Franco Arcalli. *Bernardo Bertolucci's Last Tango in Paris: The Screenplay*. New York: Delacorte Press, 1973.

Bhabha, Homi K. *The Location of Culture*. London: Routledge, 1994.

Biasion, Renzo. *Sagapò*. 1953; Turin: Einaudi, 1991.

Biasion, Renzo, and Giorgio Pavanello. *Ricordi di guerra e di prigionia: I disegni di Renzo Biasion della Fondazione Giorgio Cini*. Venice: Marsilio, 2004.

Biasion, Renzo, Mario Tobino, and Mario Rigoni Stern. *The Lost Legions: Three Italian War Novels*. London: McGibbon and Kee, 1967.

Biddle, Francis. *In Brief Authority*. 1962; rev. ed., New York: Praeger, 1976.

Bidussa, David. *Il mito del bravo italiano*. Milan: Il Saggiatore, 1994.

Blight, David W. *Race and Reunion: The Civil War in American Memory*. Cambridge, MA: Harvard University Press, 2001.

Boetticher, Bud. *When in Disgrace*. Santa Barbara, CA: Neville, 1989.

Bogle, Donald. *Toms, Coons, Mulattoes, Mammies, and Bucks: An Interpretive History of Blacks in American Films*. New York: Continuum: 2002.

Bondanella, Peter E. *Italian Cinema: From Neorealism to the Present*. New York: Continuum, 2001.

Bibliography

Bondanella, Peter E. *The Italian Cinema Book*. London: Palgrave Macmillan, 2014.

Bondanella, Peter, and Federico Pacchioni. *A History of Italian Cinema*. London: Bloomsbury, 2017.

Borde, Raymond, and Etienne Chaumeton. *A Panorama of American Film Noir, 1941–1953*. Translated by Paul Hammond. San Francisco: City Lights Books, 2002.

Brando, Marlon, and Robert Lindsey. *Brando: Songs My Mother Taught Me*. New York: Random House, 1994.

Brothers, Peter H. *Mushroom Clouds and Mushroom Men: The Fantastic Cinema of Ishiro Honda*. Seattle, WA: CreateSpace Books, 2013.

Broughton, Lee, ed. *Critical Perspectives on the Western: From "A Fistful of Dollars" to "Django Unchained."* Lanham, MD: Rowman & Littlefield, 2016.

Brown, Gene. *Movie Time: A Chronology of Hollywood from Its Beginnings to the Present*. New York: Macmillan, 1997.

Bruckner, Ulrich P., ed. *Für ein paar Leichen mehr: Der Italo-Western von seinen Anfängen bis heute*. Berlin: Schwarzkopf & Schwarzkopf, 2002.

Brunetta, Gian Piero. *Buio in sala: Cent'anni di passioni dello spettatore cinematografico*. Venice: Marsilio, 1989.

Brunetta, Gian Piero. *Il cinema neorealista italiano: Storia economica, politica e culturale*. Rome: Laterza, 2009.

Brunetta, Gian Piero. *Il ruggito del leone: Hollywood alla conquista dell'impero dei sogni nell'Italia di Mussolini*. Venice: Marsilio, 2013.

Brunetta, Gian Piero, ed. *Storia del cinema mondiale*. Turin: Einaudi, 1999.

Brunetta, Gian Piero. *Storia del cinema italiano*, vol. 2, *L'Europa: Miti, luoghi, divi*. Turin: Einaudi, 1999.

Brunetta, Gian Piero. *Storia del cinema italiano*, vol. 3, *Dal neorealismo al miracolo economico*. Rome: Editori Riuniti, 1993.

Burgio, Alberto, ed. *Nel nome della razza: Il razzismo nella storia d'Italia 1870–1945*. Bologna: Il Mulino, 2000.

Burke, Frank. *A Companion to Italian Cinema*. Chichester: John Wiley & Sons, 2017.

Burnham, James. *Suicide of the West: An Essay on the Meaning and Destiny of Liberalism*. New York: John Day, 1964.

Cain, James M. *Double Indemnity*. New York: Vintage Books, 1992.

Cain, James M. *The Postman Always Rings Twice*. New York: Vintage Books, 1992.

Calamandrei, Paolo, and Renzo Renzi, eds. *Il Processo s'agapò: Dall'Arcadia a Peschiera*. Bari: Laterza, 1954.

Caminati, Luca. *Orientalismo eretico: Pier Paolo Pasolini e il cinema del terzo mondo*. Milan: Mondadori, 2007.

Cardone, Lucia. *Franco Solinas: Il cinema, la letteratura, la memoria atti del Covegno di Studi Sassari, 3–5 dicembre 2007*. Pisa: Edizioni ETS, 2010.

Bibliography

Carolan, Mary Ann McDonald. *The Transatlantic Gaze: Italian Cinema, American Film*. Albany: State University of New York Press, 2014.

Castaldi, Rita, and Antonietta Molinari. *Scritti su Bassani: Articoli, testimonianze e interviste tra storia, letteratura e cinema*. Edited by Maurizio Villani. Bologna: Diogene, 2016.

Casty, Alan. *Robert Rossen: The Films and Politics of a Blacklisted Idealist*. Jefferson, NC: McFarland and Co., 2013.

Cawelti, John G. *The Six-Gun Mystique*. Bowling Green, OH: Bowling Green State University Popular Press, 1999.

Cecchi, Emilio. *Saggi e viaggi*. Edited by Margherita Ghilardi. Milan: Mondadori, 1997.

Cendrars, Blaise. *Hollywood, la mecca del cinema*. Translated by Emanuela Stella. Rome: Lucarini, 1989.

Césaire, Aimé. *Discours sur le colonialism*. Paris: Réclame, 1950. English ed., *Discourse on Colonialism*. Trans. Joan Pinkham. With a new introduction by Robin D. G. Kelley. New York: Monthly Review Press, 2001.

Chemotti, Saveria, ed. *Il mito americano: Origini e crisi di un modello culturale*. Padua: Cleup, 1980.

Chiti, Roberto, Roberto Poppi, and Enrico Lancia, eds. *Dizionario del cinema italiano*. Rome: Gremese, 1991.

Cooper, Anna, and Russell Meeuf. *Projecting the World: Representing the "Foreign" in Classical Hollywood*. Detroit: Wayne State University Press, 2017.

Corsi, Barbara. *Con qualche dollaro in meno: Storia economica del cinema italiano*. Rome: Editori Riuniti, 2001.

Costigliola, Frank. *France and the United States: The Cold Alliance since World War II*. New York: Twayne, 1992.

Cosulich, Callisto, ed. *Verso il Neorealismo: Un critico cinematografico italiano degli anni quaranta*. Rome: Bulzoni, 1982.

Cripps, Thomas. *Making Movies Black: The Hollywood Message Movie from World War II to the Civil Rights Era*. New York: Oxford University Press, 1993.

Custen, George F. *Twentieth Century's Fox: Darryl F. Zanuck and the Culture of Hollywood*. New York: Basic Books, 1997.

de Baecque, Antoine. *La Cinéphilie: Invention d'un regard, histoire d'une culture, 1944–1968*. Paris: Fayard, 2003.

De Bernardinis, Flavio. *Nanni Moretti*. Rome: Il Castoro, 2001.

de Grazia, Victoria. *Irresistible Empire: America's Advance through Twentieth-Century Europe*. Cambridge, MA: Harvard University Press, 2006.

de Vincenti, Giorgio, eds. *Bernardo Bertolucci*. Venice: Marsilio, 2012.

Debord, Guy. *Complete Cinematic Works: Scripts, Stills, Documents*. Oakland, CA: AK Press, 1994.

Decherney, Peter. *Hollywood: A Very Short Introduction*. New York: Oxford University Press, 2016.

Bibliography

359

del Boca, Angelo. *I gas di Mussolini: Il fascismo e la guerra d'Etiopia*. Rome: Editori Riuniti, 1996.

del Boca, Angelo. *Italiani, brava gente?* Vicenza: Neri Pozza, 2005.

del Boca, Angelo. *L'Africa nella coscienza degli italiani: Miti, memorie, errori, sconfitte*. Rome: Laterza, 1992.

del Buono, Oreste, and Lietta Tornabuoni, eds. *Era Cinecittà: Vita, morte e miracoli di una fabbrica di film*. Milan: Bompiani, 1979.

del Pero, Mario. *L' alleato scomodo: Gli USA e la DC negli anni del centrismo (1948–1955)*. Rome: Carocci, 2001.

Della Casa, Stefano, ed. *Capitani coraggiosi: Produttori italiani 1945–1975*. Milan: Electa, 2003.

Della Coletta, Cristina. *When Stories Travel: Cross-Cultural Encounters between Fiction and Film*. Baltimore: Johns Hopkins University Press, 2012.

Deloria, Philip J. *Playing Indian*. New Haven, CT: Yale University Press, 1998.

Dixon, Wheeler Winston. *Death of the Moguls: The End of Classical Hollywood*. New Brunswick, NJ: Rutgers University Press, 2012.

Djelic, Marie-Laure. *Exporting the American Model: The Post-War Transformation of European Business*. Oxford: Oxford University Press, 2001.

Doherty, Thomas. *Hollywood and Hitler, 1933–1939*. New York: Columbia University Press, 2013.

Dost, Michael, Florian Hopf, and Alexander Kluge. *Filmwirtschaft in der BRD und in Europa. Götterdämmerung in Raten*. Munich: Carl Hanser Verlag, 1973.

Du Bois, W. E. B. *The Souls of Black Folk*. Edited by Henry Louis Gates Jr. and Terry Hume Lewis. 1903; New York: W. W. Norton, 1999.

Du Bois, W. E. B., and David L. Lewis. *W.E.B. Du Bois: A Reader*. New York: H. Holt and Co, 1995.

Duclert, Vincent and Christophe Prochasson, eds. *Dictionnaire critique de la République*. Paris: Flammarion, 2002.

Dudziak, Mary L. *Cold War Civil Rights: Race and the Image of American Democracy*. Princeton, NJ: Princeton University Press, 2011.

Duggan, Christopher, and Christopher Wagstaff, eds. *Italy in the Cold War: Politics, Culture and Society 1948–58*. Oxford: Berg, 1995.

Eckstein, Arthur M., and Peter Lehman, eds. The Searchers: *Essays and Reflections on John Ford's Classic Western*. Detroit: Wayne State University Press, 2004.

Eleftheriotis, Dimitris. *Popular Cinemas of Europe: Studies of Texts, Contexts, and Frameworks*. New York: Continuum, 2001.

Ellwood, David W. *The Movies as History: Visions of the Twentieth Century*. Stroud, UK: Sutton, 2000.

Ellwood, David W. *The Shock of America: Europe and the Challenge of the Century*. Oxford: Oxford University Press, 2012.

Ellwood, David, and Rob Kroes, eds. *Hollywood in Europe: Experiences of Cultural Hegemony*. Amsterdam: VU University of Amsterdam Press, 1994.

Elmer, Greg, and Mike Gasher, eds. *Contracting Out Hollywood: Runaway Productions and Foreign Location Shooting*. Lanham, MD: Rowman & Littlefield, 2005.

Faldini, Franca, and Goffredo Fofi. *L'avventurosa storia del cinema italiano raccontata dai suoi protagonisti, 1935–1959*. Milan: Feltrinelli, 1979.

Falola, Toyin, and Kevin D. Roberts, eds. *The Atlantic World, 1450–2000: Blacks in the Diaspora*. Bloomington: Indiana University Press, 2008.

Fanon, Frantz. *Black Skin, White Masks*. Translated by Richard Philcox. New York: Grove Press, 2008.

Farassino, Alberto, ed. *Neorealismo: Cinema italiano 1945–49*. Turin: E.D.T., 1989.

Farassino, Alberto, Tatti Sanguineti, and Jean A. Gili. *Lux film: Esthétique et système d'un studio italien*. Locarno: Editions du Festival international du film de Locarno, 1984.

Fehrenbach, Heide. *Race after Hitler: Black Occupation Children in Postwar Germany and America*. Princeton, NJ: Princeton University Press, 2005.

Ferguson, Suzanne, and Barbara Groseclose, eds. *Literature and the Visual Arts in Contemporary Society*. Columbus: Ohio State University Press, 1985.

Fischer-Hornung, Dorothea, and Alison D. Goellker, eds. *Embodying Liberation: The Black Body in American Dance*. Berlin: Lit Verlag, 2001.

Fisher, Austin. *Radical Frontiers in the Spaghetti Western: Politics, Violence and Popular Italian Cinema*. London: I.B. Tauris, 2014.

Fleischer, Hagen. *Im Kreuzschatten der Mächte—Griechenland 1941–1944: Okkupation—Resistance—Kollaboration*. Frankfurt am Main: Lang, 1986.

Foa, Vittorio. *Questo novecento*. Turin: Einaudi, 1997.

Focardi, Filippo. *La guerra della memoria: La Resistenza nel dibattito politico italiano dal 1945 a oggi*. Bari: Laterza, 2020.

Fojas, Camilla. *Border Bandits: Hollywood on the Southern Frontier*. Austin: University of Texas Press, 2008.

Forgacs, David, and Stephen Gundle. *Mass Culture and Italian Society from Fascism to the Cold War*. Bloomington: Indiana University Press, 2007.

Fraccaroli, Arnaldo. *Hollywood paese d'avventura*. Milan: Fratelli Treves, 1929.

Frayling, Christopher. *Sergio Leone: Something to Do with Death*. London: Faber and Faber, 2000.

Frayling, Christopher. *Spaghetti Westerns: Cowboys and Europeans from Karl May to Sergio Leone*. London: I.B. Tauris, 2006.

Fridlund, Bert. *The Spaghetti Western: A Thematic Analysis*. Jefferson, NC: McFarland and Co., 2006.

Gabutti, Diego. *C'era una volta in America: Un'avventura al saloon con Sergio Leone*. Milan: Le milieu, 2015.

Bibliography 361

Gallagher, Tag. *The Adventures of Roberto Rossellini: His Life and Films*. New York: Da Capo, 1998.

Gandin, Piero Berengo, ed. *Alberto Lattuada fotografo: Dieci anni di Occhio Quadrato*. Florence: Alinari, 1982.

Gane, Nicholas. *The Future of Social Theory*. London: Continuum, 2004.

García, Hugo, Mercedes Yusta Rodrigo, Xavier Tabet, and Cristina Clímaco, eds. *Rethinking Antifascism: History, Memory, and Politics, 1922 to the Present*. New York: Berghahn Books, 2016.

Gasparetto, Pier Francesco. *Sogni e soldi: Vita di Riccardo Gualino*. Turin: Nino Aragno, 2007.

Gilroy, Paul. *The Black Atlantic: Modernity and Double Consciousness*. Cambridge, MA: Harvard University Press, 2003.

Giovacchini, Saverio. *Hollywood Modernism*. Philadelphia: Temple University Press, 2001.

Giovacchini, Saverio, and Robert Sklar, eds. *Global Neorealism: The Transnational History of a Film Style*. Jackson: University Press of Mississippi, 2012.

Girlanda, Elio. *Stefania Sandrelli*. Rome: Gremese, 2002.

Giusti, Marco. *Dizionario del western all'italiana*. Milan: Oscar Mondadori, 2007.

Giusti, Marco, and Enrico Ghezzi, with Sergio Grmek Germani. *Kim Arcalli: Montare il cinema*. Venice: Marsilio, 1980.

Gramsci, Antonio. *Quaderni del carcere*. Edited by Valentino Giarratana. Turin: Einaudi, 2001.

Grandi, Aldo. *La generazione degli anni perduti: Storia di potere operaio*. Turin: Einaudi, 2003.

Grattarola, Franco, and Giuseppe Pollicelli. *Pasolini, una vita violentata: Pestaggi fisici e linciaggi morali: Cronaca di una via crucis laica attraverso la stampa dell'epoca*. Rome: Coniglio, 2005.

Greene, Shelleen. *Equivocal Subjects: Between Italy and Africa—Constructions of Racial and National Identity in the Italian Cinema*. New York: Bloomsbury Academic, 2014.

Grimm, Reinhold, and Jost Hermand, eds. *Blacks and German Culture: Essays*. Madison: University of Wisconsin Press, 1986.

Guback, Thomas H. *The International Film Industry: Western Europe and America since 1945*. Bloomington: Indiana University Press, 1969.

Guerrero, Ed. *Framing Blackness: The African American Image in Film*. Philadelphia: Temple University Press, 1993.

Gundle, Stephen. *Glamour: A History*. Oxford: Oxford University Press, 2009.

Hargrove, Hondon B. *Buffalo Soldiers in Italy: Black Americans in World War II*. Jefferson, NC: McFarland and Company, 1985.

Harper, John Lamberton. *American Visions of Europe: Franklin D. Roosevelt, George F. Kennan, and Dean G. Acheson*. Cambridge: Cambridge University Press, 1994.

Hartz, Louis. *The Liberal Tradition in America: An Interpretation of American Political Thought since the Revolution*. Introduction by Tom Wicker. San Diego: Harcourt Brace Jovanovich, 1991.

Heffernan, Kevin. *Ghouls, Gimmicks, and Gold: Horror Films and the American Movie Business, 1953–1968*. Durham, NC: Duke University Press, 2004.

Hershfield, Joanne, and David Maciel, eds. *Mexico's Cinema: A Century of Film and Filmmakers*. Wilmington, DE: Scholarly Resources, 1999.

Hillier, Jim, ed. *Cahiers du Cinéma*, vol. 1, *The 1950s: Neo-Realism, Hollywood, New Wave*. Cambridge, MA: Harvard University Press, 1986.

Hoberman, J. *The Dream Life: Movies, Media, and the Mythology of the Sixties*. New York: New Press, 2005.

Höhn, Maria. *GIs and Fräuleins: The German-American Encounter in 1950s West Germany*. Chapel Hill: University of North Carolina Press, 2002.

Horak, Jan-Christopher. *Fluchtpunkt Hollywood: Eine Dokumentation zur Filmemigration nach 1933*. Münster: MAkS, 1986.

Iaccio, Pasquale. *Cinema e storia: Percorsi, immagini, testimonianze*. Naples: Liguori, 1998.

Iaccio, Pasquale, ed. *Non solo Scipione: Il cinema di Carmine Gallone*. Naples: Liguori, 2003.

Ibekwe, Chinweizu. *The West and the Rest of Us: White Predators, Black Slavers, and the African Elite*. New York: Vintage Books, 1975.

Izod, John. *Hollywood and the Box Office, 1895–1986*. New York: Columbia University Press, 1988.

Jacobs, Diane. *Hollywood Renaissance*. New York: Dell, 1980.

Johnson-Yale, Camille. *A History of Hollywood's Outsourcing Debate: Runaway Production*. London: Lexington Books, 2017.

Jones, Christopher M. *Boris Vian Transatlantic: Sources, Myths, and Dreams*. New York: Peter Lang, 1998.

Joseph, Gilbert M., Anne Rubenstein, and Eric Zolov, eds. *Fragments of a Golden Age: The Politics of Culture in Mexico since 1940*. Durham, NC: Duke University Press, 2001.

Judt, Tony. *Postwar: A History of Europe since 1945*. New York: Penguin, 2005.

Kaplan, Amy. *The Anarchy of Empire in the Making of U.S. Culture*. Cambridge, MA: Harvard University Press, 2005.

Kezich, Tullio, and Alessandra Levantesi. *Dino De Laurentiis, la Vita e i film*. Milan: Feltrinelli, 2001.

Kitses, Jim. *Horizons West: Anthony Mann, Budd Boetticher, Sam Peckinpah: Studies of Authorship within the Western*. Bloomington: Indiana University Press, 1969.

Klimke, Martin. *The Other Alliance: Student Protest in West Germany and the United States in the Global Sixties*. Princeton, NJ: Princeton University Press, 2010.

Kolker, Robert Phillip. *Bernardo Bertolucci*. London: British Film Institute, 1985.

Koppes, Clayton R., and Gregory D. Black. *Hollywood Goes to War: How Politics, Profits, and Propaganda Shaped World War II Movies*. Berkeley: University of California Press, 1990.

Koster, Henry. *Henry Koster*. Interviewed by Irene Kahn Atkins. Metuchen, NJ Scarecrow Press, 1987.

Koszarski, Richard. *Hollywood on the Hudson: Film and Television in New York from Griffith to Sarnoff*. New Brunswick, NJ: Rutgers University Press, 2008.

Kramer, Stanley, and Thomas H. Coffey. *A Mad, Mad, Mad, Mad World: A Life in Hollywood*. New York: Harcourt Brace, 1997.

Kroes, Rob, Robert W. Rydell, D. F. J. Bosscher, and John F. Sears, eds. *Cultural Transmissions and Receptions: American Mass Culture in Europe*. Amsterdam: VU University Press, 1993.

Krutnik, Frank. *"Un-American" Hollywood: Politics and Film in the Blacklist Era*. New Brunswick, NJ: Rutgers University Press, 2007.

Kuisel, Richard F. *Seducing the French: The Dilemma of Americanization*. Berkeley: University of California Press, 1997.

Labanca, Nicola. *Oltremare: Storia dell'espansione coloniale italiana*. Bologna: Il Mulino, 2002.

Lake, Marilyn, and Henry Reynolds. *Drawing the Global Colour Line: White Men's Countries and the International Challenge of Racial Equality*. Cambridge: Cambridge University Press, 2008.

Lattuada, Alberto. *Occhio Quadrato*. Milan: Edizioni di Corrente, 1941.

Lawson, John Howard. *Processional: A Jazz Symphony of American Life in Four Acts*. New York: Thomas Seltzer, 1925.

Lawson, John Howard. *Roger Bloomer: A Play in Three Acts*. New York: Thomas Seltzer, 1923.

Lazzeretti, Luciana. *Creative Industries and Innovation in Europe: Concepts, Measures and Comparative Case Studies*. New York: Routledge, 2013.

Lev, Peter. *The Euro-American Cinema*. Austin: University of Texas Press, 1993.

Liehm, Mira. *Passion and Defiance: Film in Italy from 1942 to the Present*. Berkeley: University of California Press, 1984.

Lizzani, Carlo. *Attraverso il Novecento*. Turin: Lindau, 1998.

Lizzani, Carlo. *Il mio lungo viaggio nel secolo breve*. Turin: Einaudi, 2007.

Longo, Luigi, Carlo Salinari, and Palmiro Togliatti, eds. *Per la Costituzione Democratica e per una libera cultura: Rapporti alla sessione del CC del PCI del 10–12 Novembre 1952*. Rome: Istituto Gramsci, 1953.

Lucia, Cynthia A. Barto, Roy Grundmann, and Art Simon, eds. *The Wiley-Blackwell History of American Film*. Oxford: Wiley-Blackwell, 2012.

Luconi, Stefano, and Guido Tintori. *L'ombra lunga del fascio: Canali di propaganda fascista per gli 'italiani d'America.'* Milan: M&B Publishing, 2004.

MacMaster, Neil. *Racism in Europe, 1870–2000*. New York: Palgrave, 2001.

364 Bibliography

Magrini, Ornella. *Una scomoda ossessione: Ultimo Tango a Parigi, memorie da un film proibito*. Arezzo: Zona, 2006.

Malaparte, Curzio. *Diario di uno straniero a Parigi*. Florence: Vallecchi, 1966.

Malaparte, Curzio. *La pelle*. In *Opere Scelte*. Milan: Mondadori, 1997.

Marcus, Millicent. *After Fellini: National Cinema in the Postmodern Age*. Baltimore: Johns Hopkins University Press, 2002.

Marcus, Millicent. *Italian Film in the Light of Neorealism*. Princeton, NJ: Princeton University Press, 1986.

Martin, Mel. *The Magnificent Showman: The Epic Films of Samuel Bronston*. Albany, GA: BearManor Media, 2007.

Martinez, Dolores P. *Remaking Kurosawa: Translations and Permutations in Global Cinema*. New York: Palgrave Macmillan, 2009.

Mazierska, Ewa, and Laura Rascaroli. *The Cinema of Nanni Moretti: Dreams and Diaries*. London: Wallflower Press, 2004.

McGilligan, Patrick, and Paul Buhle. *Tender Comrades: A Backstory of the Hollywood Blacklist*. Minneapolis: University of Minnesota Press, 2012.

McKenna, A. T. *Showman of the Screen: Joseph E. Levine and His Revolutions in Film Promotion*. Lexington: University Press of Kentucky, 2016.

McNeill, William Hardy. *The Rise of the West: A History of the Human Community*. Chicago: University of Chicago Press, 1963.

Miccichè, Lino, ed. *Il neorealismo cinematografico italiano*. 2nd ed. Venice: Marsilio, 1999.

Miller, Toby, Nitin Govil, John McMurria, and Richard Maxwell. *Global Hollywood*. London: BFI, 2001.

Minotti, Gianluca. *Valerio Zurlini*. Milan: Il Castoro, 2001.

Mishra, Pankaj. *Age of Anger: A History of the Present*. New York: Farrar, Straus and Giroux, 2017.

Molho, Anthony, and Gordon S. Wood, eds. *Imagined Histories: American Historians Interpret the Past*. Princeton, NJ: Princeton University Press, 1998.

Monteleone, Enzo. *Mediterraneo*. Milan: Baldini and Castoldi, 1992.

Murray, Edward. *Nine American Film Critics: A Study of Theory and Practice*. New York: Ungar, 1975.

Murray, William. *The Fugitive Romans*. New York: Vanguard Press, 1955.

Muscio, Giuliana. *Napoli/New York/Hollywood: Film between Italy and the United States*. New York: Fordham University Press, 2019.

Museo Nazionale del Cinema. *Rosso fuoco: Il cinema di Giuseppe De Santis*. Edited by Sergio Toffetti. Turin: Lindau, 1996.

Nacci, Michela. *L'antiamericanismo in Italia negli anni Trenta: Con otto fotografie di Berenice Abbott*. Turin: Bollati Boringhieri, 1989.

Naremore, James. *More Than Night: Film Noir in Its Contexts*. Berkeley: University of California Press, 2008.

Nichols, Bill, ed. *Movies and Methods: An Anthology*. Berkeley: University of California Press, 1976.

Nicoli, Marina. *The Rise and Fall of the Italian Film Industry*. New York: Routledge, 2017.

Noble, Peter. *Il negro nel film*. Rome: Bocca, 1956.

Nowell-Smith, Geoffrey, and Steven Ricci, eds. *Hollywood and Europe: Economics, Culture, National Identity, 1945–95*. London: BFI, 1998.

Office National Hellenique des Criminels de Guerre. *Les atrocités des quattres envahisseurs de la Grèce. Allemandes, Italiens, Bulgares, Albanais*. Athens: ONHCG, 1946.

Olla, Gianni. *Franco Solinas: Uno scrittore al cinema*. Cagliari: CUEC, 1997.

Pacht Bassani, Paola, and Massimo Raffaeli. *Se avessi una piccola casa mia: Giorgio Bassani, il racconto di una figlia*. Milan: La nave di Teseo, 2016.

Paggi, Leonardo, ed. *La memoria del nazismo nell'Europa di oggi*. Florence: La nuova Italia, 1997.

Pardini, Giuseppe. *Curzio Malaparte: Biografia politica*. Milan: Luni, 2020.

Parigi, Stefania, ed. *Paisà: Analisi del film*. Venice: Marsilio, 2005.

Paris, Michael. *Repicturing the Second World War: Representations in Film and Television*. New York: Palgrave Macmillan, 2007.

Passerini, Luisa. *Europe in Love, Love in Europe: Imagination and Politics between the Wars*. New York: New York University Press, 1999.

Passerini, Luisa. *Love and the Idea of Europe*. New York: Berghahn Books, 2009.

Patriarca, Silvana. *Race in Post-Fascist Italy: "War Children" and the Color of the Nation*. Cambridge: Cambridge University Press, 2022.

Pavese, Cesare. *The Moon and the Bonfires*. Translated by R. W. Flint, introduction by Mark Rudman. New York: New York Review Books, 2002.

Pavese, Cesare. *Vita attraverso le lettere*. Edited by Lorenzo Modo. Turin: Einaudi, 2004.

Pavese, Cesare, and Mariarosa Masoero. *Il serpente e la colomba: Scritti e soggetti cinematografici*. Edited by Mariarosa Masoero. Turin: Einaudi, 2009.

Pells, Richard H. *Not Like Us: How Europeans Loved, Hated, and Transformed American Culture since World War II*. New York: Basic Books, 1997.

Pensel, Hans. *Seastrom and Stiller in Hollywood: Two Swedish Directors in Silent American Films, 1923–1930*. New York: Vantage Press, 1969.

Pérez Melgosa, Adrian. *Cinema and Inter-American Relations: Tracking Transnational Affect*. New York: Routledge, 2014.

Perlstein, Rick. *Nixonland: The Rise of a President and the Fracturing of America*. New York: Scribner, 2008.

Perret, Geoffrey. *Days of Sadness, Years of Triumph: The American People, 1939–1945*. New York: Coward, McCann, and Geoghegan, 1973.

Peterson del Mar, David. *African, American: From Tarzan to Dreams from My Father—Africa in the US Imagination*. London: Zed Books, 2017.

Petrie, Graham. *Hollywood Destinies: European Directors in America, 1922–1931*. Detroit: Wayne State University Press, 2002.

Pezzotta, Alberto. *Il western italiano*. Milan: Il Castoro, 2012.

Pintor, Giaime. *Il sangue d'Europa: Scritti politici e letterari*. Edited by Valentino Giarratana. Turin: Einaudi, 1950.

Pirro, Ugo. *Le soldatesse*. Milan: Bompiani, 1965.

Pirro, Ugo. *Soltanto un nome nei titoli di testa: I felici anni sessanta del cinema italiano*. Turin: Einaudi, 1998.

Poiger, Uta G. *Jazz, Rock, and Rebels: Cold War Politics and American Culture in a Divided Germany*. Berkeley: University of California Press, 2000.

Polenberg, Richard. *War and Society: The United States, 1941–1945*. Philadelphia: J.B. Lippincott, 1972.

Prashad, Vijay. *The Darker Nations: A People's History of the Third World*. New York: New Press, 2008.

Prime, Rebecca. *Hollywood Exiles in Europe: The Blacklist and Cold War Film Culture*. New Brunswick, NJ: Rutgers University Press, 2014.

Quaglietti, Lorenzo. *Storia economica-politica del cinema italiano*. Rome: Editori Riuniti, 1980.

Rashkin, Esther. *Unspeakable Secrets and the Psychoanalysis of Culture*. Albany: State University of New York Press, 2008.

Regev, Ronny. *Working in Hollywood: How the Studio System Turned Creativity into Labor*. Chapel Hill: University of North Carolina Press, 2018.

Ricci, Steven. *Cinema and Fascism: Italian Film and Society, 1922–1943*. Berkeley: University of California Press, 2008.

Rieupeyrout, Jean-Louis. *Le Western ou le cinéma Américain par excellence*. Paris: Éditions du Cerfs, 1953.

Robinson, Greg. *By Order of the President: FDR and the Internment of Japanese Americans*. Cambridge, MA: Harvard University Press, 2001.

Rochat, Giorgio. *Il colonialismo italiano*. Turin: Loescher, 1996.

Rochat, Giorgio. *Le guerre italiane 1935–1943: Dall'impero d'Etiopia alla disfatta*. Turin: Einaudi, 2005.

Roeder, George H. *The Censored War: American Visual Experience during World War Two*. New Haven, CT: Yale University Press, 1993.

Roediger, David R. *The Wages of Whiteness: Race and the Making of the American Working Class*. London: Verso, 2022.

Roger, Philippe. *The American Enemy: A Story of French Anti-Americanism*. Chicago: University of Chicago Press, 2005.

Rondolino, Gianni. *Luchino Visconti*. Turin: UTET, 2006.

Rose, Peter I., ed. *The Dispossessed: An Anatomy of Exile*. Amherst: University of Massachusetts Press, 2005.

Ross, Steven. *Hollywood Left and Right: How Movie Stars Shaped American Politics*. New York: Oxford University Press, 2011.

Rosten, Leo. *Hollywood: The Movie Colony, the Movie Makers*. New York: Arno Press, 1970.

Bibliography

Roveri, Alessandro. *Giorgio Bassani e l'antifascismo (1936–1943)*. Ferrara: 2 G Editrice, 2002.

Rydell, Robert W., and Rob Kroes. *Buffalo Bill in Bologna: The Americanization of the World, 1869–1922*. Chicago: University of Chicago Press, 2013.

Santini, Aldo. *Tombolo*. Milan: Rizzoli, 1990.

Schary, Dore. *Heyday: An Autobiography*. Boston: Little, Brown, 1979.

Schatz, Thomas. *Boom and Bust: American Cinema in the 1940s*. Berkeley: University of California Press, 1999.

Schatz, Thomas. *Hollywood Filmmaking in the Studio Era*. New York: Metropolitan Books, 1996.

Schillace, John A. *The Tragic Forest: Tales of the Forest of Tombolo*. New York: Exposition Press, 1951.

Schivelbusch, Wolfgang. *Three New Deals: Reflections on Roosevelt's America, Mussolini's Italy, and Hitler's Germany, 1933–1939*. New York: Picador, 2006.

Schoonover, Karl. *Brutal Vision: The Neorealist Body in Postwar Italian Cinema*. Minneapolis: University of Minnesota Press, 2012.

Schwartz, Thomas Alan. *Lyndon Johnson and Europe: In the Shadow of Vietnam*. Cambridge, MA: Harvard University Press, 2003.

Schwartzel, Erich. *Red Carpet: Hollywood, China, and the Global Battle for Cultural Supremacy*. New York: Penguin, 2022.

Shaw, Tony, and Denise J. Youngblood. *Cinematic Cold War: The American and Soviet Struggle for Hearts and Minds*. Lawrence: University Press of Kansas, 2010.

Sherman, Vincent. *Studio Affairs: My Life as a Film Director*. Lexington: University Press of Kentucky, 1996.

Sklar, Robert. *Movie-Made America: A Cultural History of American Movies*. New York: Vintage Books, 2010.

Slotkin, Richard. *Gunfighter Nation: The Myth of the Frontier in Twentieth-Century America*. Norman: University of Oklahoma Press, 1998.

Smith, William Gardner. *Return to Black America*. Englewood Cliffs, NJ: Prentice-Hall, 1970.

Smyth, J. E., ed. *Hollywood and the American Historical Film*. New York: Palgrave Macmillan, 2012.

Snead, James A. *White Screens/Black Images: Hollywood from the Dark Side*. Edited by Colin MacCabe and Cornel West. New York: Routledge, 1994.

Socci, Stefano. *Bernardo Bertolucci*. Milan: Il Castoro, 1996.

Solinas, Franco. *Squarciò e altri scritti*. Nuoro: Ilisso, 2001.

Sollima, Sergio. *Il Cinema in USA*. Rome: Veritas, 1947.

Sparrow, James T. *Warfare State: World War II Americans and the Age of Big Government*. New York: Oxford University Press, 2013.

Spoto, Donald. *Stanley Kramer, Film Maker*. Hollywood: Samuel French, 1990.

Steinhart, Daniel. *Runaway Hollywood: Internationalizing Postwar Production and Location Shooting*. Berkeley: University of California Press, 2019.

Stephan, Alexander, ed. *Americanization and Anti-Americanism: The German Encounter with American Culture after 1945*. Oxford: Berghahn, 2007.

Stevens, George, and American Film Institute, eds. *Conversations with the Great Moviemakers of Hollywood's Golden Age at the American Film Institute*. New York: Alfred A. Knopf, 2006.

Strand, Paul, and Cesare Zavattini, eds. *Un Paese: Portrait of an Italian Village*. New York: Aperture, 1997.

Strode, Woody, with Sam Young. *Goal Dust: An Autobiography*. Lanham, MD: Madison Books, 1990.

Thompson, Kristin. *Exporting Entertainment: America in the World Film Market 1907–1934*. London: BFI Books, 1985.

Thornton, John. *Africa and Africans in the Making of the Atlantic World, 1400–1800*. Cambridge: Cambridge University Press, 1992.

Tirard, Laurent. *Moviemakers' Masterclass: Private Lessons from the World's Foremost Directors*. London: Faber, 2003.

Tomlinson, John. *Cultural Imperialism: A Critical Introduction*. Baltimore: Johns Hopkins University Press, 1991.

Tonti, Aldo. *Odore di Cinema*. Florence: Vallecchi, 1964.

Torriglia, Anna Maria. *Broken Time, Fragmented Space: A Cultural Map for Postwar Italy*. Toronto: University of Toronto Press, 2002.

Treveri Gennari, Daniela. *Post-War Italian Cinema: American Intervention, Vatican Interests*. New York: Routledge, 2009.

Trouillot, Michel-Rolph. *Silencing the Past: Power and the Production of History*. Boston: Beacon Press, 1995.

Vaccarella, Cristina, and Luigi Vaccarella. *Anna Magnani, Quattro storie americane*. Rome: Nuova Arnica editrice, 2003.

Vasey, Ruth. *The World according to Hollywood, 1918–1939*. Madison: University of Wisconsin Press, 1997.

Viano, Maurizio. *A Certain Realism: Making Use of Pasolini's Film Theory and Practice*. Berkeley: University of California Press, 1993.

Villa, Federica. *Il cinema che serve: Giorgio Bassani cinematografico*. Turin: Edizioni Kaplan, 2010.

Vitti, Antonio. *Giuseppe De Santis and Postwar Italian Cinema*. Toronto: University of Toronto Press, 1996.

Wagstaff, Christopher. *Italian Neorealist Cinema: An Aesthetic Approach*. Toronto: University of Toronto Press, 2007.

Wallis, Hal, and Charles Higham. *Starmaker: The Autobiography of Hal Wallis*. New York: Macmillan, 1980.

Bibliography   369

Warshow, Robert. *The Immediate Experience: Movies, Comics, Theatre, and Other Aspects of Popular Culture*. New York: Atheneum, 1970.

Williams, Alan Larson. *Republic of Images: A History of French Filmmaking*. Cambridge, MA: Harvard University Press, 1992.

Wright, Will. *Sixguns and Society: A Structural Study of the Western*. Berkeley: University of California Press, 1977.

Wyatt, Justin. *High Concept: Movies and Marketing in Hollywood*. Austin: University of Texas Press, 1994.

Xavier, Ismail. *Allegories of Underdevelopment: Aesthetics and Politics in Modern Brazilian Cinema*. Minneapolis: University of Minnesota Press, 1997.

Zagarrio, Vito, ed. *Carlo Lizzani: Un lungo viaggio nel cinema*. Venice: Marsilio, 2010.

Zagarrio, Vito, ed. *Non c'è pace tra gli ulivi: Un neorealismo postmoderno*. Rome: Fondazione Scuola nazionale di cinema, 2002.

Archives and Collections

Billy Rose Collection, New York Public Library, New York, New York.

California State Archives, Sacramento, California.

Cedric Belfrage Papers, Tamiment Library, New York University, New York, New York.

Department of Defense Film Collection, Georgetown University, Washington, DC.

De Santis Archive, Scuola Nazionale di Cinematografia, Rome, Italy.

De Santis Papers, Cineteca Nazionale, Rome, Italy.

Fondo Luchino Visconti, Fondazione Gramsci, Rome, Italy.

Gil Kurland Collection, Margaret Herrick Library, Academy of Motion Picture Arts and Sciences, Los Angeles, California.

Giuseppe De Santis Collection, Z. Smith Reynolds Research Library, Wake Forest University, Winston-Salem, North Carolina.

Giuseppe De Santis Papers, Cinecittà, Rome, Italy.

John Huston Papers, Margaret Herrick Library, Academy of Motion Picture Arts and Sciences, Los Angeles, California.

Katherine Dunham Papers, Manuscript Division, Library of Congress, Washington, DC.

Museum of Science and Industry, California State Library, Sacramento, California.

National Archives, College Park, Maryland.

Paramount Pictures Production Records, Margaret Herrick Library, Academy of Motion Picture Arts and Sciences, Los Angeles, California.

Schomburg Center, New York Public Library, New York, New York.
Stanley Kramer Papers, Department of Special Collections, UCLA, Los Angeles, California.

Index

1900, 287–88

Accord Marchandeau, 37
addiction, 86, 180, 275
Adorno, Theodor, 3, 5, 7, 10, 13–14
Agee, James, 88, 90, 106, 182;
  names *Open City* best film, 89;
  praises John Kitzmiller, 156
Alfieri Law, 27, 65
Algeria, 229, 249; Western
  intervention in, 18, 257, 280–81,
  284
America Amara, 65, 66, 148
American Civil War, 203, 230, 233,
  234, 250
American exceptionalism, 17, 147,
  186
Americanization: accusations of
  corruption associated with,
  146; connection to Fordist
  consumption, 101; of Italian
  culture, 73, 107, 268; prevalence
  of, in Western Europe, 97–98
Amidei, Sergio, 28, 66
Anaclerio, Gabriele, 283
anti-Americanism: based on
  aversion to modernity, 60; in

European context, 248, 256–57;
  as product of international
  context, 103; spaghetti westerns
  engaging with, 190
anticolonialism: African revolution,
  225; in spaghetti westerns, 236,
  237; of Marlon Brando, 278, 279,
  280; social movements abroad,
  233; struggle, 178
Antonioni, Michelangelo, 9, 38, 243
Appiah, Kwame Anthony, 235.
Appaloosa, The, 214–15, 218
Auerbach, Jonathan, 69
Axum Obelisk, 246, 247

Baldwin, James, 176
Balio, Tino, 22, 50, 52, 206
Belmonte, Laura, 33
Ben-Ghiat, Ruth, 161
Bergfelder, Tim, 21, 30, 169
Bertellini, Giorgio, 15
Bondanella, Peter, 155, 265
Bassani, Giorgio, 70–72, 84–85
Bataan, 112
Battle of Algiers, The, 133, 225, 226
Bazin, André, 14, 24, 197, 202, 220,
  252

Bell for Adano, A, 115–16, 123
Bellissima, 6, 47
Bergman, Ingrid, 47, 99
Bernstein, Irving, 44, 261, 289
Bertolucci, Bernardo, as director of *1900*, 287–88; as director of *Last Tango in Paris*, 256, 268–75, 278–84; as screenwriter, 194, 210, 223
Bicycle Thieves, 8, 103, 105, 106
Bitter Rice. See *Riso Amaro*
Blum-Byrnes Agreement, 37, 39
Boetticher, Budd, 197–203, 215–17, 223, 233–34
Bogart, Humphrey, 111–13
Brando, Marlon, 103, 225; as actor in *The Appaloosa*, 214–15; as actor in *Last Tango in Paris*, 257, 270–72, 274–75, 283–85; as actor and director in *One-Eyed Jacks*, 204–205, 233; as critic of colonialism, 278–80
Broken Lance, 195–97
Bronston, Samuel, 22, 49, 196
Brunetta, Gian Piero, 14, 58, 90, 95
bullfighting, 198–99
burbankization, 287–88
Burke-Hardtke Bill, 262–63, 289

Cain, James M., 68–73, 76–77; as archetypal American hardboiled writer, 87
Cameron, Earl, 143–44
Caminati, Luca, 233
Cannes, 38, 170, 206; John Kitzmiller awarded best male performance, 17, 170, 175; premiere of *Bitter Rice*, 99; Sophia Loren attends, 53; world premiere of *Two Women*, 22
capitalism, 7, 148, 208, 232; American, 60, 134, 146; consumer, 90

Carolan, Mary Ann McDonald, 15, 204
Casablanca, 40
Castel, Lou, as actor in *Quien Sabe?*, 226, 231; as actor in *Requiescant*, 203, 234, 239–42; as highbrow actor, 227
Cecchi, Emilio, 65–66, 67, 148
Celluloid Atlantic: as a category of analysis, 214; coalescence of, 137; decline of, 256; emergence of, 27; governmental underpinning of, 34; as integrated cultural zone, 10; three pillars of, 107–109
censorship, 73, 229, 270; American, 101–102, 130–31, 185; anxieties about, 73; Fascist, 61, 71, 81, 85
Centro Sperimentale di Cinematografia, 27, 42, 72, 239
Césaire, Aimé, 8, 221
Chaplin, Charlie, 62, 78–79, 81, 87
Chiarini, Luigi, 42, 106, 163
Cinecittà, 6, 53–55, 60, 265; decline of, 257; emergence of, 27–28, 29; as refugee camp, 87; resurgence in 1960s, 38; state-owned facilities, 44
Cinema Novo, 8
Cold War, 139, 146, 180, 258, 264; hemispheric romances, 200; relaxation of, 137–38; role of media during, 248; strained climate of, 92, 164
Coletti, Duilio, 125–26, 143–46, 170
colonialism: Euro-American, 221; in the context of *Last Tango in Paris*, 275–76, 281, 284; in the work of Fanon, 229, 235–36, 247; Italian, 131, 148, 157–58, 186; Marlon Brando as critic of, 278, 279
Columbia Pictures, 48, 55, 118, 125

Index

communism, 103, 146, 180, 183, 287–88; in Hollywood, 26–27, 39, 112, 260; Italian, 91, 93, 98

Cooper, Gary, 203–204, 223

Coppola, Francis Ford, 279, 290, 291, 292

Corri, Uomo, Corri, 227, 232, 241, 243

Corsi, Barbara, 29, 266

Costigliola, Frank, 257

creolization, 10, 73, 84

cultural imperialism, 7–8, 35, 60, 247, 248

culture industry, 5–7

Debord, Guy, 249

decolonization, 190, 210, 220, 222, 257

De Laurentiis, Dino, closes Italian studio, 289; partnership with Carlo Ponti, 42–44, 51, 53–54; as producer, 32, 130–31, 183–84

Del Boca, Angelo, 117, 148, 186

Del Buono, Oreste, 248–49

Della Casa, Stefano, 54, 220

Della Colletta, Cristina, 78

Deloria, Philip, 253, 254

Del Pero, Mario, 146

De Napoli, Olindo, 148, 174

Department of Defense, 91, 118, 119

De Santis, Giuseppe, 70–72, 123–24; as director of *Riso Amaro*, 93–101, 135–41; as reviewer, 66, 156

De Sica, Vittorio, 52, 103, 106, 124, 258

Django, 10, 204, 217, 222, 232

Dowling, Constance, 182–83

Dowling, Doris, 94–96, 98, 99

Du Bois, W. E. B., 148, 180

Duck, You Sucker!, 211, 214, 223, 224, 232

Eastwood, Clint, 190, 192, 250, 251, 255; as actor in westerns, 203, 216–17, 229–30, 250; as Sergio Leone collaborator, 196, 211–12, 215, 251

Ebert, Roger, 230, 251

Ebony Magazine, 168, 183, 184, 185

Eco, Umberto, 57, 63

El Alamein, 117, 118–19, 126. *See also* Second World War

Ellwood, David, 59

Embassy Pictures, 49, 50, 52, 137, 288

Ethiopia, Italian conquest of, 65, 148, 157–58, 161, 246

exceptionalism, in American history, 147, 186; in Italian history, 147–48, 168, 186

Faccia a Faccia, 243–45

Faldini, Franca, 226, 249

Falk, Peter, 137, 139–40

Fanon, Frantz, 228–29, 235–37, 246–47

Fanonism, 231, 234, 237, 239, 244

Farassino, Alberto, 41, 98

Fehrenbach, Heide, 147

Fellini, Federico, 52, 162, 167, 215, 291–92

film noir, 12, 87, 140, 165–66, 243

Fisher, Austin, 191, 192, 225, 229

Fistful of Dollars, A, 190–94, 211, 220, 240

Five Graves to Cairo, 109–11

Foa, Vittorio, 61

Fofi, Goffredo, 179, 226, 249

Fordism, 4–5, 24, 41, 61, 146

Ford, John, 150, 189, 197, 237

Frayling, Christopher, 189, 212, 213

French New Wave, 9, 14, 290. *See also* Jean-Luc Godard

Gallone, Carmine, 66, 123

Garbo, Greta, 11, 31, 47, 58
Getino, Octavio, 9, 237
Gilroy, Paul, 148
Giuliani, Gaia, 181
global South, 207, 209–11, 214, 237
Godard, Jean-Luc, 268, 274, 291
government, American, 32, 35, 37, 39, 261
Gramsci, Antonio, 4–6, 146, 228, 233
Greece, Italian occupation of, 126, 128–29, 133–35
Griffith, D.W., 87, 181, 267, 287
Gualino, Renato, 21, 30, 31, 32
Gualino, Riccardo, 41, 42, 44, 98
Gundle, Stephen, 6

Harder They Come, The, 222, 236
Harlem, 66, 71
Hartz, Louis, 147
Hays Code, 65
Hayworth, Rita, 95, 99, 204
Hecht, Ben, 43, 106
Henzell, Perry, 222, 249
Heston, Charlton, 258–59, 261
Hollywood: beginning of spaghetti revolution in, 203; as brand, 55; contempt for, 291; cooperation with government, 32; engagement with Mexico, 197–98; evolution and translation of Westerns, 211; fragmentation of studio system, 26; Golden Age of, 39; unions in, 258, 261–62
House Committee on Un-American Activities, 26, 27, 32, 43, 183
humanism, 74, 134
Huston, John, 40, 193

Ibekwe, Chinweizu, 8, 187
Italiani Brava Gente (film), 135–40

Italiani Brava Gente myth, 128, 249; comedic inflections, 124; counter representations, 131–35; as deflector of Italian guilt, 129, 157–58, 186; prevalence after World War II, 108–109
Izod, John, 30, 31

James Bond films, 22, 145, 175, 194, 217
Johnny Guitar, 195, 197, 220, 252
Johnson, Dots, 121–22, 143, 153, 165
Judt, Tony, 36, 248

Kaplan, Amy, 186
Kennan, George, 33, 146
Kezich, Tullio, 32, 43
Kitzmiller, John, 149, 165–70, 175–84; as actor in *Dolina Miru*, 170–72; as actor in *Senza Pietà*, 98, 143; as actor in *Tombolo Paradiso Nero*, 158, 160–62; as actor in *Vite Perdute*, 172–75; as actor in *Vivere in Pace*, 155–58; beginning of Italian film career, 150–51, 153; death of, 180
Korda, Zoltan, 111–13
Koszarski, Richard, 290
Kroes, Rob, 73
Kurosawa, Akira, 205–11, 269

La grande speranza, 125–26, 143–45, 156, 170
Lancaster, Burt, 47, 178, 203–204, 216
Lang, Fritz, 12, 43, 63
Last Tango in Paris, 18, 256–58, 266, 268–83
Latin America, 198, 199, 223, 242, 266. *See also* Mexico

Index

Lattuada, Alberto, 63–64, 87, 258; as director of *Senza Pietà*, 161, 162–68
Lawson, John Howard, 64, 112
Leone, Sergio, 86, 190–91, 192–94, 210–15, 222–25, 239–40
Le Soldatesse, 132, 135, 243
Levantesi, Alessandra, 32, 43
Levine, Joseph, death of, 289; as producer, 49–53, 137, 139; role of, in *Showman*, 19–20, 22
Libya, 109, 114, 116, 157–58, 161
Liehm, Mira, 82, 291
Lombardi-Diop, Cristina, 181
Loren, Sophia, 22, 43, 53, 267, 289
Lux Film, 21, 41–44, 98, 101
lynching, 78, 176, 202, 210, 267

Magnani, Anna, 6–7, 46–48, 258
Magnificent Seven, The, 205, 207, 210–11, 216–17
Mailer, Norman, 55, 272
male bonding in film, 231, 256, 288
Malaparte, Curzio, 153, 154, 169
Mambo, 43, 44, 183–86
Mamoulian, Rouben, 66, 72
Marcuzzo, Elio, 78–79, 81
Marshall Plan, 33–34, 44, 220, 246
Marxism, 153, 228, 250, 268, 271
Mayer, Louis B., 24, 25, 26
Maysles, Albert and David, 19–20, 49, 53
McKenna, A.T., 53
McMasters, The, 218, 229, 230, 250
Melgosa, Adrián Pérez, 200, 266, 267
memory, 13, 28, 131, 133–34, 281
Mexican Revolution, 191, 201, 224, 231, 249
Mexico, 197–205 passim, 209–10, 215, 232–33
MGM, 26, 49, 55, 58, 60, 73

Miccichè, Lino, 220
Milian, Tomas, 135, 241–46
Miller, Toby, 40
mise-en-scène, 212, 227, 236, 238, 250
misogyny, 18, 77, 145, 270–73, 283
modernity, 64, 89, 205; American, 42, 60, 69, 74, 96; capitalist, 146, 232; democratic, 86, 226, 228; postwar, 95, 199; uncertainties of, 73, 167
Monteleone, Enzo, 127, 128, 129
Motion Picture Export Association, 33, 39, 259
Murphy, Audie, 120–22, 199
Muscio, Giuliana, 12, 15, 197
Mussolini, Benito, 48, 60, 83, 84, 116, 117
Mussolini, Vittorio, 60, 82, 90

Nacci, Michela, 60
Naremore, James, 12, 87
Native Americans, in film, 193, 195–96, 230, 231, 250–54; countercultural portrayals of, 213; Marlon Brando as activist for, 279, 280
NATO. *See* North Atlantic Treaty Organization
Neorealism, 28–29, 30, 32, 87–88, 90, 102, 107, 115, 123, 129, 135–39; autochthony of, 12–13; compared with French New Wave, 14; and John Kitzmiller, 154, 166; and Last Tango in Paris, 274–75; obscuring of its Atlantic connections, 92; and spaghetti Westerns, 220–21
Nicoli, Marina, 41
Nixon, Richard, 18, 257, 259–60, 263; administration, 15, 262, 265

Index

nonprofessional actors, 87, 138, 139, 163, 172
North Atlantic Treaty Organization, 15, 146, 248, 257

Office of War Information, 116–17; reaction of, to wartime films, 111, 114–15; role of, during World War II, 109
Once Upon a Time trilogy, 192–94, 211, 223–24
Open City, 47, 88–89, 123, 155–56
Ossessione, 67–68, 70–79, 81–88, 101
Outlaw Josey Wales, The, 229, 230, 250
Outrage, The, 209, 223, 230, 251

Paisà, 89–90, 121–25, 165–66
Parigi, Stefania, 166
Pasolini, Pier Paolo, 227, 233–34, 240, 269
Patriarca, Silvana, 161
Pavese, Cesare, 61–64, 71–72, 226, 274
Peckinpah, Sam, 198, 204, 217, 224, 227
Pells, Richard, 8, 147
Pezzotta, Giulio, 197, 198, 205
Pintor, Giaime, 36
Pirro, Ugo, 98, 126, 132–35
plagiarism, 93
Poitier, Sidney, 182, 213, 227
political activism, 135, 279
Ponti, Carlo, partnership with Dino De Laurentiis, 42–44, 46, 51, 53–54; as producer, 21, 31–32, 150; retires from film production, 289
postcolonialism, 198, 207, 221–25, 257
Postman Always Rings Twice, The, 68–73, 76; echoes of, in *Last Tango in Paris*, 274

Prime, Rebecca, 46
prisoners of war, 114, 125, 144–45
Production Code Administration, 101–102
Professionals, The, 177–78, 215, 216, 224
propaganda, 116, 118, 129; American, 108, 109; Italian Fascist, 60, 61, 80; role of cinema as, 33, 35
prostitution, 127–28, 133, 154, 163, 182
protectionism, 21, 29, 262, 264

Quaglietti, Lorenzo, 40, 165
Quien Sabe?, 216, 226, 241–42; Gian Maria Volonté in, 240; Lou Castel in, 239; synopsis of, 231

racism, 149, 181–82, 187, 213, 281–82; American, 145–48, 156, 164, 176, 194; Italian, 145, 148, 174, 186; Hollywood, 180, 202
racist caricature: blackface, 144, 145, 162, 178–79; brownface, 208, 214, 224, 230, 234, 243, 244–45, 246, 249; redface, 195, 196, 230, 249, 250, 251; yellowface, 278
Ranown cycle, 199, 200, 202
Rashkin, Esther, 284
Rashomon, 206–207, 209–10, 214, 269
Ricci, Steven, 28
Reagan, Ronald, 260–61
Renoir, Jean, 67–68, 70, 83, 274
Renzi, Renzo, 129–30, 132
Revenue Act of 1951, 45–46
Riso Amaro, 93–94, 96, 98–101; as box office hit, 102
RKO, 26, 47, 198, 206
Rocha, Glauber, 8–9, 237–38
Roediger, David, 58
Roger, Philippe, 248, 253, 257
Rondolino, Gianni, 67

Index

Roosevelt, Franklin, 4, 108; administration, 26, 108
Rommel, Erwin, 109–11, 118, 120, 276
Rose Tattoo, The, 31, 46, 47, 48
Rossellini, Roberto, 88, 91, 92; as director of *Paisà*, 89, 121–22, 124, 139, 153; similarities to Kurosawa, 206

Sahara, 111–19, 126
Salinari, Carlo, 36, 248
Sand Creek Massacre, 229, 231, 250
Santarelli, Lidia, 127
Schatz, Thomas, 24
Schoonover, Karl, 12, 17, 90
Second World War, 6, 131, 136; authoritarian climate of, 206; battles of, 111, 116, 120, 135; films depicting, 109, 112, 117, 120, 124, 138, 143
Secret of Santa Vittoria, The, 48
Selim, Monique, 253
Senza Pietà, 98, 161–66, 175, 182
Seven Samurai, 205, 207–209
sexual assault, 174, 201, 206, 211; as portrayed in *The Birth of a Nation*, 267; as portrayed in *For a Few Dollars More*, 215; as portrayed in *La Pelle*, 153; as portrayed in *Last Tango in Paris*, 257, 270, 273, 283; as portrayed in *Le Soldatesse*, 132–34; as portrayed in *Mediterraneo*, 127–28; in Greece during World War II, 126; in postwar Italian cinema, 130
Shaw, Irwin, 43
silent majority, 259–60
Six-Pack, 255–57
Sklar, Robert, 12, 17, 291
Slotkin, Richard, 112, 219, 220

Smith-Mundt Act, 34–35, 220, 257
Smith, William Gardner, 150, 168, 183, 187
Snead, James, 167
socialism, 61, 90, 249
Solanas, Fernando, 9, 237
Soldier Blue, 213, 229, 230, 250–52
Solinas, Franco, 102–103, 133–34, 225–28
Soviet Union, 90, 135–39; conflict with West, 38–39, 209, 212; prewar cinema, 252
stereotypes in film, ethnic, 112–13, 118, 129, 140
Strand, Paul, 105–106
Strode, Woody, 150, 177–78, 216
Sturges, John, 205, 207–10, 212, 216–17
subtitles, 205

Tarantino, Quentin, 10, 11, 12, 13
Tax Revenue Act (1971), 15, 257, 263
taxes: on earnings in British market, 36–37; federal income, 258; on film imports, 21, 51; incentives, 45–46; proposed exemptions, 261; tax cuts, 21. *See also* Congressional acts telefoni bianchi *see* white telephone films
television: 31, 50, 52, 263, 280; actors, 192, 217, 240; conquers America, 23; rise of, in America, 39, 52, 278; rise of, in Italy, 266; threat to Hollywood, 19, 29–30
Toffetti, Sergio, 99
To Hell and Back, 120–22
Tombolo Paradiso Nero, 158–63, 164, 172–73, 181–82
Tomlinson, John, 7, 247
Trouillot, Michel-Rolph, 157

Ulysses, 43–44

378 Index

unions: American Federation
of Labor, 44, 259, 262;
Conference of Studio Unions,
39; International Alliance of
Theatrical and Stage Employees,
39, 40, 259, 262, 263
United States v. Crescent Amusement,
23
United States v. Paramount, 19, 23,
39, 102
Universal Studios, 31, 36, 40, 58

Vergès, Françoise, 148
Vidor, King, 44, 87, 103, 156, 285
Vietnam War, 2, 249, 279;
alongside rise of the colonial
world, 228; Atlantic spirit eroded
by, 257; concept of cultural
West untenable after, 18, 257;
European headlines occupied by,
134; masking as colonial subject
in the age of, 253; opposition to,
260, 280
Visconti, Luchino, 6, 9, 59, 91,
94, 106, 153, 243; as director
of *Ossessione*, 67–68, 70–74, 76,
77–88, 274; as member of Italian
Communist party, 93; use of
nonprofessional actors, 140
Vite Perdute, 172–75, 181
Vivere in Pace, 156, 164; as
compendium of racist jokes and
stereotypes, 157; hailed as rebirth
of Italian cinema, 155; role of
John Kitzmiller in, 158, 160, 177,
182
Volonté, Gian Maria, 211, 215,
218, 244; as highbrow actor,
227; as impersonator of Mexican
stereotypes, 240–42; as politically
progressive, 231

Wagstaff, Christopher, 265, 266
Walk in the Sun, A, 120
Wallis, Hal, 40, 41, 46–48
Warner Brothers studio, 40, 288, 289
Warner, Jack, 24, 26. *See also*
Warner Brothers studio
Warshow, Robert, 124, 125
Wayne, John, 197
Western, American, 190, 204, 218,
221; characteristics of, 194, 197, 224
Western, Spaghetti, characteristics
of, 195, 197, 203–204, 224;
definition of, 191; golden decade
of, 192; sensibility of, 212, 222,
225, 228, 234–35, 238–39, 244,
246–47, 249, 254
white telephone films, 28, 82
Wild Bunch, The, 217, 224
Wilder, Billy, 38, 92, 98; as director
of *Five Graves to Cairo*, 109–10; as
director of *Sunset Boulevard*, 25;
portrayal of American troops, 91;
as practitioner of film noir, 12;
use of real exteriors, 89
Williams, Alan, 70
Williams, Tennessee, 46, 48
Wings of the Hawk, 199–200, 203

Yojimbo, 207, 210, 211, 214
Yordan, Philip, 49, 194–97, 203, 252

Zagarrio, Vito, 273
Zampa, Luigi, 150, 155, 168, 179
Zavattini, Cesare, 8, 12, 88, 92,
105–106
Zinnemann, Fred, 105, 130–31,
191, 267
Zurlini, Valerio, 38, 105, 240; as
director of *Le Soldatesse*, 132,
134–35, 243; as friend of Woody
Strode, 177